International Handbooks on Information Systems

Series Editors

Peter Bernus, Jacek Błażewicz, Günter Schmidt, Michael Shaw

Titles in the Series

Heimo H. Adelsberger

Kinshuk • Jan Martin Pawlowski

Demetrios Sampson (Eds.)

Handbook on Information Technologies for Education and Training

Second edition

 Springer

Editors

Prof. Dr. Heimo H. Adelsberger
University of Duisburg-Essen
Information Systems for Production
and Operations Management
Universitätsstraße 9
45141 Essen
Germany
heimo.adelsberger@icb.uni-due.de

Prof. Kinshuk
Athabasca University
School of Computing
and Information Systems
1 University Drive
Athabasca AB T9S 3A3
Canada
kinshuk@ieee.org

Prof. Dr. Jan M. Pawlowski
University of Jyväskylä
Information Technology
Research Institute (ITRI)
Agora PL 35
40014 Jyväskylä
Finland
jan.pawlowski@titu.jyu.fi

Prof. Demetrios G. Sampson
Department of Digital Systems
University of Piraeus
and
Advanced e-Services
for the Knowledge Society Research Unit
Informatics and Telematics Institute
Center for Research
and Technology - Hellas
150 Androutsou Str.
GR-18532, Piraeus
Greece
sampson@unipi.gr, sampson@iti.gr

ISBN 978-3-540-74154-1   e-ISBN 978-3-540-74155-8

Library of Congress Control Number: 2008925556

© 2008 Springer-Verlag Heidelberg

Cover design: WMXDesign GmbH, Heidelberg

Printed on acid-free paper

9 8 7 6 5 4 3 2 1

springer.com

Editors' Foreword

Education and training have faced many challenges in the past five years – political, educational, and technological trends such as the European Bologna process, Lifelong Learning and the use of Social Software are just a few of the factors influencing this field. Furthermore, technology-enhanced learning has become the mainstream of educational and training innovation.

Within this context, this second edition of the Handbook on "Information Technologies for Learning, Education, and Training" attempts to capture the state-of-the-art in technology-enhanced learning, as it has emerged during the last years and anticipates important future developments.

As the Handbook Editors, we have aimed to provide a comprehensive guide for both researchers and practitioners working in the field of Technology-enhanced Learning and Training. Our overall objective is to enable the reader to gain a deep understanding of the past, present, and future research and applications in this field.

From a research perspective, the readers will obtain an in-depth understanding of the complex theories, strategies, concepts, and methods of Technology-enhanced Learning. Based on these fundamentals they will be able to develop new and innovative approaches for the next generation of Technology-enhanced Learning.

From an application perspective, the readers will obtain an insight into the fundamentals of technology-enhanced learning and how they can be used for designing and building best practice cases. Based on this insight, they should be able to identify opportunities for technologically enhanced educational innovation in various fields of formal and informal learning, improving the educational services they offer to the society.

The Handbook consists of four sections:

The first section on *Enabling Technologies* describes state-of-art information and communication technologies and their potential use in educational contexts. It covers basic technologies which are already widely accepted, but also presents new developments and the potentials of emerging technologies in supporting the agenda of technology-enhanced learning.

The second section deals with an important trend in the field, namely, *re-usability and interoperability*. A main advantage of digital technologies is the potential to share and re-use educational resources, activities, scenarios, practices, experiences, and expertise. This new culture of open educational communities can lead to enormous synergies and dramatic changes in the education and training of the digital natives.

The third section deals with *pedagogical issues* of technology-enhanced learning. It covers a wide range of concepts and approaches and discusses the implications of the use of digital technologies. This section aims to provide an insight into the rethinking of what will constitute pedagogical innovation in the digital world.

The fourth section takes a broader view and discusses the *organizational perspective,* as well as the successful best practice examples of the use, adoption and deployment of new technologies and pedagogical concepts.

As the Handbook Editors, we thank the authors of the chapters of this Handbook, who accepted our invitation to share years of research and experience with our readers. Furthermore, we would also like to thank the reviewers who graciously contributed to ensuring the quality of the chapters: Steve Corich, Jon Dron, Dragan Gasevic, Tiong Goh, Sabine Graf, Kim Hagen, Lynn Jeffery, Russell Johnson, Ilkka Jormanainen, Chung Hsien Lan, Kathryn MacCallum, Chiara Moroni, Niko Myller, Ali Fawaz Shareef, Jarkko Suhonen, Karen Stauffer, Charalambos Karagiannidis, Michael Verhaart and Jiz Zhou. Finally, we thank the series editors and our publisher, Springer, for their continuous support and their efforts to make this handbook possible.

We hope that this handbook contributes to the discourse in the researchers' and practitioners' communities and will lead to new ideas and advancements in the field of learning, education and training.

Heimo H. Adelsberger, University of Duisburg-Essen, Germany
Kinshuk, School of Computing and Information Systems, Athabasca University, Canada
Jan M. Pawlowski, Information Technology Research Institute, University of Jyväskylä, Finland
Demetrios G. Sampson, Department of Digital Systems, University of Piraeus, Greece

Contents

**17   The Role of Competence Assessment in the Different Stages
of Competence Development** **317**
J. Schoonenboom, C. Tattersall, Y. Miao, K. Stefanov,
A. Aleksieva-Petrova

List of Contributors

Editors

Heimo H. Adelsberger
Information Systems for Production and Operations Management
University of Duisburg-Essen
Universitätsstr. 9
45141 Essen
Germany
heimo.adelsberger@icb.uni-due.de

Adelina Aleksieva-Petrova
Faculty of Math and Informatics
University of Sofia "St. Kliment Ohridski"
5 James Bouchier Blvd.
Sofia 1164
Bulgaria
adelina@fmi.uni-sofia.bg

Peter Bateman
Faculty of Education and Language Studies Department of Education
The Open University
Walton Hall
Milton Keynes
MK7 6AA
United Kingdom
p.bateman@open.ac.uk

Sue Bennett
Faculty of Education
University of Wollongong
Wollongong NSW 2522
Australia
susan_bennett@uow.edu.au

Markus Bick
Business Information Systems
ESCP-EAP European School of Management
Heubnerweg 6
D-14059 Berlin
Germany
markus.bick@escp-eap.de

Paul De Bra
Department of Computer Science
Eindhoven University of Technology
P.O. Box 513
5600 MB Eindhoven
The Netherlands
debra@win.tue.nl

Glen Bull
Center for Technology and Teacher Education
University of Virginia
Ruffner Hall
405 Emmett Street
Charlottesville, VA 22904-4261
USA
gbull@virginia.edu

Nian-Shing Chen
Department of Information Management
National Sun Yat-Sen University
No. 70 Lien Hai Rd.
Kaohsiung
Taiwan
nschen@faculty.nsysu.edu.tw

Yi-Ru Chen
Department of Information Management
National Sun Yat-Sen University
No. 70 Lien Hai Rd.
Kaohsiung
Taiwan
pcdou213@gmail.com

Johannes Cronje
Faculty of Informatics and Design
Cape Peninsula University of Technology
PO Box 652
Cape Town 8000
South Africa
cronjej@cput.ac.za

Darina Dicheva
Department of Computer Science
Winston-Salem State University
3206 E.J. Jones Computer Science Building
601 S. Martin Luther King, Jr. Drive
Winston Salem, N.C. 27110
USA
dichevad@wssu.edu

Ulf-Daniel Ehlers
Information Systems for Production and Operations Management
University of Duisburg-Essen
Universitätsstr. 9
45141 Essen
Germany
ulf.ehlers@icb.uni-due.de

Dieter Euler
Institute of Business Education and Educational Management
University of St. Gallen
Dufourstrasse 40a
CH-9000 St. Gallen
Switzerland
dieter.euler@unisg.ch

David. Fabri
Dipartimento di Ingegneria Informatica, Gestionale
Università, Politecnica delle Marche
e dell'Automazione
Ancona, 60131
Italy

Carla Falsetti
Dipartimento di Ingegneria Informatica, Gestionale
Università, Politecnica delle Marche
e dell'Automazione
Ancona, 60131
Italy

Demetrios Fytros
Department of Digital Systems
University of Piraeus
and
Center for Research and Technology - Hellas (CERTH)
Informatics and Telematics Institute (ITI)
Advanced e-Services for the Knowledge Society Research Unit (ASK)
150 Androutsou Str.
GR-18532, Piraeus
Greece
dfytros@iti.gr

Sabine Graf
Graduate Institute of Learning and Instruction National Central University
No. 300, Jhongda Rd.
Jhongli City, Taoyuan 32001
Taiwan
sabine.graf@ieee.org

Tom Hammond
College of Education
Lehigh University
Iacocca Hall, 111 Research Drive
Bethlehem, PA 18015
USA
hammond@lehigh.edu

G. Li Hui
Faculty of Engineering, Dept. of Information Science
and Intelligent Systems
University of Tokushima
2-1, Minamijosanjima, Tokushima 770-8506
Japan
jeanniegan@hotmail.com

Annalisa Iezzi
Dipartimento di Ingegneria Informatica, Gestionale
Università, Politecnica delle Marche
e dell'Automazione
Ancona, 60131
Italy

Kinshuk
School of Computing and Information Systems
Athabasca University
1 University Drive
Athabasca, AB T9S 3A3
Canada
kinshuk@ieee.org

Rob Koper
OTEC
Open University of the Netherlands
Postbus 2960
6401 DL Heerlen
Netherlands
Rob.koper@ou.nl

Tyge F. Kummer
Business Information Systems
ESCP-EAP European School of Management
Heubnerweg 6
D-14059 Berlin
Germany
tyge.kummer@escp-eap.de

Tommaso Leo
Dipartimento di Ingegneria Informatica, Gestionale
Università, Politecnica delle Marche
e dell'Automazione
Ancona, 60131
Italy
tommaso.leo@univpm.it

François Magnan
CICE Research Chair, LICEF Research Center
Télé-université
4750 avenue Henri-Julien
Montréal, Québec
Canada
francois.magnan@licef.ca

Rory McGreal
Associate Vice President Research
Athabasca University
1 University Drive
Athabasca, AB T9S 3A3
Canada
rory@athabascau.ca

Yongwu Miao
Educational technology expertise centre (OTEC)
Open University of the Netherlands
P.O. Box 2960
NL-6401 DL Heerlen
The Netherlands
yongwu.miao@ou.nl

Franziska Zellweger Moser
Institute of Business Education and Educational Management
University of St. Gallen
Dufourstrasse 40a
CH-9000 St. Gallen
Switzerland
Franziska.Zellweger@unisg.ch

Hiroaki Ogata
Faculty of Engineering, Department of Information Science
and Intelligent Systems
University of Tokushima
2-1, Minamijosanjima, Tokushima 770-8506
Japan
ogata@is.tokushima-u.ac.jp

Gilbert Paquette
CICE Research Chair, LICEF Research Center
Télé-université
4750 avenue Henri-Julien
Montréal, Québec
Canada
gpaquett@teluq.uquebec.ca

Jan M. Pawlowski
Information Technology Research Institute
University of Jyväskylä
PO Box 35
40014
jan.pawlowski@titu.jyu.fi

Sulmana Ramazzotti
Dipartimento di Ingegneria Informatica, Gestionale
Università, Politecnica delle Marche
e dell'Automazione
Ancona, 60131
Italy

Peter Reimann
CoCo Research Centre University of Sydney
Education Building, A35, Room 244
NSW 2006
Australia
p.reimann@edfac.usyd.edu.au

Demetrios G. Sampson
Department of Digital Systems
University of Piraeus
and
Advanced e-Services for the Knowledge Society Research Unit (ASK)
Informatics and Telematics Institute (ITI)
Center for Research and Technology - Hellas (CERTH)
150 Androutsou Str.
GR-18532, Piraeus
Greece
sampson@unipi.gr, sampson@iti.gr

Judith Schoonenboom
SCO Kohnstamm Institute
University of Amsterdam
P.O. Box 94208
NL-1090 GE Amsterdam
The Netherlands
j.i.schoonenboom@uva.nl

Sabine Seufert
Institute of Business Education and Educational Management
University of St. Gallen
Dufourstrasse 40a
CH-9000 St. Gallen
Switzerland
Sabine.Seufert@unisg.ch

Marcus Specht
OTEC
Open University of the Netherlands
Postbus 2960
6401 DL Heerlen
Netherlands
marcus.specht@ou.nl

J. Michael Spector
Department of Educational Psychology and Learning Systems
Learning Systems Institute
Florida State University
307 Stone Building
Tallahassee, FL
USA
mspector@lsi.fsu.edu

Krassen Stefanov
Faculty of Math and Informatics
University of Sofia "St. Kliment Ohridski"
5 James Bouchier Blvd.
Sofia 1164
Bulgaria
krassen@fmi.uni-sofia.bg

Colin Tattersall
Educational Technology Expertise Centre
Open University of the Netherlands
Sopheon
Gaetano Martinolaan 95
6229 GS Maastricht
The Netherlands
colin.tattersall@sopheon.com

Silvia Rita Viola
Dipartimento di Ingegneria Informatica, Gestionale
Università, Politecnica delle Marche
e dell'Automazione
Ancona, 60131
Italy

William Yu Chung Wang
School of Information Management
Victoria University of Wellington
Room EA226, extn 6857, Easterfield Building, Kelburn Parade,
Wellington 6015
New Zealand
yuchung.wang@vuw.ac.nz

Chun-Wang Wei
Department of Information Management
National Sun Yat-Sen University
No. 70 Lien Hai Rd.
Kaohsiung
Taiwan
cw.wei@msa.hinet.net

Volker Zimmermann
imc information multimedia communication AG
Altenkesseler Str. 17/D3
66115 Saarbruecken
Germany
volker.zimmermann@im-c.de

Section 1:
The Enabling Technologies

Section 1.1:
Enabling Technologies

1 A Typology of Learning Object Repositories

R. McGreal

In this paper, the investigator attempts to create a comprehensive listing of learning object repositories (LORs) and address the following research questions:

1. What types of LORs are available on the Internet?
2. What are the principal features of these LORs?
3. What features are more or less universal and which are specific to certain types of repositories?
4. With the vast amounts of information available on the Internet, is there a need for LORs?

1.1 Background

LORs are becoming important resources for both learners and instructors as the quantity and quality of the learning objects (LOs) increases. The recycling and re-use of learning resources encapsulated as LOs in standards-based repositories can significantly increase the cost effectiveness of both online and blended education. With wise and considered implementation and integration of LOs and the removal of intellectual property barriers, we can reduce what is perhaps the largest barrier to participation in higher education, namely, the high and growing individual and societal cost, while increasing quality and opening up mass participation in learning.

In order to take full advantage of LOs, instructors, developers and learners need to know about LORs and have some training in how to make optimal use of them. The best strategies for incorporating components into lessons and LOs into modules and courses have yet to be identified, yet there is growing evidence that LOs can be used effectively (Flexible Learning

Advisory Group 2003; Han 2006). In this emergent stage, users need to learn which LORs are available, how to make use of them for learning and how to easily and quickly evaluate their efficacy in particular contexts. LORs are being used in 2007 and the number of LOs being accessed is growing. The seamless interoperability of LOs housed in different LORs has yet to be achieved as they have, for the most part, developed independently with some notable attempts at rendering them interoperable. The ability to use learning objects (LOs) seamlessly and consistently in different application environments has only been partially achieved (Liu et al. n.d.; eduSource 2005; Sampson and Karampiperis 2004; Osborne 2005). Nevertheless, in maximizing the capabilities of the WWW, external LOs can be successfully integrated with course materials if not in a fully interoperable manner.

One necessary component of interoperability is the absence of digital rights management (DRM) software. DRM can be a significant impediment to interoperability. LOs must be usable without the necessity of entering into a special contractual arrangement with an offering party or parties. Licensing, subscriptions and other digital rights paraphernalia restrict the use of LOs. The need for copyright clearances, contracts and licenses inhibit reuse. When access is hindered by these DRM devices, users just turn away. Open access overcomes these difficulties, facilitating access and the integration of content into lessons and courses.

For this reason "closed" LORs such as the "Annenberg Media Learner" and "Blackboard CE & Vista Epacks" will not be considered in this study. Most of the repositories examined use some form of open access permission, such as the Creative Commons license limiting use to individuals and educational institutions or to organizations with no commercial motive, retaining only attribution rights. A significant problem arises when copyright owners choose to prohibit "derivative works". This restriction may make sense in a software context in which altering of code often improves or allows performance in different contexts. However learning objects, to be effective, often have to be easily altered (by language, previous student knowledge level, tool access or cultural sensibilities, etc.) Thus, useable LOs are best licensed with no restrictions on derivative works.

1.1.1 Reuse and Repurposing

One criticism of LORs continues to be the issue of reuse. Some argue that, because learning must be contextualized, LOs, which are only relevant in a particular context, cannot be easily "reused". South and Monson (2000) called this the "reusability paradox", because they felt that LOs had to be designed for reusability in different learning contexts. Therefore, they concluded that LOs must be designed in a highly decontextualized manner. Dodani (2002) referred to this as "the cornerstone of the promise of learning objects". For example, a statistics package may be considered generic, but when it comes to using it, it must be placed in a particular context that differs depending on the learning environment and subject area.

Hodgins (2006) addresses the argument by posing the difference between "reuse" and "repurposing". He limits the definition of "reuse" to applying the LO in the same context for which it was designed, for example, taking a psychology lesson and reusing it in a wide variety of psychology courses with the same or similar curriculum items. This differs from "repurposing" which, he accepts, is more problematic. Repurposing is where that same psychology module is used in a course in a different subject area, for example in a nursing or literature course. Nevertheless, LOs can be useful even if they are only ever reused and never repurposed, if the number of students and other learners who are taking similar psychology courses that could benefit from pedagogically relevant LOs are considered.

1.1.2   Federated Searches and Harvesting

Another issue is that of searching among different repositories. This can be conducted as federated searches or through the harvesting of metadata, later searching through this subset. Federated searches are conducted by search engines accessing many different databases with the same query. A search string is input by the user and this is sent through the Internet, searching and retrieving selected metadata about individual objects from distributed databases. Harvesting, on the other hand, refers to the gathering of metadata from a number of distributed repositories into one portal websites such as Google, Yahoo or EduRSS to facilitate searching. MMLOM is a metadata mapping tool designed to facilitate searches among disparate repositories (Liu et al. n.d.).

With a little structure in the html, applications such as Dapper (http://www.dappit.com/) and Kapow (http://www.kapowtech.com/) can be used to facilitate the conversion of search results into RSS (Davies 2007). In this way, LO results can be fed out directly from the LORs to the learner based on a user profile.

1.1.3   Learning Object Criticisms

To date there have been many critics of learning objects and learning object repositories. Researchers from a critical perspective such as Friesen (2005) and Leinonen (2006) decry them as militarist. Others, like Berkun

(2005) focus on information science concerns, notably the non-use of standards that is probably a more appropriate criticism. Wilson (2005) claimed that they just "don't work", although he claims that they could if they were open source, easy to edit and repurpose, and easy to create. Even Wiley (n.d.), one of the earliest proponents of Los, is having second thoughts on their potential for reusability.

Are these and other criticisms justified? Are LOs not being used as the critics are claiming? Or are there enough easy-to-use, open-access LOs available to make a difference? The Learning Federation of Australia (2006) claims that the use of LOs in their database has been increasing, and that LOs are the most highly utilised resource in their Resource Centre. Borgne et al. (2006) studied the activities of student teachers and found that 57% are using Internet resources in the preparation of their lessons. Robertson (2006) found that 70% of teachers in his study were using these resources, with 26% knowing about and accessing specific French LORs. Han (2006) reports that LOs account for more than 50% of the traffic, with a 200% increase to the GROW Engineering LOR. *Connexions* (2007) reports that more than one million people from 194 countries are tapping into their 3,820 modules and 204 courses. Not surprisingly, MIT reported more than 8.5 million visits to its open courseware site, which was a 56% increase over the previous year. In addition, more than 350 courses have been translated and 70 mirror sites set up globally. MIT's courses are being widely distributed offline to secondary audiences (MIT Open Courseware 2005). So, although there are reasons to be skeptical of LORs, it seems that there has been substantial growth and reason to expect this growth to continue in the future.

The examples and argument above illustrate that there are many levels and types of LOs. In addition, there is no agreed-upon definition of LOs. Definitions range from LOs as anything and everything (Downes 2003) to more focused LOs as specific digital lessons (McGreal 2004). When discussing search options, there are descriptions of the repositories that store these objects, ranging from Google to highly structured domain-specific databases. These illustrate the need for taxonomical clarification.

1.2   Types of LORs

Learning object repositories (LORs) are databases used for storing and/ or enabling the interoperability of LOs. There is some confusion as to whether or not an LOR stores Los, or simply the metadata describing them, with associated links. In fact, some repositories store their content locally only within that repository. While one might argue the relative merits of both centralized and distributed approaches, it is important to specify the nature of the different repositories to reduce misconceptions when building, linking to or accessing them. For these reasons I have categorized repositories based on the locality of the LOs. Type 1: Those that house content primarily on site; Type 2: Those that mainly provide metadata with links to LOs housed at other sites; and Type 3: Hybrid sites that provide both content and links to external content. These repositories include both general repositories that host learning resources from a wide variety of subject areas and those that are focused on specific themes or topics. Still others focus on a specific educational level. The majority of these repositories are open to all users; other repositories require users to subscribe or sign in. Sign-in is generally required when submitting materials, as a form of quality control.

The granularity of objects ranges from simple components like text or pictures, to Java applets and flash animations, to lessons, modules and full courses. Most sites provide (or link to) a wide variety of components, lessons or media types. Others are more specialized. For example, the BioDiTRL repository and the Digital Scriptorium limit their hosting to manuscripts and pictures of biological organisms. The Wisconsin Online Resource Center uniquely houses Flash animations. Other sites, such as the National Academies Press host only books. Still other sites, like Carnegie Mellon's OLI host full courses.

Type 1 repositories that store content on site exclusively follow a centralised model in which the learning objects are located on a single server or website. These repositories range from the widely known MIT Open Courseware site, with more than 500 course curricula, to the focused SOFIA (Sharing of Free Intellectual Assets) website that hosts only eight courses for community college level students. Curriki is an ambitious project that aims to become a central repository for storing large numbers of learning objects, presently focusing on K-12 materials, but intending to expand to other levels. The Monterey Institute's National Repository of Online Courses requires instructors to register, but allows students free access to lessons.

The number of LOs available for use in a repository is also an important consideration. These numbers range from more than a million component objects in the NSDL Library to as few as forty in ESCOT or just eight in SOFIA. The larger ones generally consist of components and the smaller ones can be full courses or specialised multimedia applications (see Table 1.1).

Table 1.1. Type 1 repositories storing content with very limited linking

Name	URL	Level	Granularity	Total Number	Content Type	Meta-data	Comments
BioDiTRL Biological Digital Teaching Resource Library	http://bio-ditrl.sunsite.ualberta.ca/	University	Components	8869	Images	taxonomies	Subscription requested
ConneXions	http://cnx.org/	University & other	Courses	+2000	Variety	Simple	True repository not links; XML
Curriki Global Education & Learning Community	http://www.curriki.org/	K12	Various	+750	Variety	IEEE LOM	Content repository not links; SUN Microsystems
ESCOT: Educational Software Components of Tomorrow	http://www.escot.org/	Middle School	Lessons	+40		Simple	Problem solving; Javascript
Exploratories	http://www.cs.brown.edu/exploratories/ freeSoftware/home.html	University	Lessons	+60	Java applets	Simple	Computer Graphics
Exploratorium Digital Library	http://www.exploratorium.edu/educate/ dl.html	All levels	Various	+100s	Variety	Simple	Arts & Science
Explore Learning with Gizmos	http://www.explorelearning.com/	K12	Lessons	+100	gizmos	None	Math & Science
Fathom archive	http://www.fathom.com/	University	Lessons	+100	Variety	Simple	No longer working
Free-ed Net	http://www.free-ed.net/free-ed/	ComCollege	Courses	+100	Variety	Simple	
General Physics Java Applets	http://www.surendranath.org/	University	Lessons	+60	Java	None	Simulations
Geometry Center U. of Minnesota	http://www.geom.uiuc.edu/	University	Lessons	+25	Java Web	None	Simulations. Now closed but usable
Harvey Project	http://opencourse.org/Collaboratories/ harveyproject	University	Lessons	+40	Flash, Java	Simple	Reusable Learning Assets
Illumina: National Science Digital Library	http://www.illumina-dlib.org/	University	Various	?	Variety	MARC NSDL	Chemistry, biology, physics, math & computer science
IU: The UC Berkeley Interactive University Project	http://interactiveu.berkeley.edu:8000/DLMIndex/	University & K12	Lessons	+100	Variety	Simple	University repository with some links
LOLA Exchange: Wesleyan U	http://www.lolaexchange.org/	University	Lessons	+100	Variety	Dublin Core, IMS, CanCore	Univ developed materials mainly for information literacy
MLX: Maricopa Community College Learning Exchange	http://www.mcli.dist.maricopa.edu/mlx/	ComCollege	Lessons	1477	Variety	Simple	College repository
MIT Open Courseware	http://ocw.mit.edu/	University	Courses	+500	Variety	OAI-PMH	Content repository

Table 1.1. (cont.)

Name	URL	Level	Granularity	Total Number	Content Type	Meta-data	Comments
National Learning Network UK	http://www.nln.ac.uk/Materials/default.asp	Upper Secondary	Lessons	+60	VLE	IMS	Sign on to VLE. Access restricted
National Repository of Online Courses (Monterey Institute)	http://www.montereyinstitute.org/nroc/index.html	All levels	Courses & lessons	+30	Variety	Simple	Closed to members; Full courses. Student access is free
Open Course Collaboratories	http://opencourse.org/	University	Lessons	+100	Variety	Simple	Includes Harvey project et al.
Open Learning Initiative (OLI) Carnegie Mellon	http://www.cmu.edu/oli/	University 1st Yr.	Courses	+10	Variety	Simple	Available free to universities granting credit. Student access is free
PBS Teacher Source	http://www.pbs.org/teachersource/	K12	Various	+3000	Variety	Simple	Sign on required
Physics Education & Technology PhET U. of Colorado	http://phet.colorado.edu/web-pages/index.html	University	Lessons	+60	Flash	None	Physics
SOFIA Sharing of Free Intellectual Assets	http://sofia.fhda.edu/	ComCollege	Courses	8	Variety	Simple	A few full courses
Tufts Open Courseware	http://ocw.tufts.edu/	University	Various	+30	Variety	Simple	Life sciences international
Webcast UC Berkeley	http://webcast.berkeley.edu/	University	Lectures	+100	Webcasts	None	Time-limited
Wisconsin Online Resource Center	http://www.wisc-online.com	ComCollege	Lessons	2184	Flash	Simple	Free for educators sign up needed

Type 2 repositories can be considered to be "portals" that provide links to educational content provided by others. Many of them do house some content locally, but they are primarily aggregators of links. The most well-known such portal is MERLOT, which links to a wide variety of peda-gogical content. Others, like the massive CITIDEL portal, provide links to a wide variety of subject matter, ranging from research papers, notes and lesson plans to multimedia applications and videos (see Table 1.2).

Type 3 repositories combine both functions as a content host and as portals to other sites. These include massive sites like the NSDL, with links to more than 1.5 million educational resources, and the smaller and more targeted Math Forum@Drexel site with hosting of (or links to) just over 1,000 mathematics resources. Several popular international sites, such as the multilingual ARIADNE repository in Europe and the Common-wealth of Learning's COLLOR, are examples of this type. Edna in Australia is one of the more comprehensive repositories, enabling access to a wide range of hosted and linked educational content (see Table 1.3).

Repositories can also be categorized as those hosting a wide variety of content and contrasted with those that hold content in a specific subject area such as physics (General Physics Java, Heal Health) or that rely on a special application type such as gizmos (Explore Gizmos), video (Website UC Berkeley) or flash (Flashchild) (see Tables 1.4 and 1.5).

Instructors will have a special interest in repositories that provide access to full courses (see Table 1.6). These sites range from full content LORs like Curriki, although much of their content is aggregated from other sites but stored locally (Kurshan 2006). These sites also include the Connexions LOR, with external links as well as locally stored content, and the MIT LOR, which hosts only its own curriculum content. Other large sites, such as the University of Texas's World Lecture Hall, provide primarily links. Other sites only hold a small number of locally produced courses (e.g., OLI, Free Ed Net, National Repository of Online Courses).

Other LOR classifications include those that require a subscription or membership or even a payment to view or use their materials (see Table 1.7). Another useful classification is that of information objects in repositories such as Gutenberg or Battleby's (see Table 1.8). Examples of these types of repositories are provided, but there are many others available online.

Table 1.2. Type 2 repositories that store no content and are made up of links (metadata repositories)

Name	URL	Level	Granularity	Total Number	Content Type	Meta-data	Comments
AT&T Blue Web'n	http://www.kn.sbc.com/wired/blueweb n/	All levels	Various	2040	Variety	Simple	Dewey Decimal system; sites rated
CAREO: Campus Alberta Repository of Educational Objects	http://careo.ucalgary.ca	University & other	Various	4146	Variety	Simple	No longer supported
CITIDEL: Computing and Information Technology Interactive Digital Educational Library	http://www.citidel.org/	University	Various	488,279	Variety	Simple	Assets only
DLESE: Digital Library for Earth System Education	http://www.dlese.org/dds/histogram.d o?group=subject	All levels	Various	13138	Variety	Simple	
Educational object economy (eoe)	http://www.natomagroup.com/eoe.htm l		Components	+2000	Applets	Simple	Java simulations; no longer accessible
EducaNext Portal	http://www.educanext.org/ubp	University	Various	+1000	Variety	Simple	ProLearn project many languages
Educational Software Directory	http://www.educational-software-directory.net/	K12	Various	+2000	Variety	None	Links
Flashchild	http://flashchild.com/all-games/	All levels	Components	+1000	Flash	None	Games
FLORE: French Learning Object Repository for Education	http://flore.uvic.ca/welcome.php	University	Lessons	+1000?	Variety	Simple	Mainly K12
GEM Exchange Gateway to Educational Materials	http://www.thegateway.org/browse	K12	Various	+45000	Variety	Simple	Stopped in 2005?
INTUTE UK	http://www.intute.ac.uk/	University	Various	114893	Variety	Simple	Rated resources for learning
LearningLanguages.net	http://www.learninglanguages.net/	All levels	Various	+1000	Variety	Simple	All levels
Learning and Skills Web	http://www.lsweb.ac.uk/	ComCollege	Variety	+200	Variety	IMS	Sign on requested; Links
Learning about Learning Objects	http://www.learning-objects.net/modules.php?name=Web_Links	All levels	Various	?	Variety	Simple	Links not rated
LRC3: U21 Consortium	http://www.lrc3.unsw.edu.au/	University	Various	?	Variety	Simple	Closed
MERLOT	http://www.merlot.org/Home.po	All levels	Various	16166	Variety	IEEE LOM	Peer review, some copyright issues fair use ok
Needs Digital Library	http://www.needs.org/needs/	University	Various	?	Variety	IEEE LOM	University
NIME GLAD: Gateway to Learning for Ability Development	http://nime-glad.nime.ac.jp/	University	Various		Variety	Simple	Links to MIT, Utah State Japanese Univs etc.
ScienceNet Links	http://www.sciencenetlinks.com/resou rce_index.htm	K12	Various	+500	Variety	None	K12
SMETE	http://www.smete.org/smete/	All levels	Various	+6000	Variety	IEEE LOM	

Table 1.3. Type 3 repositories with both content and a significant number of links

Name	URL	Level	Granularity	Total Number	Content Type	Meta-data	Comments
ARIADNE - European Knowledge Pool System	http://www.ariadne-eu.org/	University	Various	?	Variety	IEEE LOM	English, French, Dutch, German
Commonwealth of Learning LOR	http://www.collor.org/col/	University	Various	?	Variety	IEEE LOM	Federated search; limited
ConneXions	http://cnx.org/	University & other	Modules Courses	+4000	Variety	Simple	204 full courses
Digital Scriptorium Columbia University	http://www.scriptorium.columbia.edu/	University	Components		Images	Simple	Columbia Univ.
edna: Educational Network of Australia	http://www.edna.edu.au/edna/go	K12 & other	Various	+16000	Variety	Simple	Review all sites
HEAL: Health Education Assets Library	http://www.healcentral.org/index.jsp	University	Lessons	+10000	Variety	OAI-PMH & IMS	High quality
IDEAS: Interactive Dialogue with Educators Across the State	http://ideas.wisconsin.edu/	K12	Lessons	+2000 est.	Variety	Simple	Teachers' sharing
ILife Apple Learning Interchange	http://ali.apple.com/ali/resources.shtml	K12	Lessons	+2000	Variety	Simple	Primarily links
Internet Mathematics Library: Math Forum@Drexel	http://mathforum.org/library/	All levels	Various	+1000s	Variety	Simple	Many multimedia lessons
NSDL National Science Digital Library	http://nsdl.org/search/	All levels	Various	+1.5 million	Variety	Simple	Science oriented & permissions may be needed
Problem Based Learning Clearing House	https://chico.nss.udel.edu/Pbl/	PBS only	University	Lessons		Variety	Simple
SchoolNet Canaca	http://www.schoolnet.ca/	K12	Lessons Modules	+7000	Variety	Simple	Selected by educators; French
Scottish Institute for Excellence in Social Work Education	http://www.sieswe.org/	University	?	?	?	?	Defunct
World Lecture Hall U. of Texas	http://web.austin.utexas.edu/wlh/	University	Courses	+2000	Variety	Simple	Comprehensive resource

Table 1.4. Generic learning object repositories

Type	Name	URL	Level	Granularity	Total Number	Content Type	Meta-data	Comments
3	ARIADNE - European Knowledge Pool System	http://www.ariadne-eu.org/	University	?		Variety	IEEE LOM	English, French, Dutch, German
2	AT&T Blue Web'n	http://www.kn.sbc.com/wired/bluewebn/	Various	Various	2040	Variety	Simple	Dewey Decimal system; sites rated
2	CAREO: Campus Alberta Repository of Educational Objects	http://careo.ucalgary.ca	University & other		4146			No longer supported
3	Commonwealth of Learning LOR	http://www.collor.org/col/	University	Various	?	Variety	IEEE LOM	Federated search; limited
1	ConneXions	http://cnx.org/	University & other	Courses	+2000	Variety	Simple	True repository not links; XML
?	COSTP: California Open Source Textbook Project	http://www.opensourcetext.org/	K12	Components	?	Books	Simple	Startup in conceptual stage; not completely open
1	Curriki Global Education & Learning Community	http://www.curriki.org/	K12	Various	+750	Variety	IEEE LOM	Content repository not links; SUN Microsystems
3	edna: Educational Network of Australia	http://www.edna.edu.au/edna/go	K12 & other	Various	+16000	Variety	Simple	Review all sites
2	Educational object economy (eoe)	http://www.natomagroup.com/eoe.html		Components	+2000	Applets	Simple	Java simulations; no longer accessible
2	EducaNext Portal	http://www.educanext.org/ubp	University	Various	+1000	Variety	Simple	ProLearn project many languages
2	Educational Software Directory	http://www.educational-software-directory.net/	K12	Various	+2000	Variety	None	Links
1	Fathom archive	http://www.fathom.com/	University	Lessons	+100	Variety	Simple	No longer maintained. Personal use only
1	Free-ed Net	http://www.free-ed.net/free-ed/	ComCollege	Courses	+100	Variety	None	
2	GEM Exchange Gateway to Educational Materials	http://www.thegateway.org/browse	K12	Various	+45000	Variety	Simple	Stopped in 2005?
3	IDEAS: Interactive Dialogue with Educators Across the State	http://ideas.wisconsin.edu/	K12	Lessons	+2000 est.	Variety	Simple	
3	ILife Apple Learning Interchange	http://ali.apple.com/ali/resources.s html	Primarily K12	Lessons	+2000	Variety	Simple	Primarily links
1	IU: The UC Berkeley Interactive University Project	http://interactiveu.berkeley.edu:8000/DLMIndex/	University & K12	Lessons	+100	Variety	Simple	Content repository
2	INTUTE UK	http://www.intute.ac.uk/	University	Various	114893	Variety	Simple	Rated resources for learning
2	LRC3: U21 Consortium	http://www.lrc3.unsw.edu.au/	University	Various	?	Variety	Simple	Closed
2	Learning and Skills Web	http://www.lsweb.ac.uk/	ComCollege	Variety	+1000	Variety	IMS	Sign on requested; Links

Table 1.4. (cont.)

Type	Name	URL	Level	Granularity	Total Number	Content Type	Meta-data	Comments
2	Learning Objects.net	http://www.learning-objects.net/modules.php?name=Web_Links	Diverse	Various	+200	Variety	Simple	Links not rated
1	LOLA Exchange: Wesleyan U	http://www.lolaexchange.org/	University	Lessons	+100	Variety	Dublin Core, IMS, CanCore	Univ developed materials
1	MLX: Maricopa Community College Learning Exchange	http://www.mcli.dist.maricopa.edu/mlx/	ComCollege	Lessons	1476	Variety	Simple	College repository
2	MERLOT	http://www.merlot.org/Home.po	All levels	Various	16166	Variety		Peer review; some copyright issues fair use ok
1	MIT Open Courseware	http://ocw.mit.edu/	University	Courses	+500	Variety	OAI-PMH	Content repository
1	National Learning Network UK	http://www.nln.ac.uk/Materials/default.asp	Upper Secondary	Lessons	+60	VLE	IMS	Sign on to VLE
2	NIME GLAD: Gateway to Learning for Ability Development	http://nime-glad.nime.ac.jp/	University	Various		Variety	Simple	Links to MIT, Utah State Japanese Univs etc.
1	National Repository of Online Courses (Monterey Institute)	http://www.montereyinstitute.org/nroc/index.html	All levels	Courses & lessons	+30	Variety	Simple	Closed to members; Full courses. Student access is free
3	NSDL National Science Digital Library	http://nsdl.org/search/	All levels	Various	+1.5 million	Variety	Simple	Science oriented & permissions may be needed
1	Open Course Collaboratories	http://opencourse.org/	University	Lessons	+100	Variety	Simple	Includes Harvey project et al.
1	Open Learning Initiative (OLI) Carnegie Mellon	http://www.cmu.edu/oli/	University 1st Yr.	Courses	+10	Variety	Simple	Available free to universities granting credit. Student access is free
1	PBS Teacher Source	http://www.pbs.org/teachersource/	K12	Various	+3000	Variety	Simple	Sign on required
3	SchoolNet Canada	http://www.schoolnet.ca/	K12	Lessons Modules	+7000	Variety	Simple	Selected by educators; French
1	SOFIA Sharing of Free Intellectual Assets	http://sofia.fhda.edu/	ComCollege	Courses	8	Variety	Simple	
1	Webcast UC Berkeley	http://webcast.berkeley.edu/	University	Lectures	+100	Webcasts	None	Time-limited materials. Can't copy
1	Wisconsin Online Resource Center	http://www.wisc-online.com	ComCollege	Lessons	2184	Flash	Simple	Free for educators sign up needed
1	World Lecture Hall U. of Texas	http://web.austin.utexas.edu/wlh/	University	Courses	+2000	Variety	Simple	

Table 1.5. Targeted learning object repositories

Type	Name	URL	Subject(s)	Level	Granularity	Total Number	Content Type	Meta-data
1	BioDiTRL Biological Digital Teaching Resource Library	http://bio-ditrl.sunsite.ualberta.ca/	Biology	University	Components	+10 000	Images	taxonomies
2	CITIDEL: Computing and IT Interactive Digital Educational Library	http://www.citidel.org/	Computer Science	University	Various	488,279	Variety	Simple
2	DLESE: Digital Library for Earth System Education	http://www.dlese.org/dds/histogram.do?group=subject	Earth Science	All levels	Various	13138	Variety	Simple
1	Digital Scriptorium Columbia University	http://www.scriptorium.columbia.edu/	Medieval Manuscripts	University	Components		Images	Simple
1	ESCOT: Educational Software Components of Tomorrow	http://www.escot.org/	Math.	Middle School	Lessons	+40		Simple
1	Exploratories	http://www.cs.brown.edu/exploratories/freeSoftware/home.html	Computer Graphics	University	Lessons	+60	Java applets	Simple
1	Exploratorium Digital Library	http://www.exploratorium.edu/educate/dl.html	Arts & Science	All levels	Various	+100s	Variety	Simple
1	Explore Learning with Gismos	http://www.explorelearning.com/	Math & Science	K12	Lessons	+100	gizmos	None
2	FLORE: French Learning Object Repository for Education	http://flore.uvic.ca/welcome.php	French	University	Lessons	+1000?	Variety	Simple
1	General Physics Java Applets	http://www.surendranath.org/	Physics	University	Lessons	+60	Java	None
1	Geometry Center U. of Minnesota	http://www.geom.uiuc.edu/	Geometry	University	Lessons	+25	Java Web	None
3	GROW Geotechnical Rock and Water Resources Library	http://www.grow.arizona.edu/	Geology & Water	University	Lessons	1039	Variety	Simple
1	Harvey Project	http://opencourse.org/Collaboratories/harveyproject	Human Physiology	University	Lessons	+40	Flash, Java	Simple
3	HEAL: Health Education Assets Library	http://www.healcentral.org/index.jsp	Health Sciences	University	Lessons	+10000	Variety	OAI-PMH & IMS
1	Illumina: National Science Digital Library	http://www.illumina-dlib.org/	Math, Biol, CS, Ch&Ph,	University	Various	?	Variety	MARC NSDL
3	Internet Mathematics Library: Math Forum@Drexel	http://mathforum.org/library/	Math	All levels	Various	+1000s	Variety	Simple
2	LearningLanguages.net	http://www.learninglanguages.net/	French Japanese Spanish	All levels	Various	+1000	Variety	Simple

Table 1.5. (cont.)

Type	Name	URL	Subject(s)	Level	Granularity	Total Number	Content Type	Meta-data
2	Needs Digital Library	http://www.needs.org/needs/	Engineering	University	Various	?	Variety	IEEE LOM
1	Physics Education & Technology PhET U. of Colorado	http://phet.colorado.edu/web-pages/index.html	Physics	University	Lessons	+60	Flash	None
3	Problem Based Learning Clearing House	https://chico.nss.udel.edu/Pbl/	PBS only	University	Lessons		Variety	Simple
2	ScienceNet Links	http://www.sciencenetlinks.com/resource_index.htm	Science	K12	Various	+500	Variety	None
3	Scottish Institute for Excellence in Social Work Education	http://www.sieswe.org/	Social Work	University	?	?	?	?
2	SMETE	http://www.smete.org/smete/	Science, Math, Eng, Tech & Ed	All levels	Various	+6000	Variety	IEEE LOM
1	Tufts Open Courseware	http://ocw.tufts.edu/	Life Sciences International	University	Various	+30	Variety	Simple
1	University Channel Princeton University	http://uc.princeton.edu/main/	Public & affairs	University	Lectures	+100	Video, podcasts	Simple
1	Zona Land Science & Mathematics	http://id.mind.net/~zona/	Science & Math	University	Lessons	+50	VRML	None

Table 1.6. Full course repositories

Name	URL	Level	Granularity	Total Number	Content Type	Meta-data	Comments
ConneXions	http://cnx.org/	University & other	Courses	+204	Variety	Simple	+3800 other modules
Free-ed Net	http://www.free-ed.net/free-ed/	ComCollege	Courses	+100	Variety	None	
MIT Open Courseware	http://ocw.mit.edu/	University	Courses	+500	Variety	OAI-PMH	Content repository
National Repository of Online Courses (Monterey Institute)	http://www.montereyinstitute.org/nroc/index.html	All levels	Courses & lessons	+30	Variety	Simple	Closed to members; Full courses. Student access is free
Open Learning Initiative (OLI) Carnegie Mellon	http://www.cmu.edu/oli/	University 1st Yr.	Courses	+10	Variety	Simple	Available free to universities granting credit. Student access is free
SOFIA Sharing of Free Intellectual Assets	http://sofia.fhda.edu/	ComCollege	Courses	8	Variety	Simple	
World Lecture Hall U. of Texas	http://web.austin.utexas.edu/wlh/	University	Courses	+2000	Variety	Simple	

Table 1.7. Membership required to enter repository

Type	Name	URL	Level	Granularity	Total Number	Content Type	Meta-data	Comments
$	Annenberg Media Learner.org	http://www.learner.org/index.html	K12 & University	Courses	+50	TV	Simple	Closed. Fees apply. Some free student activities
1	BioDiTRL Biological Digital Teaching Resource Library	http://bio-ditrl.sunsite.ualberta.ca/	University	Components	+10000	Images	Taxonomies	Biology; subscription requested
$	Blackboard CE & Vista Epacks	http://webct.com/content/viewpage?name=content_showcase	ComCollege & University	Modules	+1000	Multimedia	Simple	Closed. Fees apply
3	CLOE:Cooperative Learning Object Exchange	http://cloe.on.ca/	University	Lessons	?	Variety	Simple	Closed. 17 university consortium in Ontario; true repository
2	FLORE: French Learning Object Repository for Education	http://flore.uvic.ca/welcome.php	University	Lessons	+1000	Variety	Simple	Sign in
3	Learn Alberta	http://www.learnalberta.ca/	K12	Various	+2000 est	Variety	Simple	Partially closed. Content with links
1	National Repository of Online Courses (Monterey Institute)	http://www.montereyinstitute.org/nroc/index.html	All levels	Courses & lessons	+30	Variety	Simple	Closed to members; Full courses. Student access is free
1	National Learning Network UK	http://www.nln.ac.uk/Materials/default.asp	Upper Secondary	Lessons	+60	VLE	IMS	Sign on to VLE
1	PBS Teacher Source	http://www.pbs.org/teachersource/	K12	Various	+3000	Variety	Simple	Sign on required
1	Problem Based Learning Clearing House	https://chico.nss.udel.edu/Pbl/	University	Lessons	???	Variety	Variety	Simple; PBS only
1	SOLR Shareable Online Learning Resources BC Campus	http://solr.bccampus.ca/intro/	ComCollege & University	Various	+ 300	Variety	Simple	BC limited for many materials

Table 1.8. Open archives of information objects (examples)

Name	URL	Level	Granularity	Total Number	Content Type	Meta-data
Bartleby.com	http://www.bartleby.com/	All levels	Books	+3000	Ebooks	Simple
Harvard University Library Open Collections Program	http://ocp.hul.harvard.edu/	University	Concepts	+100000	Images documents	DC
National Academies Press	http://www.nap.edu/	University	Books	+3000	Ebooks	Simple
Open Video Project	http://www.open-video.org/index.php	All Levels	Concept	+1000	Videos	Simple
Oracle ThinkQuest Library	http://www.thinkquest.org/library/index.html	University	Various	+1000	Variety	None
Project Gutenberg	http://www.gutenberg.org/wiki/Main_Page	All levels	Books	+10000	eBooks	Simple
Varsity Notes	http://www.varsitynotes.com/	University	Lectures	+600	Notes	None

1.3   LOR Features

Australian practitioners have identified the following features they would like to see in a learning object repository from an end user's perspective:

- Being able to see the object up front before entering into any contractual obligations
- Simple, non-intimidating design and structure
- Being able to get the object that you want straightaway
- Being able to store the object on your own computer or on the web-based repository associated with your login
- Simple versus advanced

(Flexible Learning Advisory Group 2003)

As a matter of course, all the open-access repositories allow viewing and use of the objects with only limited contractual obligations, which are explicit in the type of creative commons license available. Some do require subscribing to the site and this is often a deterrent to users. There is a wide variety of designs, but for the most part designs are simple, accessible and not intimidating, especially for the growing number of digital natives or experienced immigrants who are comfortable dealing with web interfaces to backend databases such as Amazon, Google, etc. The search features of the different repositories offer various search capabilities that either ease or hinder the access to the content. A simple browse feature (allowing serendipitous retrieval of LOs sharing a descriptive tag such as subject, grade level, discipline, etc.) that is common in many repositories is a real aid to discovery. Many sites offer an advanced search feature for more sophisticated searches. And, because this study is limited to open-access repositories, many sites allow copying and re-storing of LOs and metadata on the user's computer or server.

Moving beyond end-user needs to the needs of repository managers and contributing users, Higgs et al. (2003) highlighted the growing need for LOR models to provide management and administrative functions. They listed the following operations as supporting the functionality of LORs:

1. *Search/find* – the ability to locate an appropriate learning object. This can include the ability to browse
2. *Quality control* – a system that ensures learning objects meet technical, educational and metadata requirements
3. *Request* – a learning object that has been located in the database
4. *Maintain* – appropriate version control
5. *Retrieve* – receive an object that has been requested

6. *Submit* – provide an object to a repository for storage
7. *Store* – place a submitted object into a data store with unique, registered identifiers that allow it to be located
8. *Gather* (push/pull) – obtain metadata about objects in other repositories for wider searches and information via a clearing house function
9. *Publish* – provide metadata to other repositories (p. 72)

1.4   Discussion

In interpreting these functions for this study, the following approaches seem reasonably consistent with Higgs, Meredith and Hand's intent. A discussion of each feature follows (see Table 1.9):

1. *Search/find.* The LORs investigated in this study all have, to varying degrees, the ability to search/find objects through metadata searching. However, some have no browse or "surf" feature, making it difficult for users to survey and serendipitously access different objects. This is analogous to libraries that allow browsing the stacks and those that require patrons to order books, which are then delivered by library staff.
   Judgment. A browse feature was almost universally present in all three types of repository. The few exceptions were primarily in types 2 and 3. The type 1 content repositories (with one exception, PhEt) all had working browse features.
2. *Quality control* is a serious issue for pedagogical, logistical and technical reasons. Some of the LORs do have quality control measures in place, but they are often not fully implemented. Others simply accept whatever LOs are provided.
   Judgment. The majority of LORs exerted some form of quality control. This of course is the justification for their existence in many cases. Type 1 content repositories all had quality controls in place. Type 2 and 3 LORs had only limited quality control over their links and more often than is comfortable, links were broken and could not be accessed. It can be argued that, in choosing a site to link to, someone has made a judgment as to its pedagogical or research value. This cannot always be assumed, however, the controls varied considerably.

3. *Requesting an LO* is a simple action in most repositories. Many permit searches of the entire database, but some limit searches to one section at a time. Of course in type 2, since the object itself is not housed, but merely described in the repository, additional intellectual property hurdles may have to be overcome at the actual location where the object is hosted.

   Judgment. With two significant exceptions (ESCOT and Exploratorium), type 1 LORs allowed comprehensive searchers. In type 2 and 3 LORs, this search feature was absent in a small but significant number of sites (14).

4. Maintaining *the LOs* and updating versions appropriately is a major task for LOR managers. For the most part, LORs have limited provision for continuous versioning and maintenance. Many LORs have none at all.

   Judgment. Maintaining a living LOR is a continuous task. In all categories, there were problems in updating and verifying information. Type 1 content sites, which control their own materials, are in a better position to sustain their collections than the other types that must rely on the survivability of the link sites. The Curricki LOR has been specifically set up to address the issue of sustainability of LOs, hoping to become a repository for content that will not move or drop off the Internet. Some sites (e.g., Fathom) that no longer add content have no need for updating. Much work needs to be done on conceptually understanding appropriate maintenance protocols as we evolve into massive re-use and recycling of objects. When is an LO altered enough to be considered a new version? How can an author update the original version, when it is has been used and further modified in many other objects? While not unique to learning objects, means to effectively manage all content (wikis, collaborative blogs, games and documents) are challenging and will likely take some time to resolve across the Net.

5. *Retrieving metadata on an LO* is more robust in those that house the content on site (type 1). It becomes problematic when accessing them through links to external websites, and sometimes even internal linking is deficient.

   Judgment. It might be expected that type 1 repositories would allow for robust retrieval. However there are some significant exceptions (e.g., NSDL and NROC) that limit their retrieval of metadata, based on business models that classify the metadata as their own asset. Type 2 and 3 LORs vary from facilitating robust retrieval to not allowing it at all. Some require membership or a subscription to access the materials (see Table 1.8).

6. *Submitting LOs by non-members* is possible for many LORs. Most exercise some form of quality control and some require that non-members open a subscription before being allowed to submit. *Judgment.* Type 1 LORs, for the most part, do not allow for submissions because they create and control their own content. Some type 1 repositories accept submissions, but these submissions must be made by vetted subscribers. Type 2 and 3 LORs also generally require either a subscription or at least a contact from the submitter before acceptance. This feature is often implemented to prevent the processing of content submitted by spambots.

7. *Storing with unique identifiers* is possible in the content-only repositories (Table 1.1). Those sites that depend on links often find that the objects can disappear into the ether as their URLs are dropped or they are moved by their owners.
   Judgment. As per the description, only type 1 content repositories uniquely store their content in their own LOR. Type 3 repositories store their own content and also link to outside content. Type 2 only link to outside content and do not store any of their own.

8. *Gathering of metadata about other objects* is conducted by the LORs that link to LOs at other websites. These LORs are aggregators and often do not store LOs themselves (types 2 and 3).
   Judgment. Type 1 LORs do not gather or link to outside LOs. This refers only to types 2 and 3.

9. Publishing *of metadata to other LORs* is allowed, but copying and storing of the LOs is often not permitted. Use is permitted but no copying. This can be problematic for course developers who want to integrate specific LOs into their courses and be assured of continuous access to that content.
   Judgment. Most type 1 LORs fully allow copying and external publishing to non-profit organizations and individuals, but some have only limited rights to the content and, as a result, users often must approach them individually. Other sites only allow use of the LOs at their site and do not permit copying. Nearly all type 2 sites have such limited rights as they do not own or control the content that they link to. Type 3 LORs have their own and external content links, so they normally have a mixed set of rights for users to meander through.

The categorization of LORs according to these criteria can be found in Table 1.9.

Table 1.9. Higgs' criteria for learning object repositories

	Name	1. Search Browse	2. Quality	3. Request Search All	4. Maintain	5. Retrieve Metadata	6. Subscribe to submit	7. Store	8. Gather	9. Publish
3	ARIADNE	Y	L	Y	N	Y	Y	N	Y	Y
2	AT&T Blue Web'n	Y	Y	N	N	N	N	N	N	N
1	BioDiTRL	Y	L	Y	L	S	Y	Y	N	Y
2	CAREO	Y	L	Y	N	N	N	N	N	N
2	CITIDEL	Y	Y	Y	Y	Y	N	N	Y	L
3	COLLOR	N	L	N	L	N	N	L	N	N
1	Connexions	Y	Y	Y	L	Y	N	N	N	L
1	Curriki	Y	Y	Y	Y	Y	Y	Y	Y	Y
2	DLESE	Y	Y	Y	N	Y	Y	N	Y	L
3	Digital Scriptorium	N	Y	Y	Y	Y	N	Y	N	N
3	Edna	Y	L	N	L	N	N	N	N	N
2	EducaNext portal	Y	Y	N	N	N	Y	N	Y	N
2	Educational software	Y	Y	Y	N	N	Y	N	Y	L
1	ESCOT	Y	Y	N	Y	Y	N	Y	N	N
1	Exploratories	Y	Y	Y	Y	Y	N	Y	N	Y
1	Exploratorium	Y	Y	N	Y	Y	N	Y	N	Y

1.5   Conclusion

1.5.1   What Types of LORs Are Available on the Internet?

Based on the analysis conducted, there are three principal types of LORs: content repositories, linking or metadata repositories, and hybrid repositories that host content and link to external LOs.

1.5.2   What Are the Principal Features of These LORs?

The principal features identified are those that Higgs et al. (2003) listed: search/find, quality control, request, maintain, retrieve, store, gather, and publish.

1.5.3   What Features Are More or less Universal and Which Are Specific to Certain Types?

The search/find/browse feature; requesting and retrieving are more or less universal as present features. Maintenance and updating are problems that all LORs struggle with. Publishing external to the LOR is also problematic among all types of LOR. Some allow for copying and reuse, but many others have limited control over digital rights. Quality control is more problematic in the linking types. Storage is manageable for the content repositories that house their own content, but is not possible in the linking and hybrid LORs. The content LORs do not gather LOs as do the other two types.

1.5.4   With the Vast Amounts of Information Available on the Internet, Is There a Need for LORs?

As the quantity of information increases on the Internet, easy access to relevant quality information (and for learners, learning materials) at the appropriate level becomes an expanding problem. Any attempts to provide quality content in interoperable formats (such as content LORs) are to be encouraged. The linking LORs help by sifting through the information, providing LOs from a trusted and knowledgeable source.

References

Berkun, S. (2005). Why does freesound succeed when so many learning object repositories fail? (electronic version). Edtech Post. http://edtechpost.ca/wordpress/2005/12/14/Why-does-'Freesound'-succeed-when-so-many-learning-object-repositories-fail. Accessed 25 September 2007.

Borgne, P. L., Fallot, J. -P., Lecas, J. -F., & Lenfant, A. (2006). Usages des technologies par les élèves professeurs: analyse à partir de questionnaires (electronic version). La Revue internationale des technologies en pédagogie universitaire. http://www.profetic.org/revue/IMG/pdf/ritpu_0203_leborgne.pdf. Accessed 18 February 2007.

Connexions (2007). Connexions is growing. http://cnx.org. Accessed 19 February 2007.

Davies, D. (2007). Could Yahoo Pipes make repository interoperability obsolete? http://david.davies.name/weblog/2007/02/23/could-yahoo-pipes-make-repository-interoperability-obsolete/. Accessed 23 February 2007.

Dodani, M. II. (2002). The dark side of object learning: learning objects (electronic version). *Journal of Object Technology*, 1(5), 37–42. http://www.jot.fm/issues/issue_2002_11/column3. Accessed 19 February 2007.

Downes, S. (2003). Paper tissue argument. http://www.downes.ca/cgi-bin/website/refer.cgi?item=1049084977&sender=. Accessed 25 September 2007.

eduSource (2005). eRiB: eduSource repository-in-a-box. http://edusource.licef.teluq.uquebec.ca/ese/en/install_erib.htm/.

Flexible Learning Advisory Group (2003). VET learning object repository: green paper for discussion. http://pre2005.flexiblelearning.net.au/projects/resources/VLOR_green_paper.doc. Accessed 20 February 2007.

Friesen, N. (2005). Some objections to learning objects. In R. McGreal (Ed.), Online Education using Learning Objects (pp. 59–70). London: Taylor and Francis.

Han, Y. (2006). GROW: building a high-quality civil engineering learning object repository and portal (electronic version). Ariadne, (49). http://www.ariadne.ac.uk/issue49/yan-han/. Accessed 18 February 2007.

Higgs, P., Meredith, S., & Hand, T. (2003). *Technology for sharing: researching learning objects and digital rights management.* Flexible Learning Leader Report 2002.

Hodgins, W. (2006). C-ing the future: content, competencies and context. In First Latin American Conference on Learning Objects. Guaaquil, Ecuador. http://www.slideshare.net/WayneH/keynote-laclo-latin-america-conference-on-learning-objects/. Accessed 25 January 2007.

Kurshan, B. B. (2006). Curriki – global education and learning community: bringing curricula into the participation age (electronic version). http://www.curriki.org/xwiki/bin/download/Coll_curriki/CurrikiWhitePaper/CurrikiWhitePaperfinaljan82007.pdf. Accessed 12 February 2007.

Leinonen, T. (2006). Learning objects – is the king naked? http://flosse.dicole.org/?item=learning-objects-is-the-king-naked. Accessed 24 March 2007.

Liu, X., Abdulmotaleb, & Saddik, E. (n.d.). Multimedia learning object metadata management and mapping tool. http://www.elg.uottawa.ca/~elsaddik/abedweb/publications/MMLOM.pdf

McGreal, R. (Ed.) (2004). *Online Education Using Learning Objects.* London: RoutledgeFalmer.

MIT Open Courseware (2005). 2005 MIT Program evaluation findings report. http://ocw.mit.edu/OcwWeb/Global/AboutOCW/evaluation.htm. Accessed 19 February 2007.

Osborne, G. T. (2005). *Towards an interoperable approach: recommendations for an institutional learning object repository.* Unpublished Master's thesis, Athabasca University, Athabasca, AB.

Robertson, A. (2006). Introduction aux Banques d'objets d'apprentissage en français au Canada. (electronic version). Réseau d'enseignement francophone à distance REFAD. http://www.refad.ca/recherche/intro_objets_apprentissage/pdf/RapportObjetsapprentissage2006.pdf. Accessed 18 February 2007.

Sampson, D., & Karampiperis, P. (2004). Reusable learning objects: designing metadata management systems supporting interoperable learning object repositories. In R. McGreal (Ed.), *Online Education Using Learning Objects* (pp. 207–222). London: RoutledgeFalmer.

South, J., & Monson, D. (2000). A university-wide system for creating, capturing, and delivering learning objects. In D. A. Wiley (Ed.), *In the Instructional Use of Learning Objects*, online version.

The Learning Federation (2006). Accessing TLF objects and digital resources (for DoE educators only). Retrieved February 18, 2007, from http://www.thelearningfederation.edu.au/node617.

Wiley, D. (n.d.). Learning objects: difficulties and opportunities (electronic version). Open content. http://wiley.ed.usu.edu/docs/lo_do.pdf. Accessed 18 February 2007.

Wilson, S. (2005). Learning resources: a personal education view from the UK. http://www.knownet.com/writing/elearning2.0/entries/scott_wilson_on_using_resources/scottwilson-eduresources.pdf/attach/scottwilson-eduresources.pdf. Accessed 18 February 2007.

2 Adaptive Hypermedia

P. De Bra

Adaptive hypermedia makes it possible to author learning material once and generate a personalized learning experience for every user. The information that is presented, the way in which it is presented and the possible ways for the user to navigate through it can all be adapted. This chapter presents the most common adaptive hypermedia methods and techniques and shows examples of how they can be (and are) used in existing adaptive hypermedia systems and in adaptive online educational material.

2.1 Introduction

Learning, and education in general, has long been approached with a "one size fits all" attitude. When the Web became popular, authors of educational material started putting textbooks on the Web, thereby using hypertext links to give learners the freedom to study the material in any way (or order) they liked. The newly created navigational freedom was an illusion, however: the textbooks were not written with studying the topics out of the original order in mind. When you open a textbook at chapter 5, you do not really expect to understand everything as you know you have missed chapters 1 through 4. However, when you open an online textbook that shows links to each chapter, you do expect to be able to go directly to chapter 5 and understand what is written there. This is reasonable, because the existence of the link to chapter 5 suggests that the author has written the textbook in such a way that going directly to chapter 5 is "normal". However, writing a textbook in such a way that everything can be understood in any reading order is an impossible task. This is where adaptive hypermedia (or AH) comes to the rescue.

The basic idea in AH is that by observing what the learner does (what she reads, what scores she obtains on tests, etc.), the system can get a detailed impression of the user's knowledge. The presence or absence of knowledge about a topic can be used to insert or remove explanations, depending on whether they are still needed, and it can also be used to guide the user towards topics she can study next. Brusilovsky (2001) has presented an overview of the AH field as it existed in 2001.

Adaptive hypermedia methods and techniques can be used to overcome the difficulties caused by the navigational freedom that is typical for hypertext. AH can be used to guide users towards the topics they are ready to study at any given time. It can be used to insert prerequisite explanations when needed, and to show additional detailed information to interested and advanced learners. It is also possible to change the guidance depending on the learner's cognitive style (or learning style) or to present topics differently, depending on that style, e.g., through text, images or video, when desired.

In order to make it possible to adapt learning material (or any other type of information) to the user, the system must get to know the user in two ways: (a) the system must follow the learning process in order to decide which topics are studied by the user, and (b) the system must know the learning style of the user, or any other aspect of the context in which the system is being used. We will concentrate on adaptation to the evolving knowledge of the user, and not on the learning styles (which are supposedly more stable and only lead to some stereotypical forms of adaptation).

Adaptive hypermedia techniques are appearing in all kinds of applications, such as personalized search engines, personalized advice on online shopping sites, recommender systems (e.g., a personalized TV guide), context-sensitive help systems, etc. However, adaptive educational hypermedia is the most popular application area for this technology, both in research and in actual full-fledged applications.

Adaptive educational applications rely heavily on a structured description of the subject domain of the application or course. In this chapter, we will base adaptation mostly on such a structural description (and only sometimes on domain-independent aspects). The chapters on metadata and on ontologies explain how such descriptions can be created using standards that often came into existence much later than the adaptive hypermedia systems and applications we describe in this chapter.

2.2   Adaptation Methods in Educational Hypermedia

Adaptation is used either to alleviate problems that users encounter (if there is no adaptation) or to improve an otherwise already normal, or at least acceptable, experience.

In most courses, there are not only links to several chapters right from the starting page, but there are also a lot of cross-references between different chapters/sections. In a normal paper textbook, the author knows whether such a reference is a forward or a backward reference, and thus whether or not the reference is to a concept already encountered when following the linear order of the book. In an online course with navigational freedom, the author cannot know whether, for a given learner, a reference will be a forward or backward reference. However, it isn't difficult for a system to track a user's path through the course text, and thus to know whether a reference leads to new information or to a previously visited page or concept. There are now two possibilities:

1. The author can create two versions of a page or the relevant part of a page (also called a fragment): one for learners who have studied the required concepts before, and one for learners who have not (and thus may need a more introductory version or an extra explanation). The system can choose which version to present, based on the user's knowledge when following the reference link.
2. The author can also determine what the conditions are (in terms of knowledge of concepts) under which it is a good idea to follow a cross-reference link. The system can check whether the learner has the required knowledge and can hide, disable or annotate the link accordingly.

These two possibilities represent the two largest categories of adaptation techniques: content adaptation (called adaptive presentation in Brusilovsky (2001)) and link adaptation (called adaptive navigation support in Brusilovsky (2001)).

Content adaptation, based on the learner's knowledge, typically comes in three forms (see also Brusilovsky (2001)):

1. When a page refers to or uses a concept the learner does not yet know, and of which at least some understanding is needed, a short prerequisite explanation can be inserted. This lets the learner continue with the chosen subject, rather than requiring a jump to the prerequisite concept in order to study that in detail first.

2. Sometimes the current concept can be elaborated upon in case a related concept is already known, or when the knowledge level of the learner is already high. For these "expert" users an additional explanation can be given that is beyond the level of the average learner (at the time of visiting the current page).

3. Sometimes an interesting comparison is possible with another concept, but only if that other concept is already known. Such a comparative explanation between the concepts can automatically be shown on the page of the second of the two concepts studied by the learner, regardless of which of the two is second in the chosen reading order.

An additional issue with content adaptation is the issue of stability. When a prerequisite explanation is shown on a page, and the learner later revisits the page after obtaining all prerequisite knowledge, should the prerequisite explanation remain or should it be removed? And if a comparative explanation is shown on the page explaining the second concept, should the comparison also be shown on the page explaining the first concept when that page is revisited later? In our online course on the topic of hypermedia (http://wwwis.win.tue.nl/2L690/), we apply no stability and learners, when revisiting a page, have never commented that the contents had changed. Figure 2.1 shows an example from this course. This of course does not mean that nobody has ever noticed a change.

- Before reading about Xanadu the URL page shows:

   …

   In Xanadu (a fully distributed hypertext system, developed by Ted Nelson at Brown University, from 1965 on) there was only one protocol, so that part could be missing.

   …

- After reading about Xanadu this becomes:

   …

   In Xanadu there was only one protocol, so that part could be missing.

   …

Fig. 2.1. Content adaptation in the hypermedia course

Link adaptation comes in two forms: the system can make suggestions as to which links to follow or avoid, and the system can change links so that they appear, disappear or lead to a different destination depending on the learner's knowledge:

When the system knows the user's goal, because that is defined as a task in the course, because it is specified by the user, or because the system can determine a "preferred" reading order, it may sort or reorder links that appear in a list. Link sorting is always performed by search engines, and it can be made adaptive by taking information about the user's knowledge or goals into account.

In a list of links, it is not only possible to use sorting to suggest a preference for a certain link destination. Links that are deemed inappropriate because the user is missing too much prerequisite knowledge, for instance, can be removed entirely. This adaptive link removal technique should be used with great care. When used on a list of chapters of a course text it may suggest that the course consists of only a few chapters and the learner may be (unpleasantly) surprised to find out there are many more chapters that only become available later. (In a very informal user study we found that users strongly preferred a list with some disabled links over a list with the unsuitable links removed.)

In normal paragraphs of text, sorting and removal are not possible (as they would disrupt the flow of the text). It is still possible to indicate desirability of links by using adaptive link annotation. The suitability of links has already been indicated using link anchor colors in the pre-Web ISIS Tutor (Brusilovsky and Pesin 1994). Later systems, including ELM-ART (Weber and Brusilovsky 2001) and its descendent, Interbook (Brusilovsky et al. 1998), use icons such as colored balls (● ● ●) to indicate whether a link is interesting or not. They may also use other icons such as checkmarks (✓ ✓ ✓) to indicate a knowledge level. Figure 2.2 shows a partial screen shot from an Interbook application.

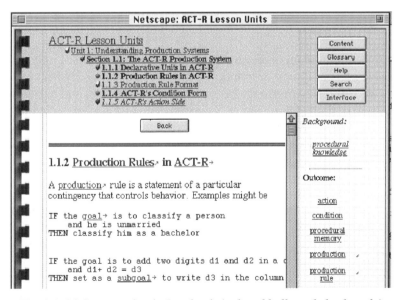

Fig. 2.2. Link annotation in Interbook (*colored balls and checkmarks*)

- Instead of indicating an undesired link through an icon such as the red ball (●), systems like AHA! (De Bra and Calvi 1998; De Bra et al. 2006) can also adaptively hide and/or disable links. When the link anchor is shown in the same color as normal text (and not underlined), the learner will most likely not notice it is there. In addition, the anchor text may also be turned into plain text, removing its link functionality. The advantage of hiding annotation is that the learner is not distracted by non-recommended links. The drawback is that links that are initially hidden and start to appear later may surprise or even confuse the learner, especially when it turns out there is unexpectedly more material to learn.
- Another way to manipulate links is by changing their destination. When a page contains a "next" button for instance, this may lead to the most appropriate page to read next. The learner's goals and knowledge may influence the decision as to which page should be next. But the destination for other links may vary as well. For a novice, a link may lead to an introduction about a topic whereas the same link may lead to a detailed or advanced discussion for a knowledgeable learner. Depending on how such adaptive link destinations arc implemented, the different link destination may be visible to an observant user (when the URL is different) or not (when the same URL is used to serve different page content).

2.3 Overlay User Models

Adaptive educational hypermedia applications or courses rely on the existence of a structured description of the domain. The AHAM model (De Bra et al. 1999) shown in Fig. 2.3 shows a domain model and a user model at the core of an AH application. These two models are connected through a teaching model, which we later renamed to adaptation model. AHAM is based on the Dexter Hypertext Reference Model (Halasz and Schwartz 1994), which shows a five-layer architecture of hypermedia applications. We concentrate on the middle layer: the storage layer.

Structure is often thought of as being hierarchical. A course text typically consists of a number of chapters, each divided into sections and subsections, down to small chunks of information such as a definition, a theorem, an example or an explanation of a certain topic. As the learner builds up knowledge of the course by studying the small topics, thus gathering knowledge of larger concepts and eventually the whole course, it makes sense to keep track of the evolving knowledge using a similarly structured user model, which we call an overlay model. (The user model is an overlay of the domain model.)

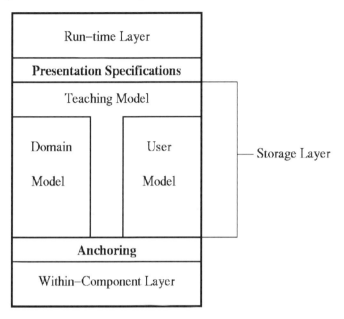

Fig. 2.3. The AHAM reference model

2.3.1   Registering Changes in Learners' Knowledge

In adaptive educational hypermedia applications there are essentially two ways in which the system can know that a learner has acquired knowledge about a topic: by observing that the learner has read a page or by evaluating answers to a test (often multiple-choice).

- Reading pages: When learning is not done through lectures (in class or on video), it is typically at least partially done through reading. (It can also partly be done through exercises and assignment work.) Since the learning material in an online course often consists of web-pages, a server-side program can register the pages a learner accesses, and conclude that the learner will study (and later, has studied) these pages. Whether this means that the learner then has full knowledge of the corresponding concept(s) is impossible to deduce with absolute certainty. If there is missing prerequisite knowledge, the learner will most likely not understand everything the page explains. And if the learner visits the page only briefly, she will not have read everything. A simple approach to decide whether the learner has studied a page is to also register the time between page accesses, in order to deduce the reading time. A more elaborate approach is taken by the AdeLE project (Mödritscher et al. 2006), which uses eye-tracking to decide what the learner has actually seen. It is not yet clear whether registering reading time or even eye movements enables adaptation that is so much better that the overall learning outcome of a course is significantly better.

- Multiple-choice tests: Verification of learners' knowledge has been done through exams for a very long time. A thorough analysis of answers to difficult questions is very hard, if not impossible, to automate. No existing software can analyze an answer to a question like "Why did Germany start World War II?" (or almost any other *why* question). However, skilled teachers often manage to create multiple-choice questions with several believable wrong answers (and one or more correct answers as well). We won't go into detail on how to create good multiple-choice questions, but note that such tests are a popular way to check a learner's knowledge level about a concept. Through such tests an AH system may verify whether its belief about the learner's knowledge is justified.

When the learning process stops, the learner's knowledge of the studies' concepts does not remain constant. Bielikova and Nagy (2006) suggest repeating prerequisite knowledge at the start of a new lesson as a remedy for the learner's imperfect memory (and make other suggestions as well). They have implemented a model for the "decay" of human memory in an extension of the AHA! system. The extended system registers the access time of each page and uses an activity-in-memory attribute of concepts to register that a concept is being used and thus refreshed. Bielikova and Nagy (2006) use an English-Slovak vocabulary application as an example, and each time a word is used it becomes active in memory. In applications with a more complex concept structure, it may be more difficult to implement the activity of refreshing the learner's memory, especially for higher-level concepts.

2.3.2 Deducing Knowledge About Higher Level Concepts

By registering page accesses (or even more detailed information about the learner's interaction with the adaptive application), the AH system creates a very fine-grained model of the learner's knowledge of the subject domain of a course. Using this detailed information in determining whether the learner has enough prerequisite knowledge to visit a page or chapter is impractical. Adaptation is often based on the knowledge of higher-level concepts (with "higher-level" meaning higher up in the concept hierarchy that describes the subject domain of a course). There are essentially two ways to implement a user model in which the knowledge of higher-level concepts is represented. From publications about systems, it isn't always clear which implementation choice was made in these systems:

- Systems like KBS Hyperbook (Henze and Nejdl 1999) use an inference engine to deduce estimated knowledge of higher-level concepts from knowledge of pages. The basic idea is that by knowing how much knowledge each page (or lowest-level information item) contributes to a higher-level concept (perhaps going through some intermediate levels of concepts as well), the knowledge of a high-level concept can be quickly calculated from its contributing page-level knowledge values. The calculation is only done when the knowledge value is actually needed, for instance, in order to decide whether a prerequisite for a concept is satisfied.

- An alternative is to use the concept hierarchy to transfer knowledge from pages to higher-level concepts each time the knowledge level of a page changes. This may imply that the knowledge of a high-level concept is updated several times without that value being needed. On the other hand, when the knowledge value is needed in order to decide on a prerequisite, it is immediately available and need not be inferred from all the lower-level values. In the AHA! system (De Bra et al. 2006), attributes of concepts (including the knowledge attribute) can be declared volatile or persistent. The value of a volatile attribute is calculated when needed, whereas the values of persistent attributes are stored. AHA! can thus support both implementation choices.

Figure 2.4 shows a screenshot of the Graph Author tool, which is part of AHA! (De Bra et al. 2006). It is used to create the conceptual structure of a course. The left part shows (part of) the concept hierarchy. The right part shows a graph of concept relationships, which in this case are (almost all) prerequisites. The concept hierarchy defines how knowledge is propagated up the concept hierarchy, from pages to sections to chapters to the whole course. This hierarchy thus deals with the conceptual content level. The concept relationship defines a pedagogical structure. In order to decide on how to perform adaptation, we have to consider the following questions: What happens when the learner studies pages with missing prerequisites? How much knowledge is required before we consider a prerequisite satisfied (or should we also consider partially satisfied prerequisites)? Are prerequisites necessarily transitive? We will now deal with each question in turn:

- When a prerequisite for a page is not satisfied, we may expect the learner to not fully understand what the page is trying to explain. If a bit of missing prerequisite knowledge can be compensated for by inserting an additional explanation into the page, we should consider the prerequisites for the page as a whole to be satisfied. When the page as a whole is not suitable for the learner, an AH system typically assigns partial knowledge to the knowledge attribute of the concept. The standard behavior of AHA! (which can be changed) is that revisiting a page while it is still not recommended does not increase the knowledge beyond that partial-knowledge level (which is set to 35 by default, with 100 meaning full knowledge). In Interbook, on the other hand, revisiting a non-recommended page does keep increasing the knowledge, so full knowledge can be obtained by studying the page several times. Links to non-recommended pages are typically hidden or annotated, so the learner clearly knows when she is following a link to such a page. Depending on the AH system used (or how it is configured), the non-recommended status of a page might also be visible on the page itself. In Interbook, a green or red horizontal line near the top of the page indicates whether the page is recommended (green) or not (red).
- When knowledge is propagated from pages to higher-level concepts, a wide range of knowledge values becomes possible. In the hypermedia course 2L690, the first three chapters form a prerequisite for the remaining advanced chapters. Since in AHA! (used to serve the course), knowledge is a value between 0 and 100, we have to decide how much knowledge of the combined first chapters is needed before the learner is advised, or at least allowed, to start studying the advanced chapters. In AHA! prerequisites by default require 50% knowledge in order to be satisfied. (This number can be changed by an author for any or all of the prerequisites.) The choice of 50% knowledge for prerequisites and 35% knowledge for studying non-recommended pages has an interesting consequence: it makes prerequisites transitive. If A is a prerequisite for B and B for C, then 50% knowledge of A is needed to make B recommended, and 50% knowledge of B is needed to make C recommended. Should the learner visit concept B while not knowing enough about A, then only 35% knowledge of B will be recorded, meaning that the prerequisite B for concept C will not be satisfied. So because A was not sufficiently known, concept C will not be recommended even when B is visited. Making prerequisites transitive makes creating a graph of prerequisite relations easy, and results in a graph that is easy to understand.

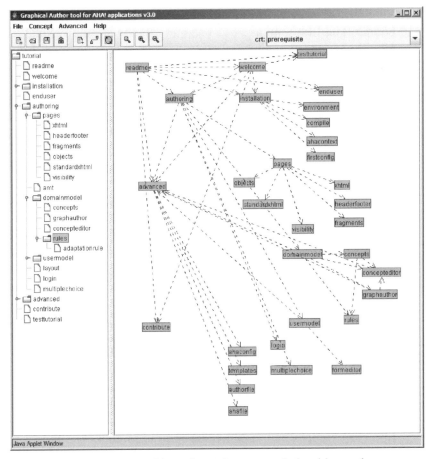

Fig. 2.4. Concept hierarchy and concept relationship graph

2.3.3   Which User Model State to Use in Adaptation?

As we have seen above, the user's knowledge state is updated each time a page is read (or a concept visited, or a test performed), and the user's knowledge state is used to determine how the presented information should be adapted (as shown in Figs. 2.3 and 2.4). But how do the user model updates and the adaptation interact with each other? When the user clicks on a link (anchor), is the requested page adapted to the current user-model state, and is the state updated afterwards? Or is the user-model state updated first and the page adapted to the new state? Both approaches have positive and negative side-effects:

- Suppose we want to use a specific example in several places in a course. The first time a page containing the example is visited, the learner should see the whole example. Subsequent visits to the example (on the same page or on other pages) may briefly recall or summarize the example instead of explaining it completely. If the presentation of the example depends on the knowledge of the example, it will be presented completely the first time, when the knowledge is still 0, and briefly on subsequent visits, when the knowledge is above 0. In order for this scheme to work, information (fragments, pages and concepts) must be presented before the user model is updated.

- Suppose we want to present a page A containing all the prerequisite knowledge for a concept B that should be studied immediately after. Page A will therefore contain a link to B. Since the user will have all the required prerequisite knowledge for B, the link pointing to B should be recommended to this user. But the link to B will only be recommended if the link is adapted to the user's knowledge state after reading page A. Since a page, once presented, cannot be changed while the user is reading it, the link must already be recommended when the user starts reading. Hence the knowledge of A must be updated before the page is presented.

- It is clear that no AH system can implement both approaches simultaneously. The second approach is the most common one. When knowledge is updated first, and adaptation performed second, the link adaptation works as expected. As for the prerequisite explanation (or example), an easy workaround is to count the number of visits, starting at 0, and know that upon the first visit to a concept its visit counter will already be 1 when the concept is presented.

2.4 Adaptation to Other Aspects Besides Knowledge

Brusilovsky (2001) states that in AH, adaptation can be done to a user's individual traits, which includes all user features that together define a user as an individual, and to the user's environment. We will briefly consider adaptation to the learner's cognitive style or learning style in this chapter (and, for simplicity, consider these equivalent), and also look at adaptation to the user's browsing device and network characteristics.

2.4.1   Adaptation to Learning Styles

Many theories on cognitive and learning styles exist. This results in a plethora of terms, many of which are more or less equivalent, and in a lot of advice on how to adapt to a learner's cognitive abilities and preferences, (some also conflicting, and some even suggesting that it may be better to adapt *against* the learner's cognitive style rather than *for* it (Smith et al. 2002)) in order for learners to also train their not-preferred skills. We base our suggestions in this chapter mostly on an extensive report by Coffield et al. (2004) that considers 71 learning-style models worthy of consideration (out of over 100 models they found). Some of the most important models for our description are that of Dunn and Dunn (1978), Witkin et al. (1977), and Honey and Mumford (1992). We highlight a few aspects of these models below:

- Sensory modalities (as used in Dunn and Dunn's study (Dunn and Dunn 1978), for instance) describe how learners best sense or perceive information. Auditory students learn best through verbal lectures. They like listening to and discussing with others. Visual students learn through seeing. This can be through pictoral (images, video) or textual material. Tactile or kinesthetic students learn best through a hands-on approach. When forced to read from paper, they underline or mark with a magic marker.
- Psychological modalities describe how learners best learn (Dunn and Dunn 1978). Analytic students prefer to learn one detail at a time, and later put the parts together to complete the big picture. Global students, on the other hand, first need to see the whole meaning (the big picture) before they deal with the individual details that together form that whole. This classification by Dunn and Dunn roughly corresponds to the field-independent and field-dependent styles of Witkin.
- Honey and Mumford suggest the following terms for the different ways in which a learner likes to learn. An activist likes to "have a go, and see what happens". These students like to experiment, often in groups, in order to deduce a theory. A reflector likes to "gather information and mull things over". These students gather data, analyze it and delay reaching conclusions. A theorist likes to "tidy up and reach some conclusions". These students think things through in logical steps, for models, and only later try to apply them. The pragmatist likes "tried and tested techniques". These students seek quick decisions, resulting in practical step-by-step procedures that work, without long discussions and theory.

- We chose to discuss only these learning styles because we can supply some concrete adaptation for them, as done by Stash and De Bra (2004) and Papanikolaou et al. (2003).
- In order to accommodate the verbalizer and imager styles, an application can offer the same (or similar) information in textual form and through images or video. Auditory users can have the text spoken out loud. Technically this adaptation is very easy using content adaptation, but it does require the information to be produced several times, once for each media type.
- Global/analytical or field dependent/independent users can be helped by changing the order in which concepts are presented. Global and field-dependent users need an overview before studying details. In order to achieve this, the system can guide the users in a breadth-first way through the top-level concepts. These users wish to know what a whole course is about before studying the details of a single topic. Analytical or field-independent users do not need such an overview. They can either navigate freely or receive guidance to navigate in a depth-first way. The required guidance can easily be generated using adaptive link hiding or annotation.
- To accommodate activists, reflectors, theorists and pragmatists, the learning material needs to be divided into objects of different types. Papanikolaou et al. (2003) suggest that an activist start with an activity, such as an exercise. A reflector should see some examples first, followed by the theory, and then solve an exercise. The theorist starts with theory, then gets some examples to illustrate the theory and finally performs some exercises. The pragmatist starts with an exercise, and then goes to examples and finally the theory. If the different pieces are small, they can be presented as fragments of a page and sorted according to the learner's cognitive style. If the pieces are too big to be presented all at once, the system can present the first item and place a sorted list of links to the other items at the bottom of the page that presents the first item.

2.4.2 Adaptation to the Browsing Environment

When dealing with online adaptive systems, the information content and structure should be independent of the actual presentation form. Viewing a website on a large monitor, with a computer on a high-speed connection, provides an experience that is very different from that of viewing the site on a personal digital assistant (PDA) with relatively low processing power and a slow wireless connection. Adaptation (other than the common adaptability by selecting different presentation skins) involves mostly the aspects of size and of bandwidth.

- Adaptation to varying screen sizes involves more than scaling objects. A decision has to be made when to change the presentation structure globally or locally. For instance, text may have to be summarized in order to fit on the screen. A page that displays a number of images may have to be replaced by a slideshow (automated or through links) showing one image at a time. Adaptation to the browsing environment may thus involve more than just adapting each information object, but may involve changing the navigation structure as well. Figure 2.5 from (Fiala et al. 2004) illustrate such adaptation. Research in this area has resulted in the AMACONT (Fiala et al. 2003) and Cuypers engines (van Ossenbruggen et al. 2001).
- Adaptation to variations in bandwidth has been attempted by various research teams. We note the work of Muntean and McManis (2006) because it evaluates the effect of different "quality of experience" factors in courseware based on an extension of the AHA! system. Quality of experience is not just a function of bandwidth but is defined using performance metrics download time, round-trip time, throughput and user tolerance for delays.
- In the study, it turned out that reducing the image or video quality in order to avoid delays allowed students to complete a course (part) equally well and faster, whereas they did not consider the quality of the presentation insufficient. Clearly users are willing to accept less perfect images and videos in order to receive them faster and without interruption.

2.5 Summary/Conclusions

Adaptive hypermedia enables automatic personalization of online course material. In this chapter, we have seen that adaptation can be applied to the information content (in order to ensure that the learner receives understandable), to the navigation structure (either by restricting possible navigation by removing or disabling links or by guiding the user through link annotation and sorting), and also to the layout and presentation (in order to match the capabilities of the browsing device and network).

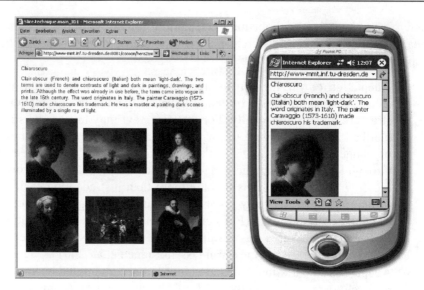

Fig. 2.5. Adaptation to the browsing device (screen size)

Adaptation is typically performed based on an estimate of the learner's knowledge of the subject domain. In order to do so, an overlay user model is constructed and maintained. But adaptation to the learner's cognitive abilities and preferences is also possible. We have shown how an AH system can adapt to various learning styles. Researchers do not yet agree on the question of whether or not adaptation to learning styles is always beneficial, so there is certainly room for future work in this area.

References

Bielikova, M., Nagy, P. (2006). Considering human memory aspects for adaptation and its realization in AHA! In *EC-TEL 2006: Technology Enhanced Learning* (pp. 8–20), LNCS 4227. Berlin Heidelberg New York: Springer.

Brusilovsky P. (2001). Adaptive hypermedia. *User Modeling and User Adapted Interaction*, 11(1–2), 87–110.

Brusilovsky, P., Pesin, L. (1994), ISIS-Tutor: an adaptive hypertext learning environment. In *Japan-CIS Symposium on Knowledge Based Software Engineering, Proc. of JCKBSE'94* (pp. 83–87).

Brusilovsky, P., Eklund, J., Schwarz, E. (1998). Web-based education for all: a tool for developing adaptive courseware. *Computer Networks and ISDN Systems (Proceedings of Seventh International World Wide Web Conference)*, 30(1–7), 291–300.

Coffield, F., Moseley, D., Hall, E., Ecclestone, K. (2004). Learning styles and pedagogy in post-16 learning: a systematic and critical review. Learning and Skills research center. http://www.lsda.org.uk/files/pdf/1543.pdf

De Bra, P., Calvi, L. (1998). AHA! An open adaptive hypermedia architecture. *The New Review of Hypermedia and Multimedia*, 4, 115–139.

De Bra, P., Houben, G. J., Wu, H. (1999). AHAM: a dexter-based reference model for adaptive hypermedia. *ACM Conference on Hypertext and Hypermedia* (pp. 147–156).

De Bra, P., Smits, D., Stash, N. (2006). The Design of AHA!. In *Proceedings of the ACM Conference on Hypertext and Hypermedia* (p. 133) and on-line version at http://aha.win.tue.nl/ahadesign/.

Dunn, R., Dunn, L. (1978). *Teaching Students Through Their Individual Learning Styles: A Practical Approach*. Reston, VA: Reston.

Fiala, Z., Hinz, M., Meissner, K., Wehner, F. (2003). A component-based approach for adaptive dynamic web documents. *Journal of Web Engineering*, 2, 058–073.

Fiala, Z., Frasincar, F., Hinz, M., Houben, G. J., Barna, P., Meissner, K. (2004). Engineering the presentation layer of adaptable web-information systems. In *Proceedings of the International Conference on Web Engineering* (pp. 459–472), LNCS 3140. Munich, Germany, July 2004.

Halasz, F., Schwartz, M. (1994). The dexter hypertext reference model. *Communications of the ACM*, 37(2), 30–39.

Henze, N., Nejdl, W. (1999). Adaptivity in the KBS hyperbook system. In *Second Workshop on Adaptive Systems and User Modeling on the WWW*.

Honey, P., Mumford, A. (1992). *The manual of Learning Styles*. Maidenhead: Peter Honey.

Mödritscher, F., Garcia-Barrios, V. M., Gütl, C., Helic, D. (2006). The first AdeLE prototype at a glance. In *Proceedings of ED-MEDIA* (pp. 791–798).

Muntean, C., McManis, J. (2006). The value of QoE-based adaptation approach in educational hypermedia: empirical evaluation. In *Proceedings of the Fourth International Conference on Adaptive Hypermedia and Adaptive Web-Based Systems* (pp. 121–130), LNCS 4018. Dublin.

van Ossenbruggen, J., Geurts, J., Cornelissen, F., Hardman, L., Rutledge, L. (2001). Towards second and third generation web-based multimedia. In *The Tenth International Conference on the World Wide Web*, WWW10, (pp. 479–488). Hong Kong: ACM.

Papanikolaou, K., Grigoriadou, M., Kornilakis, H., Magoulas, G. D. (2003). Personalising the interaction in a web-based educational hypermedia system: the case of INSPIRE. *User Modeling and User-Adapted Interaction*, 13(3), 213–267.

Smith, W., Sekar, S., Townsend, K. (2002). The impact of surface and reflective teaching and learning on student academic success. In *Proceedings of the seventh Annual European Learning Styles Information Network Conference* (pp. 407–418). Ghent.

Stash, N., De Bra, P. (2004). Incorporating cognitive styles in AHA! (The Adaptive Hypermedia Architecture). In *Proceedings of the International Conference Web-Based Education* (pp. 378–383). Innsbruck, Austria.

Weber, G., Brusilovsky, P. (2001). ELM-ART: an adaptive versatile system for web-based instruction. *Journal of Artificial Intelligence in Education* 12, 351–384.

Witkin, H., Moore, C., Goodenough, D., Cox, P. (1977). Field-dependent and field-independent cognitive styles and their educational implications. *Review of Educational Research*, 47(1), 1–64.

3 Ontologies and Semantic Web for E-Learning

D. Dicheva

This article discusses the area of ontologies and semantic web technologies in E-Learning and compares the state of research in years 2004 and 2006. It considers the impact of ontologies on the web-based educational systems (WBES). It then presents an ontology of the area of ontologies for education along with a community web portal (O4E) driven by that ontology. Finally, it presents a use case of semantic web technologies as enabling technologies for building WBES: the case of TM4L. Topic Maps for E-Learning (TM4L) is an authoring environment for building ontology-aware standards-based repositories of learning materials (objects).

3.1 Introduction

The semantic web (SW), envisioned as an extension of the current web (Berners-Lee et al. 2001), was proposed to provide enhanced access to information based on the use of machine-processable metadata annotating the web resources. A key enabling technology for the semantic web are ontologies. Ontologies offer a way to cope with heterogeneous representations of web resources and their interoperability. An ontology representing a model of a specific domain can be used as a unifying structure for giving information a common representation and semantics. Ontologies are becoming very popular due to their promise to allow a shared and common understanding of a domain that can be communicated between people and applications (Davies et al. 2003).

For educational system researchers and technologists, the semantic web vision opened a new venue promising to meet the increasing challenges E-Learning was facing due to the fast-growing web. Although some early efforts of using ontologies in intelligent educational systems can be found (see Ikeda et al. 1995; and Mizoguchi et al. 1996), the initial SW in educa-tion-related activities can be linked to year 1999, when the first ontology-focused workshop (collocated with AIED'99) (AIED 1999) took place. Among the pioneering projects employing ontologies and SW standards in education were SmartTrainer Authoring Tools (Jin et al. 1999), Edutella (Nejdl et al. 2001), the LOM RDF binding project (Nilsson et al. 2003), etc. Several SW-related projects were reported at the Workshop on Con-cepts and Ontologies in Web-Based Educational Systems (ICCE 2002) and at the Workshop on Semantic Web for Web-based Learning (CAISE 2003). The year 2004, however, can be considered the breakthrough point, when three workshops (Adaptive Hypermedia 2004; ITS 2004; ISWC 2004) took place, and the first special journal issues focused on the appli-cation of Semantic Web and Ontologies in E-Learning (three that year alone!) were published (Sampson et al. 2004; Dicheva and Aroyo 2004b; Anderson and Whitelock 2004). In addition, a number of papers appeared in other related conferences (e.g., Dolog et al. 2004; Gašević et al. 2004), journals (e.g., Devedžic 2004a) and books (e.g., Mizoguchi 2004; Brase and Wolfgang 2004).

This article presents the area of ontologies and semantic web techno-logies in E-Learning and compares the state-of-the-art in 2004 and 2006. It further focuses on considering the impact of ontologies on the web-based educational systems (WBES). An ontology of the area of ontologies for education (O4E) and a community web portal, driven by that ontology, are presented. Finally, a use case of semantic web technologies as enabling technologies for building WBES is discussed. The use case is TM4L, an authoring environment for building ontology-aware standards-based repositories of learning materials.

3.2   Overview of WBES

Web-based educational systems are employing semantic web technologies in an effort to better serve the increasing and complicated needs of the education community.

3.2.1   WBES at a Glance

The development of WBES has distinct generations that have different fea-tures with their own particular challenges:

1st generation WBES:

- *Challenges*: Centralizing and unifying sporadically appearing online courses and learning materials in order to better support them from administrative, technical, software and authoring perspectives
- *Distinguishing features*: Centralized (typically client–server) architecture, employing web technologies, a proprietary format for representing the maintained learning resources
- *Representatives*:
  - o Learning Management Systems (LMS), aimed at supporting various teaching, learning and administrative activities to allow web-enhanced courses (e.g., BlackBoard, WebCT (Blackboard n.d), Moodle (Moodle 2007))
  - o Educational portals and digital libraries, including online educational resources and functionality for manual indexing, annotation and archiving of content as well as for finding, accessing and using the resources (e.g., Merlot (Merlot 2007), NSDL (NDSL n.d))

2nd generation WBES:

- *Challenges*: Intelligent support for learners and authors, including personalization and adaptation to the users
- *Distinguishing features*: Centralized (typically client–server) architecture, employing AI and web technologies, domain conceptualization and concept-based presentation of the maintained resources, ensuring personalization through adaptation to the learner's needs and interests, still in a proprietary format
- *Representatives*:
  - o Educational adaptive hypermedia (e.g., AHA! (De Bra and Calvi 1998), InterBook (Brusilovsky et al. 1998))
  - o Task-centered educational information systems (e.g., AIMS (Aroyo and Dicheva 2001))
  - o Intelligent web-based educational systems, employing AI techniques to improve web-based teaching and learning, e.g., for curriculum sequencing, solution analysis, and problem-solving support (e.g., SQL-Tutor (Mitrovic and Hausler 2000), ELM-ART (Weber and Brusilovsky 2001), PAT Online (Ritter 1997), DCG (Vassileva and Deters 1998))
  - o Web-based collaborative learning environments, focusing on group formation, peer help, coaching, learning companions and/ or others (e.g., PHelpS (Greer et al. 1998), Epsilon, etc.)

While the second generation WBES are "intelligent" and adaptive, they are still small-scale, closed-corpus projects. They work with a relatively limited set of learning resources and employ proprietary internal representation of learning content. Thus they are not interoperable. Typically they are used by one instructor or at best in one school.

3rd generation WBES: Semantic WBES (SWBES)

- *Challenges*: Scalability, reusability of educational material, interoperability (across multiple tools and platforms), affordability (increasing learning efficiency and productivity while reducing time and costs), durability of educational material (across revisions of operating systems and software)
- *Distinguishing features*: Typically service-based architecture, ontology-aware software, reusability, exchangeability, and interoperability of the maintained learning resources and components, based on the standardization brought by the use of ontologies and of the enabling semantic web standards and technologies
- *Representatives*: WBES employing semantic web technologies

3.2.2 Semantic WBES

The semantic web is a space understandable and navigable by both human and software agents. It adds structured meaning and organization to the navigational data of the current web, based on formalized ontologies and controlled vocabularies with semantic links to each other. From the E-Learning perspective, it aids learners in locating, accessing, querying, processing, and assessing learning resources across a distributed heterogeneous network; it also aids instructors in creating, locating, using, reusing, sharing and exchanging learning objects (data and components).

Devedžic describes a vision of SW-based E-Learning in which learners are supported by educational agents that access educational servers through educational services (Devedžic 2004a). The educational servers host repositories of standardized learning objects and services and support personalization.

Aroyo and Dicheva suggest further that the semantic web-based educational systems need to interoperate, collaborate and exchange content or re-use functionality (Aroyo and Dicheva 2004). A key to enabling the interoperability is to capitalize on (1) semantic conceptualization and ontologies, (2) common standardized communication syntax, and (3) large-scale service-based integration of educational content and functionality provision and usage.

This view is also supported by Anderson and Whitelock's fundamental affordances for the semantic web: "The vision of the educational semantic web is based on three fundamental affordances. The first is the capacity for effective information storage and retrieval. The second is the capacity for nonhuman autonomous agents to augment the learning and information retrieval and processing power of human beings. The third affordance is the capacity of the Internet to support, extend and expand communications capabilities of humans in multiple formats across the bounds of time and space" (Anderson and Whitelock 2004).

Thus the vision of the semantic web-based E-Learning is founded on the following major premises:

- Machine-understandable educational content
- Shareable educational ontologies, including
    o Subject matter ontologies
    o Instructional ontologies (representing different instructional models, learning theories, approaches)
    o Authoring ontologies (modeling authors' activities)
- Educational semantic web services, for supporting
    o Learning, e.g., information retrieval, summarization, interpretation (sense-making), structure-visualization, argumentation, etc.
    o Assessment, e.g., tests and performance tracking
    o Collaboration, e.g., group formation, peer help, etc.
- Semantic interoperability

Semantic interoperability, the key promise of the semantic web, is defined as a study of bridging differences between information systems on two levels (Aroyo et al. 2006): (1) on an access level, where system and organizational boundaries have to be crossed by creating standardized interfaces that share system-internal services in a loosely-coupled way; and (2) on a meaning level, where agreements about transported data have to be made in order to permit their correct interpretation. Interoperability requires the use of standard SW languages for representing ontologies, educational content, and services. The W3C standards include RDF, RDF-Schema, and OWL (Web Ontology Language) (RDF 2007). These languages are well supported with tools such as APIs (e.g., Jena (Jena 2007) and Sesame (Sesame 2007)), editors and browsers (e.g., Protégé (Protégé 2007) and KAON (KAON 2007)). An alternative SW technology is the ISO standard XML Topic Maps (XTM) (XML Topic Maps 2007), with similar supporting tools, such as APIs (e.g., TM4J, TMAPI) (TMAPI n.d.), editors and browsers (e.g., TM4L (TM4L n.d.), Ontopoly (Ontopoly 2007)). A comprehensive introduction to the semantic web standards can be found in (Antonio and van Harlemen 2004); a comparison of available ontology editors is given in (Mizoguchi 2004); a nice introduction to engineering semantic web-based educational systems is presented in (Devedžic 2006).

In 2004 we analyzed the state of research in the field of semantic web in E-Learning by summarizing the tendencies exhibited in the papers presented at the three sessions of the International Workshop on Semantic Web in E-Learning (SWEL 2004), held in conjunction with the International Conference on Adaptive Hypermedia (AH'04), the International Conference on Intelligent Tutoring Systems (ITS'04) and the International Semantic Web Conference (ISWC'04). (All papers are available at the SWEL Workshop website (SWEL n.d.) and are not referenced individually here).

To present the results, we proposed a 2D classification of the research projects, with the following categories along the *e-Learning* and *Semantic Web* axes (see Fig. 3.1).

- E-Learning related categories:
  - o Learning Objects
  - o Learning Designs
  - o Educational Adaptive Hypermedia
  - o Learner Modeling
  - o WBES Frameworks/Architectures

- Semantic web related categories:
  - o Ontologies
  - o SW Annotation (including semantic annotation tools and [semi-] automatic generation of metadata)
  - o Mapping educational standards to SW standards (including extending educational standards and binding educational with SW standards)
  - o Agents/Distributed Systems/SW Services

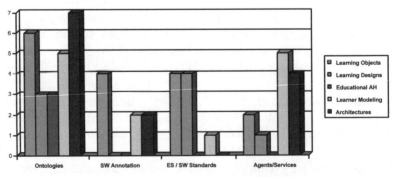

Fig. 3.1. 2004 Classification of SWEL projects, representing current tendencies

The general picture suggested tendencies to novel modularized WBES architectures that:

- Utilize concepts and ontologies to open, share, reuse and interchange educational content
- Employ semantic web compliant educational standards to provide common syntax in the communication
- Make use of semantic web (educational) services targeting a large-scale service-based integration of educational content and functionality

Two years later, we summarized the SWEL papers, presented at the 2005–2006 sessions of the workshop, held in conjunction with four other major conferences in the field: the International Conference on Artificial Intelligence in Education (AI-ED'05), the International Conference on Advanced Learning Technologies (ICALT'05), the International Conference on Knowledge Capture (K-CAP'05), and the International Conference on Adaptive Hypermedia (AH'06), as well as articles published in the special issue on semantic web for E-Learning of the *British Journal of Educational Technology (BJET)* (Naeve et al. 2006). In summarizing and clustering those works, we found out that some of the 2004 categories were not assigned any new projects, while new clusters appeared (see Fig. 3.2).

The first noticeable fact was the strong clustering of the current research and development work into two groups: creating/maintaining/using subject ontologies, and semantic annotation of learning objects (resources). In a way, this indicated maturing of the field. After the initial inclination to propose generic frameworks and abstract architectures with suggested hypothetical use of semantic web technologies for implementing some of their components, it was realized that the way to the educational semantic web required concrete semantic annotation of learning resources, which in turn should be based on using ontologies. Thus, the results were not a surprise.

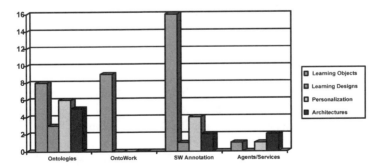

Fig. 3.2. 2006 Classification of SWEL projects, representing the current tendencies

The second noticeable fact was the departure from the initial enthusiasm to map or extend the existing educational standards, such as LOM (LOM 2007) and SCORM (SCORM 2007) to SW standards. This also didn't come as a surprise, given that the current educational standards are not concerned with the actual meaning (i.e., semantics) of the annotated resources/ activities. Very little interest was also shown in employing SW technologies for learning designs, or in the educational adaptive hypermedia.

At the same time, two new tendencies were noticed, which led to a new classification to better present the state of research: (1) The previous focus on learner modeling was shifted to personalization and contexts in SWES; and (2) A distinctive branch of the general "ontologies" category appeared, related to comparing/integration/validation/evaluation of ontologies (labeled in Fig. 3.2 with "OntoWork"). The latter also indicates maturing of the SW in Education field.

3.3   Ontologies in Education

The benefits of educational use of ontologies have been recognized relatively recently (Mizoguchi and Bourdeau 2000; Mitrovic and Devedžic 2002; Dicheva and Aroyo 2002; Devedžic 2003; Apted and Kay 2004). The term "ontology", which is borrowed from philosophy, is defined as "a particular theory about being or reality" (Gruber 2003). So, an ontology provides a particular perspective on some part of the world. While knowledge representation formalisms specify how to represent concepts, ontologies specify what concepts to represent and how they are interconnected. Thus an ontology can be seen as a well-founded and broadly agreed-upon system of concepts in a particular subject domain together with the relationships between those concepts. Specialized subject ontologies can be used as a semantic backbone for courseware or repositories of learning materials (objects). By providing agreed-upon vocabularies for domain knowledge representation, ontologies can support sharing, reuse and exchange of courseware units. Ontologies also facilitate machine readability of web content.

A number of papers have been devoted to the analysis of the ontologies in the education field, providing overviews of different aspects. Mizoguchi and Bourdeau, in their seminal work (Mizoguchi and Bourdeau 2000), enlisted a number of challenges that have not yet been met by the AI-ED technologies and proposed a roadmap of how the application of ontological engineering could assist in dealing with those challenges. Similar work is reported in several publications (Devedžic 2001; Dicheva and Aroyo 2004a), and (Devedžic 2004b) for the more specific domain of web-based intelligent systems. Several overviews of existing tools or created domain ontologies have also been performed. Examples of the former are the overview and comparison of ontology engineering environments (Mizoguchi 2004) and the analysis of semantic annotation tools for learning material (Azouaou et al. 2004). An example from the latter group is the overview of ontologies in the domain of engineering design (Kitamura and Mizoguchi 2004).

In spite of the fact that the field of SWEL is fairly young, it is already quite broad and fuzzy, partly because of the involvement of technologies from various areas of information and pedagogical sciences. To facilitate the research, Dicheva et al. (2005) collected and classified information in the field and used it to build an ontology-driven web portal, Ontologies for Education (O4E) (The O4E Portal 2007).

3.3.1 The O4E Ontology

In the O4E project, as in many other ontology-based applications, we dealt with two types of knowledge, subject domain and structural, which led to two types of ontologies. A domain ontology represents the basic concepts of the domain under consideration with their interrelations and basic properties. A structure ontology defines the logical structure of the content. It is generally subjective and depends greatly on the goals of the ontology application. It typically represents hierarchical and navigational relationships. While a domain ontology can be used as a mechanism for establishing a shared understanding of a specific domain, a structure ontology enforces a disciplined approach to authoring, which is especially important in collaborative and distributed authoring.

The process of creating an ontology is a time- and mind-consuming iterative procedure of categorization or laddering, together with disintegration or detailing. It is a totally informal analytical design, and output structures are rather subjective and sometimes awkward.

One of the guidelines with regard to creating structure ontologies relates to the clarity and mapability of the structure. It should be taken into account that an ontology is to be used not only as a knowledge component of an information system but also as a mind tool for manual information search and navigation. Authors should thus try to follow the principles of clarity and good shape, which is an accepted practice in basic scientific abstraction and modeling (e.g., physics, chemistry, etc.) (Dicheva et al. 2005).

Figure 3.3 shows the O4E domain ontology. The top-level meta-concepts of the domain ontology divide the whole field according to the role ontologies play in the research. When an ontology is considered as an object (the result of an activity), the research is focused on the theoretical

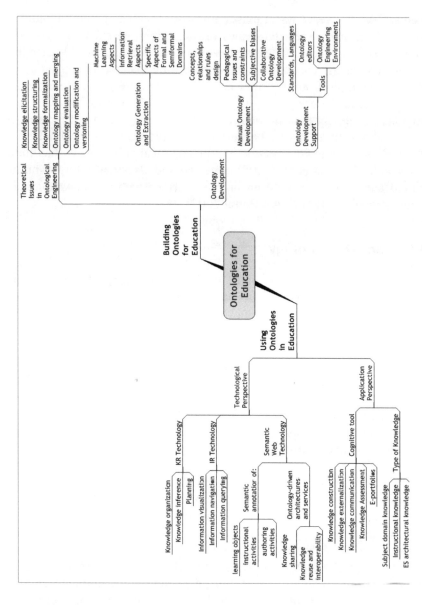

Fig. 3.3. The O4E domain ontology

and/or practical issues of the ontological engineering that are specific to the educational context. Ontologies might also serve as a technology, facilitating the solution of some educational problems such as the interoperability of knowledge-based systems and components, or the assessment of structural knowledge.

Building Ontologies for Education

When analyzing resources focused on different tasks of educational ontology development, we identified two naturally separated areas of research. While some papers study mostly the theoretical issues of ontology engineering, another large set of resources relates to the practical aspects of ontology development. Three major categories could be identified within the latter set:

- Automatic and semi-automatic ontology generation and extraction using different kinds of sources and technologies
- Manual ontology development, with a focus on problems either related to the ontology engineering process or specific to educational technology
- Research on using different standards and languages for ontology implementation, including attempt to bind semantic web and educational (e.g., LOM or SCORM) standards or reporting case studies on implementing general-purpose ontological formalisms in educational settings

Using Ontologies in Education

This field combines diverse research on different educational applications of ontologies. We tried to look at this branch from two perspectives depending on what kind of technology is implemented (technological perspective) and what role an ontology plays within a project (application perspective). We defined three main areas within the technological perspective, two of which (knowledge representation and information retrieval) are like technological donors for the ontological research, while the third one (semantic web) benefits from it the most. As for the application perspective, ontologies have been considered for a long time only as a technical artifact acting as a knowledge base component.

The field of education is one of the first in which ontologies were employed as a cognitive tool. In many respects, this was due to the widespread use of the constructivist paradigm of learning and the broad use of such knowledge technologies as concept maps, mind maps and others for learning purposes.

3.3.2   The Ontologies for Education Portal

The created ontology was used in the development of the O4E Web Portal (Fig. 3.4). The O4E Portal is aimed to serve as a single web access point, where relevant research publications and projects and successful practices are classified and annotated. The ontology is represented as a topic map (XML Topic Maps 2007), which is created and maintained with the TM4L Editor (see Sect. 3.4). The Topic Maps (TM) semantic web technology is very appropriate for formalization of lightweight ontologies and for structuring and representing ontology-based web information.

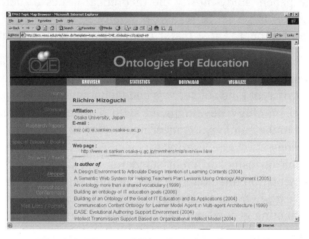

Fig. 3.4. The ontologies for education portal

3.3.3   The OMNIBUS Project: An Ontology of Learning, Instruction and Instructional Design

Among the most significant up-to-date contributions in the area of Ontologies for Education is the framework for building ontology-based instructional systems, proposed by Mizoguchi and Bourdeau (2000), and recently implemented within the OMNIBUS project. According to the authors, the OMNIBUS ontology is not a lightweight ontology but a heavyweight ontology. It is based on philosophical consideration of all the concepts necessary for understanding learning, instruction and instructional design. Although it is full of axioms, the GUI of Hozo Ontology Editor makes it easier to read it. However, readers are expected to have basic knowledge of ontology and the Hozo way of role representation. The ontology is released on the OMNIBUS site for evaluation and the complete ontology is discussed in (Mizoguchi et al. 2007).

3.4   Topic Maps for E-Learning (TM4L)

TM4L is an authoring environment for building discipline-specific ontology-aware repositories of learning objects, which are efficiently searchable, reusable and interchangeable. These repositories are based on topic maps. The two aspects, domain conceptualization, which supports findability, and ontologies, which support standardization and reusability, are incorporated uniformly in the topic maps. With regard to reusability and interoperability, learning objects must comply not only with knowledge standardization (consensus on the meaning of the educational content) but also with technological standardization (use of standard formalisms, including educational standards such as LOM and SCORM).

Domain conceptualization is used for the structuring and classification of learning content. Classification involves linking learning objects (content) to the relevant ontology terms (concepts), that is, using the ontological structure to index the repository content. Therefore, by browsing the map, learners gain insight into the domain. Moreover, understanding the relationships between the resources ensures efficient topical access to them.

The TM4L learning repository has a layered information structure consisting of three layers (see Fig. 3.5):

- Resource layer: contains a collection of diverse information resources (learning objects) associated with the specific knowledge domain
- Semantic layer: contains a conceptual model of the knowledge domain in terms of key concepts and relationships among them
- Context layer: contains specifications of different views (contexts) on the repository resources depending on a particular goal, type of user, etc., by dynamically associating components from the other two layers

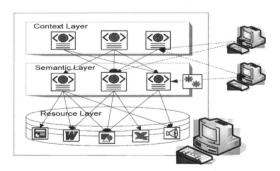

Fig. 3.5. The layered structure of a semantic learning object repository

TM4L provides support in conceptual structure design and maintenance through its functionality for editing, browsing, and combining such structures, coupled with support for relating concepts, linking concepts to resources, merging ontologies, external search for resources, defining perspectives, etc. (Dicheva and Dichev 2006). The environment consists of a Topic Map Editor and a Topic Map Viewer.

3.4.1 TM4L Editor

The TM4L Editor is an ontology editor that allows the user to build ontology-driven learning repositories using topic maps. It provides ontology and metadata engineering capabilities coupled with basic document management facilities. The TM4L Editor benefits from the Topic Maps' fundamental feature to support easy and effective merging of existing information resources while maintaining their meaningful structure. This allows for flexibility and expediency in re-using and extending existing repositories. The learning content created by the editor is fully compliant with the XML Topic Maps (XTM) standard and is thus interchangeable with other standard XTM tools. The main objects that the TM4L Editor manipulates are topics (representing domain ontology concepts), relationships between them, resources and contexts (represented by themes). Screenshots from the TM4L Editor interface are shown in Fig. 3.6.

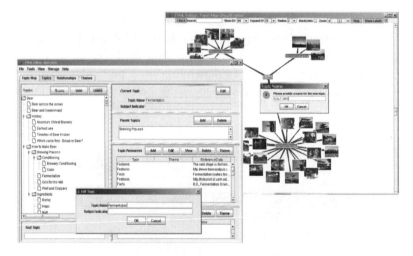

Fig. 3.6. Screenshots from the TM4L Editor: textual and visual topic editing

The most widely used ontology editor for creating educational ontologies is Protégé (Protégé 2007). Other ontology editors include KAON
(KAON 2007), OntoEdit (OntoEdit 2007) and Hozo (Hozo Ontology
Editor 2007). TM4L differs from them in two ways: (1) it allows direct
indexing of resources with concepts from the ontology; (2) it is designed
with an educational use in mind. Thus it contains pre-defined relationship
and resource types, specifically useful for learning repositories.

3.4.2   TM4L Viewer

In relation to topic map browsing, authors and learners typically differentiate in their: (1) navigation and query formulation strategy; and (2) vocabulary knowledge. The different ways of browsing and searching reflect the
gaps in terms of knowledge and perception between authors and learners.
In general, learners need to alternate phases of browsing the topic map
content with phases of querying it. In querying, they often need to refine
their selection criteria according to the obtained results. To enable multi-
purpose exploration, TM4L supports multiple views: graph view, text view
and tree view. A screenshot from the TM4L Viewer is shown in Fig. 3.7.

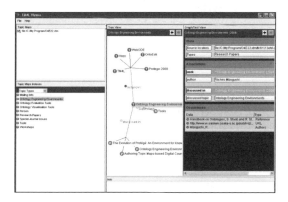

Fig. 3.7. A screenshot from the TM4L Viewer

Acknowledgements

The O4E ontology was created in collaboration with Sergey Sosnovsky,
Tanya Gavrilova and Peter Brusilovsky. TM4L and the O4E Portal resulted from the efforts of the Intelligent Information Systems group at
WSSU. This work was supported in part by the NSF Grants DUE-0333069
and DUE-0442702.

References

Adaptive Hypermedia (2004). Workshop on applications of Semantic Web technologies for educational adaptive hypermedia, in conjunction with AH'04, Eindhoven, The Netherlands, August 23–26, 2004 http://www.win.tue.nl/~laroyo/swel/2004/swel-ah.html.

AIED (1999).Workshop on ontologies for intelligent educational systems, in conjunction with AI-ED'99, Le Mans, France, July 18–19, 1999. http://aied.inf.ed.ac.uk/abstracts/Vol_10/ontologies.html.

Anderson, T., & Whitelock, D. (Ed.) (2004). The educational Semantic Web: visioning and practicing the future of education. *Journal of Interactive Media in Education*, (1), special issue.

Antonio, G., & van Harlemen, F. (2004). *A Semantic Web Primer*. Cambridge, MA: MIT.

Aroyo, L., & Dicheva, D. (2001). AIMS: learning and teaching support for WWW-based education. *IJCELLL*, 11(1/2), 152–164.

Aroyo, L., & Dicheva, D. (2004). The new challenges for e-learning: the educational Semantic Web. *Journal of Educational Technology and Society*, 7(4), 59–69.

Aroyo, L., Dolog, P., Houben, G.-J., Kravcik, M., Naeve, A., Nilsson, M., & Wild, F. (2006). Interoperability in personalized adaptive learning. *Journal of Educational Technology and Society*, 9(2), 4–18.

Azouaou, F., Desmoulins, C., & Chen, W. (2004). Semantic annotation tools for learning material. In *Workshop SW-EL'04*, Eindhoven, The Netherlands, August 23–26, 2004.

Berners-Lee, T., Hendler, J., & Lassila, O. (2001). The Semantic Web. *Scientific American*, 284, 34–43.

Blackboard (n.d.). Blackboard & WebCT. http://www.blackboard.com/us/index.Bb.

Brase, J., & Wolfgang, N. (2004). Ontologies and metadata for e-learning. In Staab, S., & Studer, R. (Ed.). *Handbook on Ontologies* (pp. 555–573). Berlin Heidelberg New York: Springer.

Brusilovsky, P., Eklund, J., & Schwarz, E. (1998). Web-based education for all: a tool for developing adaptive courseware. In *Proceedings of Seventh International World Wide Web Conference* (pp. 291–300).

CAISE (2003).Workshop on Semantic Web for Web-based Learning, in conjunction with CAISE'03, Klagenfurt/Velden, Austria, June 2003. http://www.sw-wl03.bessag.net/.

Davies, J., Fensel, D., & van Harmelen, F. (2003). Towards the Semantic Web: Ontology-Driven Knowledge Management. New York: Wiley, pp. 4–5.

De Bra, P., & Calvi, L. (1998). AHA!: a generic adaptive hypermedia system. In *Workshop on Adaptive Hypertext & Hypermedia*, Pittsburgh, PA, USA.

Devedžic, V. (2001). The Semantic Web – implications for teaching and learning. In *Proceedings of ICCE 2001* (pp. 26–28). Seoul, Korea.

Devedžic, V. (2003). Next-generation Web-based education. *International Journal for Continuing Engineering Education and Life-long Learning*, 11(1/2), 232–247.

Devedžic, V. (2004a). Education and the Semantic Web. *International Journal of Artificial Intelligence in Education*, 14, 39–65.

Devedžic, V. (2004b). Web Intelligence and artificial intelligence in education. *Journal of Educational Technology and Society*, 7 (4), 29–39.

Devedžić, V. (2006). *Semantic Web and Education*. Berlin Heidelberg New York: Springer.

Dicheva, D., & Aroyo, L. (2002). Concept and ontologies in WBES. In *Proc. ICCE Workshop Concepts & Ontologies in WBES* (pp. 3–4). Auckland, NZ, 2002.

Dicheva, D., & Aroyo, L. (Ed.) (2004b). Concept and ontologies in web-based educational systems. *Intlernatonal Journal of Continuous Engineering Education and Life-long Learning*, 14 (3), special issue.

Dicheva, D., Sosnovsky, S., Gavrilova, T., & Brusilovsky, P. (2005). Ontological Web portal for educational ontologies. In *Workshop on Applications of Semantic Web in E-Learning* (SWEL) AIED'05. Amsterdam, The Netherlands.

Dolog, P., Henze, N., Nejdl, W., & Sintek, M. (2004). Personalization in distributed e-learning environments. In *Proceedings of the 13th International World Wide Web Conference*. New York, May 2004.

Gašević, D., Jovanović, J., & Devedžić, V. (2004). Enhancing learning object content on the Semantic Web. In *Proceedings of the 4th IEEE Intl Conference on Advanced Learning Technologies* (pp. 714–716). Joensuu, Finland.

Greer, J., McCalla, G., Collins, J., Kumar, V., Meagher, P., & Vassileva, J. (1998). Supporting peer help and collaboration in distributed workplace environments. *International Journal of AI and Education*, 9, 159–177.

Gruber, T. (2003). *A Translation Approach to Portable Ontology Specifications*. San Diego: Academic.

Hozo Ontology Editor (2007). http://www.hozo.jp/. Accessed 14 June 2007.

ICCE (2002). Workshop on concepts and ontologies in Web-based educational systems, in conjunction with ICCE'02, Auckland, New Zealand, Dec. 3–6, 2002. http://icce2002.massey.ac.nz/workshop_4.html.

Ikeda, M., Hoppe, H. U., & Mizoguchi, M. (1995). Ontological issues of CSCL systems design. In *Proceedings of Intl Conf. on Artificial Intelligence in Education* (pp. 242–249). AIED'1995.

ISWC (2004). Workshop on applications of Semantic Web technologies for e-learning, in conjunction with ISWC'04, Hiroshima, Japan, November 7–11, 2004. http://www.win.tue.nl/~laroyo/swel/2004/swel-iswc.html.

ITS (2004). Workshop on applications of Semantic Web technologies for Web-based ITS, at ITS'04, 30 August – 03 September 2004, Maceió-Alagoas, Brazil. http://www.win.tue.nl/~laroyo/swel/2004/swel-its.html.

Jena (2007). http://jena.sourceforge.net/. Accessed 14 June 2007.

Jin, L., Chen, W., Hayashi, Y., Ikeda, M., Mizoguchi, M., Takaoka, Y., & Ohta, M. (1999). An ontology-aware authoring tool – functional structure and guidance generation. In *Proc. of AIED '99* (pp. 85–92). Le Mans France, 1999.

KAON (2007). http://kaon.semanticweb.org/. Accessed 14 June 2007.

Kitamura, Y., & Mizoguchi, R. (2004). Ontology-based systematization of functional knowledge. *Journal of Engineering Design*, 15(4), 327–351.

LOM (2007). Learning object metadata. http://ltsc.ieee.org/wg12. Accessed 14 June 2007.

Merlot (2007). http://www.merlot.org/merlot/index.htm. Accessed 14 June 2007.

Mitrovic, T., & Devedžic, V. (2002). A model of multitutor ontology-based learning environments. In *ICCE Workshop on Concepts and Ontologies in WBES* (pp. 15–22). Auckland, New Zealand, 3–6 December, 2002.

Mitrovic, A. & Hausler, K. (2000). Porting SQL-tutor to the Web. In *Proc. ITS'2000 Workshop on Adaptive and Intelligent WBES* (pp. 37–44).

Mizoguchi, R. (2004). Ontology engineering environments. In Staab, S., & Studer, R. (Ed.). *Handbook on Ontologies* (pp. 275–295). Berlin Heidelberg New York: Springer.

Mizoguchi, R., & Bourdeau, J. (2000). Using ontological engineering to overcome common AI-ED problems. *International Journal of Artificial Intelligence in Education*, 11(2), 107–121.

Mizoguchi, R., Sinitsa, K., & Ikeda, M. (1996). Knowledge engineering of educational systems for authoring system design – a preliminary results of task ontology design. In *Proc. of European Conf on AIED* (pp. 329–335). Lisbon.

Mizoguchi, R., Hayashi, Y. & Bourdeau, J. (2007). Inside theory-aware and standards-compliant authoring System. In *Intl AIED'07 Workshop on Ontologies and Semantic Web for e-Learning (SWEL'07)*, Los Angeles, California, July 9–13, 2007.

Moodle (2007). http://moodle.org/. Accessed 14 June 2007.

Naeve, A., Lytras, M., Nejdl, W., Balacheff, N., & Hardin, J. (Ed.) (2006). The Semantic Web for e-learning. *British Journal of Educational Technology*, 27 (3), special issue.

NDSL (n.d.). The National Science Digital Library (NSDL). http://nsdl.org/.

Nejdl, W., Wolf, B., Staab, S., & Tane, J. (2001). Edutella: searching and annotating resources within an RDF-based P2P network. In *WWW2002 Semantic Web Workshop*, Hawaii, USA, May 2002.

Nilsson, M., Palmer, M., & Brase, J. (2003). The LOM RDF binding – principles and implementation. In *3rd Annual Ariadne Conference*, Leuven, Belgium, 20–21 November 2003.

OntoEdt. (2007). http://ontoedit.com/. Accessed 14 June 2007.

Ontopoly (2007). http://www.ontopia.net/. Accessed 14 June 2007.

Protégé (2007). http://protege.stanford.edu/. Accessed 14 June 2007.

RDF (2007). http://www.w3.org/RDF. Accessed 14 June 2007.

Ritter, S. (1997). PAT online: a model-tracing tutor on the World-Wide Web. In *Proc of Workshop "Intelligent Educational Systems on the World Wide Web"*. 8th World Conference of the AIED Society, Kobe, Japan, 18–22 August.

Sampson, D., Lytras, M., Wagner, G., & Diaz, P. (Ed.) (2004). Ontologies and the Semantic Web for e-learning. *International Journal on Education Technology and Society*, 7(4), special issue. http://www.ifets.info/others/issues.php?id=25.

SCORM (2007). Sharable Content Object Reference Model. ttp://www.adlnet.gov/. Accessed 14 June 2007.

Sesame (2007). http://www.openrdf.org/. Accessed 14 June 2007.

SWEL (n.d.). Workshop on application of the Semantic Web technologies in e-learning (SWEL). http://compsci.wssu.edu/iis/swel/index.html.

The O4E Portal (2007). http://iiscs.wssu.edu/o4e/. Accessed 14 June 2007.

The Omnibus Project (2007). http://edont.qee.jp/omnibus/doku.php. Accessed 14 June 2007.

TM4L (2007). http://compsci.wssu.edu/iis/nsdl/download.html. Accessed 14 June 2007.

TMAPI (2007). http://tmapi.org/. Accessed 14 June 2007.

Vassileva, J., & Deters, R. (1998). Dynamic courseware generation on the WWW. *British Journal of Educational Technologies*, 29(1), 5–14.

Weber, G., & Brusilovsky, P. (2001). ELM-ART: an adaptive versatile system for Web-based instruction. *International Journal of Artificial Intelligence in Education*, 12(4), 351–384.

XML Topic Maps (XTM) (2007). http://www.topicmaps.org/xtm.

4 Design and Case Studies on Mobile and Wireless Technologies in Education

H. Ogata and G. Li Hui

4.1 Introduction

Generally, a lot of educational software systems for training, learning and instruction have been developed using desktop computers. However, learners have to be in a static position when learning, and find it difficult to move with desktop computers. Therefore, those systems hardly support learning anywhere at anytime.

Compared with desktop computer assisted learning, mobile learning is fundamentally about increasing learners' capability to physically move their own learning environment with them (Ogata and Yano 2004). Mobile learning is implemented with lightweight devices such as PDAs (personal digital assistants), cellular mobile phones, and so on. Those mobile devices can connect to the Internet with wireless communication technologies. In this situation, learners can seamlessly and flexibly obtain information about the context of his/her learning.

The main characteristics of mobile learning are shown as follows (Chen et al. 2002; Curtis et al. 2002):

1. Permanency: Learners never lose their work unless it is purposefully deleted. In addition, all the learning processes are recorded continuously everyday.
2. Accessibility: Learners have access to their documents, data, or videos from anywhere. That information is provided based on their requests. Therefore, the learning involved is self-directed.
3. Immediacy: Wherever learners are, they can get any information immediately. Thus, learners can solve problems quickly. Conversely, the learner can record the questions and look for the answers later.

4. Interactivity: Learners can interact with experts, teachers, or peers in the form of synchronous or asynchronous communication. Hence, the experts are more reachable and the knowledge becomes more available.

5. Situation of instructional activities: The learning could be embedded in our daily life. The problems encountered and the knowledge required are all presented in their natural and authentic forms. This helps learners notice the features of problem situations that make particular actions relevant.

6. Collaborative learning: Regardless of the physical learning scenario, mobile devices can help people learn together in an intellectual effort. The boundaries and restrictions are reduced in a collaborative learning environment, thus enhancing the overall learning process.

7. Malleability: Mobile learning gives users the opportunity to be creative and flexible. Because of the mobility characteristic, various learning systems in which creativity knows no boundary can be created.

8. Simplicity and pleasurability: More pleasure and sense of achievement is obtained in mobile learning. This is because mobile learning provides a paperless, movable and interactive learning environment. Simplicity is also the key to more effective and fun learning, because unnecessary and complicated procedures are reduced, and more time is spent on the learning itself.

We have described the introduction in this chapter. Section 4.2 explains mobile technologies such as mobile devices, wireless networks and their issues and limitations. Section 4.3 concentrates on mobile technologies in education. We will investigate more on learning theories and applications developed for mobile learning.

4.2 Mobile Technologies

4.2.1 Mobile Devices

One category of the most common mobile devices is laptops or notebook computers. They are mobile computers with the same capabilities as desktop computers. Since its creation, the notebook computer has gone through numerous culminations of advances and evolutions, with the Tablet PC one of the latest versions of the notebook computer. The mobility features allows the user to carry it around, but the dimension and weight of the notebook computer becomes an obstacle when a learner needs to constantly move around in the learning environment. The limited battery life and difficulty in extensibility and upgrading are also some of the disadvantages that come with notebook computers. Thus, much research and development has been conducted to increase the usability of notebooks. One good example is the latest development of the USD100 Laptop by the Massachusetts Institute of Technology (MIT) for children in poorer nations to provide them with more active mobile learning. The laptop operates at 500 MHz, can be set up with wireless networks and can be powered using a hand crank when it is not possible to use a battery or reliable electricity supply.

The PDA is another very popular handheld device, and its data can be synchronized with a desktop computer. Some even have communication function with Bluetooth and/or WiFi network. Various operating systems have been developed: PDA Palm OS, Windows CE/PocketPC/Windows mobile, embedded Linux and other original OS. The input method of the majority of these devices is through a pen-like instrument called a stylus, but in minor cases, some of them include small built-in or attachable keyboards.

Mobile phones and smart phones can also provide a fine platform for mobile learning. "i-mode" is a wireless Internet service for mobile phones, which has been provided by NTT-DoCoMo in Japan since 1999. i-mode enables browsing of the the light version of HTML, such as the wireless application protocol (WAP) and sending/receiving email. Now similar services such as short message service (SMS) and multimedia messaging service (MMS) are available in other types of mobile phones. In addition, television and radio services for mobile phones are available in some countries. For example, a mobile terrestrial digital audio/video data broadcasting service in Japan, called "1-seg" was officially offered in 2006.

There are many other mobile appliances, for example, music players such as the iPod, portable game devices such as Nintendo, DS and PSP. Those devices can also be used to realize mobile learning.

Despite some limitations and issues concerning mobile learning, mobile devices are fascinating. Researchers and developers are interested in developing more mobile learning applications.

4.2.2 Wireless Networks

Over the years, many different means of data and information exchange between mobile devices have appeared. Wireless networking in different forms enables users not only to have synchronous and asynchronous communication between them, but many other benefits, such as file sharing, collaborative work and learning, Internet browsing, knowledge resource inquiries, etc. Those communication methods are described as follows:

Infrared port: The IrDA (Infrared Data Association) represents a standard as a wireless communication link between two devices in which the information is transmitted using infrared light. This technology is similar to the one employed in remote controllers. IrDA technology has the limitations of only being applicable between two IrDA-enabled devices; and these two devices have to be closely located, and there should not be any kind of obstacles between them. The advantages of this technology are the low implementing price, inherent security, high-speed communication, and the fact that it has been a proven technology since 1997 in different platforms and devices, including phones, pagers, laptops, PDAs, digital cameras, handheld scanners, etc.

WiFi networking: WiFi (Wireless Ethernet 802.11b) is one of the most popular standards for WLAN (Wireless Local Area Networks). WiFi WLANs operate using unlicensed spectrum in the 2.4 GHz band. Modern WLANs support up to 11 Mbps data rates within 100 m of the base station. In most cases, WiFi WLANs are configured to give network connectivity to a group of computers or other devices free of charge to the end users in corporate enterprises or academic institutions. Each device that connects to one of these networks requires a special adapter card.

Bluetooth: The Bluetooth wireless technology was proposed in 1998 as a license-free specification for wireless connectivity for handheld devices using a special radio frequency of 2.45 GHz, formed by the strategic alliance of five major computing and telecommunications companies: Ericsson, IBM, Intel, Nokia and Toshiba. Bluetooth was designed originally as a short-range connectivity solution for personal, portable, and handheld electronic devices, where the networking configuration needs very few users' input or no input at all. This is because each Bluetooth device can automatically find others in the ranged network, without interference between them, due to the "spread-spectrum frequency hopping" technique, which reduces the frequency jamming among other devices and frequencies. Most Bluetooth-enabled devices have a built-in adapter. One of the disadvantages of this technology is the fact that, due to its complexity, not every commercial company is willing to adapt to its specifications.

3G/4G: 3G refers to the third generation of developments in wireless technology, especially mobile communications. The third generation, as its name suggests, follows the first generation (1G) and the second generation (2G) in wireless communications. 3G is generally considered applicable mainly to mobile wireless. A 3G system should be operational from any location on, or over, the earth's surface, including in homes, businesses, schools, libraries, museums, and so forth. 3G offers the potential to keep people connected at all times and in all places, and its data communication allows at most 384 Kbps.

Similar to the other abbreviations, 4G stands for fourth-generation wireless, the stage of broadband mobile communications that will supersede the 3G. While neither standards bodies nor carriers have concretely defined or agreed upon what exactly 4G will be, it is expected that end-to-end IP and high-quality streaming video will be among 4G's distinguishing features, with at least 100 Mbps data communication. Technologies employed by 4G may include software-defined radio (SDR) receivers, orthogonal frequency division multiplexing (OFDM), orthogonal frequency division multiple access (OFDMA), multiple input/multiple output (MIMO) technologies and more. All of these delivery methods are typified by high rates of data transmission and packet-switched transmission protocols.

3G technologies, by contrast, are a mix of packet- and circuit-switched networks. 4G is expected to enable pervasive computing and create new markets and opportunities for both traditional and startup telecommunications companies.

WiMAX: WiMAX, which stands for worldwide interoperability for microwave access is a wireless industry coalition for broadband wireless access (BWA) networks. WiMAX 802.16 technology is expected to enable multimedia applications with wireless connections. WiMax also has a range of up to 30 miles, presenting provider networks with a viable wireless last-mile solution. This means it can provide fixed, nomadic, portable and mobile wireless broadband connectivity without the need for direct line-of-sight with a base station. WiMAX systems are expected to deliver capacity of up to 40 Mbps per channel, for fixed and portable access applications. WiMAX will also aid in certifying the compatibility and interoperability of devices based on the 802.16 specification, and to develop such devices for the marketplace.

4.2.3   Issues and Limitations

It is crucial to understand both the capabilities and limitations of technologies in order to know the potential they offer for educational practices (Song 2006). Currently, the following are issues limiting educational applications:

1. Small screen size: Because of the limitations of the screen size, resources with longer texts have been considered inappropriate for viewing on handheld devices. In addition, though some effort has been made to develop learning environments capable of adapting to heterogeneous computing environments, the stability of these environments has not been sustained.

2. Short battery life: Mobile device users need to have a reliable source of power. Applications are hindered by short battery life. Notebook computers and PDAs in particular are prone to this problem. Thus, the most desirable feature of a next generation mobile device is a battery that lasts much longer.

3. Difficulty of text input: It was reported that text input using a stylus on handheld devices was troublesome. Some usability evaluation studies report that up to 30 min of training is required to adapt to the input methods of PDAs in order to obtain satisfactory results. There-fore, it is necessary to work on modern, easier-to-use, richer and better interfaces for future mobile devices.

4. Wireless connectivity: The fact that wireless connectivity is limited to certain situations is a barrier for anytime/anywhere learning and data collection in the field. For example, for WiFi to work there must be sufficient access points to access the network. The current infrastructure still restricts the use of WiFi because access points have to be in place to access the Internet. On the other hand, i-mode, which does not require access points, is a popular wireless Internet service provider, particularly in Japan. Unfortunately, there are still restrictions when using i-mode in terms of speed (64–384 kbps) versus WiFi (11 Mbps).

5. Lack of standard platform across different devices: Standardization for different devices does not exist. Software developers can only use the subset of the classes or libraries of development tools. The commonly known subsets are Java J2ME (Java 2 Platform, Micro Edition), embedded Visual Basic and embedded Visual C++. Other examples of non-standardizations are various HTML versions, such as wireless markup language (WML) for WAP Internet service and Compact HTML (cHTML) for i-mode.

6. Connection with other devices: Some mobile devices have limitations regarding connecting with other supporting devices such as a global positioning system (GPS) and radio frequency identification (RFID) tag reader. Connection with mobile devices such as notebook com-puters or even the PDA can be done rather easily, but it gets compli-cated when there is a need for connection with cellular phones.

However, with the development of the mobile technology, more and more inadequacies have been resolved. This, with proper pedagogic de-sign, will help boost the use handheld applications in higher education. Nevertheless, even if handheld devices are developed to be as powerful as desktops, they still will not be able to replace traditional computers because they are based on different technologies.

4.3   Case Studies and Examples

4.3.1   Learning Theories for Mobile Learning

Mobile learning is advocated by pedagogical theories such as on-demand learning, hands-on or minds-on learning, and authentic learning (Ogata and Yano 2004). Mobile learning systems provide learners on-demand information such as advice from teachers. Brown et al. (1989) defined authentic learning as coherent, meaningful and purposeful activities. Classroom activities related to the real world help enrich students' educational experience. There are four types of authentic learning: action, situated, incidental and experimental. Action learning is a practical process in which students learn by doing, observing and imitating an expert. Then feedback is received from teachers and peers while connecting knowledge with workplace activities.

Situated learning is similar to action learning in that trainees are sent to school-like settings to learn and understand new concepts and theories through authentic activities and important social interactions. Cognitive apprenticeship methods try to "enculturate students into authentic practices through activity and social interaction in a similar way evident in craft apprenticeship" (Brown et al. 1989, p. 37).

Incidental learning involves unintentional and unexamined learning from mistakes, unexpected incidents, etc. Learners discover one thing while they are doing something else. Knowledge from incidental learning develops self-confidence and increases self-knowledge in learning.

Lastly, experimental learning includes a future search process (explained in more detail below) and outdoor education. The future search process is to develop thinking and understanding. It involves developing insights, understanding, learning from others and reducing misunderstandings. Outdoor education is an outdoor program of team members applying their new knowledge learned during an outdoor experience to the job in order to gain more insights through challenging activities. Upon their return, learners integrate thoughts and actions with reflection from the outdoor experiences.

4.3.2   Mobile Learning Applications

Roschelle (2003) made a study about the different applications of mobile devices and wireless networks. He classified the available systems into four categories:

1. Classroom response systems allow teachers to obtain responses from students in a classroom. The system can collect the students' answers and, if applicable, create tables, histograms or any other graphs (statistical studies, polls, etc.). The teacher is then aware of the learners' individual performance. The classroom response system has obtained many good results in practice, improving the students' participation in class.

2. Participatory simulations coordinate a group of learners to conduct simulations through the data exchange among students. The students are able to learn about many scientific phenomena acting as agents of simulations of real phenomena. For example, the Virus Game was developed by the MIT (Colella et al. 1998) to explain the process of how a virus is spread. Also, PSSLSA (Yin et al. 2006) allows participatory simulation for learning to sort algorithms in which learners switch positions in ascending or descending sequence.

3. Collaborative data-gathering systems help learners gain experience from real life and deeply understand what they have learned. The learners touch and feel actual objects, take photos or them and bring them back to the classroom. For example, a bird-watching assistance system (Chen et al. 2002) enables students to take photos of birds outside the classroom with handheld devices and exchange the data with teachers and other students.

4. There are many other applications for mobile learning. For example, PiCo map allows learners to make their own concept maps with a Palm handhelds and exchange them by beaming them to one another. Also, basic support for ubiquitous learning (BSUL) (Saito et al. 2005) and Poodle (Houser and Thornton 2005) are learning management system (LMS) and content management system (CMS) for mobile devices, used in order to facilitate learning at anytime and anywhere.

4.3.3   Mobile Language Learning Applications

Language learning is one of the important application domains of mobile learning, because language is contextualized and the language-thinking pattern is assimilated in the real world (LaPointe and Barrett 2005). Notice for example, the vocabulary teaching experiment by Miller and Gildea (1987), in which they describe how children acquire vocabulary faster with the method used outside of school, by relating words to ordinary conversation, than with the traditional method based upon abstract definitions and sentences taken from external contexts.

A lot of mobile language learning systems have been developed. For example, the learning on the move (LOTM) system sends English vocabulary material to Japanese students using Short Messaging Service (SMS) (Thornton and Houser 2004). Also, PhotoStudy (Joseph et al. 2005) supports learning vocabulary by sharing photos taken with mobile phones with built-in cameras. Uther et al. (2005) developed a mobile learning application for speech/audio language training using Java J2ME. In addition, there are a lot of commercial products and podcast content to support mobile language learning. These systems are based upon learners' location and in addition, the authors have developed a location-based language learning system called LOCH (language-learning outside the classroom with handhelds).

LOCH was conceived to assist overseas students in learning Japanese while they are involved in real-life situations. Using the provided interfaces, the teacher assigns tasks for students to perform around town (Fig. 4.1a) using items including PDA, GPS and data commutation card, personal handy-phone system (PHS) via a mobile-phone network, and interaction with native speakers, as shown in Fig. 4.1b, and invites them to bring back their findings and/or questions. By carrying out the tasks, overseas students can enhance their communication skills in Japanese and perceive and familiarize themselves with aspects of the local culture such as food, activities, etc. Students can use their PDAs for writing down annotations, recording questions, taking pictures and reporting back to the teacher. At any time, the teacher can monitor the position of the students and establish communication with them, as shown in Fig. 4.1c. Then, the

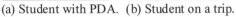

(a) Student with PDA.   (b) Student on a trip.   (c) Teacher's desk.

Fig. 4.1. One day trip with LOCH

teacher guides the students through the task's activities, giving suggestions or hints (such as "Ask somebody how to get there" or "You have to find the post office first").

After all the students conclude their tasks, they meet together in the classroom. All the gathered information is displayed and discussed, and each student explains his/her strategies to the rest of the group. Similar situations are identified, and their solutions are shared under the guidance of the teacher. Also, the teachers link the problems and the knowledge taught during the course. This is a kind of "seamless learning", in which students can seamlessly learn Japanese language not only inside the classroom but also outside the classroom.

4.4   Conclusion and Further Research

Schools will still be around in the future, but education and teaching will be a combination between just-in-case learning only in classrooms and just-in-time learning anytime and anywhere. The challenge in an information-rich world is not only to make information available to people at any time, at any place, and in any form, but specifically to say the right thing at the right time in the right way. Therefore, it is very important to realize right time and right place learning (RTRPL). RTRPL hopes to be a comprehensive method of learning and, as a result, produce a better learning environment with the aid of mobile devices. Every learning subject is unique depending on the culture and social background. We will need more research and development to strike a balance between the usage of mobile devices and traditional learning.

References

Brown, J.S., Collins, A., & Duguid, P. (1989). Situated cognition and the culture of learning. *Educational Researcher*, 18(1), 32–42.

Chen, Y.S., Kao, T.C., Sheu, J.P., & Chiang, C.Y. (2002). A mobile scaffolding-aid-based bird-watching learning system. In *Proceedings of IEEE International Workshop on Wireless and Mobile Technologies in Education WMTE'02* (pp. 15–22).

Colella, V., Borovoy, R., & Resnick, M. (1998). Participatory simulations: using computational objects to learn about dynamic systems. In *Proc. of CHI 98 conference summary on Human factors in computing systems* (pp. 9–10).

Curtis, M., Luchini, K., Bobrowsky, W., Quintana, C., & Soloway, E. (2002). Handheld use in K-12: a descriptive account. In *Proceedings of IEEE International Workshop on Wireless and Mobile Technologies in Education WMTE'02* (pp. 23–30).

Houser, C., & Thornton, P. (2005). Poodle: a course-management system for mobile phones. In *Proc. of International Workshop on Wireless and mobile Technologies in Education* (pp. 211–215).

Joseph, S., Binsted K., & Suthers, D. (2005). PhotoStudy: vocabulary learning and collaboration on fixed and mobile devices. In *Proc. of WMTE 2005* (pp. 206–210).

LaPointe, D., & Barrett, A. (2005). Language learning in a virtual classroom: synchronous methods, cultural exchanges. In *Proceedings of Computer Supported Collaborative Learning 2005* (pp. 368–372).

Miller, G.A., & Gildea, P.M. (1987). How children learn words. *Scientific American*, 257, 94–99.

Ogata, H., & Yano, Y. (2004). Context-aware support for computer supported ubiquitous learning. In *Proc. of IEEE International Workshop on Wireless and Mobile Technologies in Education (WMTE) 2004* (pp. 27–34). IEEE Computer Society Press.

Roschelle, J. (2003). Unlocking the learning value of wireless mobile devices. *Journal of Computer Assisted Learning*, 19(3), 260–272.

Saito, N., Ogata, H., Paredes, R., Yano, Y., & Ayala, G. (2005). Supporting classroom activities with the BSUL environment. In *Proc. of WMTE 2005* (pp. 243–250).

Song, A. (2006). What consequences have handheld educational uses brought about? In *Proc. of international workshop on mobile and ubiquitous learning environments in conjunction with ICCE2006* (pp. 1–8).

Thornton, P., & Houser, C. (2004). Using mobile phones in education. In *Proc. of International Workshop on Wireless and mobile Technologies in Education* (pp. 3–10).

Uther, M., Zipitria, I., Uther, J., & Singh, P. (2005). Mobile adaptive CALL: a case-study in developing a mobile learning application for speech/audio language training. In *Proc. of WMTE2005* (pp. 187–191).

Yin, C., Ogata, H., & Yano, Y. (2006). PSSLSA: participatory simulation system for learning sorting algorithms. In *Proc. of International Conference on Advanced Learning Technologies (ICALT2006)* (pp. 843–844).

5 Ambient Intelligence and Ubiquitous Computing

M. Bick and T.-F. Kummer

Ambient intelligence and ubiquitous computing characterize intelligent, pervasive and unobtrusive computer systems embedded into human environments, tailored to the individual's context-aware needs. Such miniaturised modern information and communication technology (ICT) supports humans by offering information and guidance in various application areas. Ambient intelligence leads to ambient learning by embedding individual learning activities in every day life. The learners participate and co-operate in, for example, syndicating, re-mixing, or creating learning materials and environments. The main objective of this chapter is to describe the general concepts of ambient intelligence and ubiquitous computing. Thereby, we introduce and analyse various approaches and examples to discuss how the vision of ambient intelligence can support work, learning and knowledge processes.

5.1 Introduction and Definitions

The recent advances in information and communication technology (ICT) evolution will definitely influence human life, especially in terms of communication and interaction:

A German salesman of a big European company takes part in an international exchange program and has to travel to Japan for the first time. As he already knows, there are various cultural differences between Europe and Asia in general and specifically between Germany and Japan. To prepare for his visit, he tries to learn some polite Japanese phrases. To collect additional cultural as well as historical information, he also visits a local museum that is, fortunately, hosting a Japanese exhibition at this time. The exchange-program participants are supported by an ambient learning environment that connects teachers and learners permanently also during the journey. With his personal digital assistant (PDA), the learner can store useful expressions that are linked to specific situations. Aiming at the support of everyday life situations, the corresponding ad-hoc classroom system enables teacher and students to establish a context-aware virtual classroom dynamically, independent of location and time. Additionally, the salesman uses his PDA as an electronic guide while visiting the museum. This solution offers the opportunity to combine the "real" museum with a web-based system that not only delivers text, images, digital audio and video, but also enables the visitor to construct a personal record of his visit by bookmarking exhibit content, taking digital pictures with a camera and accessing this information later on during his stay.[1]

This fictitious case illustrates that modern ICT – in a third wave of computing (Fig. 5.1) – will increasingly become invisible, be embedded in our natural surroundings, present whenever needed, and be adaptive to the users (Weber et al. 2005).

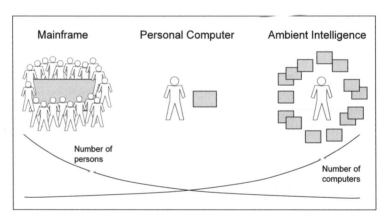

Fig. 5.1. From mainframe to ambient intelligence

Corresponding visions and terms have been coined in the last years.

- *Ubiquitous Computing*
  Ubiquitous computing is the method of enhancing computer use by providing numerous computers throughout the physical environment,

---

[1] The case study is based on recent research work by Ogata and Yano (2003a, b) as well as Bomsdorf (2005).

but making them effectively invisible to the user. This is different from just using, for example, a PDA. Ubiquitous or "everywhere" computing does not live on a personal device of any sort but in the woodwork everywhere (Weiser and Brown 1996; Weiser 2001).

- *Ambient Intelligence*
  The European Union's Information Society Technologies Program Advisory Group (ISTAG 2003) introduced the term ambient intelligence in a similar fashion to describe a vision of environments equipped with advanced technologies and computing to create an ergonomic space for the occupant in an invisible way (Bohn et al. 2005; Remagnino et al. 2005). Correspondingly, Weber et al. (2005) define ambient intelligence as the "[...] vision that technology will become invisible, embedded in our natural surroundings, present whenever we need it, enabled by simple and effortless interactions, attuned to all our senses, adaptive to users and context-sensitive, and autonomous".

- *Pervasive Computing*
  Pervasive computing is defined by IBM (Hansmann et al. 2001) as "[...] the convenient access, through a new class of appliances, to relevant information with the ability to easily take action on it when and where you need it". Within pervasive computing environments, computing is spread throughout the environment, users are mobile, information appliances are becoming increasingly available, and communication is made easier – between individuals, between individuals and things, and between things (Ark and Selker 1999).

These three terms are often used interchangeably. Extending ubiquitous computing, the term ambient intelligence focuses on the architecture and more general aspects of how such vision could be integrated into human daily life. In principle, ambient intelligence means largely the same as the more technical term, ubiquitous computing. Authors often prefer a specific notion to emphasize a particular direction of their work (Bomsdorf 2005). Consequently, we will mainly stick to the term ambient intelligence to characterize the vision of intelligent computer systems that are non-invasively embedded into human environments and are tailored to the individual's context-aware needs.

The vision of a future filled with smart and interacting everyday objects offers a whole range of fascinating possibilities. Consequently, industry has quietly begun setting its sights on the corresponding business potentials (Bohn et al. 2005). Typically, ambient intelligence is used in logistics and supply-chain management, applying wireless sensors, radio frequency identification (RFID) tags and/or positioning systems. In principle, two general economic aspects can be distinguished: a decrease of cost of a better localization of various objects or an increase of sales as a result of new "smart" products and services (Fleisch et al. 2005). Further application areas can be identified, for example, healthcare, tourism or learning.

The remainder of this chapter is organised as follows. Firstly, technological aspects will be described in Sect. 5.2. With regard to the above-mentioned possibilities, we will introduce various fields of application in depth in Sect. 5.3. While developments in information and communication technology never had the explicit goal to change society but rather did so as a side effect (Weber et al. 2005), we will also briefly describe various social and ethical implications. Considering the great variety of application possibilities, it is important that ambient intelligence will be both reliable and socially acceptable.

As already mentioned, ambient intelligence will support a paradigm shift in learning. In Sect. 5.4 we will focus on ambient learning. With regard to the definitions of ambient intelligence and the related concepts, ambient learning goes far beyond typical mobile learning scenarios. Finally, a concluding summary and some recommendations for further work will be given.

5.2   Technology

Ambient intelligence describes an environment in which the technology is embedded and hidden in the background and interacts sensitively, adaptively and responsively to people and objects (Weber et al. 2005). Therefore, computers have to be integrated parts of the reality. They disappear as visible locally separate items. Objects of our daily life, in combination with information technology, become hybrid objects, that is, things that think, or "smart devices" (Gershenfeld 1999). Consequently, the real world is the interface capable of aiding daily chores and professional duties (Remagnino et al. 2005). However, computers have to adapt to users' real world and not squeeze the user into a computer world. Thus, ambient intelligence is used to support people by offering information and guidance whenever needed (Weber et al. 2005).

To implement such environments, we must focus on two main aspects. Firstly, an ambient environment has to know and support the users' needs by enabling individual configurable services. To reach this, the environment must offer a high degree of personalization. Secondly, the system must offer anytime/anyplace computing. Therefore, three dimensions must be taken into account: mobility of the user, hardware and software.

5.2.1 Technology Trends

Various technological trends directly lead to ubiquitous computing respectively ambient intelligence. In the following we will briefly introduce the main drivers (Krcmar 2005) (Table 5.1).

Table 5.1. Main technological drivers

Computing power	The number of transistors doubles every 18 months
Miniaturization	The involves devices becoming smaller
Energy consumption	Better media are to be found for the storage of energy
Networking	Existing networks are used more effectively
Materials	New materials offer additional opportunities and functions
Sensors	Support collection of information and communication

The integral technological developments are the ongoing device miniaturization and the simultaneous increase of computing power. According to Moor's law, the number of transistors on integrated circuits doubles every 18 months (Moore 1965). This law worked quite precisely in the past. Despite the decreased energy consumption of single transistors, overall energy consumption has increased. Therefore, better solutions have to be found for the storage of energy. Passive energy transfers, such as the transmission via electromagnetic fields by using radio frequency identification (RFID) tags (see following section) or lasers, may be alternatives in the future (Fabian and Hansen 2006). Another important aspect is the technological advance in networking/communication. The average bandwidth utilisation of existing networks is increasing; the costs per data packet approach zero. This enables new applications with high data transfers and more linked systems (Krcmar 2005). Therefore, research in new materials, for example, light-emitting polymers or composite materials, offer new opportunities and additional functions such as deformation by activation (Fabian and Hansen 2006). Additionally, sensors support the collection of information concerning the environment and the communication with other devices in the system (Krcmar 2005).

5.2.2 Sensors

Sensors became a paradigm for new possibilities of continuing the miniaturization in microtechnologies and thus of ambient intelligence. Early studies underline the high potential of these technologies (Fleisch et al. 2005).

Today, sensors cover a broad range of devices that are able to detect objects, temperature, smells, sounds and gestures in the environment (Aarts 2004; Snijders 2005). Through these technologies, the context can be covered and the system can react without human intervention.

Basically, sensors require two major technologies. The first one focuses on the information that the device sends. This can be, for instance, an identification code, the data on temperature or a combination of both. Also needed is a sending station, which enables communication with the middleware. For further discussion, see (Anastasopoulos et al. 2006).

Transfer mode systems such as Bluetooth or wireless local area networks (WLAN) can be integrated in a embedded wireless system. Each of these technologies has its own pros and cons. For example, Bluetooth on one hand enables communication between various devices and sensors, including wearable objects such as clothing, in a personal area network (PAN); on the other hand, Bluetooth allows no accurate tracing (Jovanov et al. 2001; Bardram et al. 2006).

Another important technology is RFID-technology. It is expected that RFID-technology will be one of the main drivers of future ambient intelligence (EU 2005). Nevertheless, the discussions concerning security, privacy, data protection and safety issues should be taken seriously for all kinds of these sensor technologies. Accordingly, one integral issue is the protection of personal data, that is, any information relating to an identified or identifiable natural person (EU 2005; Langheinrich 2005). Correspondingly, current approaches suggest giving the user full control of the technology, that is, the ability to disable or even destroy sensor tags.

In general, sensors can be divided into two groups: active tags and passive tags. Passive RFID tags, for instance, do not have their own energy source and use radio frequency to send short information. Additionally, the storage space is limited to single bits and the range is limited to approximately 20–30 cm. In contrast, active tags have their own energy source. Hence, their range is up to several meters. However, if the battery is discharged, the complete tag becomes useless (Fabian and Hansen 2006). Therefore, as shown above, the development of new and better energy sources will be a main aim of the next years.

5.3 Architectures

Ambient intelligence has to deal with a great variety of heterogeneous devices, networks and services. Such an environment has to be compatible to devices such as mobile phones, sensors, and the above-mentioned different types of communication networks (e.g., WLAN, Bluetooth, RFID, etc.). Additionally, ambient intelligence has to be highly dynamic and flexible with regard to the concrete setting of devices that change in time, for instance, a new type of mobile phone. The corresponding reconfiguration could take place in real-time in order to directly integrate a device that is needed for the service of another device Bartelt et al. (2005) and Klus et al. (2006). For example, if a display is needed for illustration, the environment could be searched for a device with a display close to the user (Anastasopoulos et al. 2005, 2006). Consequently, the user will not always be conscious of which components are actually integrated into the ambient intelligence system.

With ambient intelligence, the user is situated in the centre (Fig. 5.2). The architecture consists of fixed and mobile computers and sensor devices provided by the middleware. These components support the collection of information relating to the user as well as to the environment, for example, biometrical data, an empty fridge or incoming e-mail. In this context, ambient intelligence could be understood as a supporting shield.

Ambient intelligence is based on a layered system (Fig. 5.3). The lower layer supports the collection of required information. Through various sensors and tags, this information gets transferred to the middle layer by applying specific control units and the transfer mode system. This way, information can be collected from the physical environment as well as from users or from the computer systems they use (Magerkurth et al. 2006).

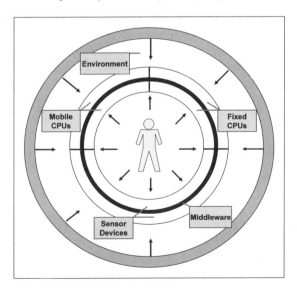

Fig. 5.2. Ambient intelligence architecture around the user

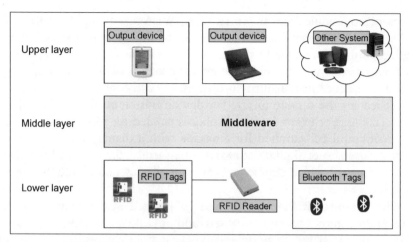

Fig. 5.3. Layered system of ambient environments

The middle layer supports address issues, for example, the interoperability of various devices, appliances, protocols, services, security aspects and scalability. Furthermore, so-called intelligent user services have to be supported. These user services have adaptive capabilities with regard to awareness to the usage conditions, physical context and social situations (Magerkurth et al. 2006). Consequently, in contrast to the lower layer, the middle layer needs specific computing power to manage the devices and support corresponding infrastructure decisions.

In the upper layer, collected information is used for value-added services such as statistical data or business process integration (Anastasopoulos et al. 2005). Output devices provide information to user devices such as laptops or desktop computers. Nevertheless, components on the upper layer can also act like devices on the lower layer. That is, output devices such as PDAs could act as sensors.

5.4   Standards

To achieve such highly integrated environments, specific standards must be taken into account. Ambient technology standards mainly focus on wireless networks and telecommunication among the various involved devices.

The information transfer from the lower layer to the upper layer (see previous section) has to emphasize wireless technology standards and corresponding data exchange standards as well as specific middleware technologies.

Common wireless protocols such as Bluetooth, general packet radio service (GPRS) or universal mobile telecommunication system (UMTS) can be used to attach the frequency of RFID tags. Current research work focuses especially on standardization activities to harmonize the different RFID tag frequencies, focusing on a worldwide-accepted format that offers RFID readers the opportunity to handle various frequencies. Correspondingly, the transnational standardization community EPCglobal promotes the global standardization of RFID tags.[2]

In addition, specific data exchange standards are required. Commonly, four groups of exchange formats can be distinguished: comma-separated values (CSV), electronic data interchange (EDI), extensible markup language (XML) and miscellaneous (Leukel 2004). Recently, ambient-specific standards have been established, for example, the physical markup language (PML) (Brock 2001). PML has been designed to standardize the description of physical objects for use in remote monitoring and control of the physical environment. The development of PML resulted in the foundation of EPCglobal. The EPC information service delivers different data to the involved objects, applying a specific transponder such as a RFID-transponder. The EPC information service comprises historical information, which enables track and trace processes. Furthermore, general information from various devices or from different data sources is available (Flörkemeier 2005).

To obtain integrated ambient intelligence, appropriate middleware technologies must be taken into account. In principle, an ambient-specific middleware could be understood as a further development of common middleware approaches for distributed systems (Coulouris et al. 2001). The corresponding infrastructure standards have to deal with the interoperability of software applications and database systems as well as with the coordination of functions that manage, control and monitor corresponding processes. The common object request broker architecture (CORBA) is probably the most common exponent of an infrastructure standard. Recent middleware technologies involve web services as part of a service-oriented architecture as a means of integration (Deitel et al. 2003). Currently, there are no formal infrastructure standards in the field of ambient intelligence and ubiquitous computing. There are various projects underway that aim to develop more or less proprietary approaches (Römer et al. 2002; Schoch 2005; Anastasopoulos et al. 2006). With regard to the involved project, partners such as Microsoft and EasyLiving (Brumitt et al. 2000) or HP and CoolTown (Kindberg and Barton 2001), various market-based de-facto standards will be developed.

---

[2] For further discussion cf. http://www.epcglobalinc.org.

5.5 Application Areas

Ambient intelligence can support humans in multitudinous application areas. Following a recent study carried out by the EU commission (EU 2006), logistics is still regarded as the application area where stimulation of ambient technology based applications might be beneficial. In addition, healthcare and government, followed by pharmaceuticals, supply-chain management and manufacturing processes, are regarded as potential implementation areas. Lastly, public transport and library systems are considered useful fields of application.

Additionally, the use in other application areas such as shops, museums, tourism, zoological fieldwork or university education, was analysed in various research projects. However, for privacy reasons, only application areas with no sensitive information or a high appreciation of sensitive information have been focused on recently (Bardram et al. 2006).

In the following, we will briefly introduce the two main areas of the above-mentioned study (logistics and healthcare) as well as university education, with regard to the objectives of this handbook.

5.5.1 Logistics

In the area of logistics, companies began to use sensors for tracking and tracing comparatively early (Flörkemeier 2005). Here, automatic inventory scanning or better fraud resistance for goods can be supported. Additionally, sensors offer the opportunity to design a smart warehouse that identifies the incoming and outgoing goods automatically and directly orders new goods if necessary.

Various case studies (Fleisch et al. 2005) underline the efficiency of ambient environments in this field of application. The customer acceptance is relatively high because no specific personal information is used in typical business-to-business processes applying passive RFID tags.[3]

Nevertheless, companies have to communicate the reasons why they have applied such technologies recently. They have to underline that sensors are only used for tracking and tracing to reduce a typical kind of hostility and to avoid possible boycotts by their customers (Thiesse 2005).

---

[3] Strassner and Eisen (2005) identified in a case study how the efficiency of loading equipment in transport could be increased significantly using RFID tags. In this field of application no personal information related to the end-customer was collected.

This field of application, of course, also relates to learning processes. For example, the learning material (e.g., books or a specific experimental design) could be an integral part of the ambient learning environment, offering the opportunity to manage the resources more effectively and generating a learning impact. Besides, problem-oriented learning scenarios should be mentioned: within a production process, a worker needs specific knowledge to fulfill his tasks. The environment dynamically recognizes a knowledge gap and provides certain learning materials such as an E-Learning course or it just orders a textbook. Additionally, processes or schedules can be simulated and tested in real-life scenarios by tagging objects such as containers, etc. Such simulations could also be part of a specific case study or a computer-based simulation game.

5.5.2 Healthcare

With regard to privacy issues, this field of application is definitely more complicated than transport processes in logistics. Accordingly, healthcare scenarios focused on applying RFID tags for tracking and tracing of blood transfusions. However, the possibilities are not limited to this.

Recent research projects assume that, in order for ambient intelligence to be accepted, the benefits of its applications have to outweigh privacy concerns, particularly in the case of medical care or the care of elderly people, in which personal information may be revealed. Ongoing collection of biometric information at the patient's home provides the opportunity to monitor the person's physical condition. Accordingly, ambient intelligence enables an early warning system if specific conditions change and, in an emergency, the system autonomously calls an ambulance.

Additionally, the integration of employees into such an environment is a common issue in this field of application. Bardram et al. (2006) talked to clinicians and other employees that were equipped with Bluetooth tags for tracking and status information. Most of the involved persons considered the tracking as an advantage because it facilitated finding or meeting others, for example. This case study underlines that ambient technologies are not generally unaccepted; rather that it is important to generate confidence by revealing the technologies' value to people and to make sure that the gathered information is not used in any other way (Bardram et al. 2006). Although ambient environments could provide a certain kind of control system, not every opportunity to monitor and analyse working processes should be realized. To identify areas where users accept ambient technologies because of their benefits, without fear of control, is a great challenge.

Furthermore, in the field of healthcare, we can also identify possibilities with regard to learning processes. Flexible consultations with available colleagues and support in diagnostics are just two examples.

5.5.3 University Education

In the field of university education, the development and implementation of advanced mobile devices as well as wireless communication infrastructures have already started to transform ways of learning (Hummel and Hlavacs 2003; Laroussi 2004). These current and emerging technologies have valuable potential in supporting the learning needs of an expanding, heterogeneous and mobile society, moving from a paradigm in which the computer is a tool embodied in a device to a scenario in which the computer creates an environment that assists individual in their contexts (Winters et al. 2005)

Corresponding tools and devices immerse in the learning environment and surround educators, students and the environment they operate in. Some are purely assistive and supportive in nature while others are becoming increasingly intelligent (Ktoridou and Etcokleous 2005). Typical learning services for ubiquitous learning are device and network detection services, location tracking services, calendar and social activities services, and content access services (Yang 2006).

Thus, not only the fields of application mentioned above will change by using ambient intelligence. It is expected that university education will also change significantly, moving toward more situated and context-aware educational styles (Hummel and Hlavacs 2003).

5.6 Ambient Learning

With regard to the introductory case as well as the application areas review, education and learning is a challenging field for ambient intelligence.

In the past decades, the majority of developed E-Learning environments have been implemented either as server-based or as client–server architecture. Such approaches are metaphors of real-world learning scenarios, as in student-teacher scenarios, in which teachers act as the content producers while students act as the content consumers (Yang 2006). Now the use of ambient technologies in education is making a step forward (Jones and Jo 2004). Enabling technologies foster a paradigm shift in learning by stressing communication and the direct and on-demand exchange of information between students and lecturers. Learners will participate and co-operate in, for example, syndicating, re-mixing or creating learning materials and environments (Yoshida 2006).

Ambient intelligence leads to ambient learning, allowing the embedding of individual learning activities in every day life (Laroussi 2004; Bomsdorf 2005). Thus, it is necessary to design specific tools and applications that mediate between the information-filled environment and the learner (Winters et al. 2005). Furthermore, the great potential of ambient technologies must be utilized rather than merely adapted to the pedagogies and curricula of static technologies, such as scenarios and applications designed for desktop computers or notebooks (Winters et al. 2005).

With regard to the distinctiveness of ambient learning environments, we define the term ambient learning in the following section and describe various key characteristics that have to be met by ambient learning environments. We will also consider related learning theories and briefly introduce various ambient learning research projects will.

5.6.1 Definitions

A literature review indicates that the term ubiquitous learning is more commonly known as ambient learning. One probable explanation is that, as already mentioned in the first section of this chapter, ambient intelligence represents, more or less, a specific European perspective on the vision of intelligent computer systems. Additionally, authors often use specific notions to stress their particular direction (Bomsdorf 2005). Ubiquitous computing probably focuses more on technologically oriented approaches. Nevertheless, we will use these terms synonymously.

Yang (2006) defines ubiquitous learning or ambient learning as "[...] an interoperable, pervasive, and seamless learning architecture to connect, integrate, and share three major dimensions of learning resources: learning collaborators, learning contents, and learning services". Thus, ambient learning focuses on how to provide learners with the right information at the right time in the right way (Ogata and Yano 2003a, b, 2005). This mirrors the definition of ambient intelligence in the first section of this chapter.

Following Jones and Jo (2004), an ambient learning environment (ALE) is a setting of omnipresent learning that takes place all around the student, although the student may not even be conscious of the corresponding learning processes. In an ambient learning environment, a multitude of new learning situations arise and may be supported by the surrounding context, that is, by time and space as well as by what resources and services are available, or by the learning collaborators (Ogata and Yano 2003a, b, 2005).

Most of the recent approaches (Ogata and Yano 2003a, b, 2005; Jones and Jo 2004; Yoshida 2006; Yang 2006) focus on collaborative learning processes. The main objective of an ambient learning environment – contrary to typical client–server oriented learning environments – is to provide answers to the following questions (Ogata and Yano 2003a, b, 2005): (1) who has the same problem or knowledge? (2) who has a different view about the problem or knowledge? (3) who has the potential to assist in solving the problem? Consequently, some authors, for example, Yoshida (2006), suggest the integration of so-called Web 2.0 social software tools, for example, wikis, blogs, or podcasts, in an ambient learning environment in order to turn learners into producers of learning material.

Finally, ambient learning environments are going to change the culture of learning: ambient learning "[...] is not constrained by schedules and physical spaces; rather, it is pervasive and ongoing, prevalent in many interactions among students, faculty, parents, administration, staff, a wide variety of community stakeholders, etc. (Laroussi 2004)".

5.6.2 Characteristics

With regard to the definitions mentioned above, various characteristics of ambient learning and ambient learning environments can be identified (Table 5.2). Ogata and Yano (2003a, b referencing Chen et al. 2002; Curtis et al. 2002) describe five main characteristics (see Table 5.2): permanency, accessibility, immediacy, interactivity, and situating of instructional activities. These were extended by Bomsdorf (2005) by the adaptability of

Table 5.2. Characteristics of ambient learning

Permanency	Learners can never lose their work unless it is purposefully deleted. In addition, all the learning processes are recorded continuously everyday
Accessibility	Learners have access to their documents, data or videos from anywhere. Information is provided based on their requests. Therefore, the learning involved is self-directed
Immediacy	Wherever learners are, they can get any information immediately. Therefore learners can solve problems quickly. Otherwise, the learner may record the questions and look for the answer later
Interactivity	Learners can interact with experts, teachers or peers in the form of synchronous or asynchronous communication. Hence, the experts are more reachable and the knowledge is more available
Situating of instructional activities	Learning could be embedded in our daily life. The problems encountered as well as the knowledge required are all presented in the nature and authentic forms. It helps learners notice the features of problem situations that make particular actions relevant
Adaptability	Learners can get the right information at the right place in the right way

ambient learning environments, that is, by making available the right information at the right time and right place (see previous section). Accordingly, learners will be able to select the learning methods most desired by or suited to them (Yoshida 2006).

5.6.3 Learning Concepts

The application of learning theories is an important consideration in designing ambient learning environments (Jones and Jo 2004). Although various projects provide insight into the field of applied technologies, it is necessary to design new educational modalities which would really take advantage of smart and interacting devices (Laroussi 2004).

The pedagogical challenge related to ambient learning is to find appropriate ways to successfully integrate such devices into learning activities. Following Ktoridou and Eteokleous (2005), a pedagogical opportunity is that the ambient learning widens the educational horizons of students as well as enhances the educational options for educators. For example, if students themselves understand why and how something happens in nature, rather than just being told that it is true, the information has more relevance and therefore more meaning (Jones and Jo 2004). Consequently, Ogata and Yano (2003a, b, 2005) suggest that when classroom activities are related to the real world, students find them more meaningful.

There are various corresponding learning concepts, such as on-demand learning, hands-on or minds-on learning, and authentic learning (Ogata and Yano 2003a, b). Ogata and Yano (2003a, b) distinguish between three types of learning to ensure authentic learning: action learning, situated learning and incidental learning. Action learning also refers to the experimental learning theory. There are two additional forms of experimental learning (Ogata and Yano 2003a, b), future search and outdoor education.

The development of an ubiquitous learning environment combines the advantages of an adaptive learning environment with the benefits of ambient intelligence and the flexibility of smart and interacting devices. "Students have the freedom to learn within a learning environment which offers adaptability to their individual needs and learning styles, as well as the flexibility of pervasive and unobtrusive computer systems (Jones and Jo 2004)".

Finally, from a technological as well as a pedagogical point of view, not all kinds of learning content and learning activities are appropriate for ambient learning environments (Trifonova 2003). Various devices are limited due to display size, capabilities or battery performance (Hummel and Hlavacs 2003).

5.6.4   Recent Developments

Recent developments in ambient learning focus on pedagogical as well as technological issues, applying corresponding technologies in classrooms or to support outdoor studies to overcome the restrictions of traditional learning environments (Bomsdorf 2005). In the following we will briefly introduce various approaches in order to get a general idea of how to use ambient intelligence to enhance learning processes:

- Ogata and Yano (2003a, b, 2005) focus on language learning as an application domain for their collaborative-learning support system with an ubiquitous environment (CLUE). To provide context-aware support to the learners, this environment provides knowledge awareness maps, which graphically provide the learner with visualisations of the relationships between shared knowledge as well as the current and past interactions of learners. The maps play an important role in finding peer learners and helpers, and thereby induce collaboration.
- Yoshida (2006) suggests a Web 2.0 supported ubiquitous learning environment to provide open-oriented, user-centric and networked learning. From his point of view, the movement towards the open sharing of learning materials, such as open educational resources[4] or open courseware,[5] will lead to further developments in ambient learning.
- Bomsdorf (2005) deals with the question of how to use ambient learning technologies to enhance learning processes at a university for distance education. Retaining suitability for learning in different, changing contexts the developed prototype follows the concept of plasticity of digital learning places. The prototype comprises models for the specification of attributes of the didactic profile and devices, as well as a resource model to characterize learning materials and services by means of metadata. The main objective is the adaptation of learning resources to different learning contexts, which continues to enable and support learning processes.
- Yang (2006) implemented a context-aware ubiquitous learning environment that consists of three sub-systems: a peer-to-peer content access and adaptation system, a personalized annotation management system, and a multimedia real-time group discussion system. To support this context-aware learning environment, a corresponding context model as well as a specific acquisition mechanism for collecting contextual information in the runtime were designed.

---

[4] For further discussion cf. http://www.unesco.org/iiep/virtualuniversity.
[5] For further discussion cf. http://www.ocwconsortium.org.

- Jones and Jo (2004) developed an adaptive teaching system using ambient technologies. The corresponding ubiquitous learning environment (ULE) resided within the physical environment. Microprocessors were embedded in objects and devices. The additional use of wireless telecommunication devices made them easily accessible and contributed to educational functionality. Moreover, Jones and Jo are currently developing a ubiquitous robot that uses sensor technologies.
- Bick et al. (2007) provided conceptual and technological solutions on how mobile and ambient learning environments can be developed in an interoperable way. Based on a specific ambient intelligence framework they implemented a prototype of a standard-based ambient learning environment.

Comparable to Bomsdorf's analysis (2005) most of the above-mentioned approaches still focus on the physical environment and its direct (semantic) relation to learning objectives and activities: "Information and services are 'brought' to the environment and/or situation they 'belong to' (Bomsdorf 2005)".

5.7 Conclusion and Further Research

The increasing use of miniaturised ICTs (such as tiny processors, improved wireless telecommunication capabilities, flexible software architectures and improved battery technology) will eventually result in a convergence of work, learning and knowledge processes. Consequently, learning and knowledge processes could be enriched sustainably by applying ambient intelligence. While the learners are moving with their mobile devices, the system dynamically supports their learning by communicating with embedded computers in the environment (Ogata and yano 2003a, b, 2005), allowing for personalisation and customisation of the system to their needs (Jones and Jo 2004).

However, ambient intelligence and ubiquitous computing are mostly still a dream. In this chapter, we described the technological concepts for providing corresponding learning environments. Furthermore, various fields of application in general as well as specific approaches in ambient learning were introduced to describe the current state of ambient intelligence research. The presented key characteristics, permanency, accessibility, immediacy, interactivity, situation of instructional activities and adaptability could be treated as success factors which must definitely be considered while implementing an ambient learning environment.

With regard to the recent advent of such highly integrated learning environments, additional standards must be taken into account. Ambient learning focuses on specific standardisation activities: on the one hand, recent learning technology standards are widely accepted specifications that provide a basis for reuse, recombination and re-contextualisation. On the other hand, specifically in the field of ambient learning, several issues have not yet been addressed (Bick et al. 2007). For example, the use of a variety of devices cannot be modelled yet and location and synchronisation aspects are currently not covered in such standards as Learning Object Metadata – LOM (IEEE 2002) or IMS Learning Design (IMS 2002).

A discussion concerning ambient intelligence is not only a question of standardisation issues. It is also an interdisciplinary field that needs to implicate social, economic, and ethical aspects. The recent approaches do not consider the learner's acceptance and awareness. Additionally, privacy and security policies have not yet been addressed appropriately. These are important aspects when introducing ambient learning environments.

References

Aarts, E. (2004). Ambient intelligence: a multimedia perspective. *IEEE Multimedia*, 11(1), 12–19.

Anastasopoulos, M., Bartelt, C., Koch, J., Niebuhr, D., Rausch, A. (2005). Towards a reference middleware architecture for ambient intelligence systems. In *Proc. of the Workshop for Building Software for Pervasive Computing*. 20th Conference on Object-Oriented Programming Systems, Languages and Applications (OOPSLA), San Diego, CA, USA. http://agrausch.informatik.uni-kl.de/publikationen/repository/workshops/work019/reference%20architecture.pdf. Accessed 8 November 2006.

Anastasopoulos, M., Klus, H., Koch, J., Niebuhr, D., Werkman, E. (2006). DoAmI – a middleware platform facilitating (re-)configuration in ubiquitous systems. In *Proc. of the Workshop System Support for Ubiquitous Computing (Ubisys)*. 8th International Conference of Ubiquitous Computing (Ubicomp 2006), Orange County, CA, USA. http://www.magic.ubc.ca/ubisys/positions/koch_ubisys06.pdf. Accessed 10 November 2006.

Ark, W. S., Selker, T. (1999). A look at human interaction with pervasive computers. *IBM Systems Journal* 38, 504–507.

Bardram, J., Hansen, T., Morgensen, M., Soegaard, M. (2006). Experiences from real-world deployment of context-aware technologies in a hospital environment. In Dourish, P., Friday, A. (Ed.). *Ubicomp 2006: Ubiquitous Computing, 8th International Conference* (pp. 369–386). Berlin Heidelberg New York: Springer.

Bartelt, C., Fischer, T., Niebuhr, D., Rausch, A., Seidl, F., Trapp, M. (2005). Dynamic integration of heterogeneous mobile devices. In *Proc. of the Workshop in Design and Evolution of Autonomic Application Software (DEAS 2005)*. ICSE 2005, St. Louis, MO, USA. http://dag.informatik.uni-kl.de/papers/DIoDE.pdf. Accessed 20 November 2006.

Bick, M., Kummer, T., Pawlowski, J. M., Veith, P. (2007). Standards for ambient learning environments. Submitted to *2nd Conference on Mobility and Mobile Information Systems (MMS 2007)*.

Bohn, J., Coroamă, V., Langheinrich, M., Mattern, F., Rohs, M. (2005). Social, economic, and ethical implications of ambient intelligence and ubiquitous computing. In Weber, W., Rabaey, J., Aarts, E. (Ed.), *Ambient Intelligence* (pp. 5–29). Berlin Heidelberg New York: Springer.

Bomsdorf, B. (2005). Adaptation of learning spaces: supporting ubiquitous learning in higher distance education. In Davis, N., Kirste, T., Schumann, H. (Ed.), *Mobile Computing and Ambient Intelligence: The Challenge of Multimedia*. Internationales Begegnungs- und Forschungszentrum fuer Informatik (IBFI), Schloss Dagstuhl, Germany. http://drops.dagstuhl.de/opus/volltexte/2005/371/pdf/05181.BomsdorfBirgit.Paper.371.pdf. Accessed 13 October 2006.

Brock, L. D. (2001). The Physical Markup Language. http://archive.epcglobalinc.org/publishedresearch/MIT-AUTOID-WH-003.pdf.

Brumitt, B., Krumm, J., Meyers, B., Shafer, S. (2000). Ubiquitous computing and the role of geometry. *IEEE Personal Communications*, 7, 41–43.

Chen, Y. S., Kao, T. C., Sheu, J. P., Chiang, C. Y. (2002). A mobile scaffolding-aid-based bird-watching learning system. In *Proc. of IEEE International Workshop on Wireless and Mobile Technologies in Education* (pp. 15–22). IEEE Computer Society Press.

Coulouris, G., Dollimore, J., Kindberg, T. (2001). *Distributed Systems: Concepts and Design*. Harlow: Addison Wesley.

Curtis, M., Luchini, K., Bobrowsky, W., Quintana, C., Soloway, E. (2002). Handheld use in K-12: a descriptive account. In *Proc. of IEEE International Workshop on Wireless and Mobile Technologies in Education* (pp. 23–30). IEEE Computer Society Press.

Deitel, M. H., Deitel, J. P., DuWaldt, B., Trees, K. L. (2003). *Web Services: A Technical Introduction*. London: Pearson Education.

EU (2005). *Working document on data protection issues related to RFID technology*. European Commission, Brussels, Belgien. http://ec.europa.eu/justice_home/fsj/privacy/docs/wpdocs/2005/wp105_en.pdf. Accessed 21 November 2006.

EU (2006). *The RFID revolution: your voice on the challenges, opportunities and threats – online public consultation preliminary overview of the results*. European Commission Information Society and Media. http://www.rfidconsultation.eu/docs/ficheiros/Summary_of_Consultation.pdf. Accessed 14 November 2006.

Fabian, B., Hansen, M. (2006). Technische Grundlagen. In Bizer, J., Spiekermann, S., Günther, O. (Ed.), *Taucis – Technologiefolgenabschätzung Ubiquitäres Computing und Informelle Selbstbestimmung, Studie im Auftrag des Bundesministeriums für Bildung und Forschung* (pp. 11–44). Kiel, Berlin.

Fleisch, E., Christ, O., Dierkes, M. (2005). Die betriebswirtschaftliche Vision des Internets der Dinge. In Fleisch, E., Mattern, F. (Ed.), *Das Internet der Dinge* (pp. 3–38). Berlin Heidelberg New York: Springer.

Flörkemeier, C. (2005). EPC-Technologie – vom Auto-ID Center zu EPCglobal. In Fleisch, E., Mattern, F. (Ed.), *Das Internet der Dinge* (pp. 87–100). Berlin Heidelberg New York: Springer.

Gershenfeld, N. (1999). *When Things Start to Think.* New York: Henry Holt.

Hansmann, U., Merk, L., Nicklous, M., Stober, T. (2001). *Pervasive Computing Handbook.* Berlin Heidelberg New York: Springer.

Hummel, K. A., Hlavacs, H. (2003). Anytime, anywhere learning behaviour using a web-based platform for a university lecture. In *Proc. of SSGRR 2003.* http://www.ani.univie.ac.at/~hlavacs/publications/ssgrr_winter03.pdf. Accessed 7 November 2006.

IEEE Learning Technology Standards Committee (2002). *Learning Object Metadata Standard,* IEEE 1484.12.1-2002.

IMS Global Learning Consortium (2002). IMS Learning Design Information Model. http://www.imsglobal.org/learningdesign/ldv1p0/imsld_infov1p0.html. Accessed 22 November 2006.

ISTAG – IST Advisory Group (2003). Ambient Intelligence: from vision to reality. ftp://ftp.cordis.lu/pub/ist/docs/istag-ist2003_consolidated_report.pdf. Accessed 16 November 2006.

Jones, V., Jo, J. H. (2004). Ubiquitous learning environment: an adaptive teaching system using ubiquitous technology. In Atkinson, R., McBeath, B., Jonas-Dwyer, D., Phillips, R. (Ed.), *Beyond the comfort zone: Proceedings of the 21st ASCILITE Conference* (pp. 468–474). http://www.ascilite.org.au/conferences/perth04/procs/jones.html. Accessed 28 November 2006.

Jovanov, E., Raskovic, D., Price, J., Chapman, J., Moore, A., Krishnamurthy, A. (2001). Patient monitoring using personal area networks of wireless intelligent sensors. *Biomedical Science Instrumentation,* 37, 373–378.

Kindberg, T., Barton, J. J. (2001). A web-based nomadic computer system. *Computer Networks,* 35, 443–456.

Klus, H., Niebuhr, D., Weiß, O. (2006). Integrating sensor nodes into a middleware for ambient intelligence. In *Proc. of the Workshop Building Software for Sensor Networks, International Conference on Object-Oriented Programming, Systems, Languages, and Applications (OOPSLA),* Portland, Oregon, USA. http://agrausch.informatik.uni-kl.de/publikationen/repository/workshops/work026/oopsla06.pdf.

Krcmar, H. (2005). *Informationsmanagement.* Berlin, Heidelberg New York: Springer.

Ktoridou, D., Eteokleous, N. (2005). Adaptive m-learning: technological and pedagogical aspects to be considered in Cyprus tertiary education. In *Proc. of m-ICTE 2005, 3rd International Conference on Multimedia an ICTs in Education,* Caceres, Spain. http://www.formatex.org/micte2005/375.pdf. Accessed 30 November 2006.

Langheinrich, M. (2005). Die Privatsphäre im Ubiquitous Computing – Datenschutzaspekte der RFID-Technologie. In Fleisch, E., Mattern, F. (Ed.), *Das Internet der Dinge* (pp. 329–362). Berlin Heidelberg New York: Springer.

Laroussi, M. (2004). New e-learning services based on mobile and ubiquitous computing: Ubi-Learn project. In *Proc. of CALIE 04 – International Conference on Computer Aided Learning in Engineering Education, Grenoble, France*. http://www-clips.imag.fr/calie04/actes/Laroussi_final.pdf. Accessed 20 October 2006.

Leukel, J. (2004). *Katalogdatenmanagement im B2B E-Commerce*. Lohmar/Köln: Josef Eul.

Magerkurth, C., Etter, R., Janse, M., Kela, J., Kocsis, O., Ramparany, F. (2006). An intelligent user service architecture for networked home environments. In *Proc. of the 2nd International Conference on Intelligent Environments* (pp. 361–370). Athens, Greece.

Moore, G. (1965). Cramming more components onto integrated circuits. In *Electronics*, 38, 114–117.

Ogata, H., Yano, Y. (2003a). How ubiquitous computing can support language learning. In *Proc. of KEST 2003* (pp. 1–6). Honjo, Akita, Japan.

Ogata, H., Yano, Y. (2003b). Supporting knowledge awareness for a ubiquitous CSCL. In *Proc. of eLearn 2003* (pp. 2362–2369). Phoenix, AZ, USA.

Ogata, H., Yano, Y. (2005). Knowledge awareness for a computer-assisted language learning using handhelds. *International Journal of Continuous Engineering Education and Lifelong Learning*, 14, 435–449.

Remagnino, P., Hagras, H., Monekosso, N., Velastin, S. (2005). Ambient intelligence – a gentle introduction. In Remagnino, P., Foresti, G., Ellis, T. (Ed.), *Ambient Intelligence. A Novel Paradigm*. Berlin Heidelberg New York: Springer.

Römer, K., Kasten, O., Mattern, F. (2002). Middleware challenges for wireless sensor networks. *Computing and Communications Review*, 4, 59–61.

Schoch, T. (2005). Middleware für Ubiquitous-Computing-Anwendungen. In Fleisch, E., Mattern, F. (Ed.), *Das Internet der Dinge* (pp. 119–140). Berlin Heidelberg New York: Springer.

Snijders, F. (2005). Ambient intelligence technology: an overview. In Weber, W., Rabaey, J., Aarts, E. (Ed.), *Ambient Intelligence* (pp. 255–269). Berlin Heidelberg New York: Springer.

Strassner, M., Eisen, S. (2005). Tracking von Ladungsträgern in der Logistik – Pilotinstallation bei einem Güterverladeterminal. In Fleisch, E., Mattern, F. (Ed.), *Das Internet der Dinge* (pp. 209–224). Berlin Heidelberg New York: Springer.

Thiesse, F. (2005). Die Wahrnehmung von RFID als Risiko für die informationelle Selbstbestimmung. In Fleisch, E., Mattern, F. (Ed.), *Das Internet der Dinge* (pp. 363–378). Berlin Heidelberg New York: Springer.

Trifonova, A. (2003). Mobile learning – review of the literature. Technical Report DIT-03-009. http://eprints.biblio.unitn.it/archive/00000359/01/009.pdf. Accessed 24 October 2006.

Want, R. (2006). An introduction to RFID technology. *IEEE Pervasive Computing*, 5, 25–33.

Weber, W., Rabaey, J., Aarts, E. (2005). Introduction. In Weber, W., Rabaey, J., Aarts, E. (Ed.), *Ambient Intelligence* (pp. 1–2). Berlin, Heidelberg New York: Springer.

Weiser, M. (1991). The computer of the twenty-first century. *Scientific American*, 265, 66–75.

Weiser, M., Brown, J. S. (1996). Designing calm technology. *Powergrid Journal* 1.01. http://www.ubiq.com/hypertext/weiser/acmfuture2endnote.htm. Accessed 22 November 2006.

Winters, N., Kanis, M., Agamanolis, S., Noss, R. (2005). The ubiquitous learning space. In *CAL 2005*, Bristol, UK. http://www.lkl.ac.uk/niall/Theubiquitouslearningspace.pdf. Accessed 24 November 2006.

Yang, S. J. H. (2006). Context aware ubiquitous learning environments for peer-to-peer collaborative learning. *Educational Technology and Society*, 9, 188–201.

Yoshida, M. (2006). Towards ubiquitous learning and education. In *Proc. of the 6th Distance Learning and the Internet Conference*, Tokyo, Japan. http://apru2006.dir.u-tokyo.ac.jp/pdf/1a-1.pdf. Accessed 2 November 2006.

6 Designing Contextualized Learning

M. Specht

6.1 Introduction

Contextualized and ubiquitous learning are relatively new research areas that combine the latest developments in ubiquitous and context aware computing with pedagogical approaches relevant to achieve more situated and context aware learning support. Searching for different backgrounds of mobile and contextualized learning, authors have identified the relationships between existing educational paradigms and new classes of mobile applications for education (Naismith et al. 2004). Furthermore, best practices of mobile learning applications have been identified and discussed in focused workshops (Stone et al. 2002; Tatar et al. 2002). Especially in the area of educational field trips (Equator Project 2003; RAFT 2003), in recent years innovative approaches for intuitive usage of contextualized mobile interfaces have been developed.

Recent research in human-computer interaction (HCI) describes several trends in designing new interfaces for interacting with information systems. Benford et al. (Benford et al. 2005) describe four main trends, which include growing interest and relevance of sensing technologies, growing diversity in physical interfaces, increasing mobility and physical engagement in HCI, and a shift in the types of applications for which innovative interfaces are designed. These developments also have a major impact on the development of new learning solutions and interfaces for explorative and situated learning support.

For building contextualized learning support on the one hand, an infrastructure for contextualization is needed. This builds on research works of the area of context aware systems (Zimmermann et al. 2005). On the other hand, methods for analyzing and designing context-specific appliances and tools for learning support from a human-computer interaction perspective

(Terrenghi et al. 2004) are necessary. Third, a pedagogical framework has to be defined that sets the constraints for giving contextualized support to learners in a specific learning application.

The following paper describes the motivation and background for contextualizing learning and illustrates the implementation of a service-based and flexible learning toolkit developed in the RAFT project for supporting contextualized collaborative learning support.

6.2   Contextualized Learning

Situated learning as introduced by Lave and Wenger (Wenger and Lave 1991) states the importance of knowledge acquisition in a cultural context and the integration in a community of practice. Learning, in this sense, must not only incorporate a curriculum but also the tasks, learning situations and interaction with the social environment of the learner. This is often contrasted with the classroom-based learning in which most knowledge is out of context and presented de-contextualized. On the one hand, the process of contextualization and de-contextualization might be important for abstraction and generalization of knowledge, but on the other hand, in the sense of cognitive apprenticeship (Collins et al. 1989), it is reasonable to guide the learner towards appropriate levels and context of knowledge coming from an authentic learning situation.

From a constructivist point of view, not only is knowledge always contextualized, but also the construction of knowledge (learning) is always situated within its application and the community of practice (Mandl et al. 1995). Stein defines four central elements of situated learning: the *content* emphasizes higher order thinking rather than the acquisition of facts; the *context* for embedding the learning process in the social, psychological and material environment in which the learner is situated; the *community* of practice that enables reflection and knowledge construction; and the participation in a process of reflecting, interpreting and negotiating meaning (Stein 1998). From the perspective of situated learning, several requirements for new learning tools can be stated, such as: use authentic problems, allow multiple perspectives, enable learning with peers and social interaction within communities and enable active construction and reflection about knowledge. A shift towards a new tradition of online learning is described by Herrington et al. (Herrington et al. 2002).

Moreover, the idea of situated learning is also closely related to the ideas of "blended learning" and "learning on demand", especially in educational systems for adults and at the workplace (Oppermann and Specht

2006). An important point that is not taken into account by a lot of new approaches for delivering learning on demand is the aspect that the need (demand) for knowledge and learning arises in a working context with the motivation for solving specific problems or understanding problem situations. This notion of "learning on demand" in the workplace exemplifies the potential of contextualized learning in the workplace. Learners who identify a problem in a certain working situation are highly motivated for learning and acquiring knowledge for problem solving. They have a complex problem situation as a demand, which can be used for delivering learning content adapted to their situation. Furthermore, not only the delivery of content into a certain context or practice is needed but also interaction facilities that allow an appropriate interaction and cooperation with educational systems must be provided.

The contextualization of learning on demand can not only be seen from the point of view of an actual problem or learning situation but can also be seen in a longer lasting process of integrated learning activities. Different learning activities are combined in blended learning approaches: The student prepares for a task, updates his/her base knowledge, applies the task in an actual working situation, documents solutions to the problem and reflects on the activities to evaluate the entire process.

Latest research also stresses two other dimensions of embedding learning support into everyday life: first, integration from a lifelong learning perspective and second, integration in a community of practice. Latest research into lifelong learning integrates informal and formal learning approaches and supports access to knowledge resources, learning activities, competence development and learning communities from a variety of clients built on service-oriented architectures (Koper and Specht 2006).

6.3 Designing Contextualized Learning Support for Field Trips: RAFT Project

In the context of the European funded project RAFT (remotely accessible field trips) the consortium created learning tools for field trips in schools. The system should support a variety of learners with different tasks either in the classroom or in the field.

RAFT envisioned facilitating field trips for schools and enabling international collaboration of schools. Instead of managing a trip for 30 students, small groups from the RAFT partner schools went out to the field, while the other students and classes from remote schools participate interactively from their classrooms via the Internet. The groups going to the field were equipped with data gathering devices (photographic, video, audio, measuring), wireless communication and a video conferencing system for direct interaction between the field and the classroom.

Field trips are an ideal example of an established pedagogical method that can be enhanced with computer-based tools for new ways of collaboration and individual active knowledge construction. The learners in the field can collect information and contextualize it with their own experiences and, at the same time, work on tasks with their peers and detect new perspectives and solutions to given problems. To foster the variety of perspectives and activities in the field trip process, RAFT developed tools for the focused support of different activities in the field and in the classroom. In recent years, several research projects have worked on enhanced field trip solutions with mobile technology (Concord Consortium 2003; Equator Project 2003).

The RAFT project followed a plan of functional analysis in the field, end user requirements analysis, system and service design, interface design and implementation and evaluation in the target group. In this paper we describe the process and some lessons learned through RAFT for developing and implementing contextualized learning support.

6.3.1   Prototyping and Scenario Based Analysis

In the first year of the project, the different phases and functional requirements for supporting live collaboration and information access during field trips were worked out. Field trips with school kids were held in Scotland, Slovakia, Canada and Germany in order to identify different activities in the field and in the classroom and to draw first evaluations of critical success factors. Different types of field trips were identified, including individual class field trips within one subject, cross-curricular field trips within a school, interconnection of classrooms with different remote experts, comparison field trips synchronously collecting data from different remote classes, longitudinal studies comparing data from different classes in different years, and others.

Through these trials, different phases for preparing the field trip, experiencing the field trip in the classroom and in the field, and the evaluation after the field trip were identified. Therefore the RAFT applications aimed to support the users with different tools depending on their current phase in the field trip process in general: preparation, field trip activity, or evaluation.

Judging from our experiences in the prototyping phase of the project, the implementation of different user roles and interfaces was not based on a software solution for intelligent rendering of interface components but was developed with specialized applications for the different roles and role-specific devices for fulfilling the tasks in the field and in the classroom. The RAFT applications can be seen as different components in a blended learning process that is distributed in time, location, social context in the different phases of the field trip. Furthermore, non-functional requirements highlighted the importance of specialized devices for certain tasks to reduce complexity of handling applications and also the possibility to split up tasks in learner groups because, in most field trips, the students actually worked in groups.

Workshops with end users were held to understand the handling of hardware and typical usage of devices from the end users' perspective. Furthermore, internal designer workshops allowed us to develop different notions of the integration of field trips into the classroom of the future.

6.3.2 Functional Analysis and Role Model Design

From the prototyping and use of the RAFT applications by end users we saw the following main activities as new qualities of contextualized learning approaches:

- Cooperative task work for synchronizing activities and raising interest: The distributed work on a task focuses the interaction and communication among the learners, technology moves into the background when the curiosity about the given task and its exploration in physical and knowledge space become the main interest. The context in this sense is an enabling means that allows the learners to immerse in the learning subject at hand.
- Data gathering for active construction of knowledge and learning materials: Users are much more motivated when "self made" learning materials get integrated into the curriculum and they have the possibility to extend existing structures for learning.
- Instant and multimodal messaging for a lively experience: The instant exchange of multimodal messages on different service levels was identified as a core requirement to make a live field trip experience happen between the field and the classroom.

To support a wide variety of different learning activities and the use of interfaces on different devices, the user interface of the RAFT system had to be built out of single blocks that support different client technologies and interaction styles. Therefore, based on the functional specification coming out of the requirements analysis phase, we clustered the functionality into components and recombined those components depending on the task and the interaction device that a user has available. Additionally, a webservice layer was build on the basis of the ALE LCMS (Kravcik and Specht 2004). This allowed us to give access to a wide variety of interface technologies.

An instantiation of a multimodal communication channel widget is one component of the RAFT interface. Depending on the input and output characteristics of the device of a user, messaging can be done with classical keyboard input. For example, the archiver working mainly with a classical PC terminal and web access can use the PC screen as an output channel and therefore have mostly text output. On the other hand, a scout in the field walking around with a mobile device cannot easily use text input. Most virtual keyboard input possibilities were quite unusable in the field due to lighting conditions and the difficulty of typing on the go on a mobile device. Therefore, the mobile users mainly scribbled on a notepad-like widget and input audio when the environmental conditions allowed it.

The RAFT services in this sense all build on a common infrastructure with base services such as content management, communications support and utilities for administrative support. Furthermore, it became clear that a base library for certain interface components was necessary as field trip support applications, in most cases, had to be adapted to the specific field-trip type (Fig. 6.1).

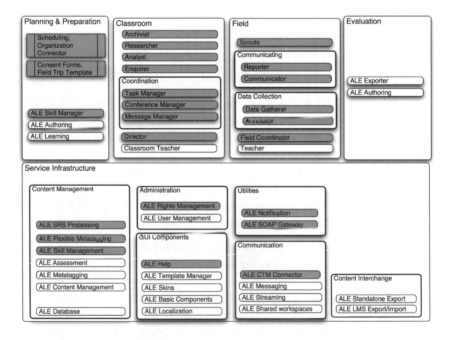

Fig. 6.1. The basic RAFT service infrastructure and functional clusters

Parallel to this functional clustering, a role model for different pedagogically motivated roles was also developed. An excerpt of those is shown in Table 6.1.

Table 6.1. Basic functional roles, their functions and examples

Role/function description	Functions	Example
Expert interviews/reporter	Structure interview, moderate questions from the classroom	A field trip class wants to learn about a defined station in a complex production process
Data gatherer/annotator: during the field trip the students gather data to support/disprove the proposed hypothesis and to find new and interesting aspects. Examples of ways to gather data: camera, video, sensor data	Collect data, annotate content with metadata, collect sensor measures, verify concrete hypotheses	Students go to the different phases of the chocolate production process and document the stages through photos
Analyse: data gained from the site is analysed and discussed during the field trip, in the classroom and after the field trip	Research online, evaluate incoming data from the field	Students look at the images taken from a biology field trip, and assess the quality and whether or not the hypotheses can be verified based on the acquired materials

6.3.3   Information Architecture and Use Case Analysis

Based on the role model and the non-functional requirements from the prototyping experiences, a basic mapping of functionality and roles was done (Table 6.2). Basically, by defining such a matrix, the focus of the role for a certain task was set and the cooperation context for different roles was defined.

Table 6.2. Mapping roles and functional widgets

Role	Task widget	Navigation widget	Messaging widget	Conference widget
Field site				
Data gatherer	+	+	+	–
Annotator	+	–	+	–
Reporter	+	+	+	–
Communicator	+	–	–	+
Classroom				
Task manager	+	–	+	–
Director	+	+	+	+
Analyst	+	–	+	–

On the one hand, learning pairs could be defined by roles such as the "data gatherer" and "annotator" pair, which have a clear division of responsibilities: while the navigator knows where to go on the map to collect certain data, the annotator looks at the collected data and annotates it with the current context. Both roles get their current context by agreeing on a common task. Another example is the "reporter" and "communicator" pair. While the reporter concentrates on the verbal communication between classroom and expert and has a moderating role, the communicator focuses on documenting and capturing the communication through conferencing and recording facilities.

On the other hand, in the classroom, the director has a moderating role for the whole class and therefore needs all information available on the classroom big screen, while the task manager concentrates only on managing and structuring tasks on the fly for the field trip. During the field trips in RAFT, it became obvious that the roles do not always need to be split between persons but several roles can also be taken over by one person if complexity allows.

For the different roles in the field trip, the information architectures for the various appliances were inferred. Figure 6.2 shows the scouting application.

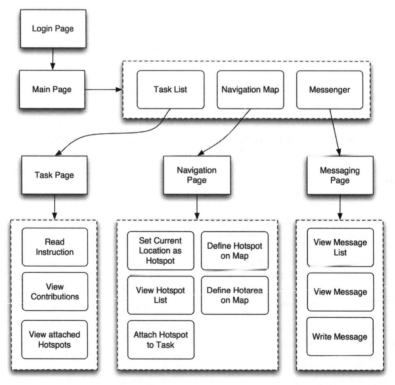

Fig. 6.2. The information architecture of the scouting application

Within this infrastructure, the RAFT partners developed a variety of interface components and widgets based on different technologies such as Java, Microsoft .NET, Macromedia Flash and others. Those widgets could then be easily combined in different applications, which would allow a highly focused and contextualized collaboration between different field trip participants.

The RAFT project raised a lot of technical and interaction issues relevant to the field of designing learning experiences for mobile and pervasive learning. In addition to the backend technology based on an LCMS and web services that allow the combination of different client technologies from electronic whiteboards to mobile telephones, the synchronization and notification of heterogenous clients accessing a persistent and consistent learning object repository became very important.

As we discovered, the field trip is a very good example of not only the synchronization between different users cooperating on a common task, but also of the distribution over the different phases of the field trip (preparation, field trip activity and evaluation), which appear to be important aspects of nomadic activities for learning and exploration.

6.4 Conclusions

The RAFT project implemented and evaluated a flexible set of tools for supporting field trips in schools. Basic experiences and conclusions include but are not limited to the following points:

- A flexible basic service infrastructure is necessary as client technologies change rapidly. Furthermore, ubiquitous access to functionality becomes more and more important, and trends like the diversification of interfaces and devices make it necessary to construct easily reusable functional components for different application scenarios.
- Restricted interaction facilities of mobile devices and new forms of sensing-based interaction make it necessary to define base contexts for cooperation and cooperative learning. Nevertheless, the main context entities can change. In the RAFT project, the tasks were the main context on which a team agrees. All members had a task widget and took this widget to set the context to which they contributed at that time.
- Contextualization of applications and the contextualized delivery and acquisition of resources appear to have different criteria and relevant methods. For contextualized learning, a pedagogical model to structure the tasks and roles and to build specialized applications

seems much more relevant than the innovative use of contextual information for on-the-fly customization of applications. Nevertheless, several results in RAFT showed that the contextual information delivery and automatic acquisition of contextual metadata is highly relevant for learning in context (Specht and Kravcik 2006).

References

Benford, S., Schnoedelbach, H., Koleva, B., Anastasi, R., Greenhalgh, C., Rodden, T. et al. (2005). Expected, sensed, and desired: a framework for designing sensing-based interaction. *ACM Transactions on Computer–Human Interaction*, 12(1), 3–30.

Collins, A., Brown, J. S., & Newman, S. E. (1989). Cognitive apprenticeship: teaching the craft of reading, writing, and mathematics. In L. B. Resnick (Ed.), *Knowing, Learning and Instruction* (pp. 453–494). Hillsdale, NJ: Lawrence Erlbaum.

Concord Consortium (2003). The Concord Consortium. http://www.concord.org. Accessed 2003.

Equator Project (2003). The EQUATOR Interdisciplinary Research Collaboration. http://www.equator.ac.uk. Accessed 2003.

Herrington, J., Oliver, R., Herrington, T., & Sparrow, H. (2002). *Towards a new tradition of online instruction: using situated learning theory to design web-based units.* Paper presented at the 17th Annual ASCILITE Conference, Lismore.

Koper, R., & Specht, M. (2006). TenCompetence: lifelong competence development and learning. In D. M.-A. Sicilia (Ed.), *Competencies in Organizational E-Learning: Concepts and Tools*. Hershey: Idea.

Kravcik, M., & Specht, M. (2004). *Flexible navigation support in the WINDS learning environment for architecture and design.* Paper presented at the Adaptive Hypermedia 2004 Conference, Eindhoven.

Mandl, H., Gruber, H., & Renkl, A. (1995). Situiertes Lernen in multimedialen Lernumgebungen. In L. J. Issing & P. Klimsa (Eds.), *Information und Lernen mit Multimedia* (pp. 167–178). Weinheim: Psychologie Verlags Union.

Naismith, L., Lonsdale, P., Vavoula, G., & Sharples, M. (2004). *Literature Review in Mobile Technologies and Learning* (Literature Review No. 11): University of Birmingham.

Oppermann, R., & Specht, M. (2006). Situated learning in the process of work. In D. Hung & M. S. Khine (Eds.), *Engaged Learning with Emerging Technologies* (pp. 69–89). Berlin Heidelberg New York: Springer.

RAFT (2003). RAFT Project Website. http://www.raft-project.net. Accessed 2003.

Specht, M., & Kravcik, M. (2006). Authoring of learning objects in context. *International Journal on E-Learning*, 5(1), 25–33.

Stein, D. (1998). Situated learning in adult education. http://ericacve.org/docs/situated195.htm. Accessed 2003.

Stone, A., Alsop, G., Briggs, J., & Tompsett, C. (2002). *M-learning and e-learning: a review of work undertaken by the Learning Technology Research Group, Kingston University, UK*. In Proceedings of the Europeain Workshop on Mobile and Contextual Learning, 20–21 June, 2002, The University of Birmingham, England.

Tatar, D., Roschelle, D., Vahey, P., & Peunel, W. R. (2002). Handhelds go to School: Lessons Learned.

Terrenghi, L., Specht, M., & Moritz, S. (2004). *Design of an interface for technology supported collaborative learning – the RAFT approach.* Paper presented at the International Conference on Entertainment Computing, Eindhoven, The Netherlands.

Wenger, E., & Lave, J. (1991). *Situated Learning: Legitimate Peripheral Participation.* Cambridge: Cambridge University Press.

Zimmermann, A., Lorenz, A., & Specht, M. (2005). Personalization and context-management. *User Modeling and User Adaptive Interaction (UMUAI), Special Issue on User Modeling in Ubiquitous Computing*, 15(3–4), 275–302.

7 Virtual and Augmented Reality

D. Fabri, C. Falsetti, A. Iezzi, S. Ramazzotti, S. Rita Viola, and T. Leo

7.1 Introduction

Virtual and augmented reality are deemed powerful learning tools because they allow, in principle, experiential learning without displacing the learner when real-experience environments are available. In order to attain satisfactory experiential learning, technology should have extremely challenging features and performances. These requirements become more and more compelling in the field of E-Learning, where the ideal of having rich individual teaching assistance for each learner is pursued (ADLNET 2004) through the exploitation of ICT.

In this contribution, we will refer to E-Learning as having a learning experience on the web. Therefore no a priori distinction between education and training will be done. Learning experiences involve a number of pedagogical, psychological and contextual aspects (see, for example, Mantovani and Castelnuovo 2003), for which the role of technology has to be suitably calibrated. Learning experiences develop according to learning process models that evolve from individual learning to social and situated learning up to knowledge creation and management. Accordingly, the requirements of technological features and performances are varied. Moreover, it is not easy to give a common definition of virtual and augmented reality, since they involve several different and heterogeneous technologies.

However, we will focus on the technical possibility of providing the user with a plausible sense of presence. Therefore this chapter will survey:

1. The evolution of the definitions of virtual reality (VR) and augmented reality (AR) in time together with the evolution of pedagogical approaches followed in both traditional learning and E-Learning

2. The evolution of the available technologies together with the improvements of the Internet
3. Examples of the applications available at present for E-Learning

Finally, a few possible research and application developments on VR and AR technology related to the enhancement of the sense of presence in E-Learning will be discussed.

7.2 Virtual Reality and Augmented Reality Versus Pedagogical Models

As far as epistemology is concerned, the meaning of "reality" should be discussed before reflecting on the "virtual" attribute. Here we will refer to the current common sense feelings about reality.

In general terms, virtual reality (VR) is a technology that allows a user to interact with a computer-synthesized environment, be it a real or an imaginary one.

According to Fitzgerald and Riva (2001), "the basis for the VR idea is that a computer can synthesize a three-dimensional (3D) graphical environment from numerical data. Using visual and auditory output devices, the human operator can experience the environment as if it were part of the world. This computer generated world may be either a model of a real-world object, such as a house; or an abstract world that doesn't exist in a real sense but is understood by humans, such as a chemical molecule or a representation of a set of data; or it might be in a completely imaginary science fiction world".

Augmented reality (AR) can be considered a particular extension of VR. The user's sensation of the world is augmented by virtual objects that provide additional data/information on the real environment. Although in the literature, different definitions of AR have been given, the following ones can be considered representative:

- Vallino (1998) states that "AR is an area of virtual reality research that concentrates on the technology to merge synthetic sensory information, usually visual information, into a user's perception of their environment. Unlike VR, which seeks to immerse the user in a completely computer-generated world, augmented reality wants to keep the user immersed in the real world and add information to their perception of it".

- Liarokapis (Liarokapis et al. 2002) states, "The main objective of AR technology is to superimpose computer-generated information directly into a user's sensory perception, rather than replacing it with a completely synthetic environment. Users within AR systems must be able to interact with the 3D information in a natural way, like they do in the real environment".
- Kauffmann and Papp (2006) state, "AR is a variation of VR. VR technology completely immerses a user inside a synthetic environment. While immersed, the user cannot see the surrounding real world. In contrast, AR allows the user to see the real world, with virtual objects superimposed upon or composed with the real world. Therefore, AR supplements reality, rather than completely replacing it. AR can be said to require the following three characteristics: (1) combines real and virtual (2) interactive in real time (3) registered in 3D".

Looking at these definitions, we see three points worthy of attention:

1. The enhancement of perception through augmented sensations (AR)
2. The aim to a natural way of interaction between user and synthetic environment (AR and VR)
3. The presumption that the user is completely immersed in the VR synthetic environment

These points are in some way permanently present in the history of VR and AR. The names "virtual reality" and "augmented reality" were proposed, respectively, in 1987 by J. Lanier and in 1990 by Boeing's researchers. The origins date back to the '50s and '60s (Brooks 1999), in the field of vehicle and flight simulators for military applications.

In the '60s, research mainly focussed on 3D interactive computer graphics. Ivan Sutherland pioneered these studies at MIT's Lincoln Laboratory. In 1963, Sutherland completed Sketchpad, a system for drawing interactively on a CRT display with a light pen and a control board. The system was useful for the interactive manipulation of images. In a few years, these studies gave rise to the head-mounted 3D computer display (HMD). In 1967, Bell Helicopters carried out tests in which a pilot wore a HMD that showed videos from a servo-controlled infrared camera mounted beneath the helicopter. The camera moved with the pilot's head, both augmenting his night vision and providing a level of immersion sufficient for the pilot to equate his field of vision with the images from the camera. This kind of system would be later named AR. In the same year, at the University of North Carolina, the first force feedback system was developed for the GROPE project (Brooks et al. 1990). The system supported the scientific visualization of molecular docking by giving graphic representation of molecules and their inter-atomic forces. Through a special hand-grip device, the user was able to change relative position and orientation of molecules to search the minimum binding energy configuration. The system evolved from 2D to full 6D (GROPE-III). During '90s, Brooks's laboratory extended the use of VR to radiology and ultrasound imaging.

Advances in flight simulators, human-computer interfaces and augmented reality systems pointed to the possibility of immersive, real-time control systems for research, training and to improve performance. VR was extended to surgery in a context of telesurgery, that is, the use of robotic devices remotely controlled with computer-mediated sensory feedback. Use of telesurgery and robot-assisted surgery is at present widespread, in particular for minimally invasive surgery and in tele-neosurgery (Wusheng et al. 2004). The first telesurgery equipment was developed at SRI International in 1993 and the first robotic surgical intervention was performed in 1998 at the Broussais Hospital in Paris.

Virtual worlds had and have elective applications in the domains of entertainment, aesthetic inspiration and socialization, where they are increasingly realistic and immersive. By 1969, Myron Krueger (University of Wisconsin) created a series of projects on the nature of human creativity in virtual environments. His VIDEOPLACE system was based on sensing floors, graphic tables, and video cameras and processed interactions between a participant's image and computer-generated graphical objects. It is worthwhile to underline that the system focused on the representation of the user's actions by the computer.

Data Glove is probably the most used device to interact with virtual worlds. The first one was developed in 1977 (University of Illinois). In 1982, Thomas Zimmerman invented the optical glove. It was meant as an interface device for musicians and was based on the common practice of playing "air guitar". This was able to track hand and finger movements to control instruments like electronic synthesizers. In 1983, the Digital Data Entry Glove was built; its features included sufficient flexibility, as well as tactile and inertial sensors to monitor hand positions for a variety of applications to comprehend data entry. In 1985, the first commercial VPL Data-Glove was produced and brought to market in 1987 by VPL Co. (California).

The time was then right to speak about immersivity, that is, a modality of human computer-interaction that is bi-directional, real-time and allows mutual reactive feedback among the two interaction actors.

The first immersive VR system – Virtual Visual Environment Display (VIVED) – was developed at NASA labs in 1985. It evolved in a virtual interface environment workstation (VIEW) in 1989. VIVED defined a de facto standard suite of VR technology, including a stereoscopic HMD, head tracker, speech recognizer, computer-generated imagery, data glove and 3D audio.

Military and medical requirements continued to drive these technologies through the 1990s, frequently by partnerships with academia or entertainment companies. With the diffusion of Internet (by the '90s), virtual worlds, AR and telepresence were successfully launched as platforms for creative work, games, training environments, research and social spaces.

VR and AR developments are strictly related to the increase of computational power. The corresponding reduction of costs brings affordability to VR and AR systems in learning and training. Edutainment and entertainment have a widespread commercial market.

The aims of creating an artificial world as realistic as possible and of providing user interaction through modalities as similar as possible to everyday experiences, are explicit. The attention is on sensations, perceptions and cognition. Sensation here refers to the elementary physiological process through which the human body receives physical energy from the external environment. It is a process that involves the organs of sense and doesn't imply a conscious involvement. Perception here refers to the process through which the sensation is organized. It is an active process happening in the brain relating the sensation to the external object and involving the experience as well. Cognition here refers to the process of the mind involving memory, imagination and representation of the world. See (Metzger 1975) for examples. In the case of AR, the human-sensitive capability is enhanced. Sensitive capability is related to the specific role that presence plays in training, in relation to the process of learning and transfer of skills. The sense of presence (Mantovani and Castelnuovo 2003) makes the learning experience engaging, and trainees will experience thoughts, emotions and behaviours similar to the ones experienced in a real-life situation, thus allowing the creation of a recallable experience.

Therefore, the potential of AR and VR with respect to learning technologies, namely in the direction of experiential learning, in light of pedagogical policies based on active, constructivist approaches and involving technology mediated/enabled learning is, in principle, universally agreed upon. The characters of technology have to be carefully tuned in to the pedagogical models and the individual learning styles involved in a specific learning experience.

Pedagogical models underlying the introduction of ICT technologies in learning refer to:

- Active learning theories, according to which learning is seen as the outcome of a process involving the direct and experiential manipulation of the field the learner is dealing with (Kolb 1984; Felder and Brent 2003)

- Constructivist learning theories, according to which learning is seen as the personal and subjective construction of the learner, according both to the experiences he/she is doing and to the ones he/she had done (Bruner 1990; Kolb 1984)
- Social and situated learning theories that generalize constructivist viewpoints to social construction shared by groups of people, depending on the particular context in which they happen (Engeström 1987; Wenger 1998)

In this latter context, an important role can be attributed to knowledge creation and management. Without entering into the discussion of the knowledge cycle (Leo 2005) it can be said that in many knowledge domains, the creation of communities of practice working on suitable virtual environments is able to promote the definition of new, relevant and exploitable knowledge.

It appears that VR is particularly suited for training in the case of emulation of real-world objects, while representation of symbolic knowledge shows better results in the implementation of constructivist approaches and for social and situated learning (involving emotional interactions too), while AR could provide its best in material knowledge sharing aimed at performance enhancement (for example, in the case of maintenance of particularly complex appliances such as air traffic control radar systems, or cabling the shell of aircrafts).

It can be argued that the more plausible they are, the stronger learning may become. To satisfy such a requirement, the main functional components of the technological suite allowing effective VR and/or AR can be classified as follows:

1. Appropriate model of phenomenon to be emulated, reaching a sufficient approximation. Sufficient approximation here refers to sensorial and perceptual human capabilities. Imagination, if properly activated, can supplement poor models but in the present context we intend to focus on enabling technologies.
2. Sufficiently powerful computational resources, in terms of processors and memory; moreover, specific languages, algorithms and architectures are needed. They can be globally named virtual engines (VE). We will consider the VE as embedded in a client–server architecture because of the assumption that the learning experience happens through the web or a private network.
3. Input/output devices. Input devices are directed towards the electronic system. Output devices are directed to the users.

4. Systems for effective interaction and reactive feedback between a user and a synthetic environment. In our view, such a class of appliances is particularly important for a simple and ecological interaction.

Regarding the forth aspect, let us underline that VR applications generate sensations that the human brain and mind are able to, and are habituated to, reconnect and reconstruct perceptual experiences and related representations according to the phylogenetic personal evolution. If this natural modality of learning is disrupted, the user may experience difficulties and fatigue.

A last point is that class 4 components are in principle able to allow virtual experiences involving non-verbal communication and interaction among persons. Examples of such technologies are virtual worlds (Virtual Worlds Review 2006) and avatar-based applications (Activeworlds 2006).

7.3   Review of the Main Enabling Technologies

We will follow the classification of technologies just proposed and point out that most review papers available in the literature about VR- and AR-enabling technologies consider only class 2 and 3 components.

Models, in particular mathematical models of physical phenomena, will not be surveyed because of their endless coverage. Every knowledge domain has elective modelling methods. In general, suitably detailed models give rise to algorithms whose implementation requires extensive computational power, and some key problems. Multiple time scales, for instance, still exist.

Our attention will be mainly focused on technologies enabling the "natural" modality of human-synthetic world interaction. We think about all sensory-motor activities a person performs to interact with and to explore the real world (walking from one place to another, speaking, watching an object modifying the peripheral field due to the movement of the head, touching an object to evaluate its consistency, hearing a sound and trying to detect its source and so on). To mimic such activities in a satisfactory manner, great computational power is required. The needed information has to be made available with the best precision and the minimum latency time to allow the user to interact in real time with the virtual world (Mäki-Patola et al. 2005). For many years, supercomputers with parallel architectures and, more recently, distributed computing, have been able to provide the needed computational power, even if at costs that are generally unaffordable in the context of learning systems. Parallel computing is the simultaneous execution of the same task, split up and specially adapted on multiple processors in order to process it faster (Atty et al. 2006; Allard et al. 2004). Computational grids (Forster and Kesselman 2003; DAME 2003) allow the sharing, selection and aggregation of a wide variety of geographically distributed computational resources (such as supercomputers, computer clusters, storage systems, data sources, instruments, people) and introduce them as a single, unified resource to solve large-scale computer and data-intensive computing applications.

7.3.1 Virtual Engine

The VE is a key component of the VR system that reads its input devices, accesses task-dependent databases, updates the state of the virtual world and feeds the results to the output displays. It is an abstraction. It can be one computer, several co-located ones, or many remote computers collaborating in a distributed simulation (Burdea and Coiffet 2003).

In our view, the VE is embedded in a client–server architecture. Therefore, it comprehends computational resources and communication services. With regard to computational resources, the following can be said:

Frequently VR/AR technologies are considered coincident with computer visualization. At the highest levels of quality (fiction movies, military applications, high tech industrial applications), this requires specific hardware and software architectures for the rendering processes, such as the creation of 2D scenes from 3D models. These processes ask for pipeline architectures.

The pipeline architecture uses parallelism and buffers, and works on three levels: application, geometry and rasterizer. The application level software reads input devices (such as gloves, trackers), changes the co-ordinate reference systems, performs collision detection and collision response and reduces model complexity.

The geometry level computes the geometric model based on coordinates and transforms and reconstructs the scene based on lighting models such as wire-framed (the simplest one shows polygon-visible edges); the flat-shaded model (which assigns the same color to all pixels in a polygon [or side] of the object); Gouraud or smooth shading (which interpolates colors inside the polygons based on the color of the edges); Phong shading (which interpolates the vertex perpendicular to the object surface before computing light intensity based on the most realistic shading model (Burdea and Coiffet 2003)). The geometry stage receives the primitives from the application stage and uses a series of geometric operations such as transformations, projections, and clippings in order to pass the new co-ordinates and the color to the rasterizer stage. This stage can be implemented by software modules, by hardware devices or by both. At the end of this stage the scene is ready to be represented. The Rasterizer hardware converts information about 2D vertices from the geometry stage (x, y, z, colour, texture) into pixel information on the screen and provides an efficient buffering system to reduce the flicker phenomenon.

The VR engine manages the objects' model too. The VR object modelling cycle is composed of I/O mapping, geometric modelling, kinematics modelling, physical modeling and object behaviours for intelligent agents.

All these duties are fulfilled by high level programming languages that exploit, for implementation, HW and SW resources available in the computers they run on (either client or server). The more used and most promising languages can be classified in two main commercial categories: open source (OS) and proprietary. In this paper we will deal with OS languages. They are listed and briefly described as follows. They are XML based. XML (Extensible Markup Language) is used for data representation and is a powerful language that describes data structures. It is a simple and very flexible text format derived from SGML (ISO 8879) and developed by W3C Consortium:

- The xVRML and VRML97 (virtual reality modelling language) specifications (VRML 2006) were created to put 3D worlds onto the Internet using an idiosyncratic notational system. The xVRML Project is focused on evolving this into a more modern approach based on using an XML-based notation and an XML schema-based definition. The xVRML Specifications (Walczak and Cellary 2002), xVRML (2003), are based on the xVRML schema, which in turn provides a model of the data in a virtual reality instance document (called a world). The xVRML schema and specifications will also form the basis for the development of "view" and "controller" software technologies to express xVRML-instance documents.

- X3D is a royalty-free OS file format and run-time architecture that represents and communicates 3D scenes and objects using XML. It is an ISO-ratified standard that provides a system for the storage, retrieval and playback of real-time graphics content embedded in applications, all within an open architecture that supports a wide array of domains and user scenarios. It has features that can be tailored for use in engineering and scientific visualization, CAD and architecture, medical visualization, training and simulation, multimedia, entertainment, education and more. The development of real-time communication of 3D data across all applications and network applications has evolved from its beginnings as the virtual reality modelling language (VRML) to the considerably more mature and refined X3D standard.

- JAVA3D (2006) introduces a new view model that takes Java's vision of "write once, run anywhere" and expands it to include display devices and six-degrees-of-freedom input peripherals such as head trackers. This "write once, view everywhere" nature means that an application (applet) written using the Java 3D view model can render images to a broad range of display devices, including standard computer displays, multiple-projection display rooms, and head-mounted displays, without modification of the scene graph. It also means that the same application, without modification, can render stereoscopic views and take advantage of the input from a head tracker to control the rendered view.[1] The quality of attainable visualization depends on the HW/Firmware available on the computer running the Java applets; at present no comparison can be made to the visualization of the computer visualization systems.

In the current implementation, Java 3D mixes a lot of Java code with OpenGL calls:

- The OpenGL® (2006) application programming interface (API) began as an initiative to create a single, vendor-independent API for the development of 2D and 3D graphics applications, to allow effective porting of applications from one hardware platform to another.
- Toolkits have to be mentioned too. They are extensible libraries of object-oriented functions designed to help the VR developer. They support various common input/output devices used in VR (so drivers need not to be written by the developer) and allow importing of CAD models, editing of shapes, specifying of object hierarchies and collision detection as well as multi-level detail, shading and texturing and run-time management. Toolkits have built-in networking functions for multi-user interactions, etc., and can be classified in various ways: text-based or graphical-programming; type of language used and library size; type of input/output devices supported; type of rendering supported; general purpose or application specific; proprietary (more functionality, better documented) or public domain (free, but less documentation and functionality).

Moreover, it should be stressed that the use of VR in E-Learning applications could require some sort of knowledge management system to allow the capture of the knowledge developed during the learning process, its

---

[1] Java 3D API Specification, Chap. 8, "View Model".

organization and its presentation back to users, for instance in the form of a richer virtual environment.

As far as communication services are concerned, let us stress that effective use of VR on the Internet requires the adoption of specific communication protocols and the ability to dynamically modify the information present in the network according to the bandwidth available. Examples of such protocols include Distributed Interactive Simulation Protocol (DIS), Transmission Control Protocol (TCP), User Datagram Protocol (UDP), Protocol Data Unit (PDU), and Network Time Protocol (NTP).

Therefore, at either the client or server side, predictive systems can be required to reduce latency (Jung et al. 2000; Furht 1998).

7.3.2   Input/Output Devices

Output devices allow the user to sense the virtual environment. Human senses need specialized interfaces, for example:

- Vision requires graphics displays, which are the physical means for visualization. In the case of individual viewing, these displays are personal displays. The image may be monoscopic or stereoscopic, monocular (for a single eye) or binocular (for both eyes).
- Sound requires interfaces that provide synthetic sound from the virtual world. The sound can be monaural (both ears hear the same sound) or binaural (each ear hears a different sound).
- Force and touch demand haptic interfaces (Kim et al. 2006; Brau et al. 2005).

At present, smell and taste interfaces are mainly rather rough prototypes (Nakaizumi et al. 2006).

A number of input devices are needed. They are available in a rich variety. We discuss in greater detail those deemed significant for natural interaction:

- *3D pointer*. A 3D pointer is a three-dimensional mouse with six degrees of freedom. The Wanda (AT 2006) was the first of the wands/3D pointers. Until now it was the most common input device for CAVE-style (2002) VR interfaces. CAVE is a multi-person, room-sized, high-resolution 3D video and audio environment invented at EVL in 1991. Graphics are projected onto three walls and the floor, and viewed through active 3D glasses.

- *Trackers*. Trackers measure the movement of "objects" such as the user's wrist or entire body by referring to a fixed system of coordinates. The underlying physical devices can be magnetic, ultrasonic, mechanical, inertial/ultrasonic or vision-based. Relevant features are the measurement rate, sensing latency, sensor noise and drift, accuracy and repeatability, sensing degradation.
- *"Powered Shoes"* (Iwata et al. 2006). Powered shoes are a type of force platform that allows the user to walk in any direction in a virtual environment. The information the powered shoes provide exploits their ability to detect walking direction in a given coordinate system. They are motorised and can be disturbing (SIGGRAPH 2006). They are apparently not useful for VR Gameworlds, but are usable for VR training, immersion and data manipulation.
- The Nintendo Wii (2006) contains a motion sensor allowing measurements of six degrees of freedom movement of the hand to be transformed into an action on a screen. It is driven by ST's micro electro-mechanical systems (MEMS) technology. The Wii's controller was designed to withstand large temperature variations. It is immune to vibration and is shock resistant up to a force of 98 N. The controller even contains a small speaker assembly, allowing it to play sounds of events happening in proximity to the player-character.

7.3.3 Interaction and Reactive Feedback Devices

VirtuSphere (2006) consists of a giant mouse ball, which the user can enter. The user can move the mouse in any direction for virtually unlimited distances by making it do the following actions: walk, jump, roll, crawl, run. The ball, which is mounted on wheels, measures the distance and the direction of the user's steps. The system informs the user through a HMD about his/her movements in the virtual environment. Alternatively, the sphere can be installed inside a CAVE VR system and synchronized with it.

7.4 Some Relevant Applications to E-Learning

Nowadays, a number of applications of VR/AR that are specifically suited for E-Learning are available. A possible way to classify these applications is to subdivide them based upon their gross educational objectives, namely, individual learning, team learning (collaborative learning) or both.

Applications addressed to improve individual skill of the learners are, in general, based on complex simulation in which the key feature is the representation of the real world, which has to be as realistic as possible. These kinds of applications are aimed at reducing cost and improving safety during training.

Several applications are in biomedicine, in which practice is needed to develop students' knowledge and skills, and simulation is the better way to manage experiential training (Zajtchuk and Satava 1997). An AR system called Standardized Patients (SPs) (McKenzie et al. 2004) is available for training in three areas: doctor-patient communication, eliciting the history and performing the physical exams. Another example is a delivery simulator (Obst et al. 2004). This system comprehends direct haptic and auditory feedback and provides important physiological data such as blood pressure, heart rates and pain and oxygen levels.

VR has been used to build a liver surgery planning system (LSPS) (Reitinger et al. 2006). It aims to support radiologists during data preparation and to give surgeons precise information for optimal decision making. It combines medical image analysis and computer graphics, which allow for innovative problem solutions, especially when user interaction with complex 3D objects is needed.

In industry, many applications are diffused for training and competence development of people involved in safety-critical jobs. In the construction industry, a simulator of a hydraulic excavator based on a VR system was developed for training machine operators (Wang et al. 2004). Many applications are available to provide training in complex technical systems. An example is the prototype of an innovative interface developed for aircraft (Haritos and Macchiarella 2005) maintenance that assists novice aircraft maintenance technicians (AMTs) with job task training. The AR system has the potential to supply rapid and accurate feedback to AMTs with any information that the user needs to successfully complete a task.

Virtual museums have profited from VR technologies such as 3D visualization and rendering. Different applications, often devoted to educational purposes, have also been developed. The Arco Project (ARCO 2003), for example, has been developed by the University of Sussex and is aimed at furnishing the infrastructures for 3D virtual exhibitions of collections of museums over the web.

Specific applications have been developed in the educational field: Magic Book, MARS and MARIE. Magic Book (McKenzie 2004) is an AR application. It superimposes on the pages of a book 3D virtual objects whose animation is sensed during interaction by means of HMD. MARS (mobile augmented reality system) (Doswell 2006) is a recent AR E-Learning project in which a learner, immersed in the real world, wears a mobile see-through display that interacts with a training/learning software. This allows users to annotate real-world objects with digital content that may combine animation, graphics, text and video. The system adapts itself to the individual learner needs and dynamically distributes suitable instructions to improve learning performance. MARIE (Liarokapis et al. 2002) uses an augmented display for learner-teacher interaction. The various objects are proposed by the teachers and can be rotated and manipulated by the participants. At this time, students can only see the objects, but future developments may give them the opportunity to smell and touch.

Systems based on a collaborative learning approach use a shared-work environment. Each user interacts with a dynamic synthetic world that changes based upon the decisions made by other users. The current usage is for simulated war or business games, largely in the educational domain. Important projects have been developed by the MIT teacher education program in collaboration with "the education arcade". They created "AR" simulations to engage people in games that combine real-world experiences with additional information supplied by handheld computers. This mode of learning appears effective in engaging university and high-school students in large-scale environmental engineering studies and in providing an authentic mode of scientific investigation.

The first game was Environmental Detectives (ED) (2003). It is an outdoor game that can be run at three sites: MIT, a nearby nature centre and a local high school. The players use GPS-guided handheld computers to uncover the source of a toxic spill by interviewing virtual characters, conducting large-scale simulated environmental measurements and analyzing data. A further game generation moved indoors using Wi-Fi enabled Pocket PCs. Mystery @ The Museum (M@M 2003) runs at the Boston Museum of Science. Players search for a fake museum item. Working in teams and within a time limit, players use virtual clues, discover and understand information contained in the museum and catch a virtual criminal using their deductive skills.

The Star School Project (Kleefeld 2005) addresses urban middle-school students in Milwaukee and Madison. Started in January 2006 and planned to run up to 2008, it tries to fill the gap between formal and informal learning through AR games, which combine physical action with virtual action using a GPS-equipped PDA.

There are systems based on VR to promote learners' active study by integrating synchronous, asynchronous and cooperative learning. Examples are Studierstube Augmented Classroom (SAC 2002) and AVEE (Huang and Chao 2005). In the SAC, small groups of students and tutors share the same AR environment. Using HMD, they can engage in face-to-face collaboration and, by using tracked gloves, can perform 3D manipulations of the virtual objects. The system is applied to train students in spatial comprehension through the software Construct3D (Kauffmann and Papp 2006) and to train medical students in surgery planning.

AR systems based on 3D visualization are used for engineering design. Designers share a conference room using an AR display. One designer can modify a prototype and the changes and adjustments are shown to other users in real time.

Various applications are available in robotics to train engineers both individually and in teams. Most applications are based on augmented display systems and allow remote users to drive a robot using images of the remote workspace. Sometimes the virtual robot image is superimposed on the real scene. The remote operator simulates the experiment to decide whether to proceed with the motion of the real robot. In other systems, the commands of the operator are executed directly on the real robot, and the AR display is used to provide a sort of immersion.

In such a context, immersion can be specified as follows: remote users will experience the presence in a real-world environment, namely a laboratory, by means of a rich, perceptive Internet-based bi-directional interaction comprising vision, hearing and perception of current modification of physical quantities. The project is used to improve collaborative learning with the remote control of robotic systems through the web in the TIGER (Telepresence Instant Groupware for higher Education in Robotics) project (Fabri et al. 2004). The project involves several universities in Italy to train control designers of robotic systems within a framework of structured and/or continuous education. It aims to represent and communicate the knowledge that can be learned by attending a robotics laboratory. It allows students to access web laboratories in different universities and to interact with real robots to control their operation during practical experiments. Students have a realistic (apparent real-time and multi-sensorial) perception of the effects of their control on the robot so that they can speculate on the effectiveness of their choices. Their reflections can be captured, assessed by the teachers and re-used for further learning and implementing knowledge sharing and knowledge creation.

In synthesis, we see an increasing attention on technologies enabling "natural" interaction between user and the synthetic world, be it virtual or remote access through the web. Knowledge creation and sharing is considered too.

7.5 Perspectives

Our point is that VR/AR can be enabling technologies for E-Learning in the context of learning experiences in which the sense of presence has to be attained by a natural (ecological) interaction with the learning environment. In such a context, VR/AR technologies can also be integrated with knowledge management tools to create, share and re-use knowledge developed by the learners themselves, provided that the new knowledge is accredited by the assessment of an expert (teacher).

Therefore, we provide indications about possible technological improvement in the direction of a more natural human-computer interaction, bidirectional with reactive feedback. We refer to developments dealing with the empowerment and refinement of interfaces.

An example of empowerment is techniques aimed at integral imaging. Recent studies (Takaki 2006; Stern and Javidi 2006) show that it is possible to construct a natural 3D display system that enables a large number of images to be displayed simultaneously in different horizontal directions to produce natural 3D images. The following relevant results were obtained: no need to wear special 3D glasses, simultaneous observation by multiple persons, no restrictions on observation position, high-presence (smooth motion parallax) images, coherence with human 3D vision (without fatigue). This promising technology could be a valid alternative to holography (Frauel et al. 2006) that generates 3D images with full-parallax and continuous viewing, but involves coherent illumination and a system that is more complex, expensive and sensitive to various factors.

Refinement concerns the inclusion of stimuli belonging to more than one sense, as mixed visual-haptic and kinesthetic stimuli. Improvements in interaction can be foreseen because of the integration of emotional aspects detected by the collection and processing of neurological or physiological signals (so-called "affective computing"). In this case, we suggest that technologies should give the user coherent sensations and perceptions.

In our view, coherence among sensations is key. Coherence among sensations means that stimuli coming from the virtual world should conform to one's perceptive and cognitive inner representations. It follows that the artificial world should be as rich and detailed as possible on one side, while, on the other side, it should produce consistent and non-contradictory perceptual experiences. In fact, in AR systems for aviation industries, if contradictions arise with the psycho-motor model of the user, the user experiences fatigue and discomfort.

To sum up, important features to consider concern the richness of stimuli that provide feedback to the human actor in the VR/AR interaction. Stimuli should be integrated, multi-channel and coherent with the learner's inner perceptive and cognitive representations.

References

Activeworlds (2006). http://www.activeworlds.com. Accessed 11 December 2006.

ADLNET (2004). SCORM. http://www.adlnet.gov. Accessed 11 December 2006.

ARCO-Augmented Representation of Cultural Objects (2003). http://www.arco-web.org. Accessed 11 December 2006.

AT-Ascention Technology (2006). http://www.ascension-tech.com. Accessed 11 December 2006.

Allard, J., Boyer, E., Franco, J. S., Ménier, C., Bruno Raffin, B. (2004). Marker-less real time 3D modeling for virtual reality. In *Proceedings of IPT'04 Symposium*.

Atty, L., Holzschuch, N., Lapierre, M., Hasenfratz, J. M., Hansen, C., Sillion, F. (2006). Soft shadow maps: efficient sampling of light source visibility. *Computer Graphics Forum* 25(4), 725–741.

Brau, E., Lallemand, J. P., Gosselin, F. (2005). Analytic determination of the tension capable workspace of cable actuated haptic interfaces. In *Proceedings of the 2005 international conference on Augmented tele-existence. ACM International Conference Proceeding Series*, vol. 157, pp. 195–200.

Brooks, F. P. Jr. (1999). What's real about virtual reality? *IEEE Computer Graphics and Applications* 19(6), 16–27.

Brooks, F. P., Ouh-Young, M. Jr., Batter, J. J. (1990). Project GROPE Haptic displays for scientific visualization. *ACM SIGGRAPH Computer Graphics Archive* 24(4), 177–185. ACM, New York, USA.

Burdea, G. C. and Coiffet, P. (2003). *Virtual Reality Technology*. 2nd Edition, Wiley, New York.

Bruner, J. S. (1990). *Acts of Meaning*. Cambridge, MA: Harvard University Press.

CAVE ® (2002). http://www.evl.uic.edu/core.php?mod=4&type=1&indi=161. Accessed 11 December 2006.

DAME-Distributed Aircraft Maintenance Environment (2003). http://www.wrgrid.org.uk/leaflets/DAME.pdf. Accessed 11 December 2006.

Doswell, J. T. (2006). Augmented learning: context-aware mobile augmented reality architecture for learning. In *Proceedings of the IEEE Sixth International Conference on Advance Learning Technologies (ICALT '06)*.

ED-Environmental Detectives (2003). http://education.mit.edu/ar/ed.html. Accessed 11 December 2006.

Engeström, Y. (1987). *Learning by Expanding: An Activity Theoretic Approach to Developmental Research*. Orienta-Konsultit, Helsinki.

Fabri, D., Falsetti, C., Ramazzotti, S., Leo, T. (2004). Robot control designer education on the Web. In *Proceedings IEEE International Conference on Robotics and Automation, Special Session on Education*, vol. 2, pp. 1364–1369.

Felder, R. M. and Brent, R. (2003). Learning by doing. *Chemical Engineering Education* (37)4, 282–283.

Fitzgerald, M. and Riva, G. (2001). Virtual reality. In Beolchi, L. (Ed.), *Telemedicine Glossary*. European Commission-DG INFSO, pp. 327–329.

Forster, I. and Kesselman, C. (2003). *The GRID: Blueprint for a New Computing Infrastucture*. Morgan Kauffman, San Francisco.

Frauel, Y., Naughton, T. J., Matoba, O., Tajahuerce, E., Javidi, B. (2006). Three-dimensional imaging and processing using computational holographic imaging. *Proceedings of the IEEE, Special Issue on 3-D technologies for imaging and display*, 94(3), pp. 636–653.

Furht (1998). *Handbook of Multimedia Computing*. CRC, Boca Raton, FL.

Haritos, T. and Macchiarella, N. D. (2005). A mobile application of augmented reality for aerospace maintenance training. In *The 24th Digital Avionics Systems Conference, DASC 2005*, pp. 5.B.3–5.1-9.

Huang, F. M., Chao, M. (2005). An architecture of virtual enviroment for e-learning (AVEE). In *Proceedings of the Fifth IEEE International Conference on Advance Learning Technologies (ICALT '05)*.

Iwata, H., Tomioka, H., Yano, H. (2006). *SIGGRAPH Conference*, Tsukuba University.

Java3D (2006). http://java3d.j3d.org. Accessed 11 December 2006.

Jung, J. Y., Adelstein, B. D., Ellis, S. R. (2000). *Discriminability of Prediction Artifacts in a Time-Delayed Virtual Environment*. HFES/IEA 2000. NASA Ames Research Center / UC Berkeley, San Diego, CA.

Kauffmann, H. and Papp, M. (2006). Learning objects for education with augmented reality. In *Proceedings of European Distance and E-Learning Network 2006*.

Kim, S., Cha, J., Kim, J., Ryu, J., Eom, S., Mahalik, N. P., Ahn, B. (2006). A novel test-bed for immersive and interactive broadcasting production using augmented reality and haptics. *The Institute of Electronics, Information and Communication Engineers Transactions*, E89-D(1), 106.

Kleefeld (2005). http://wistechnology.com/article.php?id=2416. Accessed 11 December 2006.

Kolb, D.A. (1984). *Experiential Learning: Experience as the Source of Learning and Development.* Prentice-Hall, New Jersey.

Leo, T. (2005). Guest editorial: immersive telelaboratories for engineering designer education. *Learning Technology Newsletter*, 7(3), 2–12.

Liarokapis, F., Petridis, P., Lister, P. F., White, M. (2002). Multimedia augmented reality interface for e-learning (MARIE). *World Transactions on Engineering and Technology Education*, 1(2), 173–176.

Mäki-Patola, T., Laitinen, J., Kanerva, A., Tarala, T. (2005). Experiments with virtual reality instrument. In *Proceedings of the 2005 International Conference on New Interfaces for Musical Expression (NIME05)*, Vancouver, BC, Canada.

Mantovani, F. and Castelnuovo, G. (2003). Sense of presence in virtual training: enhancing skills acquisition and transfer of knowledge through learning experience in virtual environments. In Riva, G., Davide, F., Ijsselsteijn, W. A. (Eds.), *Being There: Concepts, Effect and Measurement of User Presence in Synthetic Environments*. IOS, Amsterdam, The Netherlands.

McKenzie, J. (2004). *The eye Magic Book. A Report into Augmented Reality Storytelling in the Context of a Children's Workshop.*

McKenzie, F. D., Garcia, H. M., Castelino, R. J., Hubbard, T. W., Ullian, J. A., Gliva, G. A. (2004). Augmented standardized patients now virtually a reality. In *Third IEEE and ACM International Symposium on Mixed and Augmented Reality, (ISMAR 2004)*, pp. 270–271.

Metzger, W. (1975). *Gesetze des Sehens*. Waldemar Kramer, Frankfurt am Main.

M@M-Mystery @ The Museum (2003). http://education.mit.edu/ar/matm.html. Accessed 11 December 2006.

Nakaizumi, F., Noma, H., Hosaka, K., Yanagida, Y. (2006). SpotScents: a novel method of natural scent delivery using multiple scent projectors. In *IEEE Virtual Reality Conference*, pp. 207–214.

Nintendo Wii (2006). http://wii.nintendo.com. Accessed 11 December 2006.

Obst, T., Burgkart, R., Ruckhäberle, E., Riener, R. (2004). The delivery simulator: a new application of medical VR. In *Proceedings of Medicine Meets Virtual Reality*.

OpenGL® (2006). http://www.opengl.org. Accessed 11 December 2006.

Reitinger, B., Schmalstieg, D., Bornik, A., Beichel, R. (2006). Spatial analysis tools for virtual reality-based surgical planning. In *Proc. of the IEEE Symposium on 3D User Interfaces*.

SAC-Studierstube Augmented Classroom (2002). http://www.ims.tuwien.ac.at/research_detail.php?ims_id=classroom. Accessed 11 December 2006.

SIGGRAPH 2006 (2006). http://www.virtualworldlets.net/Shop/ProductsDisplay/VRInterface.php?ID=21. Accessed 11 December 2006.

Stern, A., Javidi, B. (2006). Three-dimensional image sensing, visualization and processing using integral imaging. *Proceedings of the IEEE, Special Issue on 3D technologies for imaging and display*, 94(3), pp. 591–607.

Takaki, Y. (2006). High-density directional display for generating natural three-dimensional images. *Proceedings of the IEEE, Special Issue on 3D technologies for imaging and display*, 94(3), pp. 654–663.

Vallino, J. R. (1998). *Interactive Augmented Reality*. Ph.D. thesis, Rochester University, New York.

Virtual Worlds Review (2006). http://www.virtualworldsreview.com. Accessed 11 December 2006.

VirtuSphere (2006). http://www.virtusphere.com. Accessed 11 December 2006.

VRML-Virtual Reality Modeling Language (2006). http://xml.coverpages.org/vrml-X3D.html. Accessed 11 December 2006.

Walczak, K. and Cellary, W. (2002). Building database applications of virtual reality with X-VRML. In *Proceedings of the seventh international conference on 3D Web technology*, Tempe, Arizona, USA, pp. 111–120.

Wang, X., Dunston, P. S., Skibniewski, M. (2004). Mixed reality technology applications in construction equipment operator training. In *18th International Symposium on Automation and Robotics in Construction (ISARC)*.

Wenger, E. (1998). *Communities of Practices*. Cambridge University Press, Cambridge.

Wusheng, C., Tianmiao, W., Yuru Z. (2004). Augmented reality based preoperative planning for robot assisted tele-neurosurgery. In *IEEE International Conference on Systems, Man and Cybernetics*.

xVRML-Extensible Virtual Reality Modelling Language (2003). http://www.xvrml.net. Accessed 11 December 2006.

Zajtchuk, R. and Satava, R. M. (1997). Medical applications of virtual reality. *Communication of the ACM*, 40(9), 63–64.

Section 1.2:
Enabling Interoperability and Re-Use

8 Learning Design: Concepts

R. Koper and S. Bennett

8.1 Introduction

Crucial in any learning process are the activities that learners undertake: reading, thinking, discussing, exploring, problem solving, etc. When learners are passive, you cannot expect them to learn much. The primary role of any instructional agent, whether it be a teacher, the learners themselves or a computer, is to stimulate the performance of learning activities that will gradually result in the attainment of the learning objectives. The instructional agent defines the tasks, provides the contexts and resources to perform the tasks, supports the learner during performance of the task and provides feedback about the results. The learning activities that are needed to obtain some learning objectives are, in most cases, carefully sequenced according to some pedagogical principles. This sequence of learning activities that learners undertake to attain some learning objectives, including the resources and support mechanisms required to help learners to complete these activities, is called a learning design.

A learning design language is a notation that describes learning designs in a machine-interpretable way. The most obvious use of such a learning design language is that it can be used to codify the learning design of a course (as a flow of activities) and then this code is interpreted with a run-time engine that can repeat the course over and over again for different users in different situations, adapted to the characteristics of the individual users in the course. When the course is designed well, the different actors do not have to be concerned much about the management of activities and information flow within the course. This is done automatically by the system in accordance with the learning design. Also the adaptation rules that are specified are applied automatically and consistently within the course runs. Furthermore, the necessary content and services are set up automatically and made available to the users at the right moment.

In this chapter we concentrate on two questions. First, how to identify high quality learning designs and second, how to codify these learning designs in a machine-interpretable way using the IMS Learning Design Specification (IMSLD 2003). In the conclusion, we identify and summarize current research issues in the field.

8.2   High Quality Learning Designs

Before using any learning design language, it is important to know which learning designs are highly effective for a certain target group, a certain domain and certain learning objectives. High quality designs are those that engage learners' prior knowledge and experiences, set learning effectively within the broader context, challenge learners through active participation, and encourage learners to articulate their understanding to themselves and peers (Boud and Prosser 2002).

The Australian project of Agostinho et al. (2002) identified high quality designs that made exemplary use of information and communication technologies in higher education. (A full description of the project and the designs collected can be found at http://www.learningdesigns.uow.edu.au.) For the purposes of this project, high quality designs were selected based on the fact that they emphasize active, constructive learning and address the need to cater to a diverse range of adult learners.

This project developed a standard format for describing designs that has since been extended and applied across education sectors. The standard learning design format provides textual information about how the design was derived from theory and/or practice, the research or evaluative evidence to support the approach, guidance about how it should be implemented and suggestions for how the design might be adapted to other learning contexts. This description is accompanied by a graphical representation developed to illustrate the learning design as it is experienced by a learner (Agostinho et al. 2002). This learning design format makes it possible to represent any learning experience of any granularity in the form of a document. Important to the learning design concept is that the description communicates the general structure and logic of the learning sequence, but does not specify either the content or the particulars of the task or support. These decisions are left to the instructional agents (e.g., teachers) acting on the guidance included in the learning design and on their understanding of the discipline and knowledge of their students and institutional require-ments. An example of the format used for the graphical representation is shown in Fig. 8.1.

This example, adapted from Bennett (2002), depicts a series of tasks that learners typically complete when undertaking an analysis of case materials, beginning with an individual analysis in which learners develop their own ideas, followed by small group and then whole class discussions in which learners refine their ideas through discussion and negotiation with other learners under facilitation by the teacher. Resources may be provided by the teacher to support the task, as the case materials are provided by the teacher in this example, or may be produced as part of the learning experi-ence to be shared with others, for example, the lists of key points derived from the cases which are refined through discussion activities. The sup-ports provided may be in the form of personal interactions with the teacher or other students, which may occur in person or may be mediated through information and communication technologies (ICTs) such as a learning management system. Support may also be provided in the form of docu-ments, in this example as written instructions, templates and guiding

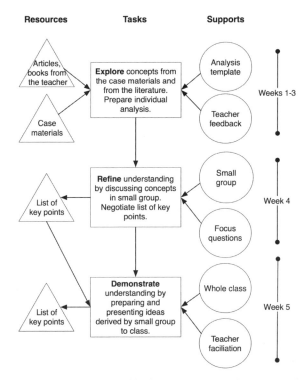

Fig. 8.1. Learning design graphical representation for case analysis tasks

questions. A timeline on the right side of Fig. 8.1 provides an indicative timeframe for the sequence. An example of the accompanying text description is available in (Bennett 2002).

The strategy of using learning designs to support the design process has its theoretical basis in case-based reasoning. Cases that describe how similar design problems have been solved have been shown to help teachers in designing new learning experiences (Bennett 2005). Teachers do this by relating proven learning designs created by others to their own contexts, and then adapting the relevant features of a design to suit their learners. When used in this way, learning designs promote a form of professional peer learning as described by Kreber (2003) in which university teachers are presented with new ideas that are grounded in the realities of teaching in higher education.

In recent research into how university teachers use learning designs, participants in a small study applied a problem-based learning design to different learning contexts, and their design decisions and outcomes were recorded and analyzed (Bennett et al. 2005). The results indicated that the learning design description supported the teachers' design processes, and that the features and underpinning rationale of the learning design was evident in the different versions developed by the participants. The findings indicate this textual and graphical form of learning design was readily understood by the participants and sufficiently flexible to be adapted to different contexts. Further research is underway to test the learning design concept across a broader range of disciplines.

8.3 Applying the Learning Designs in Online Courses

After the identification and description of effective learning designs, the next step is to provide a practical, relevant and flexible set of tools that university teachers (and others) can use to design their online courses. Despite an array of expert advice and descriptive literature about online learning, many university educators find designing effective online learning experiences a significant challenge.

Designing consists of activities, such as planning schedules, writing course outlines, preparing materials, determining assessment tasks, and anticipating students' needs (Bennett and Lockyer 2004). Designing may involve modifying a previous course, updating material or trying new strategies. Much of this design work occurs within the online environment of a learning management system (LMS) for administering, designing and facilitating online learning.

The key to using learning designs to support the design process is to provide software tools that link directly to the LMS. This strategy will provide support within the online environment, in the context and at the time it is needed. Rather than provide models to be applied or templates to be completed over which little discretion can be exercised, the strategy will give teachers the flexibility to customize the learning design to suit their context. This places the teacher in the mediating role of design decision maker rather than prescribing a particular approach, and seeks to further develop their professional knowledge and judgement. The process is depicted in Fig. 8.2.

The process begins with a teacher interacting with software tools that allow him or her to select an appropriate learning design consistent with the learning objectives required. While working with the learning design to customize and adapt it for the local situation the teacher is creating a "unit of learning", which may be a course, a subject, a module or an activity. The unit of learning, therefore, encapsulates all of the specifics of the tasks, resources and supports, which can in turn be expressed in the machine-interpretable learning-design language, IMS Learning Design (IMS LD). When the design is complete, the IMS LD document can be saved and imported into any LMS compliant with the standard.

After creating a lesson or course in an LMS and saving it as an IMS LD document, a teacher can share it within a teaching team, institution or digital library, allow it to be edited in any other LMS that complies with the standard, and save the new version as a new IMS LD document. This strategy has great potential to not only make particular lessons or courses sharable so that they can be reused and adapted by others, but also for the learning designs on which they are based to be shared and reused.

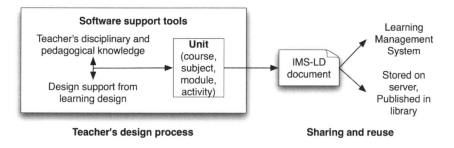

Fig. 8.2. Supporting the teacher's design process

8.4   The IMS Learning Design Specification

8.4.1   Introduction

In the previous sections we discussed how high quality learning designs could be derived from practice and how teachers can use learning design tools and high-level representations. We also discussed how these designs could be coded in IMS LD in order to be used in any compliant LMS. In this section, we will discuss the basic principles of IMS LD.

The IMS Learning Design Specification (Koper and Olivier 2004) is a standardized learning design language that was based on the work on Educational Modelling Language (EML 2000; Koper 2001; Hermans et al. 2004; Koper and Manderveld 2004) at the Open University of the Netherlands.

When we started to develop learning design language EML, we realized that we had to develop a meta-model of pedagogical approaches. There are hundreds of different pedagogical models described in the literature (for examples, see Koper 2001; Reigeluth 1983, 1999). There are many so-called lesson plans shared on the Internet (Van Es 2004), and new models, lesson plans and best practices continue to be formulated. Modelling each separate example and then developing tools to support it would be a very inefficient path to follow. For this reason we aimed at the development of a more abstract notation that is sufficiently general to represent the common structures found in these different pedagogical models. With such a notation, learning designs for concrete courses (and other units of learning, as they are called in IMS LD) can be specified that are applications of a specific pedagogical approach.

8.4.2   The Requirements

The major requirement for the development of any learning design language is to provide a containment framework that uses and integrates existing specifications as much as possible, and that can represent the teaching-learning process (the learning design or LD) in a unit of learning (UoL), based on different pedagogical models – including the more complex and advanced ones – in a formal way. More specifically, a LD specification must meet the following requirements:

1. The notation must be comprehensive. It must describe the teaching-learning activities of a unit of learning in detail and include references to the learning objects and services needed to perform the activities. This means describing:

- How the activities of both the learners and the staff roles are integrated.
- How the resources (objects and services) used during learning are integrated.
- How both single- and multiple-user models of learning are supported.

2. The notation must support mixed mode (also called blended learning) as well as pure online learning.
3. The notation must be sufficiently flexible to describe learning designs based on all kinds of theories and so must avoid biasing designs towards any specific pedagogical approach.
4. The notation must be able to describe conditions within a learning design that can be used to tailor the learning design to suit specific persons or specific circumstances.
5. The notation must make it possible to identify, isolate, de-contextualize and exchange useful parts of a learning design (e.g., a pattern) so as to stimulate their re-use in other contexts.
6. The notation must be standardized and in line with other standard notations.
7. The notation must provide a formal language for learning designs that can be processed automatically.
8. The specification must enable a learning design to be abstracted in such a way that repeated execution, in different settings and with different persons, is possible.

The IMS LD specification, following common IMS practice, consists of (a) a conceptual model that defines the basic concepts and relations in a LD, (b) an information model that describes the elements and attributes through which a LD can be specified in a precise way, and (c) a series of XML Schemas (XSD) in which the information model is implemented (the so-called "binding"), (d) a best practices and implementation guide (BPIG), (e) a binding document and sample XML documents that express a set of learning requirement scenarios. In the following sections, we will focus on the conceptual analysis work that informed the learning design specification.

8.4.3   The Conceptual Model

The pedagogical meta-model that has been developed to represent different kinds of learning designs is at the heart of the IMS LD specification. It provides the conceptual structure of the specification as well as its underlying theoretical model (see Fig. 8.3).

The core concept of LD, as expressed in Fig. 8.3, is that a learning design can be represented by using the following core concepts: A person takes on a role in the teaching-learning process, typically a learner or a staff role. In this role, he or she works towards certain learning objectives by performing learning and/or support activities within an environment. The environment consists of the appropriate learning objects and services to be used during the performance of the activities. Figure 8.4 contains an example of the use of these labels in a photograph of a classical learning design: a classroom setting.

You can imagine that this type of labelling is possible on any photograph of any teaching-learning event, whether it be classroom teaching, self-study, group collaborations, field experiments, etc. However, photographs are static and the teaching-learning process is dynamic, so merely labelling the visible entities is not sufficient. What is needed is an additional process description. This process description is provided in the method section of IMS LD. The method is designed to provide the co-ordination of roles, activities and associated environments that allows learners to meet learning objectives (specification of the outcomes for learners), given certain prerequisites (specification of the entry level for learners).

The method section is the core part of the LD specification in which the teaching-learning process is specified. All the other concepts are referenced, directly or indirectly, from the method. The teaching-learning process

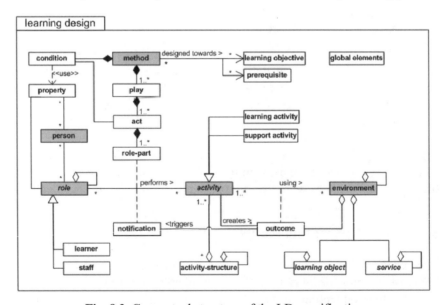

Fig. 8.3. Conceptual structure of the LD specification

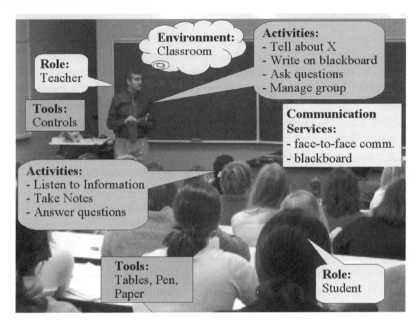

Fig. 8.4. Labelling a classroom setting with IMS LD concepts

is modelled using the metaphor of a theatrical play. A play has acts, and each act has one or more roles or parts. Acts follow each other in a sequence, although more complex sequencing behaviour can take place within an act. The roles within an act associate each role with an activity. The activity in turn describes what the person in that role is to do and what environment is available to them within the act. In the analogy, the assigned activity is equivalent to the script for the part that the role plays in the act, although less prescriptive. Where there is more than one role within an act, the roles are "on stage at the same time", that is, they run parallel. Thus a method consists of one or more concurrent play(s); a play consists of one or more sequential act(s); an act consists of one or more concurrent roles, with each role associated with an activity or activity-structure (further explained below).

The roles specified are those of learner and staff. Each of these can be specialized into sub-roles. It is left open to the designer to name the roles or sub-roles and specify their activities. In simulations and games, for example, different learners can play different roles, each performing different activities in different environments.

Activities can be assembled into activity structures. An activity structure aggregates a set of related activities into a single structure, which can be associated with a role. An activity-structure can model a sequence or a selection of activities. In a sequence, a role has to complete the different activities in the structure in the order provided. In a selection, a role may select a given number of activities from the set provided in the activity structure. This can, for instance, be used to model situations in which learners have to complete two activities, which they may freely select from a collection of five activities contained in the activity structure. Activity structures can also reference other activity structures and external UoLs, enabling elaborate structures to be defined if required.

Environments contain the resources and references to resources needed to carry out an activity or a set of activities. An environment contains three basic entities: learning objects, learning services and sub-environments. Learning objects are any entities that are used in learning, for example, web pages, articles, books, databases, software, and DVDs. The learning services specify the set-up of any service that is needed during learning, for example, communication services, search services, monitoring services and collaboration services. An example of set-up information is the specification of which LD roles have user rights in the learning service. This, for instance, enables automatic set-up of dedicated forums each time a LD is instantiated.

A method may contain conditions, that is, if-then-else rules that further refine the assignment of activities and environment entities for persons and roles. Conditions may be used to personalize LDs for specific users. An example of such a personalization condition could be: "If the person has an exploratory learning style, *then* provide an unordered set of all activities", or "If the person has prior knowledge on topic X, *then* learning activity Y can be skipped".

The "If" part of the condition uses Boolean expressions on the properties that are defined for persons and roles in the LD. Properties are containers that store information about people's roles and the UoL itself, for example, user profiles, progression data (completion of activities), results of tests (e.g., prior knowledge, competencies, learning styles), or learning objects added during the teaching-learning process (e.g., reports, essays or new learning materials). Properties can be either global or local to the run of a unit of learning. Global properties are used to model portfolio information that can be accessed in any other unit of learning that is modelled with LD, and has access to the same longterm storage for property data. Local properties are only accessible within the context of a specific run of a unit of learning and are used for temporary storage of data.

In order to enable users to set and view properties from content that is presented to them, so-called global elements are present in LD. These global elements are designed to be included in any content schema through namespaces. Content that includes these global elements is called *imsldcontent*. The preferred content schema is XHTML. Global elements can be included in the XHTML document instances to show (or set) the value of a property, for instance, a table with progression data, a report added by a learner, a piece of text or URLs added by a teacher, etc.

LDs also contain notifications, that is, mechanisms to make new activities available for a role, based on certain outcome triggers. These outcomes are, for example, the change of a property value, the completion of an activity or certain patterns in the user profiles. The person getting the notification is not necessarily the same person as the one who triggered the notification. For instance, when one learner completes an activity, then another learner or the teacher may be notified and set another activity as a consequence. This mechanism can be used to model adaptive task-setting LDs, in which the supply of a consequent activity may be dependent on the outcome of previous activities. General pedagogical rules can also be implemented using the combination of conditions and notifications, for example, "If a user has profile X, then notify learning activity Y".

8.4.4   The Information Model and XML Binding

The conceptual model is implemented as follows: A UoL is represented as an IMS Content Package (CP). A CP has an organization part that represents how items are organized in the package. Normally, the organization part represents nothing more than a hierarchy of items, but the CP specification allows replacement of the organization structure by any other structure. In IMS LD the organization part of a CP is replaced by a learning-design element (Fig. 8.5).

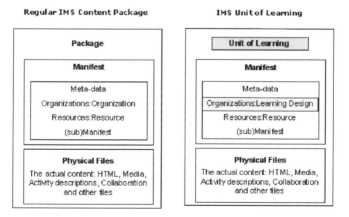

Fig. 8.5. In IMS LD the organization element of a regular IMS content package is replaced by the learning design elements

The learning-design element is a complex structure that includes elements that represent the conceptual model already outlined. The details of these elements appear in the information model document, together with their behavioural specifications.

The learning design elements have an XML schema binding that can be represented as the tree in Fig. 8.6.

The properties, activities and environments of the component element and the conditions of the method element all, in turn, have complex substructures, but these are not shown here for the sake of simplicity.

A distinction is always made between the package (reflecting the UoL at the class level) and the run of that package (an instance). In creating instances from a package, some customization and localization may typically take place.

A UoL package represents a fixed version of a UoL, with links to the underlying learning objects and service types. It may contain further XML document instances valid against the other appropriate schemas (IMS LD, IMS CP, IMS QTI, etc.) along with the physical files that are referred to in a fixed version and URIs to other resources, including services. Such a

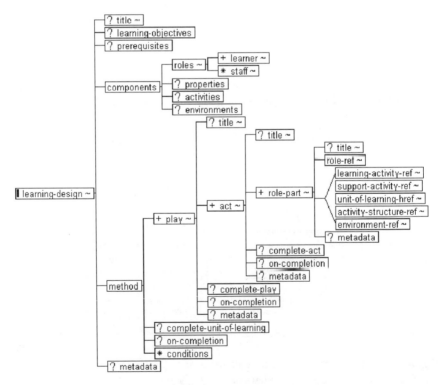

Fig. 8.6. The LD schema represented as a tree

package can be instantiated and run many times for different learners in different settings. If desired, it can also be adapted prior to instantiation in order to reflect local needs. This will create another version of the UoL and accordingly another UoL package.

8.5   Interpreting IMS LD

When a UoL is specified in IMS LD, the result is a zip file. Running this zip file requires a runtime engine that handles at least the following five tasks:

1.   Validation of the zip file to ensure that only valid IMS LD is processed. Validation includes both technical and semantic checks. Validation results are reported.
2.   Creation of one or more instances of the zip-file (this is called a run).
3.   Assignment of persons to the specific roles in the run and setup of the required communication and collaboration services, such as forums, chats and wikis.
4.   Interpretation of the IMS LD and delivery of personalized and sequenced learning activities, content and services, according to the rules defined in LD. This is achieved by keeping track of the user's progress and settings.
5.   The concept of a run is described in (Vogten et al. 2005, 2006a, b; Tattersall et al. 2005) and is comparable with parallel classes in a school. A school may have different parallel classes, each with the same objectives and content, but with different learners and teachers. The same classes (runs) are also repeated year after year with different students (and sometimes different teachers), although the versions of the learning design may be adapted in between different runs. So, a run is an instance of a course with specific learners and teachers and is executed in a specific timeframe. A runtime engine must be able to set up and manage runs of UoLs packages.

An IMS LD runtime engine must be able to interpret every IMS LD zip file package. The challenge is that LD is a declarative language, meaning that it describes *what* an implementation must do, but it does not specify *how* it should be done. Furthermore, LD is a semantically expressive language that enables expression of learning designs in a clear, natural, intuitive and concise way, closest to the original problem formulation. This expressive and declarative nature complicates the implementation of an engine that can interpret the specification. For this reason we implemented an open source runtime engine, called CopperCore (Martens and Vogten

2005; see also www.coppercore.org) to serve as a reference implementation of IMS LD handling. CopperCore can be used by any LMS to handle LD packages or be used as an example for the recoding of an LMS-native runtime engine.

The CopperCore runtime engine does not provide user interfaces: it only provides APIs to build a dedicated user interface. For demonstration purposes, CopperCore is provided with a simple user interface (CopperCore Player, see Fig. 8.7), but a better implementation of a player is the SLED player (see McAndrew et al. 2005; see also sourceforge.net/projects/ldplayer).

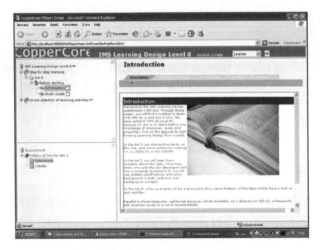

Fig. 8.7. The CopperCore player

8.6   Conclusion

In this chapter we have introduced the basic concepts in the field of learning design research. We defined what learning designs are, how high quality learning designs can be identified and described, how learning designs can be coded in IMS LD and how IMS LD code can be interpreted by a runtime engine and presented by a LD Player.

In the conclusion of this chapter we will now concentrate on the issues that have been identified and studied in the past three years. These issues are summarized from the research of many different researchers, for example, those who have reported their work in two special issues of journals (JIME 2005; ET&S 2006), an edited book (Koper and Tattersall 2005) about IMS

LD and international conferences such as ASCILITE and ICALT. The issues are summarized below.

The first issue is related to the identification of high quality learning designs. One of the ideas in this area is to identify and use learning design patterns. These patterns can be used to support learning designers in developing high quality learning designs in specific areas by combining and adapting several patterns to a course. One direction of research is to search for solutions to derive these patterns from effective IMS LD coded courses. A pattern detection mechanism will then analyze the code, looking for patterns (Brouns et al. 2005). Another approach is to capture best practices and learning design knowledge of teachers using textual descriptions and graphical representation that can be readily understood by other teachers (e.g., the approach described by Agostinho et al. (2002) and further developed by Bennett et al. (2005)).

The second issue is the development of learning design authoring tools. This includes the following issues:

(a) The development of a graphical representation for learning designs, such as the ones found in MOT+ (Paquette et al. 2006), LAMS (Dalziel 2003) and ASK-LDT (Karampiperis and Sampson 2005). Also the representation of learning designs that is described in Fig. 8.1 is an alternative.

(b) The support for reuse of the learning design knowledge of teachers and experienced instructional designers (Hernández-Leo et al. 2006).

(c) The question of how learning designers should be supported with tools and how teachers should be supported with tools in specific contexts (i.e., tools that support the teacher as a designer, Bailey et al. 2006; Bennett et al. 2006).

(d) The integration of learning design and assessment editors (e.g., IMS QTI) in a single authoring environment (Vogten et al. 2006a, b; Pacurar et al. 2006; Joosten-ten Brinke et al. 2007).

The third issue is the further development of learning design players. This includes the following issues:

(a) How to integrate the variety of specifications (e.g., IMS LD, SCORM, IMSLOM (2003), IMSQTI (2003), IMS LIP (2003)) and the connections to other systems in an E-Learning infrastructure (student administration, portfolio systems, financial systems) into a single, easy-to-use learning environment (Van Rosmalen et al. 2006)

(b) How to instantiate and integrate communication and collaboration services that are called by IMS LD, for example, forums, wikis and chats (Weller et al. 2006; Vogten et al. 2006a, b)

(c) How to design a usable, powerful and flexible graphical user-interface for a player environment
(d) How to integrate IMS LD into existing learning management systems such as Moodle, Blackboard, dotLearn and LAMS (see Berggren et al. 2005)
(e) How to integrate learning design authoring systems and learning design players, including how to deal with runtime adaptations (Zarraonandia et al. 2006)
(f) How to use an integrated set of learning design tools in an integrated way in a variety of settings, such as in universities, training, blended learning (Sloep et al. 2006)

Furthermore, there are several additional issues to mention, such as proposals to change the current XML schema binding to an ontology language such as OWL. Amorim et al. (2006) and Knight et al. (2006) propose such a binding to integrate learning objects and learning designs to represent specific pedagogical approaches and to build software agents that operate on the learning design knowledge to support the development of units of learning. A last point to mention is the work in the area of evaluation of the expressiveness of IMS LD (Caeiro-Rodriguez et al. 2005; Van Es and Koper 2006).

All this work around IMS Learning Design is aimed to provide us with a set of very flexible and usable tools that can fundamentally change the effectiveness, efficiency, flexibility, attractiveness and reuse of online learning activities and courses in the future.

Acknowledgement

The work in this chapter has been sponsored by the TENCompetence Integrated Project, funded by the European Commission's 6th Framework Programme, priority IST/Technology Enhanced Learning. Contract 027087 (www.tencompetence.org)

References

Agostinho, S., Oliver, R., Harper, B., Hedberg, H., & Wills, S. (2002). A tool to evaluate the potential for an ICT-based learning design to foster high-quality learning. In A. Williamson, C. Gunn, A. Young, & T. Clear (Eds.), *Proceedings of Australasian Society for Computers in Learning in Tertiary Education* (pp. 29–38). Auckland, NZ: UNITEC.

Amorim, R. R., Lama, M., Sánchez, E., Riera, A., & Vila, X. A. (2006). A learning design ontology based on the IMS specification. *Educational Technology and Society*, 9(1), 38–57.

Bailey, C., Zalfan, M. T, Davis, H. C., Fill, K., & Conole, G. (2006). Panning for gold: designing pedagogically-inspired learning nuggets. *Educational Technology and Society*, 9(1), 113–122.

Bennett, S. (2002). Description of a technology-supported constructivist learning environment that uses real-life cases to support collaborative project work. http://www.learningdesigns.uow.edu.au/LearningDesigns/exemplars/info/LD1/index.html. Accessed 7 November 2006.

Bennett, S. (2005). Using related cases to support authentic project activities. In A. Herrington, & J. Herrington (Eds.), *Authentic Learning Environments in Higher Education* (pp. 120–134). Hershey, PA: Idea.

Bennett, S., & Lockyer, L. (2004). Becoming an online teacher: adapting to a changed environment for teaching and learning in higher education. *Educational Media International*, 41(3), 231–244.

Bennett, S., Agostinho, S., & Lockyer, L. (2005). Reusable learning designs in university education. In T. C. Montgomerie, & J. R. Parker (Eds.), *Proceedings of the IASTED International Conference on Education and Technology* (pp. 102–106). Anaheim, CA: ACTA.

Bennett, S., Agostinho, S., Lockyer, L., Harper, B., & Lukasiak, J. (2006). Supporting university teachers create pedagogically sound learning environments using learning designs and learning objects. *International Journal on WWW/Internet*, 4(1), 16–26.

Berggren, A., Burgos, D., Fontana, J. M., Hinkelman, D., Hung, V., Hursh, A., & Tielemans, G. (2005). Practical and pedagogical issues for teacher adoption of IMS learning design standards in Moodle LMS. *Journal of Interactive Media in Education*, 2005/02. ISSN:1365-893X [jime.open.ac.uk/2005/02].

Boud. D., & Prosser, M. (2002). Key principles for high quality student learning in higher education: a framework for evaluation. *Educational Media International*, 39(3), 237–245.

Brouns, F., Koper, R., Manderveld, J., Van Bruggen, J., Sloep, P., Van Rosmalen, P., Tattersall, C., & Vogten, H. (2005). A first exploration of an inductive analysis approach for detecting learning design patterns. *Journal of Interactive Media in Education*, 2005/03. http://www-jime.open.ac.uk/2005/03/. Accessed 21 November 2006.

Caeiro-Rodriguez, M., Anido-Rifon, L., & Llamas-Nistal, M. (2005). A perspective and pattern-based evaluation framework of EMLs' expressiveness for collaborative learning: application to IMS LD. In *Proceedings of the Fifth IEEE International Conference on Advanced Learning Technologies, ICALT 2005*, Taiwan, 5–8 July 2005. http://ieeexplore.ieee.org/xpl/freeabs_all.jsp?arnumber=1508604. Accessed 21 November 2006.

Dalziel, J. (2003). Implementing learning design: the Learning Activity Management System (LAMS). http;//www.melcoe.mq.edu.au/documents/ASCILITE2003 Dalziel Final.pdf.

EML (2000). Educational modelling language (version 1.0 and version 1.1). http://dspace.ou.nl/handle/1820/81 and http://dspace.ou.nl/handle/1820/80. Accessed 21 November 2006.

ET&S (2006). Current research in learning design. *Educational Technology and Society*, 9(1), 13–175, (special issue). http://www.ifets.info/others/. Accessed 21 November 2006.

Pacurar, E. G., Trigano, P., & Alupoaie, S. (2006). Knowledge base for automatic generation of online IMS LD compliant course structures. *Educational Technology and Society*, 9(1), 158–175.

Hermans, H., Manderveld, J., & Vogten, H. (2004). Educational modelling language. In W. Jochems, J. van Merrienboer, & R. Koper, *Integrated e-Learning* (pp. 80–99). London: RoutledgeFalmer.

Hernández-Leo, D., Harrer, A., Dodero, J. M., Asension-Pérez, J. I., & Burgos, D. (2006). Creating by reusing Learning Design solutions. In *Proceedings of 8th Simposo Internacional de InformÃ¡tica Educativa, León, Spain: IEEE Technical Committee on Learning Technology*. http://dspace.ou.nl/handle/1820/788. Accessed 21 November 2006.

IMSLD (2003). IMS Learning Design. Information model, best practice and implementation guide, binding document, schemas. http://www.imsglobal.org/learningdesign/index.cfm. Accessed 21 November 2006.

IMSLIP (2003). IMS Learner Information Package. Information model, best practice and implementation guide, binding document, schemas. http://www.imsglobal.org/profiles/index.cfm. Accessed 21 November 2006.

IMSLOM (2003). IMS-LOM Metadata. Binding document, schemas. http://www.imsglobal.org/metadata/index.cfm. Accessed 21 November 2006.

IMSQTI (2003). IMS Question and Test Interoperability. Information model, best practice and implementation guide, binding document, schemas. http://www.imsglobal.org/question/index.cfm. Accessed 21 November 2006.

JIME (2005). Advances in Learning Design. *Journal of Interactive Media in Education*, 2005/01, (special issue). http://www-jime.open.ac.uk/2005/01/. Accessed 21 November 2006.

Joosten-ten Brinke, D., Van Bruggen, J., Hermans, H., Latour, I., Burgers, J., Giesbers, B., & Koper, R. (2007). Modeling assessment for re-use of traditional and new types of assessment. *Computers in Human Behaviour*, 23(6), 2721–2741.

Karampiperis, P., & Sampson, D. (2005). Designing learning services for open learning systems utilizing Learning Design. In V. Uskov, (Ed.), *Proceedings of the 4th IASTED International Conference on Web-based Education* (pp. 279–284). Anaheim, CA, USA: ACTA.

Knight, C., Gašević, D., & Richards, G. (2006). An ontology-based framework for bridging Learning Design and Learning Content. *Educational Technology and Society*, 9(1), 23–37.

Koper, E. J. R. (2001). Modelling units of study from a pedagogical perspective: the pedagogical metamodel behind EML. Heerlen: Open Universiteit Nederland. http://hdl.handle.net/1820/36. Accessed 21 November 2006.

Koper, E. J. R., & Manderveld, J. M. (2004). Modelling reusable, interoperable, rich and personalised units of learning. *British Journal of Educational Technology*, 35(5), 537–552.

Koper, R., & Olivier, B. (2004). Representing the Learning Design of units of learning. *Educational Technology and Society*, 7(3), 97–111.

Koper, R., & Tattersall, C. (Eds.) (2005). *Learning Design: A Handbook on Modelling and Implementing Network-Based Education and Training*. Berlin Heidelberg New York: Springer.

Kreber, C. (2003). The scholarship of teaching: a comparison of conceptions held by experts and regular academic staff. *Higher Education*, 46(1), 93–121.

Martens, H., & Vogten, H. (2005). A reference implementation of a Learning Design engine. In R. Koper, & C. Tattersall (Eds.), *Learning Design: A Handbook on Modelling and Delivering Networked Education and Training* (pp. 91–108). Berlin Heidelberg New York: Springer.

McAndrew, P., Nadolski, R., & Little, A. (2005). Developing an approach for Learning Design players. *Journal of Interactive Media in Education*, 2005/14. http://www-jime.open.ac.uk/2005/14/. Accessed 21 November 2006.

Paquette, G., Léonard, M., Lundgren-Cayrol, K., Mihaila, S., & Gareau, D. (2006). Learning Design based on graphical knowledge-modelling. *Educational Technology and Society*, 9(1), 97–112.

Reigeluth, C. M. (Ed.) (1983). *Instructional Design Theories and Models: An Overview of Their Current Status*. Hillsdale, NJ: Lawrence Erlbaum.

Reigeluth, C. M. (1999). What is instructional-design theory and how is it changing? In C. M. Reigeluth (Ed.), *Instructional-Design Theories and Models: A New Paradigm of Instructional Theory*, vol. II (pp. 5–29). Mahwah: Lawrence Erlbaum.

Sloep, P. B., Van Bruggen, J., Tattersall, C., Vogten, H., Koper, R., Brouns, F., & Van Rosmalen, P. (2006). Innovating education with an educational modelling language: two case studies. *Innovations in Education and Teaching International*, 43(3), 291–301.

Tattersall, C., Vogten, H., Brouns, F., Koper, R., van Rosmalen, P., Sloep, P., & van Bruggen, J. (2005). How to create flexible runtime delivery of distance learning courses. *Educational Technology and Society*, 8(3), 226–236.

Van Es, R. (2004). Overview of online databases with lesson plans and other learning design methods. http://hdl.handle.net/1820/102. Accessed 21 November 2006.

Van Es, R., & Koper, R. (2006). Testing the pedagogical expressiveness of IMS LD. *Educational Technology and Society*, 9(1), 229–249.

Van Rosmalen, P., Vogten, H., Van Es, R., Passier, H., Poelmans, P., & Koper, R. (2006). Authoring a full life cycle model in standards-based, adaptive e-learning. *Educational Technology and Society*, 9(1), 72–83.

Vogten, H., Koper, R., Martens, H. & Tattersall, C. (2005). An architecture for Learning Design Engines. In R. Koper, & C. Tattersall (Eds.), *Learning Design: A Handbook on Modelling and Delivering Networked Education and Training* (pp. 75–90). Berlin Heidelberg New York: Springer.

Vogten, H., Tattersall, C., Koper, R., van Rosmalen, P., Brouns, F., Sloep, P., van Bruggen, J. & Martens, H. (2006a). Designing a Learning Design Engine as a collection of finite state machines. *International Journal on E-Learning*, 5(4), 641–661.

Vogten, H., Martens, H., Nadolski, R., Tattersall, C., van Rosmalen, P., & Koper, R. (2006b). Integrating IMS Learning Design and IMS Question and Test Interoperability using CopperCore Service Integration. In *Proceedings of International Workshop in Learning Networks for Lifelong Competence Development*, TENCompetence Conference. 30–31 March, Sofia, Bulgaria. http://dspace.learningnetworks.org. Accessed 30 June 2006.

Weller, M., Little, A., McAndrew, P., & Woods, W. (2006). Learning Design, generic service descriptions and universal acid. *Educational Technology and Society*, 9(1), 138–145.

Zarraonandia, T., Fernández, C., & Dodero, J. M. (2006). A late modelling approach for the definition of computer-supported learning process. In *Proceedings of Adaptive Hypermedia*, June, Dublin, Ireland. http://dspace.ou.nl/handle/1820/753. Accessed 21 November 2006.

9 Competence Models in Technology-Enhanced Competence-Based Learning

D. Sampson and D. Fytros

Throughout the years competence-based management approaches have proved to be a critical tool in human resource management, vocational training and performance management. As a result, competence-based approaches are often adopted as the key paradigm in both formal or informal education and training programs. Despite this fact, the Technology-enhanced Learning (TeL) research community has only recently considered undertaking research towards technology-enhanced competence-based learning and training. To this end, there exist a number of open issues such as: how can we model competences; how can we assess competences; how can we develop training resources and training activities that target specific competences. The scope of this chapter is to contribute to this field by addressing the issue of competence modeling in technology-enhanced competence-based training, that is, how can we model and represent competence-related information in a system meaningful way.

9.1 Introduction

In recent years, Knowledge Management has become an important issue for businesses and the society in general (Marwick 2001). Knowledge Management can be seen as a cycle which begins with the discovery of knowledge, typically within an organization; continues with the description of the discovered knowledge in explicit forms; moves to the sharing of the explicitly described knowledge; and finally to the application of the tacit and explicit knowledge in day-to-day operations (Becerra-Fernandez et al. 2004).

The concept of Knowledge Management has been approached from different perspectives (Prusak 2001; Hong and Stahle 2005), namely:

- The philosophical and psychological perspective, which aims to target questions such as what knowledge is and where it comes from.
- The organisational and sociological perspective, which addresses key questions such as how we can create and master knowledge in groups, focusing on social networks and communities of practice.
- The economic and business perspective, which addresses key questions such as how to improve, in a cost-effective manner, the impact of knowledge in relation to certain organisational goal achievement.
- The technological perspective, which addresses key questions related with the design, the development and the interoperability of tools for discovering, capturing, sharing, and applying knowledge.

Competence Management is an important research issue within the research framework of Knowledge Management (Draganidis and Mentzas 2006). Tobias (2006) defines competence management as "to encompass all instruments and methods used in an organization to systematically assess current and future competences required for the work to be performed and to assess available competences of the workforce". Hamel and Prahalad (1994) anticipated that "with the passage of time, competence management will become more and more important: competence will be well recognized as extremely important for the achievement of company goals, complimentary to, for instance, core business processes, customer relationships, financial issues and so on".

Within this context, the potential benefits from the adoption of competence management are a combination of organizational and individual benefits (Hustad et al. 2004; TENCompetence 2007).

From the organizational perspective, a competence-based management approach bares the potential for identifying competence gaps within business units to ensure global competence development in targeted business sections, for designing competence development programmes that target to group performance improvement, for supporting talent management and enhance human resource potential.

From the individual perspective, a competence-based management approach bares the potential for personal competence development aiming at minimising the gap between available and desired competences within various business sections and beyond, as well as, for discovering previously hidden and/or unknown competences, enhancing possibilities for undertaking new assignments, activities or career paths.

As a result, developing the appropriate competences is a key target for in-company training programs (Kupper and van Wulfften Palthe 2001). Moreover, formal professional education and training is expected to tune their curricula towards meeting certain professional requirements, so as to appropriately equip their graduates for the labor market. Potential employers anticipate graduates who are able to operate in complex environments, as a result students need learning environments that facilitate their learning to function at the level required for starting a professional career (Weert 2004; Martin and Willems 2005).

Within this context, it appears that the results from the accomplishment of learning tasks which support a traditional knowledge-based curriculum are no longer sufficient for these dynamic social and work conditions (Westera 2001; Boon and van der Klink 2002). The gap between the knowledge-oriented education and the societal and organizational needs has lead to an increased attention on competence-based learning and training. Competence-based learning refers to the formal and informal learning and training activities that individuals and/or groups perform to improve their competences in a particular field, given some personal, societal or employment related motives (Griffin 1999; Aspin and Chapman 2000; Field 2001).

Consequenlty, technology-enhanced competence-based learning is attracting the interest of the TeL research community. For example, TEN-Competence (www.tencompetence.org) is a European Project which aims to support individuals, groups and organizations in Europe in lifelong competence development by establishing a technical and organizational infrastructure for lifelong competence development. The TENCompetence technical infrastructure is open-source and based on international specifications (Koper and Specht 2007).

Nevertheless, a number of open issues and challenges for technology-enhanced competence-based learning do exist, such as how can we model competences; how can we assess competences; how can we develop training resources and training activities that target specific competences. The scope of this chapter is to address the issue of competence modeling in technology-enhanced competence-based training, that is, how we can model and represent competence-related information in a machine-readable meaningful way so as to allow its inter-exchange in a standard and consistent way between different system implementations. This is an important issue in technology-enhanced competence-based learning since it is essential for ensuring the interoperability of these systems. As we will discuss in detail, competence-related information may refer not only to personal information, such as a learner's competence profile, but also to training curricula that were developed by linking training resources and activities with specific competences. In this context, competence models are used to inform the design of appropriate learning activities so as to minimize the gap between the expected competences of a given curriculum and the ones owned by an individual learner.

Following this short introduction to Competence Management and Competence-based Learning, in Sect. 9.2 we attempt a literature review on competence and discuss the main elements of a Competence Development Lifecycle, analyzing them through the case study of the TENCompetence Project. This discussion leads us to the need for a unified definition of competence, which can serve as the basis for developing a common Competence Model within the Competence Development lifecycle. As a result, we propose a unified definition of competence based on the analysis of the most widely referenced definitions of competence as they appear in the literature. Next, in Sect. 9.3, we discuss the concept of Competence Modeling, we identify the elements that a generic competence model ought to include based on the dimensions of the unified definition of competence proposed in Sect. 9.2, and we demonstrate its use in a real case study, namely the EuroPass Language Passport. Then, in Sect. 9.4 we discuss the current initiatives on the standardization of competence-based information, namely the IMS RDCEO (IMS RDCEO 2002), IEEE RCD (IEEE P1484.20/D01 2004) and HR-XML (HR-XML 2006) specifications, present a mapping between the elements of these specifications and offer initial discussion on their ability to meet the overall needs of competence modeling, as identified in Sect. 9.2. Finally, we discuss our conclusions from the investigation of this topic.

9.2   The Concept of Competence

9.2.1   Historical Origins

The concept of competence has a long history. The early Romans already practiced a kind of competence profiling towards the selection of the "good Roman soldier" (Mayoral et al. 2007). The Chinese Empire, for three thousand years, recognized differences in individual abilities beyond formal education by adopting civil service exams for the selection on government jobs (Hoge et al. 2005). In Medieval Times, apprentices were expected to develop specific skills they would be needed for effective job performance, as defined by the master craftsman (McLagan 1997). For hundreds of years, educators have defined the knowledge and skills to be covered in their curricula.

In recent years, McClelland in his seminal paper, "Testing for Competence Rather than for Intelligence" (McClelland 1973), introduced the concept of competence into the human resources literature. His work was developed within the context of United States Information Agency efforts to improve their personnel selection procedures. In his research, McClelland proposed numerous competences, such as interpersonal sensitivity, cross-cultural positive regards and management skills that distinguish superior from average officers.

Today, competences are proved to be a critical tool in human resource management, vocational training and performance management (Lachance 1999; Lucia and Lepsinger 1999; Sanghi 2004; Hoge et al. 2005; Otto et al. 2007):

- In human resource management, competences can be used as part of the criteria to select the most appropriate available person for a given task in hand. Competence-based selection is driven by the assumption that achieving a closer match between the requirements of the task in hand and an individual's competences will result in higher job performance and satisfaction.
- In vocational training, competences can be used as the drivers for the design of appropriate learning resources and activities, the selection of appropriate learning material, processes and eventually curricula that bare the potential to eliminate the gap identified between competences needed and those available. This is important for the adoption for on-demand training.
- In performance management, available competences and obtained results within the context of given tasks can be processed to maintain records that connect them in meaningful ways.

However, despite the fact that competences are an important tool for various fields of application, the research community has not agreed to a commonly accepted definition of the term resulting to multiple interpretations (Boon and van der Klink 2002; Delamare and Winterton 2005; Winterton et al. 2005; Sanchez-Ruiz et al. 2006). Furthermore, there is some confusion and debating concerning the difference between competence and competency. Some authors use the term competencies as the plural of the term competence or treat the two as synonymous. Others argue that competency in the American sense complements competence as used in the UK occupational standards (Boon and van der Klink 2002; Delamare and Winterton 2005; Winterton et al. 2005; Sanchez-Ruiz et al. 2006). However, it is evident that competencies are only a subset of the required competences for a given professional and/or academic field (Cheetham and

Chivers 2005). In this chapter, we use competency as a synonym of the term "skill" which is only a part of our adopted competence definition.

In the next section we review the most widely referenced definitions of competence as they appear in the literature. Tables 9.1 and 9.2 presents these definitions which were selected to provide the different perspectives of the term towards building a global understanding of the field and identifying the different issues that it involves.

9.2.2 Competence Definition: A Literature Review

The word competence is derived from Latin word "Competere" which means to be suitable (Onrec 2007). The competence concept was originally developed in Psychology referring to the individual's ability to respond to certain demands placed on them by their environment. In the tables below, we present the main definitions of competence from different authors and from different application fields, in an effort to provide a thorough understanding of the different aspects that this term involves. To this end, Table 9.1 presents examples of competence definitions in human resource management, while Table 9.2 presents examples of competence definitions in vocational training and education.

Table 9.1. Examples of competence definitions – human resource management

Competence definitions – human resource management	
Author	Definition
McClelland (1973)	The knowledge, skills, traits, attitudes, self-concepts, values, or motives directly related to job performance or important life outcomes and shown to differentiate between superior and average performers
Spencer and Spencer (1993)	An underlying characteristic of an individual that is casually related to criterion-referenced effecting and/or superior performance in a job situation. Competences can be distinguished into essential, competences which serve as the foundation of knowledge and skills needed by everyone and differentiating competences, which are used to distinguish superior performance from average performance and they may include characteristics such as self-concepts, traits and motives
Lachance (1999)	An underlying characteristic of an employee (i.e., a motive, trait, skill, aspects of one's self-image, social role, or a body of knowledge) which results in effective and/or superior performance
Treasury Board of Canada Secretariat (1999)	Knowledge, skills, abilities and behaviors that an employee applies in performing his/her work and that are the key employee-related levers for achieving results that are relevant to the organization's business strategies

Table 9.1. (Cont.)

Competence definitions – human resource management	
Author	Definition
Joint Nature Conservation Committee (1999)	A term that describes the range of knowledge, skills, behaviour, attitude and abilities an individual brings to a specific area of a job, such as team working.
Intagliata et al. (2000)	Competences provide organizations with a way to define in behavioral terms what their leaders need to do to produce the results the organization desires and do so in a way that is consistent with and builds its culture
United Nations Industrial Development Organization (2002)	A set of skills, related knowledge and attributes that allow an individual to perform a task or an activity within a specific function or job
Sinnott et al. (2002)	A characteristic of an employee that contributes to successful job performance and the achievement of organizational results. These include knowledge, skills, and abilities plus other characteristics such as values, motivation, initiative, and self-control
Missouri Library Association (2005)	An underlying characteristic of an individual that is directly related to effective or superior performance in a job. Differentiating competences distinguish superior from average performer
Cheetham and Chivers (2005)	Overall, effective performance within an occupation, which may range from the basic level of proficiency to the highest levels of excellence. A competence consists of four main components, namely, knowledge/cognitive competence, functional competence, personal or behavioral competence and values/ethical competence. Knowledge/cognitive competence is defined as "the possession of appropriate work-related knowledge and the ability to put this to effective use". Functional competence is defined as "the ability to perform a range of workbased tasks effectively to produce specific outcomes". Personal/behavioral competence is defined as "the ability to adopt appropriate, observable behaviors in work-related situations". Values/ethical competence is defined as "the possession of appropriate personal and professional values and the ability to make sound judgments based upon these in work-related situations"
Tobias (2006)	The cognitive (e.g., knowledge and skills), affective (e.g., attitudes and values), behavioral and motivational (e.g., motives) characteristics or dispositions of a person which enable him or her to perform well in a specific situation
International Board of Standards for Training, Performance and Instruction (2006)	An integrated set of skills, knowledge, and attitudes that enables one to effectively perform the activities of a given occupation or function to the standards expected in employment

Table 9.2. Examples of competence definitions – vocational training and education

Competence definitions – vocational training and education	
Author	Definition
Voorhees (2001)	A combination of skills, abilities and knowledge needed to perform a specific task
Kupper and van Wulfften Palthe (2001)	The capability of people to perform in a function or a profession according to the qualifications they have. These qualifications should be expressed in terms of knowledge, skills and attitude
Eurydice (2002)	The ability to perform a particular task
Friesen and Anderson (2004)	The integrated application of knowledge, skills, values, experience, contacts, external knowledge resources and tools to solve a problem, to perform an activity, or to handle a situation
Sanchez-Ruiz et al. (2006)	A dynamic combination of knowledge, understanding, skills and abilities

9.2.3   Competence Development

Competence development can be seen as a lifecycle which aims at the continuous enhancement and development of an individual's or a group's competences. The main steps of this lifecycle can be identified as follows: (a) the creation of a competence model through the identification of required job and task roles and relevant competences, (b) the assessment of existing competences, (c) the gap analysis between existing competences and the required competences for a specific job or task role, (d) the definition of competence development programmes or units of programmes to minimize the identified gaps and (e) the continuous performance monitoring and assessment to confirm improvement (Sinnott et al. 2002). Recently within the context of the TENCompetence Consortium, Koper (2006) proposed the TENCompetence domain model which specifies the data classes that will be represented in a competence development support system referred to as "Personal Competence Manager" (Vogten et al. 2007). The TENCompetence Domain Model defines the basic concepts of the Competence Development Lifecycle and their relationships.

Competences are anticipated to be modeled in the TENCompetence domain model as follows. Each learning network has a *competence map* that contains a series of competence profiles for roles, functions and jobs. A *competence profile*, which is an instance of a certain competence model, contains one or more *competences* that must be attained in order to meet the demands of the profile. Each profile can have various function levels (e.g., the roles of junior seaman, captain, navigating officer). The evidences that an actor needs to demonstrate as a proof of the mastering a certain competence profile are rather formal (e.g., diploma, license, certification). These formal profiles are agreed upon in certain communities like a professional association or a government.

Nevertheless, job profiles are changing over time, due to the fact that the underlying job requirements are changing or that the perceptions on the jobs are changing. In the TENCompetence framework, the technical infrastructure that facilitates capturing the competence profiles of a community is called *competence observatory* (Zervas and Sampson 2007). The results of the observatory should be represented in an interoperable manner. Also competence profiles that are created within a learning network should be exported to the competence profile observatory for further monitoring and decisions. Competence element changes within certain profiles are essential to "keep-up-to-date both the available and the required competences for a certain role, job or function". When a new competence is defined, the actors who attained the profile will be informed that a new competence is available (or required) for the profile.

From the above discussion, it becomes evident that modeling and representing competence-related information in a machine-readable meaningful way so as to allow its inter-exchange in a standard and consistent way between different system implementations, is an essential element for building technology-enhanced competence-based training systems.

9.2.4 Towards a Unified Definition of Competence

A key observation from the previous section is that one of the core issues for Competence Development is the competence modeling. However, based on the literature review on the competence term definition presented in Sect. 9.2.2, it is evident that there does not exist a commonly accepted definition of competence, which is essential for developing a competence model. This fact means that, before accepting a unified and generic definition of the term competence, it will be difficult to proceed towards a reliable competence modeling.

Let us assume a person that already has a university degree in Mathematics and he now wants to obtain a degree in Computer Science from another university. Obviously, he does not expect to participate again in classes of subjects that he has already been certified through his previous degree (such as algebra). A reasonable way to pursue this is to compare his competence profile with the competence model that the new university uses to represent the contents of its curricula and prove that the course "algebra" is one of the classes that he has already successfully attained.

It is rather reasonable to expect that training organizations' professionals are able to understand the various instances that were developed using
different competence models, ought to the fact that each institute uses its
own definition of the term competence, and manually map them. However
that could be hardly interpreted by software systems.

As a result, aiming to contribute towards facilitating the communication
and interoperability between various competence-based systems, in this
chapter we identify the adoption of a unified, generic definition of competence as an essential step. This means that, we need a definition for competence that will be able to accommodate and reconcile all the different
ways that the term competence is used in literature. Such a unified generic
definition should provide the common ground for developing a generic
competence modeling process. This can lead to the creation of multiple
instances of competence models using common elements that can be exchanged between systems dealing with competence-related information.

Based on the different issues emerging from the competence definitions
presented in Sect. 9.2.2, in this section we identify three core dimensions
of the term competence. Figure 9.1 represents these three dimensions.

The first dimension is an individual's characteristics, which refer to a set
of characteristics such as knowledge, skills, attitudes, abilities, behaviors,
traits, values, motives, self-concepts, aspects of one's self-image, social role
and/or self-control.

The second dimension is the individual's competence proficiency level.
Proficiency levels are used to classify competences at specific levels,
according to the performance of the individual when demonstrating the
competence by an action. According to the sample of the definitions, the
proficiency level may include superior and average performance, effective
and superior performance, or a range from the basic level of proficiency to
the highest levels of excellence performance of an activity.

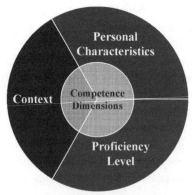

Fig. 9.1. Competence dimensions

The third dimension is the context in which the individual's competence is applied. The context may refer to a specific area of a job, to an occupation or function, to a life outcome, to work-related situations, to a specific situation, or to a specific task.

Table 9.3 examines whether the identified dimensions are incorporated in each one of the competence definitions that we recorded in Sect. 9.2.2 and to what extend.

Table 9.3. Relationship between generic competence dimensions and competence definitions

Authors	Personal characteristics	Proficiency level	Context
McClelland (1973)	✓	✓	✓
Spencer and Spencer (1993)	✓	✓	✓
Lachance (1999)	✓	✓	✗
Treasury Board of Canada Secretariat (1999)	✓	✗	✓
Joint Nature Conservation Committee (1999)	✓	✗	✓
Intagliata et al. (2000)	✓	✗	✗
Voorhees (2001)	✓	✗	✓
Kupper and van Wulfften Palthe (2001)	✓	✗	✓
Eurydice (2002)	✓	✗	✓
United Nations Industrial Development Organization (2002)	✓	✗	✓
Sinnott et al. (2002)	✓	✗	✓
Friesen and Anderson (2004)	✓	✗	✓
Missouri Library Association (2005)	✓	✓	✓
Cheetham and Chivers (2005)	✓	✓	✓
Tobias (2006)	✓	✗	✓
International Board of Standards for Training, Performance and Instruction (2006)	✓	✗	✓
Sanchez-Ruiz et al. (2006)	✓	✗	✗

It appears that these dimensions are related to all definitions examined to a certain extend, and thus, for the needs of this chapter we adopt the following generic definition of the term competence: a competence can be defined as a set of personal characteristics (e.g., skills, knowledge, attitudes) that an individual possess or needs to acquire, in order to perform an activity within a specific context. Performance may range from the basic level of proficiency to the highest levels of excellence. Based on this definition, we will next discuss the issue of competence modeling.

9.2.5 Competence Models

In general, model is an abstraction of a concept for the purpose of understanding it before building it. Hence, a competence model can be considered as a generic structure which is applicable beyond the built environment professions. Lucia and Lepsinger (1999) define competence model as "a descriptive tool that identifies the competences needed to perform a role effectively in the organization and help the business meet its strategic objectives".

For the purpose of this chapter, we suggest that the elements of a competence model should be related to the competence dimensions that we have identified in Sect. 9.2.4. These elements are captured in Fig. 9.2 and they include:

- *Name*: this element provides a short name of the competence.
- *Description*: this element provides a complete description of the competence.
- *Proficiency Level*: this element aims to describe the proficiency level of the competence. It consists of two sub-elements, namely "level" and "scale". First, the sub-element "level" aims to describe different types of proficiency level based on the facets of the dimension "Personal Characteristics" (e.g., skills, knowledge, attitudes) discussed in Sect. 9.2.4. For each characteristic the name of the proficiency level where it belongs, the type and a description of the characteristic must be given. On the other hand, as far as the sub-element "scale" is concerned, different qualitative or quantitative scales may be used in order to represent proficiency levels. The values of the qualitative scales must be represented as an ordered list, while for the quantitative scales the minimum value, the maximum value and the interval must be described.
- *Context*: this element aims is related to the dimension "context" of the unified competence definition captured in Fig. 9.1 and it can be described with two sub-elements, namely, "name" and "description".

By assigning certain values to each element of the proposed competence model, then a specific instance of a competence is generated. Next, we demonstrate a real life example of such an instance using the Europass Language Passport. This is the European common model for language competences which was developed by the Council of Europe as part of the European Language Portfolio (European Commission 2001).

The Europass Language Passport supports the description of language proficiency levels based on a six level scale retrieved from the Common European Framework of Reference for Languages (European Commission

2001). These levels are: level A1 and A2 for basic users, level B1 and B2 for independent users and level C1 and C2 for proficient users. Furthermore, the Europass Language Passport defines a competence ontology consisting of five simple competences and three complex competences (that is, any competence consisting of other – simple or complex – competences). Each of these competences is associated (directly or indirectly) with a list of language topics (see Fig. 9.3).

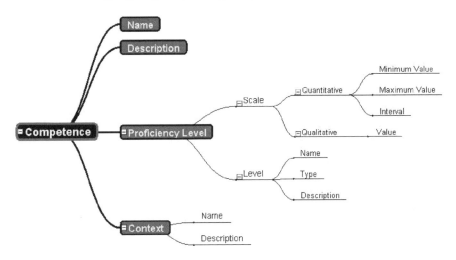

Fig. 9.2. Competence model elements

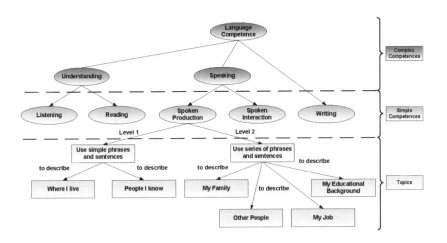

Fig. 9.3. Partial view of competence ontology used in europass language passport

Therefore according to the proposed competence model, an instance based on Europass Language Passport, has the following form:

Name: English Language Speaking
Description: The language user acts alternately as speaker and listener with one or more interlocutors so as to construct conjointly, through the negotiation of meaning following the co-operative principle, conversational discourse. Also, the language user produces an oral text which is received by an audience of one or more listeners.

Proficiency Level

- **Scale**
  - o **Qualitative**
    - ▪ **Value:** A1
    - ▪ **Value:** A2
    - ▪ **Value:** B1
    - ▪ **Value:** B2
    - ▪ **Value:** C1
    - ▪ **Value:** C2
- **Level**
  - o **Name:** B2
  - o **Type:** Knowledge
  - o **Description:** Good grammatical knowledge without much sign of having to restrict what he/she wants to say, adopting a level of formality appropriate to the circumstances.
- **Level**
  - o **Name:** B2
  - o **Type:** Skill
  - o **Description:** Can use the language fluently, accurately and effectively on a wide range of general, academic, vocational or leisure topics, marking clearly the relationships between ideas.
- **Level**
  - o **Name:** B2
  - o **Type:** Attitude
  - o **Description:** Willingness to distance oneself from conventional attitudes to cultural difference.

Context

- **Name:** Europe
- **Description:** Learning and working in Europe

In Technology-enhanced Competence-based Learning the process of competence modeling requires appropriate technological infrastructures for storing, organizing, sharing and mapping the various instances of competence models. This is essential for representing competence instances in an interoperable manner using a single, globally agreed format. To this end, international efforts are already in place towards defining specifications for competence descriptions. In the next section, we present and examine these specifications.

9.3 Competence Specifications and Discussion

Recently, specifications for competence description, such as the IMS RDCEO (Reusable Definition of Competency or Educational Objective), the IEEE RCD (Reusable Competency Definitions) and the HR-XML Competencies (Measurable Characteristics) have been proposed. These are intended as the means for facilitating interoperability across systems that deal with competence-related information by allowing them to refer to common definitions with commonly recognized values.

The IMS RDCEO specification (IMS RDCEO 2002) defines an information model for describing, referencing, and exchanging definitions of competences and educational objectives, targeting technology-enhanced competence-based training. Although the IMS RDCEO specification does not intend to offer a solution to the aggregation of complex competences from simple competences, its data model allows the integration of relational information or competence ontologies through embedding additional metadata. Furthermore, the IMS RDCEO specification does not address the issue of how competences are to be assessed, certified, recorded or used as part of a process with a wider scope, such as Competence Management (IMS RDCEO 2002).

In the same way, the IEEE RCD specification describes a Competence Definition anticipated to be used in a Learning Management System or referenced in a Competency Profile, by making direct reference of the IMS RDCEO specification (IEEE P1484.20/D01 2004).

On the other hand, the scope of the HR-XML Consortium is to define a competence description, as well as, to be able to record evidences used to substantiate a competence with ratings and weights that can be used to rank, compare, and evaluate the sufficiency or desirability of a competence (HR-XML 2006).

In Fig. 9.4, we illustrate the mapping between the elements of the IMS RDCEO and the HR-XML specifications. As we can see both the IMS RDCEO and the HR-XML specifications provide the following elements:

- *Identification*: A globally unique label assigned to identify or classify the competence.
- *Title*: A short name for the competence.
- *Description*: A narrative description of the competence.
- *Definition*: A structured description that provides a more complete definition of the competence.
- *Taxonomy*: The taxonomy where the competence belongs.
- Personal information: Information about the individual that possess the competence is described.
- while the HR-XML specification further includes elements for:
- *Measurable evidences*: Information used to prove the existence, sufficiency, or level of a competence. Evidences might include test results, certificates, licenses, or a record of direct observation, such as a report given by a former supervisor or other employment reference.
- *Measurable weights*: Information on the relative importance of the competence or the sufficiency required or other type of dimension.

Thus, we can observe that both specifications include titles and descriptors that need to be interpreted by human beings, since the information stored within these elements are in a narrative format. As a result, these elements are not directly machine-understandable. Furthermore, both specifications adopt definitions about competence, that do not take into consideration issues such as the "Proficiency Level", which is important for many definitions of the competence concept as we have seen in Sect. 9.2.2. Thus, the current scope of these specifications do not address all issues emerging from the competence dimensions identified in the unified definition provided in Sect. 9.2.4 (Karampiperis et al. 2006; Sampson et al. 2007).

More specifically, according the competence model captured in Fig. 9.3, every competence has a name and a complete description. As we can see in Fig. 9.5, both specifications include elements for supporting the naming and the description of a competence, however, this information is stored in a narrative format.

On the other hand, according to the competence model captured in Fig. 9.3, every competence incorporates various proficiency levels that can be represented via the use of different qualitative or quantitative scales. Furthermore, the characteristics of an individual (e.g., skills, knowledge, attitudes) in relation to a specific competence may differ according the proficiency level of the person.

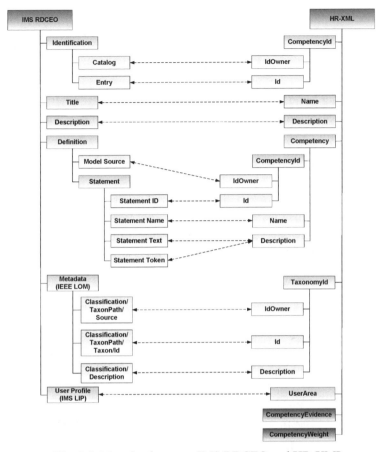

Fig. 9.4. Mapping between IMS RDCEO and HR-XML

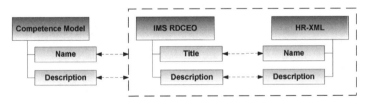

Fig. 9.5. Mapping between competence model and competence specifications (name-description)

The IMS RDCEO specification supports the representation of a competence proficiency level, only within the "Title" element. The information stored within this element is in a narrative format, thus, it is not directly machine understandable and limits the potential for systems interoperability. Moreover, the IMS RDCEO specification does not provide a way to capture the values of the scale that is used for the representation of the proficiency level or a way to describe the facets of the dimension "Personal Characteristics" that differentiate based on the proficiency level.

On the other hand, as we can see in Fig. 9.6, the HR-XML specification allows the representation of proficiency level information, within the "CompetencyWeight" element. This element contains the "Type" sub-element that is used to specify the type of the competence weight. This sub-element can be related to the "Proficiency Level" in our generic competence model. In addition, the "CompetencyWeight" element contains sub-elements that can be used for the representation of the qualitative or quantitative scales, as it can be seen in Fig. 9.6. However in the case of the qualitative scale only the minimum and the maximum value can be described, while it would be desirable to be represented all the values as an ordered list. In addition the HR-XML specification does not provide a way to describe the facets of the dimension "Personal Characteristics" of our generic competence model.

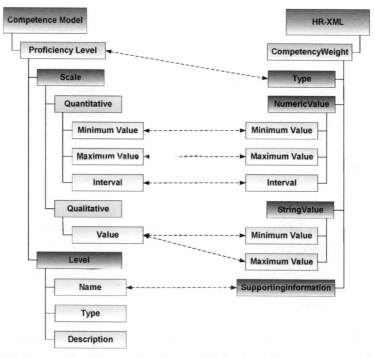

Fig. 9.6. Mapping between competence model and competence specifications (proficiency level)

Finally, it appears that both specifications do not include information about the context in their schemas. However, as discussed in Sect. 9.2, the context description is an important element for competence modelling and is anticipated to be included in the competence description.

As a conclusion of this section, both specifications, namely, the HR-XML and the IMS RDCEO, have not included in their scope important dimensions of the generic competence model presented in Sect. 9.2.

9.4 Conclusions

Throughout the years competence-based management approaches have proved to be a critical tool in human resource management, vocational training and performance management. As a result, competence-based approaches are often adopted as the key paradigm in both formal or informal education and training programs.

However, despite the fact that competences are an important tool for various fields of application, the communities of researchers and the practitioners have not agreed to a commonly accepted definition of the term competence, resulting to multiple interpretations. On the other hand, this is essential for developing a generic competence model, as a core step for Competence Development. This is a major drawback for achieving interoperability between various systems that deal with competence-related information.

Within this context, in this chapter we proposed a unified definition of the term competence that is capable to accommodate the different literature definitions and identify three dimensions that can be used for developing a generic competence description model.

In Technology-enhanced Competence-based Learning the process of competence modeling requires appropriate technological infrastructures for storing, organizing, sharing and mapping the various instances of competence models. This is essential for representing competence instances in an interoperable manner using a single, globally agreed format. To this end, international efforts are already in place towards defining specifications for competence descriptions.

Specifications for competence description, such as the IMS RDCEO (Reusable Definition of Competency or Educational Objective), the IEEE RCD (Reusable Competency Definitions) and the HR-XML Competencies (Measurable Characteristics) have been recently proposed. These are intended as the means for facilitating interoperability across systems that deal with competence-related information by allowing them to refer to common definitions with commonly recognized values.

A careful examination of these specifications reveals that they do not included in their scope important dimensions of the generic competence model proposed in this chapter. As a result, it appears that further investigations are in order, so as to facilitate the development of technology-enhanced competence-based training systems.

Acknowledgements

The work on this chapter has been sponsored by the TENCompetence Integrated Project that is funded by the European Commission's 6th Framework Programme, priority IST/Technology Enhanced Learning. Contract 027087 (www.tencompetence.org).

References

Aspin, D. N. & Chapman, J. D. (2000). Lifelong learning: concepts and conceptions. International Journal of Lifelong Education, 19(1):2–19

Becerra-Fernandez, I., Gonzalez, A. & Sabherwal, R. (2004). Knowledge Management: Challenges, Solutions and Technologies. Pearson Prentice Hall, New Jersey

Boon, J. & van der Klink, M. (2002). Competencies: the triumph of a fuzzy concept. In, Academy of Human Resource Development Annual Conference, vol. 1, pp. 327–334, Honolulu

Cheetham, G. & Chivers, G. (2005). Professions, Competence and Informal Learning. Edward Elgar, Cheltenham

Delamare, F. & Winterton, J. (2005). What is competence? Human Resource Development International, 8(1):27–46

Draganidis, F. & Mentzas, G. (2006). Competency based management: a review of systems and approaches. Information Management and Computer Security Journal, 14(1):51–64

European Commission (2001). Common european framework of reference for languages. Retrieved December 30, 2007 from http://www.coe.int/t/dg4/linguistic/Source/Framework_EN.pdf

Eurydice (2002). Key competencies: a developing concept in general compulsory education. Retrieved December 30, 2007 from http://www.mszs.si/eurydice/pub/eurydice/survey_5_en.pdf

Field, J. (2001). Lifelong education. International Journal of Lifelong Education, 20(1/2):3–15

Friesen, N. & Anderson, T. (2004). Interaction for lifelong learning. British Journal of Educational Technology, 35(6):679–687

Griffin, C. (1999). Lifelong learning and social democracy. International Journal of Lifelong Education, 18(5):329–342

Hamel, G. & Prahalad, C. K. (1994). Competing For the Future. Harvard Business School Press, Boston

HR-XML (2006). HR-XML consortium competencies (measurable characteristics). Retrieved December 30, 2007 from http://ns.hr-xml.org/2_4/HR-XML-2_4/CPO/Competencies.html

Hoge, M., Tondora, J. & Marrelli, A. (2005). The fundamentals of workforce competency: implications for behavioral health. Journal of Administration and Policy in Mental Health, 32:509–531

Hong, J. & Stahle, P. (2005). The coevolution of knowledge and competence management. International Journal of Management Concepts and Philosophy, 1(2):129–145

Hustad, E., Munkvold, B. & Moll, B. (2004). Using IT for strategic competence management: potential benefits and challenges. In, Proc. of the European Conference on Information Systems (ECIS), Turku, Finland

IEEE P1484.20/D01, (2004). Draft standard for information technology – learning technology – competency definitions. Retrieved December 30, 2007 from http://ltsc.ieee.org/wg20/files/IEEE_RDCEO_Spec.pdf

IMS RDCEO, (2002). IMS reusable definition of competency or educational objective. Retrieved December 30, 2007 from http://www.imsglobal.org/competencies/

Intagliata, J., Ulrich, D. & Smallwood, N. (2000). Leveraging leadership competencies to produce leadership brand: creating distinctiveness by focusing on strategy and results. Human Resource Planning Journal, 23(4):12–23

International Board of Standards for Training, Performance and Instruction (2006). Competencies. Retrieved December 30, 2007 from http://www.ibstpi.org/competencies.htm

Joint Nature Conservation Committee (1999). Biodiversity information assistant. Retrieved December 30, 2007 from http://www.jncc.gov.uk/pdf/job200607.pdf

Karampiperis, P., Sampson, D. & Fytros, D. (2006), Lifelong competence development: towards a common metadata model for competencies description – the case study of europass language passport. In, Proc. of the 6th IEEE International Conference on Advanced Learning Technologies (ICALT 2006), 677–681, Kerkrade, The Netherlands

Koper, R. (2006). TenCompetence domain model. Retrieved December 30, 2007 from http://dspace.ou.nl/handle/1820/649/DomainModel-version1p0.pdf

Koper, R. & Specht, M. (2007). TenCompetence: lifelong competence development and learning. In, Miguel-Angel Sicilia (Ed.), Competencies in Organizational E-Learning: Concepts and Tools. Idea, Hershey, PA, pp. 230–247

Kupper, H. & van Wulfften Palthe, A.W. (2001). Competency-based curriculum development: experiences in agri chain management in The Netherlands and in China. In, IAMA World Food and Agribusiness Conference, Sydney, Australia

Lachance, J. R. (1999). Looking to the Future: Human Resources Competencies. United States Office of Personnel Management

Lucia, A. D. & Lepsinger, R. (1999). The Art and Science of Competency Models: Pinpointing Critical Success Factors in Organizations. Jossey-Bass, San Francisco

Martin, H. & Willems, E. (2005). IT support of competence based learning in groups in a distance learning environment. The electronic Journal of e-Learning, 3(1):31–40

Marwick, D. (2001). Knowledge management technology. IBM Systems Journal, 40(4):814–830

Mayoral, M. R., Palacios, C. R., Gómez, J. M. & Crespo, A. G. (2007). A mobile framework for competence evaluation: innovation assessment using mobile information systems. Journal of Technology Management and Innovation, 2(3):49–57

McClelland, D. (1973). Testing for competence rather than for intelligence. American Psychologist Journal, 20:321–333

McLagan, P. (1997). Competencies: the next generation. Training and Development, 51(5):40–47

Missouri Library Association (2005). A behavioral approach to support staff development. Retrieved December 30, 2007 from http://molib.org/Outline.pdf

Onrec (2007). Competency profiling fits the bill. Retrieved September 30, 2007 from http://www.onrec.com/content2/news.asp?ID=12930

Otto, T., Riives, J. & Loun, K. (2007). Productivity improvement through monitoring of human resources competence level. B. Katalinic (Toim.). DAAAM International Scientific Book 2007. DAAAM International Vienna

Prusak, L. (2001). Where did knowledge management come from? IBM Systems Journal, 40(4):1002–1007

Sampson, D., Karampiperis, P. & Fytros, D. (2007). Developing a common metadata model for competencies description. Interactive learning environment, special issue on learning networks for lifelong competence development, 15(2):137–150, Routledge

Sanchez-Ruiz, L. M., Edwards, M., & Sarrias E. B. (2006). Competence learning challenges in engineering education in Spain: from theory to practice. In, Proc. of the International Conference on Engineering Education, San Juan, USA

Sanghi, S. (2004). The Handbook of Competency Mapping. Sage, London

Sinnott, G. C., Madison, G. H. & Pataki, G. E. (2002). Competencies: report of the competencies workgroup. Workforce and succession planning work Groups. New York State Governor's Office of Employee Relations and the Department of Civil Service

Spencer, L. M. & Spencer, S. M. (1993). Competence at Work. Wiley, New York

TENCompetence (2007). M6.1 Templates of the pedagogical models to be used in authoring environment; model that combines classical and new forms of assessment. European Community Information Society Technologies (IST) Programme, Contract 027087

Tobias, L. (2006). Organizational competence management – a competence performance approach. In, 6th International Conference on Knowledge Management (I-KNOW 06), Graz, Austria

Treasury Board of Canada Secretariat (1999). Framework for competency-based management in the public service of Canada. Report of joint initiative between the Treasury Board of Canada Secretariat and the Public Service Commission

United Nations Industrial Development Organization (2002). UNIDO competencies. Retrieved December 30, 2007 from https://www.unido.org/userfiles/timminsk/UNIDO-CompetencyModel-Part1.pdf

Vogten, H., Koper, R., Martens, H., & Van Bruggen, J. (2007). Using the personal competence manager as a complementary approach to IMS Learning Design authoring. *Interactive Learning Environments*

Voorhees, R.A. (2001). Competency-based learning models: a necessary future. In, R.A. Voorhees (Ed.), Measuring What Matters: Competency-Based Learning Models in Higher Education: New Directions for Institutional Research, 110. Jossey-Bass, San Francisco, pp. 5–13

Weert, T. J. (2004). ICT-rich and competency based learning in higher education. In, Proc. of the New Educational Benefits of ICT in Higher Education

Westera, W. (2001). Competences in education: a confusion of tongues. Journal of Curriculum Studies, 33(1):75–88

Winterton, J., Delamare-Le Deist, F. & Stringfellow, E. (2005). Typology of knowledge, skills and competences: clarification of the concept and prototype. Centre for European Research on Employment and Human Resources. Groupe ESC Toulouse. Research report elaborated on behalf of Cedefop/Thessaloniki

Zervas, P., & Sampson, D. (2007). The TENCompetence observatory: an enabling technology for common description of competences. In, Proceedings of the 7th IEEE International Conference on Advanced Learning Technologies, Niigata, Japan

10 Learner Modelling Through Analyzing Cognitive Skills and Learning Styles*

S. Graf and Kinshuk

Providing adaptivity in web-based educational systems supports learners in their learning process and makes learning easier for them. However, providing adaptivity requires knowing the needs of the learners. Therefore learner modelling, the process of building and updating a learner model, is a crucial aspect of adaptive systems and necessary for providing course content that fits to the learners' needs. In this chapter, we discuss recent research focusing on cognitive traits and learning styles. We show approaches by which cognitive traits and learning styles can be identified. In order to get additional data for improving learner modelling, we discuss investigations about the relationship of cognitive traits and learning styles, and the aspects of adaptation resulting from this combination.

10.1 Introduction

Different learners have different needs. They differ, for example, in their learning goals, their knowledge about the domain, their cognitive traits and their learning styles. These individual differences affect the learning process and are the reasons why some learners find it easy to learn in a particular course whereas others find the same course difficult (Jonassen and Grabowski 1993).

---

* This research has been partly funded by the Austrian Federal Ministry for Education, Science, and Culture, and the European Social Fund (ESF) under grant 31.963/46-VII/9/2002.

Several studies have been conducted considering individual differences of learners and their impact on learning and on the achievement of learners (for an overview, see Jonassen and Grabowski 1993). As Jonassen and Grabowski (1993) summarized, prior knowledge is one of the strongest and most consistent individual-difference predictors of learners' achievement. Although prior knowledge seems to account for more variance in learning than other individual differences, more recently educational researchers have focused on aspects of personal characteristics and abilities such as cognitive traits and learning styles and are investigating their impact on learning. These investigations are motivated by educational and psychological theories. For example, the cognitive load theory (Paas et al. 2003; Sweller 1988) suggests that learning happens best under conditions that are aligned with human cognitive architecture. Therefore, it is beneficial to incorporate the differences in cognitive architecture in order to avoid cognitive overload and thus a negative effect on learning. Regarding learning styles, Felder, for example, pointed out that learners with a strong preference for a specific learning style might have difficulties in learning if their learning style is not supported by the teaching environment (Felder and Silverman 1988; Felder and Soloman 1997). On the other hand, incorporating learning styles makes learning easier and leads to better achievement.

Individual differences impact learning in general, and hence also play an important role in technology-enhanced learning. Adaptive systems address this exact issue and aim at incorporating the different needs of learners by providing adapted courses. Brusilovsky, for example, defined adaptive systems as "systems which reflect some features of the user in the user model and apply this model to adapt various visible aspects of the system to the user" (Brusilovsky 1996, p. 88). Considering this definition from the viewpoint of an adaptive educational system, the adaptation process in such a system consists of two parts: first, a model of the learner has to be built (and updated) which includes all necessary information about the learner to provide adaptivity and second, this information has to be used in order to generate adapted courses.

The learner model plays a crucial role in adaptive systems. The information included in the learner model is based on the system's beliefs about the learner. The process of building and updating the learner model is called learner modelling. While Self (1994) provided a comprehensive description of learner modelling from the point of view of the formal techniques, Brusilovsky (1994, 1996) classified learner models and techniques for learner modelling based on existing systems.

Brusilovsky (1996) distinguished between two different ways of learner modelling: automatic and collaborative learner modelling. In the former, the process of building and updating the learner model is done automatically, based on the action of the learner when he/she is using the system for learning. The main problem with this approach is to get enough reliable information to build a robust student model. According to Brusilovsky (1996), a solution to this problem might be the use of additional, more reliable sources, such as the results of tests, in the learner modelling process. On the other hand, in collaborative learner modelling, the learner provides explicit feedback, which can be used to build or update the learner model. For instance, the learner can provide data for the learner modelling mechanism such as stating explicitly whether a page was relevant for his/her learning goal. Another option is to let the learner do the adaptation by himself/herself and therefore show directly what he/she expects from the system. For example, the order of links on a page can be changed by the learner, showing the preferred order to the system. Another possibility is that the learner is allowed to directly update the information of the learner model.

In a learner model, different kinds of information can be included. Brusilovsky (1994) distinguished two major groups, namely models of course knowledge and models of individual subject-independent characteristics. Both are different in terms of the form of representation of the model as well as in terms of the methods used in its construction and application. While first investigations about learner modelling were focused on models about the course knowledge, more and more research is now done on modelling individual characteristics of learners.

In the following sections, we focus on two individual characteristics, namely cognitive traits and learning styles, and describe recent research that deals with detecting such information in order to build a learner model. As discussed before, an important issue of learner modelling is to get enough reliable information about the learner that can be addressed by the use of additional information. Concerning this matter, we discuss the relationship between cognitive traits and learning styles and show how this relationship can be used to improve learner modelling. Since an aim of learner modelling is to use the gathered information to provide adaptivity, the chapter also describes how this information can be used and gives some examples on how learners can be supported by adaptive systems.

10.2 Identifying Individual Differences

Identifying the individual differences and using this information to build and update a learner model are requirements for providing suitable adaptivity regarding the respective individual differences. The more information is available, the more reliable the learner model and the better the adaptation suit will be. In the following two subsections, we introduce collaborative and automatic approaches to identify cognitive traits and learning styles. Subsequently, we discuss how both of these characteristics are related to each other and how information about this relationship can be used to improve learner modelling and subsequent adaptation.

10.2.1 Identifying Cognitive Traits

The Cognitive Trait Model (CTM) (Kinshuk and Lin 2004; Lin and Kinshuk 2005) is a learner model that profiles learners according to their cognitive traits. Four cognitive traits – working memory capacity, inductive reasoning ability, information processing speed and associative learning skills – are included in CTM so far. The CTM offers the role of learning companion, which different learning environments for a particular learner can consult and interact with. The CTM can still be valid after a long period of time due to the more or less persistent nature of cognitive traits of human beings (Deary et al. 2004). When a student encounters a new learning environment, the learning environment can directly use the CTM of the particular student, and does not need to "re-learn the student".

Collaborative Learner Modelling Approach

With regard to the collaborative learner modelling approach, information about the learners' cognitive traits can be gathered by asking them to perform tests to measure their cognitive traits. The gathered information from the tests can then be used by the CTM in order to provide adaptivity. An example for such a test is the WebOSPAN task (Graf et al. 2006), which is an online task developed to identify working memory capacity.

A drawback of the collaborative learner modelling approach is that the learners must make additional effort. In the case of cognitive traits, these tests take quite a long time and special conditions are required, for example, asking the learners that they have no interruption during a test.

Automatic Learner Modelling Approach

In contrast to the collaborative learner modelling approach, the automatic learner modelling approach collects data from the behaviour of the learner while he/she is using the educational system. Therefore, data about the cognitive traits of each learner can be collected without any additional effort of the learners.

Lin and Kinshuk (2005) describe a typical structure of an automatic learner modelling approach for the CTM (Fig. 10.1). The learner interface provides a presentation of the learning environment to interact with the learner. The interface listener component is a mechanism that can monitor events created by learner's interactions with a learning environment. Learner interactions are interpreted as a series of learner actions performed on knowledge objects. Actions are then passed on to the action history components and are stored in action history.

The performance-based model typically exists independently in the adaptive educational system. It represents a learner's domain competence and models the problem-solving process that the learner undertakes. Certain learner behaviours, called manifestation of traits (MOTs), can be used to make inferences about the cognitive capacity. Information of the performance-based model, such as passing or failing a unit, can be useful for detecting MOTs of some cognitive traits and therefore data in the performance-based model is used as a source by the MOT detector component.

Various MOTs are defined for each cognitive trait. Each MOT is a piece of an interaction pattern that manifests a learner's characteristics (e.g., low inductive reasoning ability). The MOT detector component contains knowledge about a number of MOTs and detects those MOTs within a series of actions that are requested from the action history component.

The individualized temperament network component (for a detailed description, see Lin and Kinshuk 2004) is responsible for calculating the learners' cognitive traits, which are passed through the trait model gateway and saved in the cognitive trait model.

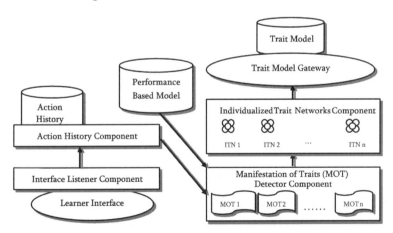

Fig. 10.1. Structural view of cognitive trait model

10.2.2 Identifying Learning Styles

Several different learning style models exist in the literature, each proposing different descriptions and classifications of learning types. These include the models by Kolb (1984), Honey and Mumford (1982) and Felder and Silverman (1988). Looking at adaptive educational systems incorporating learning styles, the Felder-Silverman learning style model (FSLSM) is one of the most often used models, and some researchers even argue that FSLSM is the most appropriate model for use in adaptive web-based educational systems (e.g., Carver et al. 1999; Kuljis and Liu 2005). As a consequence, a lot of research work related to FSLSM deals with aspects of learner modelling and adaptivity. For this reason, the discussion about identifying learning styles is focused on FSLSM as well.

According to FSLSM, learners are characterized by their preferences in four bipolar dimensions: *active* learners learn by trying things out and working with others, whereas *reflective* learners learn by thinking things through and prefer to work alone. *Sensing* learners like to learn concrete material and tend to be practical, whereas *intuitive* learners prefer to learn abstract material such as theories and their meanings and tend to be more innovative than sensing learners. *Visual* learners remember best what they have seen, whereas *verbal* learners get more out of words, regardless of whether they are spoken or written. *Sequential* learners learn in linear steps and prefer to follow linear stepwise paths, whereas *global* learners learn in large leaps and are characterized as holistic. Each learner has a preference for each of these four dimensions.

Collaborative Learning Modelling Approach

For identifying learning styles, most existing adaptive systems have used a collaborative approach by asking learners to fill out a questionnaire. To detect learning styles according to FSLSM, the Index of Learning Styles (ILS) was developed (Felder and Soloman 1997). ILS consists of 44 questions and is available online. As a result, it provides four values between +11 and −11, one for each dimension. Using the active/reflective dimension as an example, the value of "+11" means that a learner has a strong preference for active learning, whereas the value of "−11" indicates that a learner has a strong preference for reflective learning.

The ILS is an often used instrument. Several kinds of investigations have been done on ILS data. Felder and Spurlin (2005) provide an overview of studies showing the frequency of occurrence of each learning style. Furthermore, research deals with investigating the reliability and validity of ILS. While some studies conclude that ILS seems to be reliable and valid (Felder and Spurlin 2005; Litzinger et al. 2005; Zywno 2003), other studies found limitations in the reliability and validity of the instrument as well as some unexpected dependencies between learning styles (Van Zwanenberg et al. 2000; Viola et al. 2007). Besides these inconsistent results, it is argued that questionnaires have to deal with the problem that the given answers might not correspond to the real behaviour the questions aim to investigate, both intentionally and unintentionally (Draper 1996; Paredes and Rodríguez 2004).

Automatic Learner Modelling Approach

Instead of asking learners about their preferences, recent research focuses on observing the behaviour of learners during an online course and inferring from this behaviour their learning styles.

Paredes and Rodríguez (2004) introduced a mixed learner modelling approach. In the TANGOW system, learners fill out the ILS questionnaire when they log in the first time. This information is then used to initialize the learner model. To update and control the information in the learner model, the behaviour of the learners in the system is monitored. If learners behave contrary to the determined learning style preference stored in the learner model, the information in the learner model is revised. TANGOW incorporates only the sensing/intuitive and the sequential/global dimension of FSLSM. Furthermore, only four patterns, each of one learning style preference, are observed for revisions. Since only one corresponding adaptation feature exists per learning style, this approach is suitable for the system to provide appropriate adaptivity. However, it seems to not have enough information to detect completely the learning styles proposed by Felder and Silverman.

Recent research deals with a fully automatic learner modelling approach that considers several patterns for each learning style dimension to draw conclusions about the learning style preferences on the respective dimensions. García et al. (2007) proposed an automatic approach for the system SAVER and performed an experiment to show the effectiveness of their approach. The approach considers the active/reflective, sensing/intuitive, and the sequential/global dimensions. The visual/verbal dimension is not incorporated since no relevant learning material is presented in the course. Overall, 11 patterns are included for the three dimensions. Based on the data from these patterns, Bayesian networks (Jensen 1996) are used to calculate the preferences of the learning style dimensions for each learner. The evaluation of the approach shows a high degree of precision when comparing the calculated learning styles of the 10 users with their results from ILS.

Another approach for automatic learner modelling was investigated by Cha et al. (2006). They observed the behaviour of learners during an online course in an intelligent learning environment based on specific patterns. An experiment with 70 learners was conducted in order to test the effectiveness of decision trees (DT) (Dunham 2002) and hidden Markov models (HMM) (Rabiner 1989) for detecting learning styles according to FSLSM. For both techniques, several patterns were incorporated for each learning style dimension. However, only data indicating a strong or moderate preference for a specific learning style dimension (>3, according to ILS results) was included in the experiment. While for the visual/verbal dimension, DT achieved the better result, for the sequential/global dimension, the HMM performed better. This can be argued by the fact that HMM are able to consider sequences of learners' actions that might be more relevant for the sequential/global dimension. Results for the sensing/intuitive and the active/reflective dimensions were for both techniques the same, and the error rates (22.22% for sensing/intuitive and 33.33% for active/reflective) were quite high.

The above approaches were developed for specific systems and therefore used only those patterns for which the system was able to collect data. Graf and Kinshuk (2006a) proposed a tool for detecting learning styles in learning management systems (LMS) in general. The tool extracts relevant data about learners' behaviour from different LMS databases keeping in mind that different LMS have different database schemata. The patterns relevant for detecting learning styles were derived from commonly used features in LMS such as forums and exercises. Again, for each learning style dimension, several patterns were defined. The calculation of the learning styles is based on the approach used in the ILS questionnaire. Therefore, the data gathered for each pattern indicates either a preference for one or the other style of the dimension, or respectively no preference. As a result, the values of the patterns for each dimension were summed up and scaled. This approach considers that not all LMS might be able to provide data for all patterns. However, the more patterns included in the calculation process, the more stable the result. For further investigations, the learning management system Moodle (2007) was extended in order to provide all recommended data (Graf and Kinshuk 2006b).

10.2.3 Relationship Between Cognitive Traits and Learning Styles

So far, cognitive traits and learning styles were discussed separately and information was respectively gathered from the behaviour of learners during an online course. As discussed before, the challenge of the automatic learner modelling approach is to identify and collect sufficient information to make reliable and useful inferences. To support the detection process of required information, it is beneficial to find mechanisms that use whatever information about the learner is already available to obtain as much reliable information as possible to build a more robust student model.

In order to get additional information, the relationship between learning styles and cognitive traits was investigated. In web-based educational systems that consider either only learning styles or only cognitive traits, the relationship leads to more information. This additional information can be used to provide better adaptivity for combined learning styles and cognitive traits instead of only for one of them. In systems that incorporate learning styles as well as cognitive traits, the interaction can be used to improve the detection process of the counterpart. This leads to a more reliable student model. For instance, considering the learner modelling approach for cognitive traits (described above), the information about learning styles can be treated like a manifestation of traits (MOT). In the neural network, the impact of this new MOT can be calculated and the information can be used for detecting cognitive traits. For learning styles, the information about cognitive traits can similarly be seen as a pattern that gives an additional indication for a specific learning style preference.

Graf, Lin, and Kinshuk (2008) investigated the relationship between the Felder-Silverman learning style model and one cognitive trait, namely working memory capacity. They conducted a comprehensive literature review and found several studies indicating a relationship between the four dimensions of FSLSM and working memory capacity. Based on the literature, a relationship between high working memory capacity and a reflective, intuitive, and sequential learning style was identified. In contrast, learners with low working memory capacity tend to prefer an active, sensing, and global learning style. Regarding the visual/verbal dimension, it can be concluded that learners with low working memory capacity tend to prefer a visual learning style but learners with a visual learning style do not necessarily have low working memory capacity.

To verify the proposed relationship, an exploratory study of 39 students was conducted (Graf et al. 2006). The results show that the identified relationship between working memory capacity and two of the four dimensions of the learning style model – the sensing/intuitive and the visual/verbal dimension – was significantly supported. For the two remaining dimensions, only tendencies but no significant correlations were found and therefore, a further study with a larger sample size is planned.

10.3 Providing Adaptivity

In the previous section, we focused on how cognitive traits and learning styles can be detected. In most cases, the reason for detecting such information and building a learner model is to provide adaptivity. Different possibilities exist for adapting a course based on the information of the learner model. The most often used approach is to match the instructions to the preferences or abilities of the learners and teach according to the learners' strengths. This approach aims at a short-term goal, namely to make learning as easy as possible at the time learners are using the system. Looking at long-term goals, Messick (1976) suggested that learners should also train in their not-preferred skills and preferences. He argued that when learners acquire more educational experience, they are required to adapt to a variety of instructional methods and styles. The ability to adapt to different instructional styles will prepare them with important life skills. For example, providing verbal learners with only visual forms of instruction forces them to develop and use visual skills.

However, for both approaches, the needs of learners have to be identified. Then, based on this information, the respective approach can be chosen. Which approach should be applied might depend on specific conditions such as the current learning goal, the experience of the learner in a particular subject and so on.

In the following two subsections, we discuss how instructions can support specific needs, either learning style preferences or cognitive abilities. Examples are given showing how courses can match (or mismatch) to specific preferences or abilities.

10.3.1 Adaptivity Based on Cognitive Traits

Humans typically have a number of cognitive abilities. In this subsection, we focus on cognitive abilities that are important for learning. These include working memory capacity, inductive reasoning ability, information processing speed and associative learning skills. These four cognitive traits are also considered in CTM. For each of these traits, Kinshuk and Lin (2003) introduced suggestions on how to support learners with low and high cognitive abilities in adaptive educational systems. These suggestions are based on the Exploration Space Control elements (Kashihara et al. 2000), which are elements that can be changed to create different versions of courses to suit different needs. These elements include the number and relevance of paths, and the amount, concreteness and structure of content, as well as the number of information resources.

Working memory allows us to keep active a limited amount of information (roughly 7 ± 2 items) for a brief period of time (Miller 1956). Matching courses to the working memory capacity of individual learners takes into account their abilities and therefore avoids cognitive overload. For learners with low working memory capacity this can be achieved by decreasing the number and increasing the relevance of paths in a course. Furthermore, less but more concrete content should be presented and the number of available media resources should increase. In contrast, for learners with high working memory capacity, less relevant paths can be presented with an increased amount of content as well as abstractness.

Inductive reasoning skills relate to the ability to construct concepts from examples. For learners with low inductive reasoning skills, many opportunities for observation should be provided. Therefore, learning systems can support these learners by providing a high amount of well-structured and concrete information with many paths. For learners with high inductive reasoning skills, the amount of information and paths should decrease to reduce the complexity of the hyperspace and hence enable learners to grasp the concepts more quickly. Moreover, information can be presented in a more abstract way.

Information processing speed determines how fast the learners acquire the information correctly. For learners with low information processing speed, only the important points should be presented. Therefore, the number of paths and information should decrease and the relevance of paths should increase. Additionally, the structure of the information should increase in order to speed up the learning process. In contrast, for learners with high information processing speed, the information space can be enlarged by providing a high amount of information and paths.

The associative learning skills link new knowledge to existing knowledge. In order to assist the association processes during the student's learning, the instruction needs to assist the recall (revisit) of learned information, to clearly show the relationships of concepts (new to existing), and to facilitate new or creative association/insight formation by providing information of the related domain area. A high amount of information, different media resources, and many relevant paths help a learner with low associative learning skills to associate one concept to another. Furthermore, well-structured information makes linkage between concepts easier. In contrast, for learners with high associative learning skills, less structure of information allows them to navigate more freely and hence enhances the learning speed. Additionally, the relevance of the paths should decrease to enlarge the information space.

10.3.2 Adaptivity Based on Learning Styles

Looking at the Felder-Silverman learning style model, some systems exist that provide adaptivity based on dimensions of FSLSM. All these systems aim at providing courses that fit to the learning style preferences of the learners. In the following section, we discuss the possible adaptation features for each dimension of FSLSM.

The sequential/global dimension is often used in adaptive systems. For example, the TANGOW system provides adaptivity by modifying the order of tasks in the course (Paredes and Rodríguez 2004). For a sequential learning style, a more structured path through the learning material is provided, whereas global learners are presented with a more open course structure. Bajraktarevic et al. (2003) proposed a system that provides sequential learners with small chunks of text-only information and also hides all links apart from the next and back buttons for navigation in order to provide a more structured path. In contrast, for global learners, pages comprised elements such as a table of contents, summary, diagrams, overview of information and so on to give the learner an overall picture. Additionally and in agreement with Paredes and Podríguez, several links within the text were provided in order to provide an open structure. Similarly, Hong and Kinshuk (2004) suggested implementation rules to present the learning material step by step and to constrict links for sequential learners as well as to show global learners the big picture of the course and provide all links for them. The CS383 system (Carver et al. 1999) focused on the order of multimedia objects. For sequential learners, slide shows, hierarchical structured hypertext and media objects were listed with higher priority, whereas for global learners, lesson objectives, hypertext, a response system, a digital library, and media objects were recommended. Looking at learning management systems, a concept was proposed to present tests and exercises after each learning unit and therefore more frequently for sequential learners, whereas for global learners, these tests and exercises were recommended at the end of the chapter (Graf 2005). Furthermore, it is again suggested to hide links and highlight the back and next buttons for sequential learners and present outlines, show links within the text, and provide additionally a navigation menu for global learners.

With regard to the sensing/intuitive dimension, the TANGOW system provides adaptivity by modifying the order of presentation within tasks. For sensing learners, an example is presented first and then the explanation is given, whereas an intuitive learner gets first the explanation and then an example (Paredes and Rodríguez 2004). This feature is also suggested by Hong and Kinshuk (2004). Furthermore, they recommended more hands-on activities for sensing learners and more concepts and abstract content for intuitive learners. While the above-cited works adapted to the order of examples in the course, Graf (2005) suggested an increase in the number of examples for sensing learners. Furthermore, multimedia objects such as audio objects and interactive animations should be presented to sensing learners. In CS383 (Carver et al. 1999), slide shows, hypertext, a response system, a digital library and media clips are recommended for sensing learners, whereas for global learners, the learning objectives, slide shows, a response system and media objects are ranked highly.

Looking at the visual/verbal dimension, most adaptive systems work on the basis of providing visual learners with visual material such as graphics, diagrams and images, as well as animations, whereas courses for verbal learners are text-based or include audio objects (Carver et al. 1999; Graf 2005; Hong and Kinshuk 2004). Additionally, communication features are suggested for supporting verbal learners (Graf 2005).

Regarding the active/reflective dimension, Carver et al. (1999) argued that the nature of hypermedia systems inherently supports both active and reflective learning. These systems force students to make choices and look at specific learning material that facilitates active learning. On the other hand, reflective learning is supported since students can reflect and think about the material at any point in their studies. Therefore, no adaptivity regarding the active/reflective dimension is provided in CS383. Graf (2005) suggested providing more multimedia objects such as interactive animations, more exercises as well as communication features for active learners. Hong and Kinshuk (2004) agreed on the communication features and additionally suggested encouraging reflective learners to write summaries about the already-learned material.

10.4 Conclusion

In this chapter, we provided an overview about learner modelling with focus on cognitive traits and learning styles. We discussed how cognitive traits and learning styles can be identified. Investigations about the relationship between cognitive traits and learning styles were presented, showing how this additional information can be used to improve learner modelling. Since learner modelling enables a system to provide adaptivity, some adaptive features for cognitive traits and learning styles were shown.

More and more recent research is being done in modelling and providing adaptivity based on individual characteristics such as cognitive traits and learning styles. However, when considering systems that automatically detect the individual differences and use this information to provide adaptive instructions concerning short-term and long-term goals of learning, many issues are still open. For instance, further research is necessary on developing a stable approach for automatic learner modelling, which is not restricted to a specific system. Another open question concerns the application of different kinds of adaptivity. On the one hand, a short-term goal is to provide students with courses that fit their needs and make learning easier for them. On the other hand, long-term goals should include challenging learners with mismatched courses to train their weaker abilities and preferences and provide them with important life skills.

References

Bajraktarevic, N., Hall, W., Fullick, P. (2003). Incorporating learning styles in hypermedia environment: empirical evaluation. In *Proceedings of the Workshop on Adaptive Hypermedia and Adaptive Web-Based Systems*, Nottingham, UK (pp. 41–52).

Brusilovsky, P. (1994). The construction and application of student models in intelligent tutoring systems. *Journal of Computer and Systems Sciences International*, 32(1), 70–89.

Brusilovsky, P. (1996). Methods and techniques of adaptive hypermedia. *User Modeling and User-Adapted Interaction*, 6(2–3), 87–129.

Carver, C. A., Howard, R. A., Lane, W. D. (1999). Addressing different learning styles through course hypermedia. *IEEE Transactions on Education* 42(1), 33–38.

Cha, H. J., Kim, Y. S., Park, S. H., Yoon, T. B., Jung, Y. M., Lee, J.-H. (2006). Learning style diagnosis based on user interface behavior for the customization of learning interfaces in an intelligent tutoring system. In M. Ikeda, K. D. Ashley, T.-W. Chan (Eds.) *Proceedings of the 8th International Conference on Intelligent Tutoring Systems*, LNCS, vol. 4053 (pp. 513–524). Berlin Heidelberg New York: Springer.

Deary, I. J., Whiteman, M. C., Starr, J. M., Whalley, L. J., Fox, H. C. (2004). The impact of childhood intelligence on later life: following up the Scottish mental surveys of 1932 and 1947. *Journal of Personality and Social Psychology*, 86(1), 130–147.

Draper, S. W. (1996). Observing, measuring, or evaluating courseware: a conceptual introduction. In G. Stoner (Ed.), *Implementating learning technology*. Edinburgh: Learning Technology Dissemination Initiative (pp. 58–65).

Dunham, M. H. (2002). *Data mining: Introductory and advanced topics*. Upper Saddle River, NJ: Prentice Hall.

Felder, R. M., Silverman, L. K. (1988). Learning and teaching styles in engineering education. *Engineering Education*, 78(7), 674–681. Preceded by a preface in 2002: http://www.ncsu.edu/felderpublic/Papers/LS-1988.pdf Accessed 23 July 2006.

Felder, R. M., Soloman, B. A. (1997). Index of learning styles questionnaire. http://www.engr.ncsu.edu/learningstyles/ ilsweb.html. Accessed 30 April 2006.

Felder, R. M., Spurlin, J. (2005). Applications, reliability and validity of the index of learning styles. *International Journal on Engineering Education*, 21(1), 103–112.

García, P., Amandi, A., Schiaffino, S., Campo, M. (2007). Evaluating Bayesian networks' precision for detecting students' learning styles. *Computers and Education*, 49 (3), 794–808.

Graf, S. (2005). Fostering adaptivity in e-learning platforms: a meta-model supporting adaptive courses. In *Proceedings of the IADIS International Conference on Cognition and Exploratory Learning in Digital Age* (pp. 440–443). IADIS.

Graf, S., Kinshuk (2006a). An approach for detecting learning styles in learning management systems. In *Proceedings of the International Conference on Advanced Learning Technologies*. IEEE Computer Science, Alamitos, CA (pp. 161–163).

Graf, S., Kinshuk (2006b). Considering learning styles in learning management systems: Investigating the behavior of students in an online course. In *Proceedings of the First IEEE International Workshop on Semantic Media Adaptation and Personalization (SMAP 06)* (pp. 25–30). IEEE.

Graf, S., Lin, T., Jeffrey, L., Kinshuk (2006). An exploratory study of the relationship between learning styles and cognitive traits. In *Proceedings of the European Conference of Technology Enhanced Learning, Lecture Notes in Computer Science 4227* (pp. 470–475). Berlin Heidelberg New York: Springer.

Graf, S., Lin, T., Kinshuk (2008). The relationship between learning styles and cognitive traits – getting additional information for improving student modelling. *International Journal on Computers in Human Behavior*, 24(2), 122–137.

Honey, P., Mumford, A. (1982). *The Manual of Learning Styles*. Maidenhead: Peter Honey.

Hong, H., Kinshuk (2004). Adaptation to student learning styles in web based educational systems. In L. Cantoni, C. McLoughlin (Eds.), *Proceedings of World Conference on Educational Multimedia, Hypermedia & Telecommunications (ED-MEDIA)* (pp. 491–496).

Jensen, F. V. (1996). *An Introduction to Bayesian Networks*. Berlin Heidelberg New York: Springer.

Jonassen, D. H., Grabowski, B. L. (1993). *Handbook of Individual Differences, Learning, and Instruction*. Hillsdale, NJ: Lawrence Erlbaum.

Kashihara, A., Kinshuk, Oppermann, R., Rashev, R., Simm, H. (2000). A cognitive load reduction approach to exploratory learning and its application to an interactive simulation-based learning system. *Journal of Educational Multimedia and Hypermedia*, 9(3), 253–276.

Kinshuk, Lin, T. (2003). User exploration based adaptation in adaptive learning systems. *International Journal of Information Systems in Education*, 1(1), 22–31.

Kinshuk, Lin, T. (2004). Cognitive profiling towards formal adaptive technologies in web-based learning communities. *International Journal of WWW-based Communities*, 1(1), 103–108.

Kolb, D. A. (1984). *Experiential Learning: Experience as the Source of Learning and Development*. Englewood Cliffs, NJ: Prentice-Hall.

Kuljis, J., Liu, F. (2005). A comparison of learning style theories on the suitability for elearning. In M. H. Hamza (Ed.), *Proceedings of the IASTED Conference on Web Technologies, Applications, and Services* (pp. 191–197). ACTA.

Lin, T., Kinshuk (2004). Dichotomic node network and Cognitive Trait Model. In *Proceedings of IEEE International Conference on Advanced Learning Technologies*. IEEE Computer Science, Los Alamitos, CA (pp. 702–704).

Lin, T., Kinshuk (2005). Cognitive profiling in life-long learning. In C. Howard, J. V. Boettcher, L. Justice, K. Schenk, P. L. Rogers, G. A. Berg (Eds.), *Encyclopedia of International Computer-Based Learning* (pp. 245–255). Hershey, PA: Idea.

Litzinger, T. A., Lee, S. H., Wise, J. C., Felder, R. M. (2005). A study of the reliability and validity of the Felder-Soloman Index of Learning Styles. In *Proceedings of the ASEE Annual Conference*. American Society for Engineering Education.

Messick, S. (1976). Personal styles and educational options. In S. Messick (Ed.), *Individuality in Learning* (pp. 327–368). San Francisco: Jossey Bass.

Miller, G. A. (1956). The magic number seven, plus or minus two: some limit of our capacity for processing information. *Psychology Review,* 63(2), 81–96.

Moodle (2007). http://www.moodle.org. Accessed 6 January 2007.

Paas, F., Renkl, A., Sweller, J. (2003). Cognitive load theory and instructional design: recent developments. *Educational Psychologist*, 38, 1–4.

Paredes, P., Rodríguez, P. (2004). A mixed approach to modelling learning styles in adaptive educational hypermedia. *Advanced Technology for Learning*, 1(4), 210–215.

Rabiner, L. R. (1989). A tutorial on hidden Markov models and selected applications inspeech recognition. *Proceedings of the IEEE*, 77(2), 257–286.

Self, J. (1994). Formal approaches to student modelling. In G. I. McCalla, J. Greer (Eds.), *Student modelling: The Key to Individualized Knowledge-Based Instruction* (pp. 295–352). Berlin Heidelberg New York: Springer.

Sweller, J. (1988). Cognitive load during problem solving. *Cognitive Science*, 12, 257–285.

Van Zwanenberg, N., Wilkinson, L. J., Anderson, A. (2000). Felder and Silverman's index of learning styles and Honey and Mumford's learning styles questionnaire: how do they compare and do they predict academic performance? *Educational Psychology*, 20(3), 365–380.

Viola, S. R., Graf, S., Kinshuk, Leo, T. (2007). Investigating relationships within the index of learning styles: a data-driven approach. *International Journal of Interactive Technology and Smart Education*, 4(1), 7–18.

Zywno, M. S. (2003). A contribution to validation of score meaning for Felder-Soloman's index of learning styles. In *Proceedings of the ASEE Annual Conference*. American Society for Engineering Education.

11 Turning Potentials into Reality: Achieving Sustainable Quality in E-Learning Through Quality Competence

U.-D. Ehlers

11.1 Introduction

Starting from the importance of quality for today's E-Learning, in this chapter, the current debate is summarised, and a new concept of how quality can be developed in a sustainable way is presented. The concept is moving away from a mechanistic view of quality assurance to processes of quality co-development with quality-literate stakeholders and to negotiation-based permanent quality reflection in educational processes.

The previous chapters of the book showed that E-Learning as a concept refers to a variety of different forms of technology-enhanced learning, usually characterised as the use of knowledge, information and learning technology (KILT) to connect people with each other and/or to resources for learning purposes (formal, informal, non-formal). Because E-Learning can take many forms depending on the educational sector and learning scenario, related concepts of quality management, quality assurance and quality development also take many forms. It is clear today that there is no single path and no one-size-fits-all concept, but enhancing quality demands a continuous effort. Still, the question of quality gets to the heart of the learning debate – quality can be regarded more and more as a subjectively individual and collectively influential category: What should learning opportunities look like and how should they be structured, now and in the future? How do we meet the demand for high quality learning capacities that are needed to transform our societies into learning societies? Quality in the field of E-Learning is especially diverse because it brings together the fields of education, technology and economy in order to contribute to societal development, to innovate formal, non-formal and informal learning opportunities, and to empower learners as citizens to take part in our emerging learning and information societies. The debate on quality is a debate about how learning and education should look in the future and about values and cultures. It takes place on the basis of diverse experiences and convictions.

The current use of instruments and strategies shows that quality is a much sought after but diverse discussed topic: Wirth (2006) reports that an empirical study among European universities ($N = 241$) revealed that more than half of the institutions at least partly apply a quality model for E-Learning (53%) (PLS Ramboll Management 2004). The instruments used focus mainly on learner satisfaction or evaluation by external peers, creation of an internal quality system, external quality assessment, and guidelines as well as standards for course development. In addition to this, 24 universities reported that they applied the same quality assurance methods for E-Learning as they did for traditional educational settings (ibid). Research by Fraunhofer IPSI (2003) confirms these findings: in the corporate sector, user feedback is very much the focus. Only very few organisations are opting for quality certificates (7–8%, according to a study conducted by Unicmind 2002).

Balli et al. state that an increase of quality-related activities has taken place in recent years (Balli et al. 2002). In particular, the increasing number of country-, region- and even world-wide rankings and benchmarks indicate this development (see Danish Evaluation Institute 2003; Federkeil 2004). The reason for this rise in quality-related activities can be attributed to increasing competition, the improvement quality strategies themselves (see Falk 2000), a growing understanding of quality as a major differentiator on the market, and changing legal limiting factors (see Bötel and Krekel 2004, Bötel et al. 2002).

However, the debate is not so much characterised by accurate empirically defined concepts and operationalised notions but rather constituted of a dense bundle of a broad range of arguments, objectives, convictions and procedures (Terhart 2000). It is less characterised by its precise definition but rather by its positive connotation. The very impact of the word "quality" on behaviour demonstrates its meaning. The word merely signifies "composition" (Latin: *qualis*) but in everyday language it is used to distinguish a characteristic of an object as being of a higher calibre than the same characteristic of another object. Fröhlich and Jütte emphasise that, even if current quality management approaches are not completely satisfying yet, they at least must be seen as a chance to become more sensitive towards current challenges and innovative ways to solve quality issues (Fröhlich and Jütte 2004).

11.2 E-Learning Quality: A Field of Great Diversity

The following section gives an overview of the debate on quality and how it can be systematised. E-Learning quality – or educational quality in a wider context – is a diverse concept. It is not an absolute and fixed category but rather depends on the situation in which it is employed. No country has (yet) reached a social, political or academic consensus on what educational quality actually is. Different methods are used to assure quality, ranging from market-oriented instruments, government-driven consumer protection mechanisms and accreditation concepts to institutional strategies and individual instruments. Approaches can have an explicit intentional character or can be rather implicit when quality development is left to individuals' professional competences.

Defining quality is a normative act, referring to a specific context. Consequently, situations and interests always influence the definition of quality. This applies especially to quality in the sector of social and educational services, since the quality of those services is, by nature, only constituted in the moment of service provision itself and through a negotiation and co-production of the professional educational actor and the client.

To critically analyse quality, it is helpful to identify the basic points of the debate. We can distinguish between three fundamentally different aspects in the discussion (Ehlers 2003):

- Different interpretations of quality
- Different stakeholders with different perspectives on quality
- Different forms of quality (input, process, and output quality)

Together these three aspects provide a general frame of reference for the described debate.

One dimension is the different interpretation of the meaning of quality. Numerous definitions from various fields are available. For example, a widely used definition in economics is a product-oriented understanding, which views quality as a physical characteristic of an object. Of course such a definition cannot easily be transferred to the educational sector. Unlike businesses, education does not involve classic supplier-customer relationships. It is an association of co-producers. An E-Learning program supplies technology and content but it is up to the learners themselves to actively use it, that is, learn. This interaction between the learning environment and the learner is known as a co-production process. In education, we can currently identify about five different meanings of quality:

- Quality as an exception, describing the surpassing of standards
- Quality as perfection, describing the state of flawlessness
- Quality as functionality, referring to the degree of utility
- Quality as an adequate return, measured by the price-performance or cost-benefit ratio
- Quality as transformation, describing the above-mentioned co-producer relationship between the learner and the learning environment and referring to the learners' progress in terms of a learning process

However, there are not only different interpretations of quality but also different stakeholders' perspectives: the enterprise as a user of a training measure, the tutors supervising an E-Learning program, the human-resource managers who establish a framework for continuing education in their sector and the learners. Each of these players generally has divergent interests and differing quality requirements and interpretations. It is therefore important to regard quality not as a static element but as a negotiation process between different stakeholders involved in the social process.

Last but not least, quality can also refer to different educational processes or levels. We can cite the different levels of the famous quality triad by Donabedian (1980):

- E-Learning prerequisites (input or structure quality): availability or capability of the technological infrastructure, qualification of tutors, etc.
- The learning process (process quality): the interaction of learners, learning formats, corporate learning culture, learning content and desired training goals
- The result (output/outcome quality): the increase in learners' professional competence

Quality cannot be generalised. There is no direct relation between action and impact. Quality development – like education – is situated and rooted in the context of a culture and a learning environment. Defining quality, therefore, means navigating this multidimensional space. There is no easy answer or standard quality-assurance solution. We have to abandon the hope of only having to define quality criteria once to be able to appraise E-Learning services and formats properly in the future. A key factor for E-Learning thus will be a concise quality orientation that spans all processes and puts learners first. They must take the pole positions in the quality debate since their (professional) development is at stake – regardless of formal or informal environments.

Even more dimensions of diversity that influence the quality debate can be identified. There is, for example, the notion of quality in different subjects and topics. From an international perspective, cultural diversity places enormous challenges on the quality debate. Nagel (2004) reports that students' role in society is viewed quite differently in the Anglo-Saxon, Scandinavian or southern European countries. In Anglo-Saxon countries, he reports, students are seen as investors in their own career, in Scandinavian countries they are viewed as young citizens and in southern European countries as family members. It is evident that such differences in perception influence the structure of educational systems and have an impact on the answer to the quality question.

11.3 Methodology and Instruments to Develop Quality for E-Learning

Which tools and methods exist and how can they be understood and categorised? Recently there have been many efforts to design and implement instruments for quality development in education in general and in E-Learning in particular. Several publications systematically describe and explain these approaches and their respective backgrounds (see Gonon 1998; Riddy et al. 2002; Srikanthan and Dalrymple 2002).[1] The various existing publications reveal a large number of different concepts and approaches to quality management in the educational sector. Already a smaller study by the Danish Institute for Evaluation identifies and analyses up to 34 quality-assurance agencies in 24 countries (Danish Evaluation Institute 2003). A CEDEFOP study by Bertzeletou (2003) even identifies 90 national and international quality approaches for quality certification and accreditation. Woodhouse (2003) counts more than 140 quality approaches that are associated with the International Network of Quality Assurance Agencies in Higher Education (called INQAAHE). Most of these certification and accreditation bodies follow their own quality approaches and have their own evaluation, certification and accreditation offerings. Most of the mentioned studies and papers address traditional certification and accreditation frameworks for higher education. Only a few include newer quality

---

[1] See also the European Initiative, European Quality Observatory (http:/7www.eqo.info).

approaches that specifically focus on recent educational innovations and E-Learning. In the following, a brief overview of methods and instruments in the field of quality is given, based on (Ehlers and Pawlowski 2004).

11.3.1 Quality Management Approaches

Quality management (QM) approaches can be used to ensure or optimize the quality of an educational process. They generally do not follow a product-related quality understanding; they are directed at creation, implementation, and performance processes. According to this understanding, QM approaches focus on customer and, specifically, learner requirements for planning, implementing and providing a product (for example, an educational product such as an E-Learning course). Due to their generic scope, these approaches can be applied in different branches and contexts. For E-Learning, there are currently no generally recognized quality management approaches. However, there is increasing development of concepts that are based on the generic process orientation of quality management approaches, and that are then especially adapted for the educational field or E-Learning.

11.3.2 Quality Assessment on the Basis of Criteria Lists and Checklists

Quality criteria are defined as characteristic attributes of a learning program whose learning effectiveness has been proven in a validity study. Many quality criteria lists, however, contain criteria for which no explicit proof exists, but are simply assumed to be effective for learning. Most quality criteria catalogues are normative-static tools for the assessment, development and selection of learning platforms, learning software or learning environments. Assessment tools based on quality criteria lists are relevant and popular because they seem to make it relatively easy to evaluate learning effectiveness, although this is usually only possible with time-consuming empirical methods. As a result, these tools enable people to assess the quality of a learning arrangement or learning software without prior empirical studies.

Meier (1995) points out that many quality criteria lists mainly contain criteria from the area of "screen interface design" or "technical usability". However, pedagogical/didactic criteria are often underrepresented. However, metasurveys on the learning effectiveness of multimedia learning environments show that, in particular, the didactic concepts implemented in E-Learning-modules and learning arrangements have a greater effect on the learning process than the so-called "delivery technology" that is used.

11.3.3 Evaluation Approaches for E-Learning

Evaluation approaches target the actual learning processes and situations that occur when E-Learning is used. These methods do not focus on a product itself, but on a learning process, and thus makes the learners the focus of attention.[2] Specialised evaluation approaches for assessing E-Learning require a learning-theoretical basis to determine which processes in media-supported learning affect each other and how. Only by this method is it possible to investigate and evaluate assumptions about how learners learn and whether or not they are learning effectively.

11.3.4 Standards for Quality and E-Learning

Standards are often misunderstood, especially in the education community. However, the intention of standardization is not, as is often assumed, to reduce and unify the didactic or technological options, but to standardize their description. The goal is to attain a greater transparency for all users of learning technologies (learners, teachers, etc.) and a greater interoperability, as well as to improve reusability. This is more and more important in E-Learning, particularly in global education markets. A progressive understanding of standardization in this sense focuses on the structured provision of information on learning resources, to enable learners, teachers and systems to adjust to the respective teaching/learning context. The complex field of standards can be classified into three segments (Ehlers and Pawlowski 2006):

- *Quality Standards* support quality development in organizations according to their specific needs and requirements.
- *Learning Technology Standards* deal with the interoperability of components of learning environments, such as authoring systems, learning management systems (LMS), and learning resources and services. The variety of these standards cover the aspects of content, management, actors and didactics.
- *Related standards* are used within quality or learning technology standards, such as technology, process, or legal standards.

---

[2] Strictly speaking, the assessment of e-learning offers using quality criteria lists is also a form of quality evaluation, a so-called expert assessment or product evaluation. However, since it clearly differs from more process-related evaluation approaches in its conceptual approach and implementation, both types – quality criteria assessment and evaluation – are considered separately (Tergan 2000).

11.3.5 Further Quality Approaches for E-Learning

In addition to the previously described quality approaches, there are other methods for assessing or assuring quality. These include approaches such as:

- Benchmarking (for example, *Quality on the Line* by the Institute of Higher Education Policy, USA, 2001), which attempts to compare different offers (for example, from E-Learning providers) on the basis of specified criteria.
- Accreditation and certification approaches (for example, national or regional accreditation offices), in which providers of E-Learning must submit to a one-time or regular audit and are then awarded a certificate.
- Quality mark organisations (for example, the British Learning Association, eQCheck Canada and the Finnish E-Learning Quality Mark) are usually associations of several organisations in the educational field that award a mark of quality to member organisations that meet previously determined criteria.

Comparing different concepts and approaches to assure and develop quality is difficult because of the concepts' different scope and nature. However, there have been attempts to develop reference models, such as the European Quality Observatory Model (Ehlers et al. 2004) or the one made by the International Standardisation Organisation (ISO/IEC 2005). Wirth (2006) suggests a simple but effective method to categorise different quality approaches and instruments. Figure 11.1 shows that he uses the well-known Deming-Circle terminology (see, for example, Seghezzi 2003) for categorisation:

- Field 1 represents large international organisations that drive standardisation and the development of generic quality management approaches (Bötel et al. 2002; Demski and Lorenz 1995; Gonon 1998). Their transferability to the educational sector is still controversial. Therefore three developments have recently been initiated (ISO 10015, DIN PAS 1032, DIN PAS 1037) which focussed specifically on the educational context.
- In field 2, recommendations (i.e., American Federation of Teachers 2000; Hollands 2000), guidelines (i.e., Open and Distance Learning Quality Council 2001) or criteria catalogues (Gottfried et al. 2002) and checklists (American Council on Education 2001; Bellinger 2004) are listed.
- Field 3 represents accreditation and certification approaches that focus on different educational aspects and levels.
- Finally, in field 4, awards and prices are summarised.

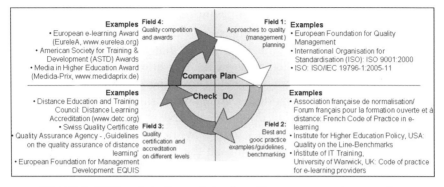

Fig. 11.1. Different starting points of quality management approaches

11.4 Quality Literacy: Competencies for Sustainable Quality Development

How can quality development lead to a sustainable improvement of educational processes? In the following section it is argued that, independently of the implementation of a specific quality management approach, the quality of its implementation process has a great effect on the improvement of the learning experiences. A comprehensive quality management system, for example, can lead to over-structured administrative processes of an organization and stifle teachers' pedagogical desires. An efficient documentation of processes or the existence of quality guidelines do not guarantee effective teaching and learning scenarios, A quality strategy in education is only sustainable if it aims at improving the competencies of the actors, who are involved in the implementation of this strategy. Actors must be able to implement a quality strategy according to their specific context and to ensure that it becomes an instance of reflection and improvement of professional pedagogical behaviour. Involvement, participation, reflection and improvement of professional pedagogical behaviour are therefore taken as the normative reference points to indicate the success, and sustainability, of a quality strategy. Such an understanding is directed towards a professionalisation of pedagogical processes and to change the actors' views of quality development towards a perspective of reflection and development of teaching practice.

The concept is highly relevant today because research indicates reservations towards the effectiveness of quality strategies to improve the quality of the learning processes in general and of E-Learning in particular (Eaton 2003; Fröhlich and Jütte 2004; Leef 2003; Simon 2001). Often it is argued that there is a danger of certified input processes and output processes to become inflexible, dictatorial rules that may stifle future innovations and quality improvements. With regard to the use of E-Learning, Tulloch and Sneed conclude that even traditional quality systems in higher education mislead many institutions toward imitating classical face-to-face training instead of fostering and leveraging strategic advantages of media-supported learning scenarios (Tulloch and Sneed 2000). Meyer in particular draws a negative picture of accreditation: Accreditation has become a battlefield between those who would use traditional accrediting standards to forestall the changes wrought by distance education and those who would change accreditation" (Meyer 2002). Friend-Pereira et al. (2002) agree to this by concluding that quality accreditation may become dangerous if it only serves legitimation purposes. They point to moving to a stage of quality development in which the stakeholders change their behaviour and reflect upon their professional values and attitudes as a result of a quality development process. Quality development in this sense becomes a matter of further developing a professional attitude stimulated by a set of processes, rules and values which are understood and incorporated, and lead to improved behaviour in educational contexts, both on the side of the provider as well as on the side of the clients (see also Sect. 11.5 for an exact account on how clients and providers are co-producing quality).

Recently, an empirical study by Lagrosen et al. (2004) indicated that internal quality evaluation gains more and more in importance compared to external quality assessments. This is also confirmed and further elaborated by an international study by Ehlers (2005), which shows that a distinction can be made between so-called explicit quality strategies (official instruments and concepts of quality development, designed either externally or internally) and implicit procedures, in which quality development is left to individuals and is not part of an official strategy:

- Quality strategies or instruments coming from externally adopted approaches such as ISO, EFQM and BAOL Quality Mark (explicit)
- Quality strategies that are developed within an organisation (explicit)
- Quality development that is not part of an official strategy but is rather left to individuals' professional activities (implicit)

The survey shows that internally (35%) and externally (26%) developed quality approaches are used. One quarter of the respondents (24%) work in institutions in which quality development is left to the staff. Around one out of six (15%) use no quality strategies for E-Learning. Overall, therefore, around four out of ten respondents (39%) do not use any official quality strategy. Of course, quality assurance also has the role of differentiating educational providers from each other but must first and foremost have an impact on the learning processes. Independent quality assurance has to meet high expectations, process complex relationships and at the same time must allow for an efficient evaluation and economic justification (Fröhlich and Jütte 2004).

Background information: The concept of quality literacy is based on the assumption that quality in education is the result of competent behaviour of stakeholders involved in an attempt to develop quality. The scientific approach that is used to derive the concept of quality literacy builds upon the concept of Total Quality Management as described by Horine and Lindgren (1995) and applies the concept of Media Literacy as formulated by Baacke (1996) to the field of quality development. This application is done on the theoretical basis of the concept of action competence relating to elaborations of Weinert (1999) and van der Blij (2002) and also taking into account the connection between knowledge, skills and competence according to North (1998, 2005). In the following section we describe a set of that are necessary to perform quality development processes.

11.4.1 The Four Dimensions of Quality Literacy

Quality literacy can be described as a set of four central elements that contribute to carrying out successful quality development in education. They do not constitute distinct factors of quality literacy, but rather differentiate the inner structure of the concept of quality literacy:

1. Dimension: Quality Knowledge
This dimension addresses the "pure" knowledge about the possibilities of today's quality development and up-to-date quality strategies in E-Learning and education. The term quality strategies refers to all guidelines, structures, rules, tools, checklists or other measures that have the goal of enhancing the quality of an E-Learning-scenario. There are two sub-dimensions to quality knowledge: informational and an instrumental, which go back to Ryle's (1949) classification of "knowing that" and "knowing how":

- *Informative*: The informational dimension refers to information and knowledge about quality systems, tools and procedures. It is about having access to information resources, primary as well as secondary, and understanding the system of quality development. Typical examples are questions such as: What is a quality approach? What is evaluation? quality management? quality assurance? quality development?

- *Instrumental*: The instrumental dimension refers to the knowledge of how to use and apply a certain specific tool, such as an evaluation questionnaire, or how to use a list of criteria or guidelines for a specific context. It answers questions such as: How can an evaluation questionnaire be applied in an educational context such as in a classroom? How can a set of benchmarks be used to assess my system against another one? It does *not*, however, relate to the competence of implementing a quality system with a certain intention, such as reducing the drop-out rate of a course. This is covered through the dimension of quality experience.

2. Dimension: Quality Experience

This dimension describes the ability to use quality strategies with a certain intention. It is based on the experiences that actors have with quality development, and with applying quality measures and strategies to educational scenarios. It can be differentiated from the instrumental knowledge dimension because it refers not only to the pure application of quality strategies or tools but also covers the feedback analysis and initiating improvement processes. That means that, in addition to the instrumental knowledge of quality strategies, this dimension also carries an intention and a goal with it. Quality experience refers to the ability to use existing quality strategies (e.g., guidance and consulting concepts) to generate data about educational processes in order to improve them. It answers questions such as: How can I use quality strategies in a certain way to improve the educational process?

3. Dimension: Quality Innovation

This dimension relates to the ability that goes beyond the simple use of existing instruments and strategies. It refers to the modification, creation and development of quality strategies and/or instruments for one's own purpose. An innovative and creative aspect is important for this dimension: Adaptation and creativity here are understood as the further development and reorganisation of existing quality strategies within a given context; innovation means inventing and developing new strategies for quality development:

- *Adaptation*: This sub-dimension refers to the ability to adapt an existing quality strategy or tool to one's own context. It goes thus beyond the pure usage of an existing tool, needs deeper understanding of it, within the given methodological framework and demands for *creativity*. Typical questions are: How can a certain quality management concept be extended to a number of processes and categories in order to adapt it to the organisation's specific needs?

- *Creation/Innovation*: The creation/innovation dimension describes the ability to think beyond existing strategies and to go further than merely modifying them. It describes the ability to invent a complete new quality system. Such self-developed systems are often used for organisations' internal purposes when existing approaches do not cover the specific goals and requirements. An example would be the development of a new evaluation questionnaire for the assessment of a course when existing tools fail to analyse the desired aspects. Also it could be the development of a new method of consultation with learners before a course starts in order to pre-assess their needs and goals.

4. Dimension: Quality Analysis

Quality Analysis relates to the ability to analyse the processes of quality development critically in light of one's own experiences and to reflect upon one's own situation and context. It enables actors to evaluate different objectives of quality development and negotiate between different perspectives of stakeholders. To "analyse critically" means to consider the ability of differentiation and reflection of existing knowledge and experiences in light of quality development challenges. For learners this would mean to be aware of the responsibility that they have for quality in education as a co-producer of learning success. For providers this means to enable flexible negotiation processes in the educational offerings, and to respect individual objectives and preferences as well as societal contexts and organisational structures in their definition of quality objectives for education. Two sub-dimensions can be differentiated: analytic and reflexive:

- *Analytic Quality Analysis*: The analytic dimension covers the process of analytically examining the meaning and the debate of quality in education. It is the ability to move within the framework of the quality discourse, to contribute analysis and to understand the different influences, starting from the market perspective and business models, taking into account technical and pedagogical aspects. Analytic quality analysis answers the question: What is the state of the quality discussion and what are important developments in the debate?

- *Reflexive Quality Analysis*: The reflexive dimension is directed towards the analysis of one's own situation. It is the ability to set quality goals for one's own individual or organisational context, and to position oneself in the quality debate. The reflexive dimension emphasises the ability to understand future challenges in educational quality development, rethink one's current quality situation and develop a strategy to meet future challenges. A typical field of the reflexive quality analysis competence is the development of future goals, leitmotivs, and strategies either for oneself as the individual learner or for an organisation.

11.5 Quality Development in Education and E-Learning: A Negotiation Process

In the following section, a quality model that shows the interactive nature of quality development in education is presented (Fig. 11.2). It is inspired by a model of Meyer and Mattmüller (1987), which is taken from the field of service quality and adapted to the context of education. It connect to the above-described characteristics of quality development and the suggested concept of quality literacy. The model shows that quality is first only a potential that has to be realised in the educational situation through mutual negotiation and stock-taking of providers and clients. It combines the concepts of Donabedian (1980) with the concepts from Grönroos (1984), and divides quality into three processes: potential, process, and outcome quality. These processes are each differentiated for both the provider and the client. The model is extended by adding phase categories: (a) needs analysis, (b) realisation and (c) incorporation. For each phase the concept of quality literacy applies in a different way.

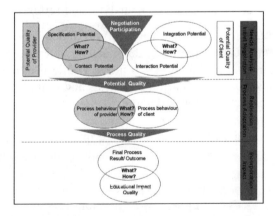

Fig. 11.2. Participative model for quality development (cited from Ehlers 2007: adaptation of Meyer and Mattmüller 1987)

Potential Quality/Needs Analysis Phase

In this phase the needs for quality, the situation and the context of the educational scenario are subject to examination. The potential quality of the provider is characterised by the capacity of its staff and the potential of its equipment, materials and infrastructure. The *specification potential* is the provider's ability to react to the client's individual needs and preferences in order to provide the educational environment. The *contact potential* is the ability to enter into a negotiation process with the client. It relates to expertise in the field of pedagogic-diagnostic abilities and also covers the means of communication and contact possibilities. The *contact potential* aims at building trust with the clients and establishing the basis for negotiation of the educational provision. All in all, the potential quality of the provider is about its capacity to interact with clients and react to their needs.

The model also sees a potential quality on the side of the client: The term *integration potential* points to the ability of the client to assess needs and to the client's self-reflection and analysis capacity. By that, the model allocates part of the responsibility for the quality of educational processes to the client. It gives importance to the fact that clients/learners have to be aware of their own needs and preferences in order to enter into a high-quality learning opportunity that is created in collaboration between themselves and the provider. A precise exploration of the integration potential by the provider can influence the educational provision enormously. The *interaction potential* further describes the client's abilities to contribute to a constructive negotiation process and to become part of a participative definition of educational quality. The client's background, former experiences and abilities to express his or her needs are influential categories for this potential.

Stakeholders who are involved in these processes need the capacity to evaluate and define the needs of all stakeholders involved in the educational scenario and negotiate between themselves to achieve a high quality of the learning environment (quality analysis). Additionally, knowledge about the possibilities of quality development and about quality strategies or good practice examples could be of help in the needs analysis phase.

The needs analysis phase leads to a decision for a quality strategy. For this, quality knowledge is needed. If none of the available strategies meet the identified requirements, a new quality strategy has to be developed. For this, two competencies are especially important: quality knowledge and quality analysis skills. For the development of an individual strategy, the ability of quality innovation, that is, the ability to creatively and innovatively develop a suitable concept, gains importance.

Process Quality/Realisation and Process Adaptation Phase

In the realisation phase, a quality strategy that corresponds to the analysed needs is implemented into an organisation and continuously adapted to the specific organisation's needs. The process quality is the result of interaction between the clients and the learning environment. The model shows that the only thing that partial qualities have in common is that they are divided into two parts. This relates back to the work of Grönroos (1984), who differentiates *what* the client and the provider co-construct and *how* they do it. An interesting notion of Grönroos's concepts is the emphasis that, apart form the purely functional process of providing a service, for all partial qualities, the emotional or human service quality is an influential factor. However, this is difficult to conceptualise into an operational model. Also Lethinen and Lethinen (1991) refer to these qualities and name them "physical quality" and "interactive quality".

In the realisation phase, quality instruments and tools can be used. The use of models and instruments for quality development, for example, checklists, process descriptions and/or evaluation questionnaires, requires a high number of quality experiences. The adaptation of these instruments and models demands innovation and modification and is conceptualised in the dimension of quality innovation. Critical analysis and assessment form an integral part of this phase. Quality Analysis thus becomes important.

Outcome Quality/Incorporation and Impact Phase

In the end, quality development is always directed towards the modification of the behaviour of individual actors of an organisation, its tutors or teachers or the authors of courses, etc. The incorporation phase relates to the actual impact, that is, the outcome of quality development. In the quality model, the resulting quality represents the educational impact that is evoked through the process of co-construction of educational opportunities. Meyer and Mattmüller (1987) subdivide this quality component into one part that is immediately recognisable and another part that is the long-term impact quality. For educational processes, this division into two types of results is important because often the long-term results are more important than the short-term effects (e.g., the competencies that can be used when the employee is back to his/her workplace).

In particular, this phase looks into the actual effect of the quality strategies. "Incorporation" means that the new values, norms and concepts that are inherent in newly introduced quality concepts have to be incorporated by the actors who use them and affect their everyday professional behaviour. For example, it is not only important that an evaluation questionnaire be selected and distributed and the feedback analysed, it is as important that the results have an impact on the educational process. In the incorporation phase, we therefore examine whether the changed processes and new values that are suggested through a new quality strategy are incorporated into the activity patterns of the stakeholders. Critical analysis skills and evaluation experiences are necessary for this phase. Quality analysis, therefore, is crucial in this phase. Table 11.1 gives an overview of the relevant questions that are addressed for each of the partial qualities.

Table 11.1. Overview of partial qualities of the participatory model for quality development (adapted from Meyer and Mattmüller 1987)

Potential quality of provider	Specification potential	Which learning opportunities and boundaries does the educational offer contain with regard to the individual situation and preference of the client? (Is it possible to choose time, place, teachers, learning groups and learning environments?) How is the educational environment adapted to the individual characteristics and preferences of the client?
	Contact potential	Which possibilities to specify their learning needs exist for the clients? (e-communication means, office hours, educational counselling offers, etc.) How competent are the contact persons? (diagnostic abilities, flexibility, communicative competencies, etc.)
Potential quality of client	Integration potential	What are the expectations and needs of the client? What is the client's attitude and preference towards the educational experience? What meaning does the educational experience have for the client?
	Interaction potential	How good is the client's capacity to communicate his/her needs or to integrate them into the educational context? (communicative abilities, self reflection processes, self-diagnostic abilities, etc.) What is the client's situation and background? Can the client enter into a beneficial educational process?
Process quality	Process be-haviour of provider	How is the educational experience structured? How is the educational environment realised? Where are the strengths and weaknesses in the educational provision?
	Process be-haviour of client	How can the client realise the educational opportunities provided for his/her benefit? Where are the client's strengths and weaknesses in the educational process? (learning problems, misunderstandings, etc.)
Final process result	Final process result	Which procedures are used to determine the final process quality? How are these procedures applied?
	Educational impact	What is the educational impact for the client (e.g., in the workplace)? Is there a service of guidance/tutoring even after the course has ended?

The questions reveal that all partial qualities require differentiated competencies in order to be realised. The quality of all phases is then the result of quality-competent behaviour. The presented quality model is of heuristic value. It combines the different partial qualities with the phases of introducing a quality strategy and helps to differentiate them from each other. The model, which was originally constructed for the field of service quality, has been adapted to the field of educational provision. This adaptation shows that the quality can combine the different concepts mentioned before: co-construction and participation, as well as quality literacy within one model.

11.6 Summary and Conclusion

The chapter argues that quality improvement should aim first and foremost at improving e-educational processes, and should not address mainly external market success (certificates), administrative procedures (like quality management strategies sometimes do) or focus purely on technological parameters. Secondly, it is highlighted that educational improvement needs methodologies that allow stakeholders to participate and negotiate in the quality development process in order to turn potential qualities into realities.

Quality development in E-Learning is described as the result of a co-production between learners and their learning environments and can, in principle, not be defined ex-ante or prescriptively. In the end, this means that the result of an educational process cannot be steered and optimised like a production process. Quality strategies therefore cannot guarantee a high quality of learning processes but should rather aim at a professionalisation of the quality development process, both on the client's side and on the provider's side. Additionally, a set of four competencies that are seen as relevant for such a professionalisation of quality development processes are outlined.

The interactive nature of quality development is reflected in a quality model in Sect. 11.5, which subdivides overall E-Learning quality into three partial quality potentials: (1) The potential quality of the provider and the client has to be realised through interaction and negotiation. Potentials are then turned into (educational) processes. (2) The process quality in turn leads to results and the (3) outcome quality, which aims at having a long-term impact. The authors suggest connecting this threefold structure to a prototypical quality development process with (a) needs analysis, (b) a realisation/adaptation and (c) an incorporation/impact phase. Quality literacy has its role as a set of competencies that are needed as specific abilities in all phases.

In conclusion, we would like to stress that quality development runs the risk of remaining a purely technocratic process when it is not linked to a process of professionalisation of the stakeholders. Quality literacy is a prerequisite for quality development in an educational setting, on both the client's side and the provider's side. The described competencies allow acting in a competent way in the field of quality development and entering into a process of stimulating a quality culture with the aim of continuous improvement. The aim of developing quality literacy is a move towards a professionalisation of the quality debate.

References

American Council on Education (2001). *Distance Learning Evaluation Guide.* Washington, DC: American Council on Education.

American Federation of Teachers (2000). Distance education: guidelines for good practice. http://www.aft.org/higher_ed/downloadable/distance.pdf. Accessed 18 November 2003.

Baacke, D. (1996). Gesamtkonzept Medienkompetenz [Media Competence]. *Agenda. Zeitschrift für Medien, Bildung, Kultur.* March/April 1996, 12–14.

Balli, C., Krekel, E. M., Sauter, E. (2002). Qualitätsentwicklung in der Weiterbildung aus der Sicht von Bildungsanbietern – Diskussionsstand, Verfahren, Entwicklungstendenzen [Quality development in ongoing education from the perspective of providers]. In C. Balli, E. M. Krekel, E. Sauter (Eds.), *Qualitätsentwicklung in der Weiterbildung – Zum Stand der Anwendung von Qualitätssicherungs- und Qualitätsmanagementsystemen bei Weiterbildungsanbietern* (pp. 5–24). Bonn: Bundesinstitut für Berufsbildung.

Bellinger, G. (2004). Systems: Understanding the Way. Internet: http://www.systems-thinking.org/systems/systems.htm (cited 2008-05-13).

Bertzeletou, T. (2003). Quality Assurance in VET, Thessaloniki.

Bötel, C., Krekel, E. M. (2004). Trends und Strukturen der Qualitätsentwicklung bei Bildungsträgern [Trends and structures of quality development of educational providers]. In C. Balli, E. M. Krekel, E. Sauter (Eds.), *Qualitätsentwicklung in der Weiterbildung – Wo steht die Praxis?* (pp. 19–40). Bielefeld: Bertelsmann.

Bötel, C., Seusing, B., Behrensdorf, B. (2002). Qualitätssicherungs- und Qualitätsmanagementsysteme bei Weiterbildungsanbietern: Ergebnisse der CATI-Befragung [Qualityassurance, qualitymanagement in training institutions]. In C. Balli, E. M. Krekel, E. Sauter (Eds.), *Qualitätsentwicklung in der Weiterbildung – Zum Stand der Anwendung von Qualitätssicherungs- und Qualitätsmanagementsystemen bei Weiterbildungsanbietern* (pp. 25–44). Bonn: Bundesinstitut für Berufsbildung.

Danish Evaluation Institute (2003). Quality procedures in European higher education: an ENQA survey. ENQA Occasional Papers 5. http://www.enqa.net/texts/procedures.pdf. Accessed 22 December 2003.

Demski, M., Lorenz, T. (1995). Zertifizierung vonQualitätsmanagementsystemen bei Bildungsträgern. Renningen-Malmsheim.

Donabedian, A. (1980). *Explorations in Quality Assessment and Monitoring.* Ann Arbor: Health Administration.

Eaton, J. S. (2004). Accreditation and Recognition of Qualifications in Higher Education: the United States, in Quality and Recognition in Higher Education, OECD.

Ehlers, U.-D., Pawlowski, J. M. (2004). Qualitätsentwicklung im E-Learning: Ein Entscheidungsmodell für die Auswahl von Qualitätsansätzen in Europa, In Fietz, Gabriele, Godio, Christina, Mason, Robin (2004): E-Learning für internationale Märkte. Entwicklung und Einsatz von E-Learning in Europa. Bielefeld.

Ehlers, U.-D. (2003). Zum Stand der Forschung: Qualität beim E-Learning [State of the art in research for quality in e-learning]. In U.-D. Ehlers, W. Gerteis, T. Holmer, H. Jung (Eds.), *E-Learning-Services im Spannungsfeld von Pädagogik, Ökonomie und Technologie.* Bielefed: L³-Lebenslanges Lernen im Bildungsnetzwerk der Zukunft.

Ehlers, U.-D. (2005). A participatory approach to e-learning-quality. a new perspective on the quality debate. *LLine – Journal for Lifelong Learning in Europe,* XI/2005.

Ehlers, U.-D. (2007). Quality literacy – competences for quality development in education and e-learning. In *Educational Technology and Society,* 10(2). North, New Zealand: Palmerston.

Ehlers, U.-D., Pawlowski, J. M. (2006). *Handbook of Quality and Standardisation in E-Learning.* Berlin Heidelberg New York: Springer.

Ehlers, U.-D., Hildebrandt, B., Pawlowski, J. M., Teschler, S. (2004). The European quality observatory. enhancing quality for tomorrow's learners. In *Supporting the Learner in Distance Education and E-Learning, Proceedings of the Third EDEN Research Workshop* (pp. 138–145), Oldenburg, Germany.

Federkeil, G. (2004). CIIE-Alumni-Ranking: Ergebnisse einer vergleichenden Absolventenbefragung Humanmedizin des Centrums für Hochschulentwick-lung. Arbeitspapier 57, Gütersloh.

Fraunhofer IPSI (2003). Gemeinsam Online-Lernen: Technologien & Lernszenarien – Auswertung einer Umfrage des Fraunhofer IPSI bei Weiterbildungsanbietern im August/September 2003 [Online Learning Communities]. http://www.ipsi.fraunhofer.de/concert/projects_new/alba/Gemeinsam_Online_Lernen.pdf. Accessed 07 March 2004.

Friend-Pereira, J. C., Lutz, K., Heerens, N. (2002). European student handbook on quality assurance in higher education. http://www.esib.org/projects/qap/QAhandbook/QAhandbook.doc. Accessed 09 February 2004.

Fröhlich, W., Jütte, W. (2004). Qualitätsentwicklung in der wissenschaftlichen Weiterbildung [Quality development in scientific training]. In W. Fröhlich, W. Jütte (Eds.), *Qualitätsentwicklung in der postgradualen Weiterbildung: Internationale Entwicklungen und Perspektiven* (pp. 9–17). Berlin: Waxmann.

Gonon, Ph. (1998). Das internationale Argument in der Bildungsreform. Die Rolle internationaler Bezüge in den bildungspolitischen Debatten zur schweizerischen Berufsbildung und zur englischen Reform der Sekundarstufe II. Bern et al.

Gottfried, J. A., O'Doherty, J., Dolan, R. J. (2002). Appetitive and Aversive Olfactory Learning in Humans Studied Using Event-Related Functional Magnetic Resonance Imaging. In *The Journal of Neuroscience*, December 15, 2002, 22(24):10829-10837. Internet: http://www.jneurosci.org/cgi/content/abstract/22/24/10829 (cited 2008-05-13).

Grönroos, C. (1984). A service-oriented approach to marketing of services. *European Journal of Marketing*, 18(4), 36–44.

Hollands, N. (2000). Online testing: best practices from the field. http://198.85.71.76/english/blackboard/testingadvice.html. Accessed 10 April 2004.

Horine, J., Lindgren, C. (1995). Educational improvement using Deming's profound knowledge. *New Era in Education*, 76(1), 6–10, London.

ISO/IEC (2005). ISO/IEC 19796-1:2005. *Information Technology – Learning, Education, and Training – Quality Management, Assurance and Metrics – Part 1: General Approach*. Final Draft International Standard (FDIS), 2005.

Lagrosen, S., Seyyed-Hashemi, R., Leitner, M. (2004). Examination of the dimensions of quality in higher education. *Quality Assurance in Education*, 12(2), 61–69.

Leef, G. C. (2003). Accreditation is no Guarantee of Academic Quality. *The Chronicle of Higher Education*, 49(30), B17.

Lethinen, U., Lethinen, J. O. (1991). Two approaches to service quality dimensions. *The Service Industries Journal*, 11(3), 287–303.

Meier, A. (1995). Qualitätsbeurteilung von Lernsoftware durch Kriterienkataloge. In Schenkel, P., Holz, H. (eds.) (1995): Evaluation multimedialer Lernprogramme und Lernkonzepte, BIBB-Reihe Multimediales Lernen in der Berufsbildung. Nürnberg, pp.149–190.

Meyer, K. A. (2002). *Quality in Distance Education*. Focus on On-Line Learning. ASHE-ERIC Higher Education Report, 29(4), 1–121.

Meyer, A., Mattmüller, R. (1987). Qualität von Dienstleistungen [Quality of services]. Entwurf eines praxisorientierten Qualitätsmodells. *Marketing ZFP*, 9(3), 187–195.

Nagel, B. (2004). Recht in der Weiterbildung, In Krug, P./ Nuissl, E. (Ed.): Rechtshandbuch Weiterbildung, Neuwieda.

North, K. (1998). *Wissensorientierte Unternehmensführung, Wertschöpfung durch Wissen* [Knowledge oriented enterprise management]. Wiesbaden: Gabler.

North, K. (2005). *Kompetenzmanagement* [Competence management]. Wiesbaden: Gabler.

PLS Ramboll Management (2004). Studies in the context of the e-learning initiative: virtual models of European Universities (Lot 1): Final Report to the EU Commission, DG Education & Culture. http://wwwupload.pls.ramboll.dk/eng/Publications/PublicAdministration/VirtualModels.pdf. Accessed 01 October 2004.

Riddy, P., Fill, K. (2002). *Technological CSFs for E-Learning implementation.* pp. 15–19. In: McPherson, M., Henderson, L., Kinshuk (Eds.): Proceedings of the Workshop on The Changing Face of HE in the 21st Century: Critical Success Factors (CSFs) for Implementing E-Learning; held in conjunction with International Conference on Computers in Education (ICCE2002), 3-6 December 2002, Auckland, New Zealand. ISBN 0-473-09631-5.

Ryle, G. (1949). *The Concept of Mind.* New York: Barnes and Noble.

Seghezzi, H. D. (2003). Integriertes Qualitätsmanagement. Das St. Galler Konzept, 2. Aufl., München, Wien.

Simon, B. (2001). E-Learning an Hochschulen: Gestaltungsräume und Erfolgsfaktoren von Wissensmedien. Köln: Eul.

Srikanthan, G., Dalrymple, John F. (2002). Developing a Holistic Model for Quality in Higher Education. In *Quality in Higher Education*, v8 n3 pp. 215–24, Nov 2002.

Tergan, S.-O. (2004). Erfolgreiches E-Learning: Die Sicht der Wissenschaft. In Schenkel, P., Tergan, S-O. (2004): *Erfolgsfaktoren für E-Learning*, Heidelberg.

Terhart, E. (2000). Qualität und Qualitätssicherung im Schulsystem. Hintergründe - Konzepte - Probleme. In *Zeitschrift für Pädagogik*, 46, pp 809–830.

Tulloch, J. B., Sneed, J. R. (2000). *Quality Enhancing Practices in Distance Education: Teaching and Learning.* Washington, DC: Instructional Telecommunications Council.

Unicmind (2002). Die Nutzung von eLearning-Content in den Top350-Unternehmen der deutschen Wirtschaft [Use of e-learning content in the top 350 enterprises of Germany]. Eine Studie im Auftrag der unicmind.com AG. http://www.unicmind.com/unicmindstudie2002.pdf. Accessed 11 February 2004.

Weinert, F. E. (1999). *Konzepte der Kompetenz.* Paris: OECD.

Wirth, M. (2006). An analysis of international quality management approaches in E-Learning: Different paths, similar pursuits. In Ehlers, U.-D., Pawlowski, J. M., (Eds.), *Handbook on quality and standardization in E-Learning.* Springer, 2006, pp. 97–108, Heidelberg.

Woodhouse, D. (2003). The quality of quality assurance agencies. http://www.inqaahe.nl/public/docs/ThequalityofEQAs.doc. Accessed 30 July 2003.

12 Integration of Learning and Working: Convergent Processes and Systems

J.M. Pawlowski and M. Bick

12.1 Introduction

Learning is no longer limited to an institutional context such as schools or higher education. In this paper, we will show how learning should be organized in different contexts, such as the workplace or during leisure time. The main corresponding trend leading to changes for organizations and individuals is the trend of convergence. Thereby, this article focuses on two issues: (a) How can learning and business processes be integrated into a common process framework? and (b) How can the related systems be integrated to enable an efficient workflow?

The trend of convergence can be identified on different levels (Wilbers 2002; Wersig 1999). In most approaches, convergence is only limited to technological issues. However, implementing integrated systems means to take organizational and cultural changes into account as well. Convergence can be observed on the following levels:

- *Cultural Level*
  One of the most significant convergence trends is the trend of globalization. National systems need to be harmonized towards a common system. As an example, higher education systems are harmonized (Adoption of Master- and Bachelor-System, Bologna Process; Dumont and Sangra 2006). One of the challenges will be the harmonization whilst keeping the characteristics of educational systems, including their cultural uniqueness.

- *Organizational/Process Level*
  In organizations, learning processes are no longer separated from work processes. Learning processes are integrated into the day-to-day work. Additionally, responsibilities are changed: every employee is responsible for his/her own training. This also means that new solutions are to be found for learning outside the workplace during leisure time. Examples are workplace-oriented learning (Illeris 2004) and game-based learning (Prensky 2001; Gibson et al. 2006).
- *Systems' Level*
  Different systems, applications and tools converge towards a common performance improvement system. This includes improvement through availability of documents (document management systems), availability and generation of adequate content (content management systems), availability and exchange of knowledge (knowledge management systems), just-in-time learning (learning systems) and other business information systems.
- *Technological Level*
  On this level, several technologies are integrated, mainly influenced by the use of the internet. Desktop PCs have merged with mobile technologies (such as PDAs, Smartphones, Tablet PCs); web technologies have merged with digital TV and other business information systems.

Therefore, the trend of convergence leads to challenges for organizations: How do these trends influence the business model of an organization? How do they influence staff members and daily operations?

It is necessary (a) to monitor those trends as constraints influencing an organization and (b) to proactively take those changes into account. As a first step, it should be analyzed how synergies can be achieved. Typical synergies include, for example, improving the efficiency of processes, shortening project duration, the availability of training, avoiding data redundancies, improving cooperation. Therefore, we focus on two of the above-mentioned levels with the most significant synergy potentials: redesigning processes and systems.

This chapter provides a framework for the integration on those two levels and recommendations for organizations how to design processes and systems for an integrated learning and working environment. To illustrate the corresponding steps, an application scenario is presented showing the steps to a successful integration towards convergent systems.

12.2 Integration

How can business and learning processes and corresponding systems be designed and connected? This is the main question for decision-makers and all actors involved. A variety of research approaches and concepts has been developed and studied for the integration of information systems, specifically business information systems (Scheer 1992; Konstantas et al. 2006). Those approaches differ in the degree of integration and their methodology. Generally, several types of integration/coupling can be distinguished, both within an organization or between organizations (cf. Linthicum 2001; Hasselbring 2000; Bick and Pawlowski 2006):

- Data integration: Data is exchanged among and retrieved from several, usually heterogeneous sources.
- Application interface integration: Well-defined interfaces define the re-use of components and the logic of programs.
- Method integration: The method to handle a business process is re-used.
- Portal integration: Portals can integrate components of heterogeneous applications.
- Process integration: Processes are re-designed, re-organized and integrated.

As a first step, an organization needs to decide on the level of integration. This leads to many changes, implementation efforts, and impact. Whereas data integration can be implemented relatively easily, it does not have the same impact and synergies as a full-process integration and re-design. An information system is valued as integrated, when the following conditions are fulfilled:

- Business processes are modeled and related to each other.
- Interfaces between the corresponding information systems are well defined and data exchange is automized.
- Relevant data are identified, not redundantly stored and used by all corresponding systems.

However, a complete integration is not always feasible in the short term. A careful analysis of the efforts as well as the expected synergies has to be done. This also includes a careful risk analysis since the integration depends on a variety of success factors (cf. Lam 2005; Mashari and Zairi 1999), such as staff involvement, change procedures and implementation concepts. However, in most cases, the synergy effects will outperform the implementation efforts.

12.2.1 Process Integration

The need to integrate working and learning processes has been discussed extensively (cf. Torraco 1999; Illeris 2004). Workplace-oriented learning is the key concept whenever a problem or, more generally, a learning need occurs. This means that a business process is directly related to the corresponding learning process. As an example, when conflicts arise within a project, conflict-management training could be started to deal with the situation. This means that the project-management process should be connected to the training process, including the relevant systems.

Several concepts have been developed to achieve workplace-oriented learning or to integrate knowledge-intensive processes and learning processes (cf. Lytras et al. 2002). Most of the approaches focus on the integration of the actual learning process and the business process. Other related processes, such as administration, management, or development processes (e.g., how to efficiently develop learning materials), are usually still isolated. An integration of all related processes can lead to greater synergy effects.

Reasons for isolated and inefficient processes are not necessarily specific to the field of learning. Several reasons can be identified leading to a lack of process integration. Most success and failure factors are similar to business process reengineering projects (for a detailed description cf. Mashari and Zairi 1999). It is not the goal of this article to fully discuss all success factors and obstacles. However, when implementing integrated processes, adopters should be aware of potential obstacles, such as organizational resistance; lack of organizational readiness for change; lack of commitment, support and leadership; improper information system integration and inadequate information system development.

In process integration projects, several typical steps have to be performed. It is obvious that processes need to be analyzed concerning their integration potentials. Typical tasks in this field are (1) process identification, (2) process modeling, (3) process analysis, (4) process management/re-design. However, processes are different from organization to organization. There is no one-size-fits-all solution. Since many organizations, especially educational organizations, have not specified and described their processes, it might be necessary to start with modeling processes and systems in an organization.

12.2.2 Process Integration Using Reference Models and Standards

With regard to the above-mentioned typical tasks we introduce an exemplary solution based on standards:

Process Modeling

To identify integration potentials, it is necessary to carefully model and analyze business as well as learning processes. To minimize modeling and specification efforts, it is useful to base process descriptions on *reference models and standards.* Those models provide a framework for processes, usually specific for a branch or sector (Fettke and Loos 2003). Generic models exist for different domains, for example, e-business organizations or educational organizations. An organization should model its business processes using these as a blueprint.

We recommend two models from the variety of reference models and use them as an example how to integrate processes: The Essen Learning Model (Pawlowski 2001) for the field of E-Learning, and the ebXML standard (UN/CEFACT OASIS 2001) for modeling generic business processes. By comparing and merging those models, we show how typical business processes are related to typical learning processes and how synergies are identified.

For the field of E-Learning, the Essen Learning Model distinguishes the following process categories and processes/components to be considered for E-Learning (Table 12.1):

Table 12.1. Typical processes for E-Learning

Category	Processes/components
Management and administration	Project management, configuration management, quality management, role administration, course administration, test administration, reporting
Development	Context modelling, content development, method selection, presentation, communication, evaluation
Learning process	Enrolment, learning activity, support, test, portfolio

As the model for generic business processes, ebXML distinguishes the following categories (UN/CEFACT OASIS 2001) (Table 12.2):

The ebXML model also provides typical sub-processes for each of those process categories, which can be used as a blueprint when modeling business processes in an organization. Furthermore, ebXML describes typical data exchanges and exchange formats to facilitate the exchange process between business partners. Those formats can be used to identify whether a typical process output can be used for learning or knowledge management processes. As an example, in the category "Human Resources", student data, enrolment data or transcripts are used. Those should be integrated with data within an LMS administration component.

Table 12.2. ebXML processes

Category	Sample processes/components
Procurement	Bid submission
	Contract negotiation
	Purchase order preparation
	Receiving
Human resources	Hiring
	Training
	Payroll management
	Personnel deployment
Transportation	Loading
	Shipping
	Packaging
Manufacturing	Product development
	Product design
	Assembly
	Quality control
Marketing & sales	Advertising use & campaigning
	Marketing management
	Sales calling
	Customer credit management
Customer service	After sales service
	Warranty construction
Financing	Loan management
	Stock subscriptions and sales
	Dividend policy
Administration	Accounting
	Financial reporting
	Executive management

As a result of this step, an organization should describe both their business and learning processes. Based on this description, the processes are analyzed in the next phase.

Process Analysis

Within the process analysis, the main question is to identify synergies between the models. As a first step, it is necessary to anticipate knowledge and learning requirements in business processes. Those requirements arise, in particular, in processes with a high degree of complexity, ill-structured processes and processes that lead to organizational changes. Therefore, the following questions arise:

- Which business processes and systems will require learning/training materials?
- Which processes will require extensive knowledge sharing?
- How can those materials be generated from existing information?
- How can the actors interact to design a common process?

From those questions, typical integration tasks can be derived:

- *Process Overlaps*: In the event of process overlaps, these connections should be well defined and lead to a connected, inter-related process. For example, for most business processes, experience sharing should be an integral part of the process and thus has to be included in the process model.
- *Shared Services and Systems*: For many processes, common services and systems can be defined. For example, "staff administration" is a service that is used by different departments or systems.
- *Information/Data Integration*: A variety of data/information can be used by different processes. For example, in many production processes a demand for learning or knowledge exchange arises. Each business process should be analyzed to see whether materials that can be used for learning purposes (e.g., scenario extraction) are produced. For example, in software testing, a variety of scenarios are developed in the test phase. Those can be used to design realistic case studies or simulations. Furthermore, in daily operations, problems occur and are solved by exchanging knowledge between staff members. To make the problem and the solution transparent, one must codify it in a knowledge base and, if the problem occurs regularly, use it to generate training materials.
- *Cooperation process*: For all of the above tasks, it is necessary to define a process to intitiate cooperative activities between staff members from different departments. Therefore, a cooperative process should be set up in order to work towards a common goal: to define an efficient business process including learning and knowledge requirements and demands.

Each process of an organization should be analyzed for possible overlaps and for learning/knowledge demands. For example, which learning demands can/will arise in the manufacturing process should be analyzed. For each process, it should be determined (1) if there is integration potential and (2) which kind of integration task is required.

The table below (Fig. 12.1) shows an analysis grid for processes, based on the standard process definitions by the Essen Learning Model and ebXML. For each process, integration potentials should be identified in the categories shown above. The table only shows a portion of the processes of an organization to illustrate the analysis process. The processes in the left column are the source processes; the processes in the first row denote the target processes. For example, the manufacturing process (source) has influences towards the authoring process (target) since problems in the manufacturing process can directly serve as scenarios for learning environments.

	Manufacturing	Human Resources	Customer Service	...	Knowledge Identification	Knowledge Sharing	...	Learning: Authoring	Learning Process	...
Manufacturing	▓				SS	PO		ID	PO	
Human Resources		▓			SS	ID		PO[4]	PO	
Customer Service			▓		PO	PO		SS[5]	PO	
...										
Knowledge Identification	PO[1]	ID[3]	PO		▓	▓		SS	SS[6]	
Knowledge Sharing	SS	SS	PO		▓	▓		SS	PO	
...										
Learning: Authoring	ID[2]	PO	PO		PO	PO		▓		
Learning Process	SS	SS	PO		SS	SS			▓	
...										

PO Process Overlap (includes SS and ID)
SS Shared Service (includes ID)
ID Information / Data Integration
▓ not subject to this analysis

Sample Integration Statements
[1] Within the design process, potential problems should be identified and added to the knowledge base
[2] Real data from manufacturing situation should be provided to training developers during the design and the production process
[3] The HR system should provide user data to the organization's yellow pages
[4] User requirements should be determined in cooperation of the HR department and course authors
[5] Developers should develop FAQ about typical requests for the customer services
[6] A common database should be provided for identifying typical problems

Fig. 12.1. Simplified process analysis framework

The table shows what kind of integration is possible and in which direction the integration potential occurs (e.g., data integration from customer service to the learning process). Each integration task should be clearly described in a separate description.

The table shows only the highest level of integration tasks (e.g., process overlaps include shared services and data integration) between the three process types (business, knowledge, learning), not the internal integration tasks. In many cases, however, internal process optimization potentials are also identified and realized.

Based on such an analysis, the following should be defined:

1. Which processes and systems can be integrated
2. Which processes should be redesigned and how
3. Which information/data should be shared
4. Which actors should be involved in cooperative processes

Using this framework, an organization can define the main overlaps as well as learning and knowledge demands. It shows how processes should be inter-related and re-designed in an integrated way.

12.3 Systems Integration Based on Learning Technology Standards

Various systems are usually used within the context of an educational organization, such as enterprise resource planning, human resources, authoring, learning management, knowledge management and document management systems (Bick and Pawlowski 2006). As shown above, there are several opportunities to relate and integrate those systems, e.g., by data or application interface integration. In this section, we will illustrate how standards, especially learning technology standards, can be used to integrate systems.

Generally, learning technology standards provide a format to exchange data on specific aspects of learning environments and scenarios. The main question is how those standards can be used to design interfaces and integrate data between business, knowledge and learning processes.

Figure 12.2 shows a classification for standards in the field of learning, education, and training. Such learning technology standards deal with the interoperability of components of learning environments, such as authoring systems, learning management systems (LMS) and learning resources and services. Different standards have been developed for the description of content (Learning Object Metadata, LOM, IEEE 2002), for the interaction between LMS and learning objects (Sharable Content Object Reference Model, SCORM, Dodds and Thropp 2004), for didactical scenarios (IMS

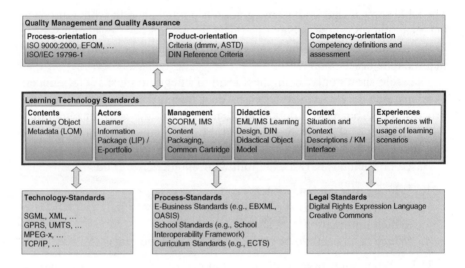

Fig. 12.2. Classification of learning technology standards (Pawlowski and Bick 2006)

Learning Design, Koper et al. 2002; DIN Didactical Object Model, DIN 2004), and for actor/user modelling (Learner Information Package, LIP, Smythe et al. 2001).

Additionally, several new specifications can be used as a tool for information/data integration. For example, the DIN Didactical Object Model can be used to describe learning/problem scenarios and experiences.

Table 12.3. Learning technology standards for systems integration

Standard/specification	Purpose
Learning object metadata	Description of resources, e.g., learning materials, knowledge objects
SCORM	Transfer of objects (e.g., learning materials, knowledge packages) across systems
Learner information package	Description of staff data, competencies, learning experiences
Learning design	Description of scenarios, extraction of scenarios from business processes
DIN didactical object model	Description of scenarios, description of context and situations, description of experiences

These standards (Table 12.3) provide a basis for the exchange of information between business and learning processes. However, several issues are not yet fully addressed (Bick and Pawlowski 2007):

- *Context Description*: One of the main advantages in E-Learning is the possibility to personalize learning processes. The adaptation of learning environments should be based on the context of the learner. However, there is currently no adequate context specification that can be used by authoring or learning management systems. Potential candidates for standardization are (a) the DIN Didactical Object Model for a rough description of the organizational context (DIN 2004) and (b) the approach of context and culture metadata (cf. Pawlowski and Richter 2007) to describe a variety of aspects, including countries, organizations, culture, technical infrastructure and legal systems.

- *Experiences*: Re-use highly depends on its usefulness for actors in a given context. To determine usefulness, it is necessary to see how previous usage scenarios have been performed and how users perceived the usage. Therefore, it is necessary to find a representation of experiences and performance indicators. A promising approach in this field is the analysis of previous usage scenarios by Wolpers et al. (2007) and again the DIN Didactical Object Model (DIN 2004; Pawlowski and Bick 2006).

The above-mentioned standards and approaches provide formats for many integration tasks. They can be used to design shared services and systems and to integrate data and information. However, currently only learning-related systems use those standards. Therefore, it is necessary to develop mappings of the specifications to other services and specifications, for example, in knowledge management systems and business information systems.

12.4 A Step-by-Step Guide Towards Process and Systems Integration Based on Standards

Following the main objective of this chapter, we illustrate how processes and systems can be designed to have a common basis for business, knowledge and learning systems. We introduce a practical application scenario and describe the phases of the integration:

- Awareness building and context setting
- Process analysis and redesign
- Designing shared services and systems
- Integrating data and information

The scenario shows samples for those steps and gives practical recommendations on how to realize integration projects.

12.4.1 Application Scenario

As an example, we will show the integration of business (production), learning and knowledge management processes (a full discussion of this sample is described in Pawlowski and Bick (2006)). The corresponding scenario stresses that related topics are handled by different departments and isolated processes. However, by integrating processes, systems and data, synergies can be created. Figure 12.3 shows typical relations between the processes:

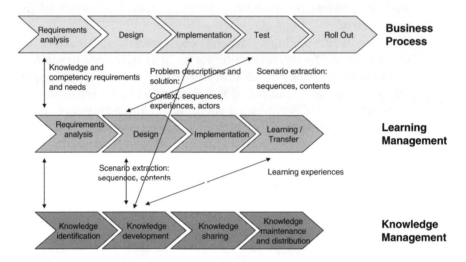

Fig. 12.3. Relations and synergies of business, knowledge and learning processes (Pawlowski and Bick 2006)

Synergy effects can occur in three situations. The interdependencies between the production, learning, and knowledge processes have to be identified as a first step. The following samples illustrate synergies when integrating processes and corresponding systems:

Production Process and Knowledge Management Process: In the production process, the user uses only directly related information systems, such as shop-floor information systems or MRP. In case of problems (e.g., delays, machine breakdown), the knowledge management system is used. The problem scenario is transferred to the knowledge management system. If there are solutions, the production process continues. If not, a new problem scenario is generated, providing solutions for future problems after the problem is finally solved.

Production Processes and Learning Processes: The production situation should be continuously monitored by external and internal evaluations. The results should be the basis for a continuous gap analysis, identifying competencies and skills to improve the production process. The learning process will be started and performed, leading to an improved production situation.

Knowledge Processes and Learning Processes: Developing real-life scenarios usually requires enormous resources. By combining learning and knowledge processes, real-life scenarios can be derived from the knowledge management system. Learning experiences can also provide suggestions for problems arising in the future and should therefore be stored in the knowledge management system.

The scenario shows synergy effects between processes to provide knowledge support for the workforce.

12.4.2 Awareness Building and Context Setting

The integration of processes and systems requires the commitment and participation of a variety of departments and actors. It means that people with different backgrounds, different languages, and different objectives need to work towards a common goal: to integrate knowledge sharing and learning in each business process and vice versa. Therefore, it is necessary to prepare an organization for this task. An organization should ensure that the integration is anchored and present in all parts of an organization.

Integration has to be contained in the organization's vision, strategy and policies. If an organization is committed to integration, this should be contained in these statements. In most organizations, knowledge sharing and learning are not adequately represented and therefore not backed by top management. Therefore, the process to improve vision, strategies and policies needs to be established. The redefinition of those statements should not be the responsibility of management alone. The process should be at least transparent to all staff members and can include participants from all staff groups to actively set new directions for the organization. For example, the strategy/policy should explain what "knowledge sharing" or "workplace-oriented learning" means with regard to the organization's core competencies and how those concepts influence the main operations.

Directly related is the process of awareness raising. The integration will not be successful if it is a top-down regulation. All members of an organization should be aware of the integration and its meaning for their personal actions.

The outcome of this phase should be revised vision, strategy and policy documents that show the organization's long-term view of integration and the consequences for all parts of an organization. All staff groups should be aware of and involved in this process.

12.4.3 Process Analysis and Redesign

The main objective of this phase is to identify integration opportunities, that is, process overlaps, shared services and systems, and data integration. As a first step, it should be analyzed which processes are overlapping or handled separately even though they should be integrated. In the application scenario, the processes of software testing and designing learning environments overlap. Software developers generate a variety of testing scenarios during the software development process. Those can be re-used to provide real data for a simulation for learning purposes. This means that the process of software development and the development process of learning environments are coupled. In this example, a process called "generating training scenarios and data" could be added in which both departments are involved. After this common process, both (former separate) processes will be performed in parallel with occasional overlap.

A second example is the generation of a knowledge base for knowledge management purposes. During the learning process in a simulation, users/learners gain experiences and work on problem solving. Solutions can then be used as initial knowledge for a knowledge management system on specific problems. Therefore, the two processes, "designing a knowledge base" and "learning: problem solving", can be coupled.

Those two examples show how processes can be coupled and how usually separated actors and departments can cooperate in order to integrate processes and gain synergy effects. To summarize the activities, this phase consists of the following steps:

- *Process Identification and Modelling*: Processes in the relevant departments are modelled, including actors involved and systems used in a formal process model. For a general discussion on process modeling techniques, see Bider (2003). For a specific approach for learning processes, see Naeve and Sicilia (2006).
- *Process Analysis*: As a second step, processes should be analyzed concerning their synergy effects (using the process analysis grid in the last section).

- *Process Redesign and Implementation*: Based on analysis, the new processes should be designed (cf. Becker et al. 2003). However, it is necessary to launch parallel cooperation processes to prepare and enable actors to work together.

The above steps are the basis for an integrated process framework in organizations.

12.4.4 Designing Shared Services and Systems

Whereas process redesign requires huge organizational changes, on this level, only systems are coupled or integrated. In the application scenario, several types of systems are involved, such as learning management systems, knowledge management systems, HR systems, manufacturing planning systems, authoring & programming systems.

The main decision is whether a system should be integrated or loosely coupled by mapping and integrating data (see next section). In a heterogeneous environment, we recommend choosing the first option in the long-term perspective, starting with data integration.

Generally, areas and entities that are relevant for more than one system must be determined. Those entities are not always obvious, since a variety of functionalities are used in different contexts: An example is user data: In HR systems or within the organization's intranet, user administration services are used (e.g., registering users, calculation performance indicators, messaging, etc.). Therefore, it has to be identified where similar services are used and how they can be implemented (e.g., web services, cf. Bick and Pawlowski 2006).

As a summary, the following steps are done in this phase:

- *Systems and service identification*: Based on the analysis grid, it should be determined which systems and, on a lower level, services are used in an organization.
- *System and service design*: It should be determined how systems and services should be coupled (integration or loose coupling). Based on this decision, the services should be redesigned to be re-used by different systems.

After this phase, clear connections between the organization's systems should be designed and implemented.

12.4.5 Integrating Data and Information

The loosest form of coupling systems is the exchange of data and information. In the application scenario, different systems are coupled using learning technology standards and specifications.

As shown in the analysis grid, the processes and systems that use similar data entities should be identified. As an example, user data are used in different systems, such as HR, knowledge management and learning management systems. Each of those systems have similar basic data (e.g., user identification, name, contact data) but specialized extensions (e.g., learner preferences, learner history).

To develop an integrated data model for an organization, the following steps should be performed:

- *Data definition*: Firstly, it is necessary to define common data classes and to determine necessary extensions.
- *Choice of specifications*: In an idealistic case, a standard should be chosen covering all aspects of the involved systems.
- *Data mapping*: In most cases, heterogeneous data descriptions exist. Therefore, mapping is necessary to define the relations between the different entities.
- *Data synchronization*: Finally, data should be stored consistently and without redundancies (e.g., in a single repository or data warehouse). In distributed environments, synchronization mechanisms have to be defined.

A promising approach to connect the above-mentioned steps is the use of ontologies and semantic web services. As an example, Dietze et al. (2007) define an ontology taking into account existing standards.

For the choice of specifications, learning technology standards cover a variety of aspects needed in all systems: learning, knowledge and business information systems. Table 12.4 shows candidates for different purposes. These can be recommended as initial specifications.

Using those descriptions, a basic format for data exchange is given. For each type of entity, extensions are necessary. Those extensions can be built as application profiles (CEN/ISSS 2006). However, they cover the most important aspects in the intersection of learning, knowledge and business information systems.

Table 12.4. Integration using learning technology standards

Aspect	Specification	Explanation
Scenarios	DIN Didactical Object Model/IMS Learning Design	Both specifications can be recommended to describe scenarios as a basis for knowledge identification and learning environments. They cover aspects such as activities, context, and services that are used in many contexts: software development, problem or situation descriptions, learning scenarios
Contents/documents	Learning Object Metadata	Learning Object Metadata cover a variety of aspects of contents (such as documents, learning modules, knowledge bits). Each can be described and related to each other
Users	Learner Information Package	This specification describes a variety of aspects on user data. It covers all necessary basic data as well as specific data for the fields of knowledge management and learning
Experiences	DIN Didactical Object Model	Experiences can be used in a variety of contexts, such as knowledge management. DIN DOM provides a format for structured description of experiences

12.5 Conclusion

This chapter shows potentials of integrating learning, knowledge and business information systems. To redesign processes and systems in an organization, it is necessary to carefully analyze the existing situation and to identify integration potentials.

Three levels of integration should be considered: processes, systems and services, as well as data. In spite of a high effort of re-designing such information systems, an integrated system will improve an organization's performance.

As a solution, a typical application scenario was shown as an exemplary solution. To design interfaces, we recommend using learning technology standards as the basis, with specific context-dependent extensions (application profiles).

The presented solution is a proposal for the future and a solution for convergent systems. However, the different communities (e.g., in the field of knowledge management and E-Learning) will need to cooperate to develop common solutions to minimize the adaptation efforts for systems' integration.

References

Becker, J., Kugeler, M., Rosemann, M. (Eds.) (2003). *Process Management – A Guide for the Design of Business Processes*, Berlin Heidelberg New York: Springer.

Bick, M., Pawlowski, J. M. (2006). Interface standards: integration of learning and business information systems. In U. D. Ehlers, J. M. Pawlowski (Eds.), *European Handbook of Quality and Standardisation in E-Learning*. Berlin Heidelberg New York: Springer.

Bick, M., Pawlowski, J. M. (2007), A Framework for integrated ambient learning and knowledge environments. In N. Gronau (Ed.), *4th Conference on Professional Knowledge Management – Experiences and Visions, Part 2* (pp. 335–342). Berlin: GITO.

Bider, I. (2003). Choosing approach to business process modeling – practical perspective. Research Report, IbisSoft, 2003, http://www.ibissoft.com/publications/HowTo.pdf.

CEN/ISSS (2006). *CEN Workshop Agreement (CWA) 15555 Building Application Profiles for eLearning*, Brussels.

Deutsches Institut für Normung (DIN e.V.) (2004). *Aus- und Weiterbildung unter besonderer Berücksichtigung von e-Learning – Teil 2: Didaktisches Objektmodell – Modellierung und Beschreibung didaktischer Szenarien* [Learning, Education and Training focussing on e-Learning – Part 2: Didactic Objects Model – Modelling and Description of Scenarios for Learning, Education and Training]. Berlin: Beuth.

Dietze, S., Gugliotta, A., Domingue, J. (2007). A semantic Web service oriented framework for adaptive learning environments. In *European Semantic Web Conference (ESWC) 2007*, Innsbruck, Austria.

Dodds, P., Thropp, S. E. (2004). SCORM 2004, 2nd edition overview. http://www.adlnet.org/downloads/70.cfm. Accessed 5 July 2005.

Dumont, B., Sangra, A. (2006). Organisational and cultural similarities and differences in implementing quality in e-learning in Europe's higher education, In. U. D. Ehlers, J. M. Pawlowski (Eds.), *European Handbook of Quality and Standardisation in E-Learning*. Berlin Heidelberg New York: Springer.

Fettke, P., Loos, P. (2003). Classification of reference models – a methodology and its application. *Information Systems and e-Business Management*, 1(1), 35–53.

Gibson, D., Aldrich, C., Prensky, M. (Eds.) (2006). *Games and Simulations in Online Learning: Research and Development Frameworks.* Hershey, PA: Information Science.

Hasselbring, W. (2000). Information system integration: introduction. *Communications of the ACM*, 43(6), 32–38.

IEEE Learning Technology Standards Committee (2002). *Learning Object Metadata Standard*, IEEE 1484.12.1-2002.

Illeris, K. (2004). A model for learning in working life. *Journal of Workplace Learning*, 16(8), 431–441.

Konstantas, D., Bourrières, J.-P., Léonard, M., Boudjlida, N. (Eds.) (2006). *Inter-operability of Enterprise Software and Applications*. London: Springer.

Koper, R., Olivier, B., Anderson, T. (2002). IMS Learning Design Information Model, Version 1.0. http://www.imsglobal.org/learningdesign/ldv1p0pd/imsld_infov1p0pd.html. Accessed 12 June 2003.

Lam, W. (2005). Investigating success factors in enterprise application integration: a case-driven analysis. *European Journal of Information Systems*, 14(2), 175–187.

Linthicum, D. S. (2001). *B2B Application Integration: e-Business Enable Your Enterprise*. Boston: Addison Wesley.

Lytras, M. D., Pouloudi, A., Poulymenakou, A. (2002). A framework for technology convergence in learning and working. *Educational Technology and Society*, 5(2), 99–106.

Mashari M. A., Zairi M. (1999). BPR implementation process: an analysis of key success and failure factors. *Business Process Management Journal*, 5(1), 87–112.

Naeve, A., Sicilia, M. A. (2006): Learning processes and processing learning: from organizational needs to learning designs. In *ADALE, International Workshop on Adaptative Learning and Learning Design*. Dublin, Ireland, June 2006.

Pawlowski, J. M. (2001). *Das Essener-Lern-Modell (ELM): Ein Vorgehensmodell zur Entwicklung computerunterstützter Lernumgebungen* [The Essen Learning Model: A model for the development of computer-supported learning environments]. Dissertation, University of Essen.

Pawlowski, J. M., Bick, M. (2006). Managing & re-using didactical expertise: the didactical object model. *Educational Technology and Society*, 9(1), 84–96.

Pawlowski, J. M., Richter, T. (2007). *Context and Culture Metadata – A Tool for the Internationalization of E-Learning*. In C. Montgomerie, J. Seale (Eds.), *ED-MEDIA* (pp. 4528-4537). Chesapeake, VA: AACE.

Prensky, M. (2001). *Digital Game-Based Learning*. New York: McGraw-Hill.

Scheer, A.-W. (1992). *Architecture of Integrated Information Systems*. Berlin Heidelberg New York: Springer.

Smythe, C., Tansey, F., Robson, R. (2001): IMS Learner Information Package, Information Model Specification, Version 1.0. http://www.imsproject.org/profiles/lipinfo01.html. Accessed 12 October 2003.

Torraco, R. J. (1999). Integrating learning with working: a reconception of the role of workplace learning. *Human Resource Development Quarterly*, 10(3), 249–270.

UN/CEFACT & OASIS (2001). Catalog of common business processes, v1.0. *Business Process Team*, 11 May 2001.

Wersig, G. (1999). Konvergenz als virtuelle Integration und Medienidentitäten [Convergence as a virtual integration and media identities]. http://kommwiss.fu-berlin.de/434.html. Accessed 10 December 2003.

Wilbers, K. (2002). E-Learning didaktisch gestalten [Didactical Design of E-Learning]. In A. Hohenstein K. Wilbers (Hrsg.), *Handbuch E-Learning* (*Kap. 4.0*) [Handbook E-Learning]. Köln: Deutscher Wirtschaftsdienst.

Wolpers, M., Najjar, J., Verbert, K., Duval, E. (2007): Tracking Actual Usage: the Attention Metadata Approach. Educational Technology and Society, 10(3), 2007.

Section 2:
The E-Pedagogy

13 Bridging the Gap Between Face-to-Face and Cyber Interaction in Holistic Blended Learning Environments

N.-S. Chen, C.-W. Wei, Kinshuk, Y.-R. Chen, and Y.-C. Wang

Previous research studies on blended learning have mainly focused on blending between either physical face-to-face and cyber asynchronous, or cyber face-to-face and cyber asynchronous environments. This research has created a holistic blended-learning environment (HBLE) in which physical face-to-face, cyber face-to-face and cyber asynchronous blended models are synthesized into one holistic blended-learning model. Such a model enables teachers and learners to do two-way interaction asynchronously and synchronously regardless of whether they are in physical space or cyber space. This research also explores whether significant differences exist in terms of effects on classroom climate and learning effectiveness between physical face-to-face groups (P-F2F) and cyber face-to-face groups (C-F2F).

The research methodology includes surveys, interviews and content analyses. Triangulation of different sources of data also prevents bias. After the collection of quantitative questionnaires on classroom climate and learning satisfaction in the middle and at the end of a semester, interviews and analyses via online discussion forums were used to supplement and explain the quantitative survey results.

The research results show that although C-F2F has a larger change on classroom climate and learning effectiveness before the mid-term and after the final exam than P-F2F, there was no significant difference in learning effectiveness between the C-F2F and P-F2F student groups. Furthermore, results show a positive correlation between classroom climate and learning satisfaction. The study validates the positive potential of implementing holistic blended learning for higher education.

13.1 Introduction

Blended learning is used not only in corporate training settings but also for instruction in conventional schools. In recent years, many scholars have focused their research studies on blended learning and view it as the future trend for academic research and pedagogical practices (Garrison and Kanuka 2004; Graham 2004). However, in the past, blended learning referred only to two blended-learning models: physical face-to-face and cyber asynchronous, and cyber face-to-face and cyber asynchronous. Although both models have the potential to provide resource sharing and learning discussions through the learning management system (LMS) over the Internet, they still have some drawbacks. The difference between the two models lies in the fact that physical face-to-face and cyber asynchronous blended learning is limited by space since it requires the teachers and learners to be in a physical classroom to have synchronous lessons. On the other hand, although cyber face-to-face and cyber asynchronous allows the teachers and learners to have synchronous lessons and see each other's facial expressions through web cams in the cyber classroom, the non-verbal behavioral interaction is still largely limited.

Due to the increasing international collaboration in education and the need for extended education, such as life-long learning and learning-on-demand paradigms, it has become necessary to provide a more flexible blended-learning environment. For example, through the synchronous learning platform, teachers can invite foreign scholars/experts to deliver professional talks for students without requiring them to actually pay a physical visit. Also, a student in an extended education program may choose to have a synchronous lesson in the physical classroom or cyber classroom and interact with other students regardless of the student's location. To make such options possible, this research has constructed a holistic blended-learning environment (HBLE) in which physical face-to-face, cyber face-to-face and cyber asynchronous learning environments have been amalgamated. To implement this kind of holistic blended-learning model, we need to build a blended synchronous classroom by integrating a physical classroom and a cyber synchronous classroom supported by the synchronous learning management platform as shown in Fig. 13.1.

In Fig. 13.1, some students participate in the physical classroom (physical face-to-face group, P-F2F) and some students participate in the cyber synchronous classroom (cyber face-to-face group, C-F2F) at the same time. In the physical classroom, there are three big, projected screens: one for displaying the videos of all students participating online, one for

Fig. 13.1. A physical classroom in a holistic blended learning environment

displaying main teaching materials and one for displaying an online chat room, including a bigger video window of the person who is presenting (typically a teacher, but may also be a student doing a presentation or an invited external expert). In the cyber synchronous classroom, students from the C-F2F group can also see the students sitting in the physical classroom, the teacher, the teaching content and the online chat room on their own computer screen (see Fig. 13.3). Through this kind of blended synchronous classroom, teachers can interact smoothly with students regardless of whether they are sitting in a physical classroom or in a cyber synchronous classroom. The same is true for participating students. Both P-F2F and C-F2F students can engage in asynchronous learning activities provided by the platform.

Many studies have shown that interaction is an important element in learning (Fernandes et al. 2005; Kerres and de Witt 2003; Leh 2002). The psychological state of the classroom, called the classroom psychological environment and also known as the classroom climate (Withall 1949), is the direct result of interaction (Good 1973; Moos 1979; Walker and Fraser 2005). Many studies have shown that such psychological climate plays an important role in the learning success of students (Hiemstra 1991; Merriam and Brockett 1997; Sisco 1991; Walker and Fraser 2005). However, since there are vast differences between the physical and cyber class (Hiltz and Wellman 1997; Stonebraker and Hazeltine 2004), the issue of whether the results of the physical class can be used to measure the relationship between classroom climate and learning effectiveness is worth delving into. Especially in the realm of the cyber class, the scope of research is often focused on the discussion of students' learning effectiveness, the attitudes of teachers and students, and the satisfaction levels of teachers and students, showing a lack of relevant research on classroom climate.

Therefore, this research sets out to examine whether there is a significant difference in classroom climate perception and learning effectiveness between P-F2F and C-F2F in this kind of holistic blended-learning environment. If no significant difference is found between P-F2F and C-F2F, then the HBLE can be said to be valuable for learners who need flexibility in the learning process. Furthermore, this study also examines whether a positive correlation exists between the classroom climate and learning effectiveness.

13.2 Literature Review

This study focuses on the differences in perceptions of the classroom climate and learning effectiveness between P-F2F and C-F2F in a holistic blended-learning environment. The related works of blended learning, classroom climate and learning effectiveness are discussed next.

13.2.1 Blended Learning

Although the term "blended learning" came into common use only recently, the idea has been in use for years. Different researchers have defined blended learning differently, so the definition of blended learning has not yet come to a conclusion. Graham et al. (2003) have summarized three types of definitions from literature about blended learning, concluding that it is a combinations of (a) different instructional methods, (b) different modalities or delivery media or (c) online and face-to-face instruction.

Because it is difficult to find a program without multiple instructional methods, modalities and delivery media, the third definition mentioned above is closer to the essence of blended learning (Graham 2004). Even though the third definition is widely accepted, many scholars have their own applications of blended learning. With the advancement of information technology and the availability of visual aids, face-to-face interaction is no longer limited to the traditional physical classroom. It can work in the cyber learning environment as well, and can be conducted using mechanisms such as cyber synchronous classroom (Chen et al. 2005). Hence, there are three scenarios for implementing face-to-face interaction, the first being Physical F2F in the physical Classroom, the second being Cyber F2F in cyber synchronous Classroom and the third being Blended F2F (Physical F2F and Cyber F2F) in the blended synchronous classroom. This study addresses the third scenario as our target environment.

13.2.2 Classroom Climate

Social psychologists were the earliest researchers to take an interest in classroom behavior. Their fundamental interests were in student/student and student/teacher interactions (Medley and Mitzel 1963). Classroom climate is sometimes referred to as the learning environment, or something related to atmosphere, ambience, ecology and milieu. The impact of classroom climate on students and teachers can be either beneficial or a barrier to learning (Adelman and Taylor 2005). Classroom climate is a perceived quality of the setting. It emerges in a somewhat fluid state from the complex transactions of many immediate environmental factors, such as physical, material, organizational, operational and social variables (Adelman and Taylor 2005).

This research considers the classroom climate as interaction among class members, physical environment and class materials to form a special emotional perception that refers to the class's psychological environment. Moreover, the classroom climate perception is difficult to change as only the students themselves can perceive the climate of their own classes.

Traditional classroom climate assessment is mainly based on the social ecology concept proposed by Moos (1976), which includes three different dimensions: relationship, personal growth, and system maintenance and change. These dimensions are most often used to evaluate classroom climate. However, the traditional instruments cannot be directly applied to a cyber classroom. It is necessary to develop specific instruments for cyber classrooms. Therefore, many cyber classroom instruments have recently been developed in succession, for example, the Distance and Open Learning Environment Scale (Jegede et al. 1995), Geography Classroom Environment Inventory (Teh 1999), Constructive On-line Learning Environment Survey (Taylor and Maor 2000), Web Based Learning Environment Instrument (Chang and Fisher 2001), and Distance Education Learning Environment Survey (DELES) (Walker and Fraser 2005). The DELES considers various factors, such as instructor support, student interaction and collaboration, personal relevance, authentic learning, active learning, and student autonomy, and is consistent with the objective of this study. Hence, our classroom climate survey was developed on the basis of DELES.

13.2.3 Learning Effectiveness

Hiltz and Wellman (1997) indicate that students' learning effectiveness is usually evaluated by their test scores. Rovai and Barnum (2003) consider that student perception is more important for evaluating students' learning effectiveness and recommend the use of students' self assessment as an index. Based on research of learning effectiveness in the cyber class in recent years, researchers divide learning effectiveness into two categories (Johnson et al. 2000; Summers et al. 2005). One of the categories is the learner's test scores, which includes pre-test, post-test, mid-term and final test. Another is the learner's learning perception, which includes satisfaction, interaction, participation and cooperation, all of which refer to learner's experiences and reactions throughout the learning process.

As a result, this research evaluates learning effectiveness based on objective test scores and subjective learning satisfaction. Test scores include mid-term and final tests, and learning satisfaction includes the learner's perception of the learning activity. The data of students' perceptions is collected by self-assessment surveys.

13.2.4 Classroom Climate and Learning Effectiveness

Much of traditional research has demonstrated that learning effectiveness, including learning satisfaction, can be predicted by classroom climate (Brookover et al. 1979; Deng 1992; Flanders 1960; Majeed et al. 2002; Moos 1979). However, recent research has focused on the development of instruments for the classroom climate (Jiang and Ting 2000; Jung et al. 2002) rather than on the relationship between classroom climate and learning effectiveness in the cyber class. The cyber class differs greatly from the physical class (Hiltz and Wellman 1997; Stonebraker and Hazeltine 2004). Therefore, it is important to find out whether the effect of the physical class may actually be applied to cyber learning. This research will discover whether classroom climate has a positive correlation with learning effectiveness in the cyber class.

13.3 Research Methodology

This research explored how classroom climate and learning effectiveness changes according to the time and environment, and examined the relationship between classroom climate and learning effectiveness in P-F2F and C-F2F. The model of the research is shown in Fig. 13.2.

In this research, the cyber-classroom climate is constructed by teacher support, student autonomy, and student interaction and collaboration, and learning effectiveness is constructed by learning satisfaction and test scores (mid-term and final tests). In addition to observation of the changes in P-F2F and C-F2F, this research analyzes the differences of learning effectiveness between them. Furthermore, this study examines the relationship between the classroom climate and learning effectiveness.

This research primarily focuses on quantitative study, supplemented with qualitative study, which includes survey, interview and data collection. The research uses Patton's (2002) triangulation method to verify the methodology. The quantitative research tools include three questionnaires, "individual background", "classroom climate", and "learning satisfaction". The individual background questionnaire (see Appendix 1) was used to analyze students' backgrounds. The classroom climate questionnaire (see Appendix 2) was created according to Walker and Fraser's (2005) DELES instrument and Darkenwald's (1989) research. The learning satisfaction questionnaire (see Appendix 3) took the research of Arbaugh (2000), Bolliger and Martindale (2004), and Hong (2002) as references to analyze student satisfaction. On the other hand, the analysis of qualitative survey was conducted through group interviews and by coding the collected data from the online discussion forum with system records such as login frequencies and the number of messages posted. The interview questions and a description of the coding are shown in Appendix 4.

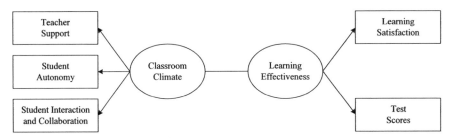

Fig. 13.2. The model of the research

The subjects of the study were selected from the students who enrolled in the course called Computer Networks, at the National Sun Yat-sen University. Holistic blended learning was applied throughout the semester in the course. The students, divided into P-F2F and C-F2F groups, used the same cyber classroom, which included the functions of cyber face-to-face and cyber asynchronous, supported by the Cyber University of National Sun Yat-sen University (http://cu.nsysu.edu.tw). There was no difference between these two sample groups in terms of learning contents, materials, assignments, exams, teaching assistants and schedule. On top of that, both P-F2F and C-F2F were allowed to interact with each other through the blended synchronous classroom. In addition to the assignments and exams, the students were asked to do a term project and to report back by the end of the semester. All students were required to attend synchronous classes every Wednesday from 6:30 pm to 9:30 pm. The only difference was that the C-F2F group attended a cyber synchronous classroom, while the P-F2F group attended a physical classroom. C-F2F students could interact with the instructor and P-F2F students through visual devices (see Fig. 13.3). On the other hand, P-F2F students could have face-to-face interaction with the instructor in the classroom and see C-F2F students through images provided by projector (see Fig. 13.4). Students from both groups could interact with one another via visual devices (see Fig. 13.5).

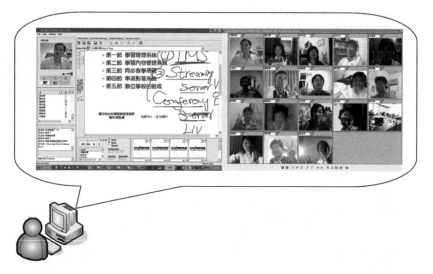

Fig. 13.3. Cyber face-to-face group (C-F2F) in the cyber synchronous classroom

Fig. 13.4. Physical face-to-face group (P-F2F) in the physical classroom

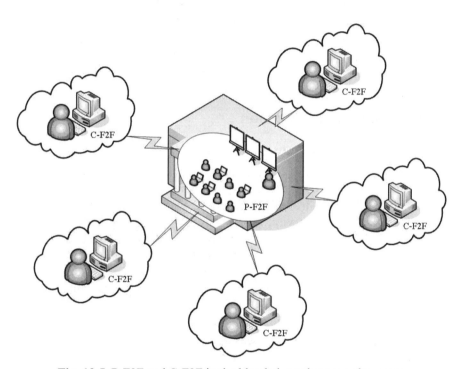

Fig. 13.5. P-F2F and C-F2F in the blended synchronous classroom

The study was conducted using a questionnaire that was first revised based on the suggestions of three domain experts, and then an analysis of factors and reliability was carried out to test the reliability of the survey. All the factors are listed in Table 13.1.

Table 13.1. The definition and reliability of variables in each construct

Construct	Variables	Definition	Cronbach's α (mid-term/final)
Classroom climate	Teacher support	The learner perceived support from the teacher	0.89/0.88
	Student autonomy	The learner perceived autonomy in learning	0.87/0.90
	Student interaction and collaboration	The learner perceived interaction and collaboration with others	0.92/0.84
Learning satisfaction	Teacher satisfaction	The learner's satisfaction level with the instructor	0.99/0.90
	System satisfaction	The learner's satisfaction level with the learning management system	0.86/0.85
	Interaction satisfaction	The learner's satisfaction level of interaction with others	066/0.65
	Course satisfaction	The learner's satisfaction level with the course	0.81/0.86

13.4 Result and Discussion

A total of 64 students were enrolled in the course, with 39 students in C-F2F mode and 55 in P-F2F mode. After discarding the invalid questionnaires due to missing data, 56 valid questionnaires were used in this study. Out of them, 24 were from C-F2F and 32 were from P-F2F. The Likert scale was used in the survey, ranging from 5 (very satisfied) to 1 (very dissatisfied). This study was aimed at observing the change and difference between the mid-term and final exams, of the classroom climate and learning effectiveness within each group and among the two groups. The variation is a score obtained by subtracting the mid-term from the final in each item of questionnaires test scores.

With regard to the individual background analysis, a chi-square test for the homogeneity of proportions was applied. The results show that no significant difference was found in the sex, age, education, major, marital status, residences, and time and number of use between the two groups (p-value > 0.05). The pre-test was used to test the prior knowledge of the students of both groups about the subject matter and was analyzed by independent t-test. Although the C-F2F received slightly higher score than the P-F2F, no significant difference was found (p-value = 0.951). Based on the results, both groups had similar background and level of prior knowledge.

13.4.1 Classroom Climate

As shown in Table 13.2, the score for the classroom climate decreased slightly in C-F2F but no significant difference was found. Although the classroom climate increased slightly in P-F2F, there was still no significant difference between the two groups. This concludes that classroom climate variations in both groups are similar. Table 13.3 shows that teacher support decreased and a significant difference was found. This is probably because C-F2F students are similar to lurkers when the teacher is delivering lessons in the real classroom and the primary impression about teachers for cyber synchronous classroom students is derived by voice and the teacher's video window. It shows that teachers need to pay more attention to looking at, and interacting with, students in cyber synchronous classroom environments. However, this would involve changing teaching style and adapting to blended synchronous classrooms. Further research should address how to resolve these issues. Another factor that also contributes to the decrease in teacher-support perception is that the teacher and teaching assistants helped students resolve many problems from the beginning of the course until the mid-term exam, after which students shifted focus to more interaction with teammates instead of with the teacher because they had to work together as a team on the term project.

Table 13.2. The variation of classroom climate between mid-term and final

Group	Number	Mean	Std. dev.	Within		Between	
				t	p	t	p
ALL	56	−0.0192	0.3306	−0.436	0.665	-	
C-F2F	24	−0.0500	0.2638	−0.929	0.363	0.353	0.725
P-F2F	32	0.0038	0.3755	0.057	0.955		

Table 13.3. The variation of classroom climate in each variable between mid-term and final

Variable	Group	Number	Mean	Std. dev.	Within		Between	
					t	p	t	p
Teacher support	ALL	56	−0.1374	0.4137	−2.486	**0.016***	-	
	C-F2F	24	−0.2500	0.4299	−2.849	**0.009****	−1.800	0.078
	P-F2F	32	−0.0530	0.3864	−0.775	0.444		
Student autonomy	ALL	56	0.0417	0.5048	0.618	0.539	-	
	C-F2F	24	0.0556	0.4132	0.659	0.517	0.177	0.860
	P-F2F	32	0.0313	0.5702	0.310	0.759		
Student interaction and collaboration	ALL	56	0.0774	0.5241	1.105	0.274	-	
	C-F2F	24	0.1111	0.4247	1.282	0.213	0.414	0.681
	P-F2F	32	0.0521	0.5933	0.497	0.623		

* $p < 0.05$, ** $p < 0.01$

13.4.2 Learning Satisfaction

Table 13.4 shows that learning satisfaction of both C-F2F and P-F2F groups increased, with a significant difference for C-F2F students. However, no significant difference was found between the changes in the two groups. It shows that both groups have good learning satisfaction but C-F2F has a greater variation. This is probably because C-F2F students did not expect that they could achieve comparably good learning results through this kind of cyber classroom. As shown in Table 13.5, a significant difference was found in the changes in student satisfaction with the system for both C-F2F and P-F2F. The changes in the interaction satisfaction for C-F2F was also a significant difference. However, there was no significant difference in changes between the two groups for system satisfaction and interaction satisfaction. Based on the interviews and the posted messages, system satisfaction for both groups increased with learners' familiarity with the system. According to the records that were tracked, there were 20 system-related problem messages posted prior to the mid-term, but only five after the mid-term. It shows that students were getting familiar with the system and both groups had similar levels of system satisfaction. However, there was a significant difference in the number of posted messages between the two groups. This is because C-F2F students had to rely on asynchronous posts for communications while P-F2F students could communicate physically within the campus. Unlike P-F2F, C-F2F students did not know their classmates before the semester. So C-F2F had lower mid-term interaction satisfaction than P-F2F. In addition, students learned individually at the course's beginning, and started working together with team members after mid-term on projects, assignments and tests. As a result, the interaction satisfaction of C-F2F became higher than P-F2F after the mid-term. This result confirms the notion that group cooperative learning is an important teaching strategy for online learning.

Table 13.4. The variation of learning satisfaction between mid-term and final

Group	Number	Mean	Std. dev.	Within		Between	
				t	p	t	p
ALL	56	0.1131	0.2809	3.013	**0.004****	-	
C-F2F	24	0.1493	0.2680	2.729	**0.012***	0.929	0.357
P-F2F	32	0.0859	0.2914	1.668	0.105		

* $p < 0.05$, ** $p < 0.01$

Table 13.5. The variation of learning satisfaction in each variable between mid-term and final

Variable	Group	Number	Mean	Std. dev.	Within		Between	
					t	p	t	p
Teacher satisfaction	ALL	56	0.0214	0.3921	0.409	0.684	-	
	C-F2F	24	0.0083	0.4021	0.102	0.920	−0.215	0.831
	P-F2F	32	0.0313	0.3906	0.453	0.654		
System satisfaction	ALL	56	0.3214	0.6137	3.919	**0.000***	-	
	C-F2F	24	0.3542	0.6833	2.539	**0.018**	0.343	0.733
	P-F2F	32	0.2969	0.5660	2.967	**0.006**		
Interaction satisfaction	ALL	56	0.1845	0.5892	2.344	**0.023***	-	
	C-F2F	24	0.3333	0.5108	3.197	**0.004***	1.663	0.102
	P-F2F	32	0.0729	0.6264	0.659	0.515		
Course satisfaction	ALL	56	0.0268	0.5429	0.369	0.713	-	
	C-F2F	24	0.0208	0.5209	0.196	0.846	−0.070	0.944
	P-F2F	32	0.0313	0.5671	0.312	0.757		

$* p < 0.05, ** p < 0.01, *** p < 0.001$

13.4.3 Test Scores

As shown in Table 13.6, the final grades of C-F2F decreased, but not significantly. The final grades of P-F2F increased slightly, but again, not significantly. The changes of grades between the two groups were not significantly different either. This implies that both C-F2F and P-F2F can achieve the same level of test scores. According to the interviews and the posted messages, the decrease in the final grades of C-F2F students was probably due to heavy non-curricular work or to the difficulty in achieving a balance between work and study. Some students pointed out that they were easily distracted by things which were irrelevant to the course, since they were studying in their own environment rather than in a physical classroom. P-F2F students participated in a physical classroom and therefore had to pay careful attention to what was going on, since no archive of interaction was available after the class. As deduced from here, C-F2F brings students a more convenient and flexible space but more distractions. Potential solutions to this problem should be another issue for further research.

Table 13.6. The variation of test scores between mid-term and final

Group	Number	Mean	Std. dev.	Within		Between	
				t	p	t	p
ALL	56	−2.3036	16.3917	−1.052	0.298	-	
C-F2F	24	−6.0417	14.9738	−1.977	0.060	−1.488	0.143
P-F2F	32	0.5000	17.0710	0.166	0.869		

13.4.4 The Correlation Between Classroom Climate and Learning Effectiveness

According to simple correlation analysis, there was a significant correlation between class climate and learning satisfaction (p-value = 0.013), but no significant correlation was found between class climate and test scores (p-value = 0.289). As shown in Table 13.7, the statistical results were consistent with the information from interviews and posted messages in which many students connected classroom climate with learning satisfaction. The results showed that classroom climate and learning satisfaction had a significant correlation. On top of that, some students thought that test scores depended mainly on students' efforts, while others thought group interaction had some indirect influences on their test scores. Besides, students believed that the interactions between the instructor and students were the major factors for establishing values in classroom climate, and the instructor and teams were the major factors in determining learning satisfaction. These results were the same as the simple correlation analysis.

Table 13.7. Inter-correlations of variation among study variables

	Classroom climate	Learning satisfaction	Test scores
Classroom climate	1		
Learning satisfaction	**0.332***	1	
Test scores	0.144	−0.082	1

$* p < 0.05$

13.5 Conclusion

Due to recent advancements in broadband Internet development, cyber face-to-face interaction is now feasible and can be conducted within the scope of cyber synchronous classrooms. There are three scenarios for implementing face-to-face interaction: the Physical F2F in a physical classroom, the Cyber F2F in a cyber synchronous classroom, and the Blended F2F in a blended synchronous classroom. This study addresses the third scenario as our target environment. This research integrated physical classroom, cyber synchronous classroom and cyber asynchronous learning into a holistic blended-learning environment. A blended synchronous classroom is built to realize this kind of blended learning, with some students participating in the physical classroom (physical face-to-face group, P-F2F) and some students participating in the cyber synchronous classroom (cyber face-to-face group, C-F2F) at the same time. The purpose of this research was to explore whether significant differences exist in terms of effects on classroom climate and learning effectiveness between the physical face-to-face group (P-F2F) and the cyber face-to-face group (C-F2F). This study also examined whether a positive correlation exists between classroom climate and learning effectiveness.

The study found that there was no significant difference in the classroom climate and learning effectiveness between C-F2F and P-F2F. There was a significant correlation between classroom climate and learning satisfaction but no significant correlation was found between classroom climate and test scores. The statistics' results were consistent with the information gained through interviews and posted messages, in which many students connected classroom climate with learning satisfaction. Based on the results, we recommend that institutions in higher education supplement the holistic blended-learning environment with synchronous lectures for both on-campus and off-campus students at the same time. Though the study proved that holistic blended learning is worth promoting, the generalization of the results is limited due to the strict selection process of subjects, which results in relatively small sample size. In order to have a more generalized application, further studies with larger sample sizes are needed.

Studies are also needed to analyze factors affecting classroom climate and learning effectiveness with regards to teacher characteristics, focusing on the important role teachers can play in improving classroom climate and learning effectiveness. The research in this chapter also indicates a significant correlation between cyber classroom climate and learning satisfaction. Based on the results, further studies should also be expanded to understand the cause and effect between these relations.

Acknowledgement

This research was supported by the National Science Council, Taiwan (NSC 95-2520-S-110-001-MY2).

Appendix

Appendix 1: Individual Background Questionnaire

Part 1: Basic Information

1. Identity: graduate student, part-time graduate student, online student, or credit student
2. Age: 21~30, 31~40, 41~50, or more than 50

3. Highest education: high school, college, university, master, or doctor
4. Current major: information management related or non information management related
5. Marriage status: married or single
6. Current job position: information management related, non information management related, or no job
7. Residences: north, middle, south, or east
8. The desire of enrolling in the cyber learning program of National Sun Yat-Sen University is: voluntarily or non-voluntarily
9. The tuition for the cyber learning program comes from: individual or company
10. The location to attend cyber learning lesson: home, office, school, or other
11. The motivation for enrolling in the cyber learning program of National Sun Yat-Sen University: personal interests, credit, knowledge, job requirement, or other
12. The average hours per week to use cyber learning system for study: less than 3 h, 4~6 h, or more than 6 h
13. The frequency per week to login at National Sun Yat-Sen Cyber University: less than 5 times, 6~10 times, or more than 10 times
14. The number of courses passed through National Sun Yat-Sen University: 0 courses, 1 course, 2 courses, 3 courses, 4 courses, 5 courses, 6 courses, or more than 6 courses

Part 2: Learning Characteristics

15. I usually created and worked with documents using computers.
16. I usually used email.
17. I usually communicated with others through the Internet.
18. I had experiences in Cyber Learning such as BBS discussion groups or online information collection.
19. I had learning experiences using cyber learning systems.
20. I had confidence in searching for desired information using the World Wide Web (WWW).
21. I was able to download required files and information from websites.
22. I believe that I have abilites in troubleshooting for Cyber Learning.
23. I could master my learning content synchronously by Internet.
24. I had the ability to review materials through the Internet to improve learning.

Appendix 2: Classroom Climate Questionnaire

Part 1: Teacher Support
1. The teacher is concerned about my feelings in the class.
2. The teacher encourages me to participate in the class.
3. The teacher seeks to understand my needs for learning.
4. The teacher responds promptly to my questions.

Part 2: Student Autonomy
5. I am allowed to set my own learning schedule.
6. I am allowed to work at my own pace.
7. I have the chance to incorporate my ideas in the class.
8. I am in control of my learning.

Part 3: Student Interaction and Collaboration
9. I can discuss my ideas with other students.
10. I have the opportunity to collaborate with others.
11. I feel good when I interact with other students.
12. I have the opportunity to share information with other students.

Appendix 3: Learning Satisfaction Questionnaire

Part 1: Teacher Satisfaction
1. I am satisfied with teacher's preparation.
2. I am satisfied with the learning method delivered by teacher.
3. I am satisfied with teacher's support.
4. I am satisfied with class discussion led by teacher.

Part 2: System Satisfaction
5. I am satisfied with user interface of the learning management system.
6. I am satisfied with function of the learning management system.
7. I am satisfied with stability of the learning management system.
8. I am satisfied with easy-to-use features of the learning management system.

Part 3: Interaction Satisfaction
9. I am satisfied with the interaction with team members.
10. I am satisfied with the interaction with other students.
11. I am satisfied with the learning activities with others.
12. I am satisfied with the discussion with others.

Part 4: Course Satisfaction
13. I am satisfied with the learning materials.
14. I am satisfied with the program scheme.
15. I am satisfied with the evaluation method.
16. I am satisfied with the delivery of materials.

Appendix 4: Coding Description

The coding for C-F2F and P-F2F represents the cyber face-to-face and physical face-to-face groups that include the number representing the sequence of the student, the respective question and the particular dialogue. For example: C-F2F-2-2-25 refers to the second student from C-F2F group answering question 2 in the 25th dialogue. Afterwards, sorted information and summarization from class discussion or group discussion forums were

Table 13.8.

Types	Codes	Code description
Learning group	C-F2F (cyber face-to-face group)	The learners in cyber synchronous classroom
	P-F2F (physical face-to-face group)	The learners in physical classroom
Discussion forum types	CDF (class discussion forum)	The discussion forum for all learners
	GDF (group discussion forum)	The discussion forum only for each individual team members
Article types in the discussion forums	COR (course)	The articles about the course
	FEL (feeling)	The articles of the learners' feelings about the course
	TEA (teacher)	The articles of the learners' feelings about the teacher
	PRO (project)	The articles about the final project
	SYS (system)	The articles about the learning system
	MID (mid-term)	The articles about the mid-term examination
	FIN (final Exam)	The articles about the final examination
	AUT (autonomy)	The articles about student autonomy
	INA (interaction)	The articles about interaction among teacher and students
Number	0–9	The sequence number of students, questions, dialogues, teams, or articles

extracted and numbered. Again, the coding for C-F2F and P-F2F represents the cyber face-to-face and physical face-to-face groups that include the attributes of the discussion forums or the team number representing the sequence of the student and the respective question. For example: C-F2F-CDF-708-SYS refers to the 708th posted message from the discussion forum of C-F2F group. Since the content was in Chinese, only the coding scheme is given here. For the complete list of coding materials, please contact the authors directly.

References

Adelman, H. S., & Taylor, L. (2005). Classroom climate. In S. W. Lee, P. A. Lowe, & E. Robinson (Eds.), *Encyclopedia of School Psychology.* Thousand Oaks, CA: Sage.

Arbaugh, J. B. (2000). Virtual classroom characteristics and student satisfaction with Internet-based MBA courses. *Journal of Management Education*, 24(1), 32–54.

Bolliger, D. U. & Martindale, T. (2004). Key factors for determining student satisfaction in online courses. *International Journal on E-Learning*, 3(1), 61–67.

Brookover, W., Beady, C., Flood, P., Schweitzer, J., & Wisenbaker, J. (1979). *School Social Systems and Student Achievement: Schools Can Make a Difference.* New York: Praeger.

Chang, V., & Fisher, D. L. (2001). A new learning instrument to evaluate online learning in higher education. In M. Kulske & A. Herrmann (Eds.), *New Horizons in University Teaching and Learning* (pp. 23–34). Perth: Curtin University of Technology.

Chen, N. S., Ko, H. C., Kinshuk, & Lin, T. (2005). A model for synchronous learning using the Internet. *Innovations in Education and Teaching International*, 42(2), 181–194.

Darkenwald, G. G. (1989). Enhancing the adult classroom environment. In E. R. Hayes (Ed.), *Effective Teaching Styles* (pp. 67–75). New Directions for Continuing Education, no. 43. San Francisco, CA: Jossey-Bass.

Deng, B. (1992). A Multilevel Analysis of Classroom Climate Effects on Mathematics Achievement of Fourth-Grade Students. (ERIC Document Reproduction Service No.ED 348222).

Fernandes, E., Roethlisberger, K., & Forte, M. W. (2005). The four dimensions of blended learning. In M. Khosrow-Pour (Ed.), *Managing Modern Organizations with Information Technology* (pp. 15–18). San Diego, CA: Idea.

Flanders, N. A. (1960). *Teacher Influence, Pupil Attitudes and Achievement.* Minneapolis: University of Minnesota.

Garrison, D. R. & Kanuka, H. (2004). Blended learning: uncovering its transformative potential in higher education. *Internet and Higher Education*, 7(2), 95–105.

Good, C. V. (Ed.). (1973). *Dictionary of Education*. New York: McGraw-Hill.

Graham, C. R. (2004). Blended learning systems: definition, current trends, and future directions. In C. J. Bonk & C. R. Graham (Eds.), *Handbook of Blended Learning: Global Perspectives, Local Designs* (pp. 3–21). San Francisco, CA: Pfeiffer.

Graham, C. R., Allen, S., & Ure, D. (2003). Blended Learning Environments: A Review of the Research Literature. Unpublished manuscript, Provo, UT.

Hiemstra, R. (1991). Aspects of effective learning environments. In R. Hiemstra (Ed.), *Creative Environments for Effective Adult Learning* (pp. 5–12). San Francisco, CA: Jossey-Bass.

Hiltz, S. R. & Wellman, B. (1997). Asynchronous learning networks as a virtual classroom. *Communications of the ACM*, 40(9), 44–49.

Hong, K. S. (2002). Relationships between students' and instructional variables with satisfaction and learning from a Web-based course. *The Internet and Higher Education*, 5(3), 267–281.

Jegede, O. J., Fraser, B. J., & Fisher, D. L. (1995). The development and validation of a distance and open learning environment scale. *Educational Technology Research and Development*, 43(1), 90–93.

Jiang, M. & Ting, E. (2000). A study of factors influencing students' perceived learning in a Web-based course environment. *International Journal of Educational Telecommunications*, 6(4), 317–338.

Johnson, S. D., Aragon, S. R., Shaik, N., & Palma-rivas, N. (2000). Comparative analysis of learner satisfaction and learning outcomes in online and face-to-face learning environments. *Journal of Interactive Learning Research*, 11(1), 29–49.

Jung, I., Choi, S., Lim, C., & Leem, J. (2002). Effects of different types of interaction on learning achievement, satisfaction and participation in Web-based instruction. *Innovations in Education and Teaching International*, 39(2), 153–162.

Kerres, M. & de Witt, C. (2003). A didactical framework for the design of blended learning arrangements. *Journal of Educational Media*, 28(2–3), 101–113.

Leh, A. (2002). Action research on hybrid courses and their online communities. *Educational Media International*, 39(1), 31–38.

Majeed, A., Fraser, B. J., & Aldridge, J. M. (2002). Learning environment and its association with student satisfaction among mathematics students in Brunei Darussalam. *Learning Environment Research*, 5(2), 203–226.

Medley, D. & Mitzel, H. (1963). Measuring classroom behavior by systematic observation. In N. Gage (Ed.), *Handbook of Research on Teaching* (pp. 247–328). Chicago: Rand McNally.

Merriam, S. B. & Brockett, R. G. (1997). *The Profession and Practice of Adult Education: An Introduction*. San Francisco, CA: Jossey-Bass.

Moos, R. H. (1976). *The Human Context: Environmental Determinants of Behavior*. New York: Wiley.

Moos, R. H. (1979). *Evaluating Educational Environments: Procedures, Measures, Findings and Policy Implications*. San Francisco, CA: Jossey-Bass.

Patton, M. Q. (2002). *Qualitative Research and Evaluation Methods*. Thousand Oaks, CA: Sage.

Rovai, A. P. & Barnum, K. T. (2003). On-line course effectiveness: an analysis of student interactions and perceptions of learning. *Journal of Distance Education*, 18(1), 57–73.

Sisco, B. R. (1991). Setting the climate for effective teaching and learning. In R. Hiemstra (Ed.), *Creating Environments for Effective Adult Learning* (pp. 41–50). San Francisco, CA: Jossey-Bass.

Stonebraker, P. W. & Hazeltine J. E. (2004). Virtual learning effectiveness: an examination of the process. *The Learning Organization*, 11(3), 209–255.

Summers, J. J., Waigandt, A., & Whittaker, T. A. (2005). A comparison of student achievement and satisfaction in an online versus a traditional face-to-face statistics class. *Innovative Higher Education*, 29(3), 233–250.

Taylor, P., & Maor, D. (2000). Assessing the efficacy of online teaching with the constructivist on-line learning environment survey. In A. Herrmann & M. M. Kulski (Eds.), *Flexible Futures in Tertiary Teaching*. Proceedings of the 9th Annual Teaching Learning Forum, Perth: Curtin University of Technology.

Teh, G. P. L. (1999). Assessing student perceptions on internet-based online learning environments. *International Journal of Instructional Media*, 26(4), 397–402.

Walker, S. L. & Fraser, B. J. (2005). Development and validation of an instrument for assessing distance education learning environments in higher education: the Distance Education Learning Environments Survey (DELES). *Learning Environments Research*, 8(3), 289–308.

Withall, J. (1949). The development of a technique for the measurement of social-emotional climate in classrooms. *Journal of Experimental Education*, 17, 347–361.

14 Complex Domain Learning

J.M. Spector

14.1 Introduction

New information and communications technologies have introduced new possibilities for learning and transformed the design of instructional and performance environments in the last 20 years or so (Ganesan et al. 2001; Morgan et al. 2006; Morgan and Spector 2004). At the same time, research in cognitive science has led instructional technologists to think about new ways to support learning and the development of expertise (Schwier et al. 2006; Spector 2004a, b, c; Spector and Anderson 2000; Spector et al. 2005a, b). Along with the advent of new technologies and approaches is an interest in and emphasis on learning and performance in complex domains (e.g., complex and dynamic systems involving tasks such as crisis management, environmental planning, social policy formulation, etc.) (Dörner 1996; Spector 2006a, b; Sterman 1994). This chapter focuses on recent research and developments involving technology-supported learning and performance in complex domains.

It is fairly well understood how to promote learning simple subject matter involving declarative knowledge and straight-forward procedures (Klein et al. 2004; Richey et al. 2001). An excellent overview of methods and approaches that work well in simpler domains can be found in Merrill (2002), who argues that instructional systems that succeed center instruction around authentic problems and can be characterized as (a) progressively and iteratively activating prior knowledge and skills, (b) demonstrating new knowledge and skills, (c) providing extensive opportunities for application of new knowledge and skills, and (d) helping learners integrate new knowledge and skills into related activities. Satisfying these principles of instruction requires blending general knowledge with regard to concepts and principles, specific portrayals of problem situations and solutions, and practice in responding to complex problem situations.

Moreover, research on learning in simpler domains suggests that two things seem to account for most of the variance in terms of learning outcomes: (a) focused time on task (Bloom 1974; Ericsson 2001; Gagné 1985), and (b) robustness of instructional strategy (R. C. Clark 2003; R. E. Clark 2003; Clark and Mayer 2003; Gagné 1985; Merrill 2002). There are of course other relevant factors such as an individual's prior knowledge and experience, interest in the subject area and the situation in which learning occurs. Meaningful feedback is a critical aspect of both focused time on task and robustness of instructional strategy (Banger-Drowns et al. 1991; Kulhavy and Stock 1989). What these and other studies have shown is that timely, informative feedback is generally supportive of learning. How often to provide feedback and how much elaboration to include depends somewhat on how advanced the individual learner is.

One can argue that a combination of these two factors is critical for learning in complex domains. That is to say that it is *effective* time on *meaningful* tasks that matters. An effective instructional strategy is one that is likely to keep learners engaged as their knowledge and skills develop. Motivation and self-regulation are then additional factors that have a strong influence on learning outcomes. If too little learning support is offered initially, learners may become confused and not develop the ability to monitor their own performance. On the other hand, if too much support is offered to advanced learners, they may regard the learning environment as too simple. The development of self-regulatory skills is a generally desirable, long-term goal of many instructional programs. The fading of instructional support as students gain competence and confidence, consistent with the notion of cognitive apprenticeship (Collins et al. 1989), can support the goal of developing self-regulatory skills.

Technology can and has been used effectively to support learning according to the above-mentioned principles and approaches (Spector 2007). However, technology can and has been misused in support of learning. In simpler subject domains that have well-structured sets of knowledge and skills along with well-formulated sets of representative problems that have standard solution approaches and solutions, it is possible to determine which uses of technologies in various situations contribute to learning and how well particular technology support mechanisms function. What is not well understood is whether and to what extent these or other principles, approaches and technologies effectively support learning and instruction in complex domains, which is the focus of this chapter.

14.2 Complex Domains

What one regards as simple or complex is somewhat dependent on the individual making the judgment. A highly experienced automobile mechanic might regard the task of diagnosing the cause for engine misfire as rather simple, whereas an apprentice mechanic might see this task as quite challenging. Apart from individual differences in terms of prior knowledge and experience, however, there are some identifiable characteristics of complex problem situations and problem-solving skills associated with these situations. For example, van Merriënboer (1997) characterizes a complex cognitive skill as one that consists of multiple constituent skills, some of which involve thoughtful processing. Examples of complex cognitive skills can be found in a variety of task domains and problem-solving situations, including air traffic control, computer programming, engineering design, environmental planning, medical diagnosis and repair and maintenance of various kinds of equipment. These task domains vary in terms of how they are complex and the problem-solving challenges they present to those involved. These types of tasks consist of sub-tasks, involve multiple constituent skills and require some thoughtful processing of information during the task. For example, a repair task such as removing and replacing the brakes on an automobile may involve knowledge about operating a hydraulic jack, the ability to remove a wheel and the operation of a brake-fluid pump. When the new brake is installed, the mechanic must check the brake system for leaks and proper operation. Multiple steps and thoughtful processing can be found in many problem and task situations in the other complex domains indicated above.

However, one is inclined to ask about different kinds of complexity, as this might affect how to design learning environments, instructional systems and performance support mechanisms. Jonassen (2004) identifies 11 kinds of problems, ranging from logic problems to dilemmas. Each type represents a particular kind of complexity and has specific characteristics; as a consequence, each problem type has associated instructional strategies and learning activities that are likely to be effective. For example, with regard to dilemmas, the goal might be to engender in the learner an appreciation for the vexing nature of particular choices. This goal might be supported by using technology to present a scenario that immerses the learner in a role-playing situation that requires a decision. For example, such scenarios and simulations can help medical personnel appreciate the consequences of (dis)continuing life support for patients who have been diagnosed as terminally ill and who have asked to be removed from life support.

What is it that makes a problem or task situation complex? One ready answer is to identify sources of complexity. One source of complexity involves the number of components or factors involved. Psychologists have studied the limits of short-term memory and generally agree that serious short-term memory limits exist (Miller 1956). When too many chunks of information are involved or when there are distractions, the cognitive load placed on a learner increases and performance drops (Sweller 1988). In short, the number of components involved is one source of complexity. This this can be called computational complexity. Strategies for addressing this source of complexity include part-to-whole sequencing and part-task training. In other words, if the only source of complexity is due to a large number of factors (many components with which to become familiar, many procedural steps to master or distracting factors), then we know how to support learning and performance, and technology is useful in doing so.

Unfortunately, there are other sources of complexity that are far more difficult to manage. Jonassen (2004) notes that it is the connectedness and types of relationships among various factors that is a primary source of complexity; he also notes that some complex problems are well structured in terms of having well-defined input states, transformation rules and desired goals; however, other problems are ill structured. It is ill-structured complex problems that present particular challenges for learners and for those who design instruction to support learning, as will be discussed subsequently. Dörner (1996) argues that non-linear relationships and those involving delayed effects present challenges for human reasoning even for those who are well educated and highly motivated. Moreover, humans tend to focus on a particular part of a complex system when things begin to go wrong. That is to say that we too easily lose sight of the whole system and the integrated and dynamic nature of its many components when dealing with specific breakdowns in a complex system.

Society confronts a wide range of problems associated with increasingly complex and dynamic systems (e.g., stabilizing national economies, sustaining responsible levels of growth and development, responding to crisis situations, designing engineering solutions for a variety of problems, delivering safe patient care, improving public health, protecting the environment, and educating society for the information age). These problems occur within the context of systems – economic systems, ecological systems, physical systems, human physiological systems, educational systems and so on – and are addressed by organizations, which comprise another kind of system: a social system. The problems themselves are becoming ever more complex due to changes in social and political systems, globalization, advances in technology and other factors. Changes in problem situations and the associated systems occur often at a fundamental level, which places severe cognitive challenges on those who are required to develop solutions and formulate policies with regard to these systems. With increasing problem complexity, it becomes increasingly difficult to understand such systems and to act effectively (Dörner 1996; Sterman 1994). This complexity is coupled with the fact that groups of individuals with differing backgrounds and levels of experience are often involved; in many cases, multiple organizations as well as multiple individuals are involved (Wang et al. 2005). Individual differences play a significant role in problem-solving efficacy, particularly varying with regard to the amount of prior relevant experience (Ericsson 2001; Krems 1995). Many problems critical to society occur within the context of complex, dynamic, multi-agent systems.

It is important for society to develop solutions and strategies for successfully confronting these problems, which some have called "wicked" (Rittel and Webber 1973). Systemic improvement in responding to such problems requires a significantly improved understanding of (a) the dynamics and complexities of these challenging problems, and (b) the ways that individuals and groups perceive situations, conceptualize the problem space and then organize and develop solutions (see Fig. 14.1).

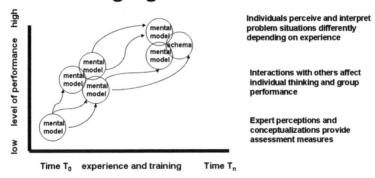

Individual and Group Behavior in Challenging Problem Situations

Individuals perceive and interpret problem situations differently depending on experience

Interactions with others affect individual thinking and group performance

Expert perceptions and conceptualizations provide assessment measures

Wild and Wicked Problems

Characteristics: Complex, ill-structured problem situations; Various individual perceptions and conceptualizations; Many interactions; Elaborated conceptualizations; Actions, decisions and changed situations

Desired Consequences: Effective action; Improved performance; Development of expertise

Fig. 14.1. Complex and ill-structured problem situations

Effective complex problem solving involves interactions between problem solvers and a particular situation, complexities inherent in the underlying system, and perceived and real constraints and requirements associated with the situation. Developing cognitive flexibility (Kozma 2000; Spiro et al. 1991) would seem to be a significant enabling factor for developing skills in solving complex problems. Complex problem solving involves both internal factors (those associated with the human characteristics of problem solvers) and systems' factors (those associated with the underlying complex system), some of which are interrelated (see Fig. 14.1). Individual recall ability is one factor that affects the performance of problem solvers (Ericsson et al. 2000; Krems 1995), but other cognitive variables (e.g., domain-specific knowledge, meta-cognitive strategies, cognitive styles) as well as non-cognitive variables (e.g., self-confidence, perseverance, motivation, enjoyment) also affect problem-solving performance (Dörner and Wearing 1995; Ericsson 2001).

Dörner (1996) addressed these issues in *The Logic of Failure*. At Chernobyl, for example, Dörner found that there were very highly trained and well-motivated individuals operating the nuclear power plant. However, things went badly wrong because these individuals did not have a systemic understanding of the nuclear facility; they conceptualized the problem in terms of a localized perspective (i.e., involving only one sub-system); and they had been reinforced to behave in ways that actually made the problem situation worse (e.g., initially ignoring some instruments that they believed were prone to malfunction, reacting immediately to an apparently local problem, etc.). Gonzalez and Sawicka (2006) provided a systemic representation of unintentional reinforcement of undesired behavior and used that system's model to predict eroding compliance with security concerns. Dörner (1996) and Gonzalez and Sawicka (2006) argue that human performance can be improved if individuals are trained, through the use of interactive simulations, to think holistically and systemically rather than exclusively in terms of particular sub-systems, checklists and standardized procedures. Evidence suggests that such simulations can improve performance and response to unexpected and unlikely situations, and they are widely used in pilot training and more recently in healthcare (Barach et al. 2001).

Conventional methods to teach problem solving are inadequate preparation for the wild and wicked problems that confront society. People are not being prepared to solve ill-structured problems; indeed, the existence of such problems is rarely acknowledged in classroom settings. Experiential instructional methods appear appropriate for ill-structured problem situations, and interactive simulations hold great potential in this regard, although substantial gaps exist in our knowledge with regard to design, use and evaluation. In any case, the situation is ripe for technology's being used to support learning, instruction and performance in complex domains. Of particular interest here is the use of networked technologies (i.e., E-Learning) to support learning in complex domains.

14.3 E-Learning

For our purposes, "E-Learning" is interpreted broadly and includes any use of computers and the Internet to support learning. Online courses delivered using such course management systems as BlackBoard, Moodle, Sakai or WebCT are obvious examples of E-Learning. Courses that are supported through the use of a CD-ROM or DVD and an authored sequence of instruction delivered on a local computer are also included in this interpretation of E-Learning. An example in this category would be an introductory course to a particular foreign language delivered via CD-ROM. Online courses have now surpassed computer-based courses as the prevalent form of E-Learning, although both forms are quite common, and some courses make use of both a local computer running a CD-ROM and Internet-based activities. Computer-based courses tend to be directed at individuals and generally allow individual pacing. Internet-based courses tend to be directed at groups and generally require scheduling within a specified time frame. Exceptions exist in both categories, of course; the point here is to note that computer-based courses are primarily a form of individualized instruction whereas Internet-based courses are primarily a form of group instruction.

There are several things worth noting about E-Learning. First, the prevalence of E-Learning has grown significantly in the last 20 years and is likely to continue to expand in the foreseeable future. Benefits include flexibility with regard to time and place and the potential for some cost savings on the part of both learners and organizations (Spector 2005; Spector et al. 2003).

Second, E-Learning is often held to inappropriate standards. Computer-based courses have often been expected to yield the two sigma benefit associated with personalized tutoring (Bloom 1984). Comparing one-to-one human tutoring with computer-based instruction is wrong-headed because too many relevant differences are entirely overlooked (e.g., the cost and qualifications of a human tutor). What is legitimate is to see to what extent students master specific subject matter and how long it takes them to do so. That is to say that it is certainly legitimate to examine learning outcomes associated with a particular form of instruction; indeed, sound educational practice requires as much. However, there is no reason to expect computer-based courses to produce two sigma improvements over traditional classroom instruction. If a computer-based course produces outcomes that are not significantly different from classroom instruction, then we still should not condemn computer-based instruction as other benefits might pertain. The finding of no significant difference can be highly significant. One might conclude in particular cases that there is no educational loss in moving to computer-based instruction and there might be advantages.

Similar ill-founded contrasts are made between online courses and traditional classroom courses, with the former being discredited as simple-minded page-turners. Again, many lectures are just as deadly boring as simple online courses and they lack the advantage of being easily revisited and accessed multiple times. Again, the finding of no significant difference in terms of learning outcomes may be a significant finding. If an online course is no worse in terms of learning outcomes than a classroom lecture, then other benefits might accrue for both learners and teachers.

Educational researchers are typically inclined to look for educational advantages, and they spend a great deal of time emphasizing the affordances of new technology (Spector 2007). This is certainly legitimate, but it is not essential in showing that E-Learning is useful. What seems pertinent is to retain Merrill's (2002) first principles of instruction and to take them into account when evaluating a particular E-Learning course (or any course). That is to say, if the course is not problem-centered and fails to support multiple applications of new knowledge and skills in a variety of problem-solving circumstances, then it is not likely to promote substantial learning. Too many courses, both traditional courses and E-Learning courses, involve too much telling and showing and too little applying and integrating. The adage that "one learns what one does" is relevant in this context. If all one does is read or listen, then one is not likely to become adept at solving complex problems.

14.4 E-Learning in Complex Domains

How well can one support the development of expertise in complex domains using various forms of E-Learning? This is an instance when the notion of an affordance (Gibson 1979) is particularly relevant. Affordances refer to the things made possible by a particular feature of an object. Ill-structured problems that arise within the context of complex and dynamic systems cannot easily be recreated in a classroom environment. As noted earlier, research clearly shows that practice is critical for the development of expertise. How then is one to achieve competency in a complex problem-solving domain unless one is able to practice on a variety of complex problems? Interactive simulations offer the relevant affordances (Alessi 2000; Milrad et al. 2002; Spector 2000; Spector and Anderson 2000). Most instructional designers and technologists argue that simulation-based instruction can support learning in and about complex domains. Interactive simulations have the affordance of being able to engage learners in situations not reasonably possible to create otherwise (Spector and Davidsen 2000, 2001). These simulations can be delivered on a stand-alone computer or through the Internet. The computer can simulate one or more of the decision-makers or intelligent agents involved in the situation. Additional affordances of interactive simulations are a result of their digital nature. Situations can be varied in terms of complexity, and a sequence of problems can be presented to learners consistent with the principles of cognitive apprenticeship (Collins et al. 1989) and model-facilitated learning (Milrad et al. 2002).

It is expensive to develop highly interactive simulations for use in E-Learning environments. Typically, such simulations require a team of developers working for one or more years in concert with subject matter experts. Validation of the simulation is an important step in the development process. The simulation must be authentic for users; the consequences of user actions and decisions must be faithful to what would happen in the actual situation. Validation of a complex simulation may take many months. Developing a robust pedagogical framework around the simulation also takes time and requires field testing. In short, while there are many learning benefits to such advanced forms of E-Learning, the associated development costs are significant.

There are other more affordable forms of E-Learning that can support learning in complex domains. For example, having access to others and asking about how they regard a particular complex problem can develop individual reflection on and analysis of various problem factors. E-mail, discussion threads, blogs and wikis can all be used for such a purpose. It is imaginable that one can develop a database containing representative problems in a particular domain along with annotated and elaborated expert solutions; these can be used to provide practice problems along with meaningful feedback to learners. This kind of system-generated feedback can also promote meta-cognitive and self-regulatory skills in a learner. For example, if a learner submits a response to a complex problem to a system with such a database, the system can respond by saying, "Thanks for your problem response. Here is a response developed by an acknowledged expert in the area. Can you identify similarities and differences between your response and this one?" Such a system could also present a learner with a problem scenario along with a prepared solution and then ask the learner to critique that solution. Once one acknowledges the importance and relevance of timely and informative feedback in the learning process, one is immediately led to issues pertaining to assessment and evaluation, which are discussed next.

14.5 Assessment and Evaluation

It was noted earlier that, with regard to simpler task domains and problem-solving situations, it is possible to determine through established individual assessment and program evaluation methods what works (and occasionally, why it works) with different learners in various contexts. However, with regard to the kinds of complex domains described here, it is quite difficult to determine what works and why. There are at least two serious challenges to the assessment and evaluation of learning in and about complex domains. First, many of the problems that arise in these situations are ill-structured and lack standard solutions. Indeed, there are often multiple acceptable approaches and responses to problems in these domains. How, then, is one to determine that individuals are improving, especially with resepct to various instructional interventions and performance support mechanisms?

Spector and Koszalka (2004) developed a method to assess progress of learning in complex domains. Basically, their approach is to identify representative problem scenarios, ask highly experienced individuals to indicate how they conceptualize the problem space, then ask learners before, during and after instruction to conceptualize the problem space and look for similarities and differences in the learners' responses. In the cases examined thus far (biology, engineering design and medical diagnosis), there have been clearly identifiable patterns among the problem conceptualizations of highly experienced individuals. Moreover, it is possible to develop metrics to see how far individual responses are from an expert response (Spector et al. 2005a, b) and how individual responses progressively develop over time and through instruction (Dummer and Ifenthaler 2005; Seel 1995; Seel et al. 2000). Other researchers also use concept mapping and systems modeling to determine how well individuals understand a particular problem situation (Clariana and Strobel 2007; Größler et al. 2003; Herl et al. 1999; O'Connor and Johnson 2004).

A second serious challenge to assessment and evaluation in complex domains results from the involvement of a requirement for multiple persons to develop responses to actual problems. The traditional unit of analysis in learning and performance has been the individual, but with regard to the kinds of complex problem-solving tasks discussed here, it is really how well a group of individuals responds that is the most relevant unit of analysis. One team member may excel in a particular component skill, but overall performance often requires competent performance by all team members. In short, not only is performance difficult to measure because there is not a single, standard solution, but team performance is of particular interest, as shown by the growing interest in collaborative learning (Dillenbourg et al. 1996). Team dynamics add an additional layer of analysis to the already difficult problem of assessment and evaluation in complex domains (O'Connor and Johnson 2004).

14.6 Future Developments

Predicting the future is problematic. There is this fundamental problem: On what evidence does one support the notion that the future will resemble the past? If one abandons the belief that the future will resemble the past in relevant ways, then predictions are entirely without foundation. For example, when the earth, moon and sun are aligned (e.g., full and new moon phases), the tides are higher than at other times. I might be able to calculate when the earth, moon and sun will next be aligned and then predict that a high tide will occur at that time. However, to make that prediction, I must assume that the past pattern of high tides occurring at times of lunar-solar alignment will continue into the future. While I might be able to generate an explanation for such an assumption involving gravity and other relevant phenomena, I cannot know that relevant aspects will not change. We rarely think about this dilemma with regard to common physical phenomena, but that is how I am inclined to think about the future of technology-enhanced learning in complex domains.

I would like to believe that we will find much less expensive ways to develop highly interactive and highly distributed simulations. I would like to believe that we will find ways to use technology to personalize instruction to approach two sigma learning benefits. I would like to believe that vast repositories of validated learning and instructional objects will be available to everyone, rich or poor, anywhere in the world. I would like to believe that we will become the knowledge planet with tolerant societies sharing information and living in peace. I would like to believe.

References

Alessi, S. (2000). Building versus using simulations. In J. M Spector and T. M. Anderson (Eds.), *Integrated and Holistic Perspectives on Learning, Instruction, and Technology: Understanding Complexity* (pp. 175–196). Dordrecht: Kluwer.

Banger-Drowns, R. L., Kulik, C-L. C., Kulik, J. A., & Morgan, M. T. (1991). The instructional effects of feedback in test-like events. *Review of Educational Research, 61*, 213–218.

Barach, P., Satish, U., & Streufert, S. (2001). Healthcare assessment and performance: Using simulation. *Simulation and Gaming, 32*, 147–155.

Bloom, B. S. (1974). Time and learning. *American Psychologist, 29*, 682–688.

Bloom, B. S. (1984). The 2-sigma problem: The search for methods of group instruction as effective as one-to-one tutoring. *Educational Researcher, 13*, 4–16.

Clariana, R. B., & Strobel, J. (2007). Modeling technologies. In J. M. Spector, M. D. Merrill, J. J. G. van Merriënboer, & M. P. Driscoll, *Handbook of Research on Educational Communications and Technology* (3rd ed.). Mahwah, NJ: Erlbaum.

Clark, R. C. (2003). *Building Expertise: Cognitive Methods for Training and Performance Improvement.* Washington DC: International Society for Performance Improvement.

Clark, R. E. (2003). What works in distance learning: Instructional strategies. In H. F. O'Neil (Ed.), *What Works in Distance Learning* (pp. 13–31). Los Angeles, CA: Center for the Study of Evaluation.

Clark, R. C., & Mayer, R. E. (2003). *E-Learning and the Science of Instruction.* San Francisco, CA: Jossey-Bass Pfeiffer.

Collins, A., Brown, J. S., & Newman, S. E. (1989). Cognitive apprenticeship: Teaching the craft of reading, writing and mathematics. In L. B. Resnick (Ed.), *Knowing, learning and instruction: Essays in honor of Robert Glaser* (pp. 453–494). Hillsdale, NJ: Erlbaum.

Dillenbourg, P., Baker, M., Blaye, A., & O'Malley, C. (1996). The evolution of research on collaborative learning. In P. Reimann, & H. Spada (Eds.), *Learning in humans and machines: Towards an interdisciplinary learning science* (pp. 189–211). London: Pergamon.

Dörner, D. (1996). *The Logic of Failure: Why Things Go Wrong and What We Can Do to Make Them Right* (R. Kimber & R. Kimber, Translators). New York: Metropolitan Books.

Dörner, D., & Wearing, A. (1995). Complex problem solving: Toward a (computer-simulated) theory. In P. A. Frensch, & J. Funke (Eds.), *Complex Problem Solving: The European Perspective* (pp. 65–99). Hillsdale, NJ: Lawrence Erlbaum.

Dummer, P., & Ifenthaler, D. (2005). *Planning and assessing navigation in learning environments: Why learners often do not follow the path laid out for them.* Presentation at the International Conference for Methods and Technologies for Teaching, Palermo, Italy, March, 2005.

Ericsson, K. A. (2001). Attaining excellence through deliberate practice: Insights from the study of expert performance. In M. Ferrari (Ed.), *The Pursuit of Excellence in Education* (pp. 21–55). Mahwah, NJ: Erlbaum.

Ericsson, K. A., Patel, V., & Kintsch, W. (2000). How experts' adaptations to representative task demands account for the expertise effect in memory recall: Comment on Vicente and Wang (1998). *Psychology Review, 107*(3), 578–592.

Gagné, R. M. (1985). *The Conditions of Learning* (4th ed.). New York, NY: Holt, Rinehart and Winston.

Ganesan, R., Edmonds, G. S., & Spector, J. M. (2001). The changing nature of instructional design for networked learning. In C. Jones, & C. Steeples (Eds.), *Networked Learning in Higher Education* (pp. 93–109). Berlin Heidelberg New York: Springer.

Gibson, J. J. (1979). *The Ecological Approach to Visual Perception*. Boston: Houghton Mifflin.

Gonzalez, J. J., & Sawicka, A. (2006). Compliance: A tension between conditioning and cognition. *Technology, Instruction, Cognition and Learning, 3*, 265–288.

Größler, A., Rouwette, E. A. J. A., & Vennix, J. A. M. (2003). *Exploring rationality with system dynamics based simulators: A literature review*. Paper presented at the International Systems Dynamics Conference, New York, July, 2003.

Herl, H. E., O'Neil, H. F. Jr., Chung, G. L., & Schacter, J. (1999). Reliability and validity of a computer-based knowledge mapping system to measure content understanding. *Computers in Human Behavior, 15*(3–4), 315–333.

Jonassen, D. II. (2004). *Learning to Solve Problems: An Instructional Design Guide*. San Francisco, CA: Pfeiffer.

Klein, J. D., Spector, J. M., Grabowski, B., & de la Teja, I. (2004). *Instructor Competencies: Standards for Face-to-Face, Online and Blended Settings*. Greenwich, CT: Information Age.

Kozma, R. B. (2000). The use of multiple representations and the social construction of understanding in chemistry. In M. Jacobson & R. Kozma (Eds.), *Innovations in Science and Mathematics Education: Advanced Designs for Technologies of Learning* (pp. 11–46). Mahwah, NJ: Erlbaum.

Krems, J. F. (1995). Cognitive flexibility and complex problem solving. In P. A. Frensch & J. Funke (Eds.), *Complex Problem Solving: The European Perspective* (pp. 201–218). Hillsdale, NJ: Lawrence Erlbaum.

Kulhavy, R. W., & Stock, W. A. (1989). Feedback in written instruction: The place of response certitude. *Educational Psychology Review, 1*(4), 279–308.

Merrill, M. D. (2002). First principles of instruction. *Educational Technology Research and Development, 50*(3), 43–59.

Miller, G. A. (1956). The magical number seven, plus or minus two: Some limits on our capacity for processing information. *Psychology Review, 63*, 81–97.

Milrad, M., Spector, J. M., & Davidsen, P. I. (2002). Model facilitated learning. In S. Naidu (Ed.), *Learning and Teaching with Technology: Principles and Practices* (pp. 13–27). London: Kogan Page.

Morgan, K., & Spector, J. M. (Eds.) (2004). *The Internet Society: Advances in Learning, Commerce and Society*. Southampton UK: Wessex Institute of Technology.

Morgan, K. M., Brebbia, C. A., & Spector, J. M. (Eds.) (2006). *The Internet Society II: Advances in Education, Commerce and Governance*. Southampton, UK: WIT.

O'Connor, D. L., & Johnson, T. E. (2004). Measuring team cognition: Concept mapping elicitation as a means of constructing team shared mental models in an applied setting. In A. J. Canas, J. D. Novak, & F. M. Gonzalez (Eds.), Concept Maps: Theory, Methodology, Technology, Vol 1. *Proceedings of the First International Conference on Concept Mapping* (pp. 487–493). Pamplona, Spain: Public University of Navarra.

Richey, R. C., Fields, D. C., & Foxon, M. with Roberts, R. C., Spannaus, T., & Spector, J. M. (2001). *Instructional Design Competencies: The Standards* (3rd ed.). Syracuse, NY: ERIC Clearinghouse on Information and Technology.

Rittel, H., & Webber, M. (1973). Dilemmas in a general theory of planning. *Policy Sciences, 4*, 155–169.

Schwier, R., Hill, J., Wager, W., & Spector, J. M. (2006). Where have we been and where are we going? Limiting and liberating forces in IDT. In M. Orey, V. J. McLendon, & R. M. Branch (Eds.), *Educational Media and Technology Yearbook 2006*. Portsmouth, NH: Greenwood.

Seel, N. M. (1995). Mental models, knowledge transfer and teaching strategies. *Journal of Structural Learning, 12*(3), 197–213.

Seel, N. M., Al-Diban, S., & Blumschein, P. (2000). Mental models and instructional planning. In J. M. Spector & T. M. Anderson (Eds.), *Integrated and Holistic Perspectives on Learning, Instruction and Technology: Understanding Complexity* (pp. 129–158). Dordrecht, The Netherlands: Kluwer.

Spector, J. M. (2000). System dynamics and interactive learning environments: Lessons learned and implications for the future. *Simulation and Gaming, 31*(3), 457–464.

Spector, J. M. (2004a). Current issues in new learning. In K. Morgan, C. A. Brebbia, J. Sanchez, & A. Voiskounsky (Eds.), *Human Perspectives in the Internet Society: Culture, Psychology and Gender* (pp. 429–440). Southampton, UK: WIT.

Spector, J. M. (2004b). Multiple uses of information and communication technology in education. In N. Seel & S. Dijkstra (Eds.), *Curriculum, Plans and Processes of Instructional Design*. Mahwah, NJ: Erlbaum.

Spector, J. M. (2004c). Problems with problem-based learning: Comments on model-centered learning and instruction in Seel (2003). *Technology, Instruction, Cognition and Learning, 1*(4), 359–374.

Spector, J. M. (2005). Time demands in online instruction. *Distance Education, 26*(1), 3–25.

Spector, J. M. (2006a). A methodology for assessing learning in complex and ill-structured task domains. *Innovations in Education and Teaching International, 43*(2), 109–120.

Spector, J. M. (2006b). From learning to instruction: Adventures and advances in instructional design. In G. Clarebout & J. Elen (Eds.), *Avoiding Simplicity, Confronting Complexity: Advances in Studying and Designing (Computer-Based) Powerful Learning Environments* (pp. 15–27). Rotterdam: Sense.

Spector, J. M. (Ed.) (2007). *Finding Your Online Voice: Stories Told by Experienced Online Educators*. Mahwah, NJ: Erlbaum.

Spector, J. M., & Anderson, T. M. (Eds.) (2000). *Integrated and Holistic Perspectives on Learning, Instruction and Technology: Understanding Complexity*. Dordrecht: Kluwer.

Spector, J. M., & Davidsen, P. I. (2000). Designing technology enhanced learning environments. In B. Abbey (Ed.), *Instructional and Cognitive Impacts of Web-Based Education* (pp. 241–260). Hershey, PA: Idea.

Spector, J. M., & Davidsen, P. I. (2001). Cognitive complexity in decision making and policy formulation: A system dynamics perspective. In R. Sanchez & A. Henee (Eds.), *A Systems Perspective on Resources, Capabilities and Management Processes* (pp. 155–171). Amsterdam: Elsevier.

Spector, J. M., & Koszalka, T. A. (2004). *The DEEP Methodology for Assessing Learning in Complex Domains* [Final report to the National Science Foundation Evaluative Research and Evaluation Capacity Building]. Syracuse, NY: Syracuse University.

Spector, J. M., Doughty, P. L., & Yonai, B. A. (2003). *Cost and Learning Effects of Alternative E-Collaboration Methods in Online Settings* [Final report for the Andrew W. Mellon Foundation Cost Effective Use of Technology in Teaching Initiative]. Syracuse, NY: Syracuse University.

Spector, J. M., Dennen, V. P., & Koszalka, T. A. (2005a). Causal maps, mental models and assessing acquisition of expertise. *Technology, Instruction, Cognition and Learning, 3*(1–2).

Spector, J. M., Ohrazda, C., Van Schaack, A., & Wiley, D. A. (Eds.) (2005b). *Innovations in Instructional Technology: Essays in Honor of M. David Merrill*. Mahwah, NJ: Erlbaum.

Spiro, R. J., Feltovich, P. J., Jacobson, M. J., & Coulson, R. L. (1991). Cognitive flexibility, constructivism and hypertext: Random access instruction for advanced knowledge acquisition in ill-structured domains. *Educational Technology, 31*(9), 22–25.

Sterman, J. D. (1994). Learning in and about complex systems. *System Dynamics Review, 10*(2–3), 291–330.

Sweller, J. (1988). Cognitive load during problem solving: Effects on learning. *Cognitive Science, 12*, 257–285.

Van Merriënboer, J. J. G. (1997). *Training Complex Cognitive Skills: A Four-Component Instructional Design Model for Technical Training*. Englewood Cliffs, NJ: Educational Technology Publications.

Wang, X., Dannenhoffer, J. F. III, Davidson, B. D., & Spector, J. M. (2005). Design issues in a cross-institutional collaboration on a distance education course. *Distance Education, 26*(3), 405–423.

15 Communities of Practice

P. Reimann

Although being essentially a descriptive social theory, the communities of practice (CoP) idea has been frequently employed to guide instructional design, in particular the design of online learning communities. The chapter sets out by relating CoP as developed by Lave and Wenger (1991) to socio-cultural theories of learning. I then critically inspect the notion of an online community, noting that most of these so-called communities fall short on the social dimension. The Inquiry Learning Forum is introduced as a typical example for an online community platform (for in-service teachers), and building on this specific instance a set of general design guidelines for online communities of learning are identified. I also sketch possible implications for the role software developers and instructional designers can play when designing for communities of users. The chapter closes by a look at recent management research relating to CoPs and identifies research desiderata.

15.1 Introduction

The invention of the community of practice (CoP) concept is attributed to Lave and Wenger's (1991) ethnographic study of situated learning in apprenticeship relations. Based on their analysis of apprenticeship relations amongst Yucatec midwives, Vai and Gola tailors, naval quartermasters, meat cutters, and non-drinking alcoholics, they define a CoP as "a system of relationships between people, activities, and the world; developing with time, and in relation to other tangential and overlapping communities of practice" (p. 98). Brown et al. (1989), among others, have developed the concept further, and Wenger (1998) provides a detailed account of a CoP in an insurance claims processing office. More recently, because of the importance the concept gained in (knowledge) management circles, Wenger et al. (2002) have made suggestions as to how organisations can foster and sustain CoPs.

Although Wenger (1998) does not include an explicit definition of CoP, approximations suggested by others such as Barab and Duffy (2000) are helpful: "Roughly, a community of practice involves a collection of individuals sharing mutually defined practices, beliefs, and understandings over an extended time frame in the pursuit of a shared enterprise" (p. 36). Building on Wenger's work and interpretations thereof, characteristics of CoPs are (1) shared knowledge, values and beliefs; (2) overlapping histories among members; (3) mutual interdependence; (4) shared enterprise; and (5) mechanisms for reproduction (Barab et al. 2004).

15.2 Learning as Participation

Learning, as employed in education, has mostly been used with a meaning best characterized by the acquisition metaphor (Sfard 1998): to learn means to acquire knowledge in the form of concepts or rules. The knowledge can then accumulate, become refined, or be combined with other knowledge. The metaphor of learning as acquisition permeates educational thought so extensively that its metaphorical impact was only open to reflection once an alternative was suggested by Lave and Wenger (1991): learning as participation. In the participation metaphor, learning is conceived as a process of becoming a member of a certain community. Becoming a member does not happen automatically, but is very much dependent on the learner actively adopting the language of the community, adapting to its norms, and, over time, negotiating new meanings and contributing to the modification of practices. The metaphor of learning as participation refers to the fact that as learners become accepted members of a community, they also participate in the creation of meaning, that is, in the creation of knowledge that has value with respect to the community's practices and values. The shift from knowledge as a material-like substrate that an individual owns to *knowing* as an activity within a social context should also be noted.

The notion of participation is central to the wider theoretical framework that sees learning as always situated in specific physical and social settings (Brown et al. 1989), and has been further developed, for instance, by Wenger in his studies on communities of practice (Wenger 1998; Wenger et al. 2002). Research in the socio-cultural and anthropological tradition that gave rise to the participation metaphor was initially conducted with respect to manual practices, such as in communities of midwives and butchers (Lave and Wenger 1991), but has been quickly applied to "cognitive" domains as well, in particular to learning mathematics (e.g., Carraher 1991) and to the practices commonly found in today's white-collar workplaces (Handley et al. 2006). Participation, not only in the sense of interacting with the social environment but also with the physical environment, is central to ecological theories of learning as well (Barab and Roth 2006).

15.2.1 Types of CoPs

Not all CoPs are alike. While the applied management literature on CoPs treats them as mostly one-dimensional, others have suggested that CoPs be distinguished by their initial purpose or their stage of development (Gongla and Rizzuto 2001). Wenger et al. (2002) note that CoPs take different forms depending on size, life span, geographic dispersion, boundary span, creation process and degree of institutionalized formalism. Dube et al. (2006) suggest a typology for virtual CoPs, also useful for face-to-face CoPs, based on their careful analysis of the research literature as well as observational studies. The main dimensions in this typology are demographics, organizational context, membership characteristics and the technological environment.

Particularly important for this chapter is the type of CoP that has a focus on learning, sometimes called communities of learning (CoLs). Although I will continue to use the term CoP, this chapter is mainly about CoLs. And CoLs themselves come in different forms. A very useful distinction has been suggested by Riel and Polin (2004): task-based, practice-based, and knowledge-based learning communities. When compared along dimensions such as membership, task features and learning goals, participation structures, and mechanisms for growth and development, these overlapping types of learning communities differ from each other and, hence, require different kinds of designs and support.

Task-based learning communities are typically groups of people with comparatively few members who work together for a specified period of time to accomplish a specific objective, such as generating a product. While not a community in the strict sense, but rather a team, team members often experience a strong sense of identification with the task, team and organization. Practice-based learning communities are larger groups with an un-specified life span, and shared, but not specific, goals. Membership is not formally defined. Such communities provide for their members "richly contextualized and supported arenas for learning" (Riel and Polin 2004), centered around shared practices. Knowledge-based learning communities, finally, are similar to communities of practice in many respects, but focus on the deliberate and formal production of external knowledge about their practice. The related notion of knowledge-building communities (Scardamalia and Bereiter 2003) focuses entirely on the practice of knowledge building.

15.2.2 Online Communities, Virtual Communities

The phrase "online community" is probably the most over-used term in the short history of the Internet. Rheingold (1993) is often cited as providing the original definition of virtual communities as "… social aggregations that emerge from the Net when enough people carry on … public discussions long enough, with sufficient human feeling, to form webs of personal relations in cyberspace" (p. 5). If community is used with the meaning common among social scientists, at least, then it becomes questionable as to whether people who participate (occasionally) in an Internet forum or a chat room can be considered to be a community; similarly, groups of professionals who come together online (or off-line, for that matter) to learn do not automatically form a community. In most cases, it would be more appropriate to speak of groups and acknowledge that developing a group into a community is a major accomplishment, requiring special processes and practices (Kling and Courtright 2003). Only few online groups can be considered CoPs when we use the characteristics mentioned above as a yardstick. Hence, virtual communities and CoPs may be more virtual than we might like them to be.

The term community is, of course, aspirational in nature, frequently used by politicians and real-estate developers, in addition to web designers. In common language, community "… usually connotes a group which shares warm, caring and reciprocal social relationships among its members" (Kling and Courtright 2003). In sociology, it was found important to distinguish community from society (the German language makes a nice distinction between *gemeinschaft* and *gesellschaft*), and community is typically used by experts for social configurations with dense and demanding social ties, ritual occasions, common beliefs and practices (Brint 2001). From a social science perspective, then, the definition suggested (and frequently employed) by Rheingold is one-sided because it focuses on the medium of a conversational forum, and thus does not provide a basis for distinguishing communities from other social configurations, such as groups, hang-outs or associations. In Preece's (2000) analysis, community, as used by the Internet community, is identical with online communication, and hence of little analytical use.

It is worth keeping in mind that the theory of CoPs as introduced by Lave and Wenger is not so much a theory of learning as it is a theory of socialization. Particularly in Lave's writings, the development of identity within social contexts is the main line of development that needs to be understood, with the production of meaning as an integrated element. Quite different from the forms of interaction we find in online environments, communities have a common cultural and historical heritage, are one system within a set of interdependent systems and have the capacity to reproduce themselves (Barab and Duffy 2000).

Because communities are mainly social spaces, those interested in capitalizing on CoPs for the purpose of the creation of intellectual and social capital (knowledge management) and for the purpose of learning/socialization face a substantial design challenge. Preece (2000) identified the maintenance of sociability as one of the biggest tasks of successful online communities, and, in turn, of those who are designing for and maintaining such communities. The challenge is even greater as sociability is not only a function of the tools, but of the emerging interactions, which are in turn affected by social awareness and trust.

Virtual cooperation can be seriously handicapped by the difficulty of accessing the non-verbal cues, which we use to create social awareness. The absence of these cues can be linked to the slow development of trust between team members and therefore a source of sub-optimal performance. Daniel et al. (2003) consider social structures as social capital and tightly interwoven with trust. One function of social capital is to enable the community or group to obtain and distribute this wealth, ultimately satisfying the members more than if they were not members. Daniel et al. identify the level of trust as a key difference between virtual learning communities and distributed communities of practice. They categorise a virtual learning community as having a low level of trust, whereas the familiar, distributed community of practice has high levels of trust.

An Example for an Online CoP

One of the best-researched virtual online communities is ILF, the Inquiry Learning Forum (http://ilf.crlt.indiana.edu), which serves a community of practice consisting of in-service and pre-service mathematics and science teachers (Barab et al. 2003). As shown in Fig. 15.1, the ILF offers a range of structures for participation, such as the lounge area and the inquiry lab. Some of the primary areas for collaboration are the ILF Classrooms, enabling members to visit the classroom of other teachers in a virtual manner.

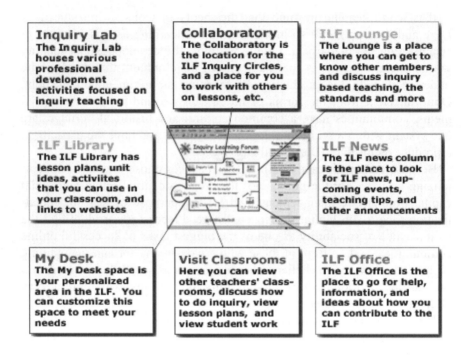

Fig. 15.1. Elements of the Inquiry Learning Forum (accessed on 18 Dec. 2006 at http: //ifl.crlt.indiana.edu)

Each classroom holds lessons taught by a specific teacher, and by selecting a specific lesson, one can watch video segments of the lesson. These shared lesson examples are important for the practices of teachers because they extend their school practices. In schools, teachers rarely visit each other's lessons. ILF provides the opportunity for teachers to learn from each other by observing and commenting on the video segments. To support this exchange of information around lessons segmented, the designers of the ILF created the collaboratory. The collaboratory is a space in which (typically small) groups of teachers can come together to exchange experiences. Each group within the collaboratory is referred to as an inquiry circle, and the contents of an inquiry circle are only visible to its members. It is probably fair to say that the ILF hosts multiple CoPs, each of them occupying an inquiry circle space.

ILF shares a number of goals and design features with Tapped In (www.tappedin.org), another online education community of practice (Schlager and Fusco 2004). Both environments are well documented and researched (see the reader edited by Barab et al. 2004).

15.3 CoP as a Metaphor for Online Design

The interest in the concept of a CoP has been tremendous, and has not been restricted to learning researchers in search of a fresh theoretical lens through which to describe and analyze complex learning. Practitioners such as managers have been attempting to employ CoPs as a means to foster knowledge building and dissemination in organizations, and instructional designers have been attempting to use CoPs as a guideline for the design of online professional development environments.

Those instructional designers who want to use this theory as a guiding metaphor have to grapple with a number of tensions, or dualities, to use Barab, MaKinster and Scheckler's (2003) term. A core challenge is the tension between CoPs as designed and emergent. Since communities are by definition self-organizing systems, emerging in response to local conditions and the needs of their members, there are definite limits to affecting them by design. Wenger (1998) himself speaks of "minimalist design", consisting of the creation of a tentative platform and then facilitating the community in growing and evolving its own space (Barab et al. 2003).

Another duality, or productive tension, built into the notion of CoPs is the one between participation and reification. It is through participation in community-recognized practices that members become part of the community, with participation at the root of both meaning-building and identity formation. When a cooperative practice is accomplished, the resulting outcome often takes the form of representational artifacts (text, drawing, calculation, etc.). These artifacts reify the experience of the practice. Because reifying helps a community to communicate and sustain its practices, it is an extremely important process. At the same time, the artifact is not the practice itself, and hence suffers from the same problems as all representations, all models: because they are necessarily incomplete, they are to some extent wrong and misleading. While practices are messy and dynamic, their reifications are neat and static – a "useful illusion" (Wenger 1998). In online communication, textual artifacts play a very central role because the technical media often do not allow the transportation of other signals. Thus, for online communities in which practices are only indirectly shared, and often only shared via textual representations, reification may come too early, too frequently and in too limited a representational format. The use of video and other "rich" media provides some relief, but does not solve all of the problems, see Barab et al. (2004).

15.3.1 Guideposts for Design

Because each CoP is unique and follows its own dynamics, no specific design guidelines have been suggested in the literature, except for the general advice to design for flexibility and sociability. The general heuristic is to avoid over-designing and to leave room for the community members to create their own place in the space provided by the designer. In general, it is easier to identify the Don'ts rather than the Do's. Schlager and Fusco (2004) discuss a number of guideposts for designing community technology, which I will summarize here.

Learning processes: As the learning processes in CoPs are essentially social and informal, occurring as a side-effect of engaging in joint practices, technology should cater to this informal nature and thus support the social structures that promote community learning processes. Software such as learning management systems with their linear structure and course-oriented navigation may not be well suited. Instead, groupware tools, with their focus on communication, artifact creation and shared ownership, are potentially better suited.

History and culture: Since the history of a CoP is substantially encapsulated in workplace artifacts (e.g., lessons plans, assessments, portfolios in the case of teachers), technology should support the creation, management, reuse and modification of these artifacts. From a design perspective, the aspects of re-use and modification are probably most relevant because they usually do not happen spontaneously. There is also the danger of offering document support functionality that is closely related to document management software used in hierarchically structured organizations. In terms of software genres, a wiki might be better suited than Lotus Notes.

Community reproduction and evolution: A pivotal resource for any CoP is its stock of senior practitioners, who might cover a wide area of diverse expertise. Technology ought to be put to use to allow CoPs to harness this expertise by making it available in the form of informal, personal relationships. Informal mentorship relations, for instance, constitute a powerful means to convey professional knowledge, but are difficult to scale to larger communities when the interaction is restricted to face-to-face contacts between mentor and mentee.

Leadership: Leadership in CoPs may intersect with, but is not identical to, organizational management structures. Community leaders primarily perform social support services: organizing, networking and brokering. E-Learning and intranet systems that come with a strong organizational/ managerial framework do not fit within the predominantly social and emergent nature of leadership in CoPs.

Local/Global: In addition to support for the building of communities, knowledge transfer into the wider community is essential – and difficult. From this perspective, dedicated groupware systems seem less than ideal, at least to the extent that they include a strong in-group/out-group element.

In addition, Schlager and Fusco (2004) mention two guideposts that are more specific to community of teaching professionals.

- Membership identity and multiplicity: CoPs in educational professions are characterized by the high diversity of tasks, roles and expertise of their members. Due to the personalized nature of classroom teaching, interests are varied and teachers come and go, leading to a high turnover. Hence, software designed to support teacher CoPs ought to support building and management of professional identity and finding the right people to cooperate with, as well as have the flexibility to allow members to function in multiple roles.
- Social networks: Teachers' CoPs tend to be more loosely structured than CoPs in other professions. Technology can be used to analyze social networks in online communities, thus identifying the substructures, such as cliques, where frequent and reciprocal interactions do take place. Likewise, identifying where those cliques overlap can lead to an approach to community-wide information exchange via bridging members.

In addition to these general functional requirements for community support software and online environments, it needs to be stressed that designers need to have a clear understanding of what practices are to be supported. While each good software design should be based on an understanding of peoples' practices, there is no question that supporting CoPs requires serious effort to that effect. And, since CoPs are self-organized, any changes to existing practices as enforced by the software environment will need to be very carefully designed and introduced, or else potential community members will vote with their mice and leave.

15.3.2 Frameworks for Design

As said before, designing online communities of practice for learning communities is a formidable challenge. These challenges centre around the tension between designing for, versus the emergence of, structures (Barab et al. 2003), around the issue of sociability of virtual environments (Preece 2000) and around the needs of autonomous life-long learners who might not comply with instructional designs (Goodyear 2005a). In the context of designing for online CoPs, the "design fallacy" is particularly problematic.

This design fallacy is the belief that all major design decisions need to be made before the software is developed and used, and that design can primarily be improved by learning ever more about the end user needs and characteristics (Williams et al. 2005). This fallacy is related to the view that places a lot of attention and importance on the initial design process and pays much less attention to the appropriation and domestication processes (Lie and Sorensen 1996) performed by users.

Seeding, Growth, Re-seeding

Gerd Fischer's SER design methodology – Seeding, Evolutionary growth, and Re-seeding – has its roots in his work with design teams and computational support for distributed design processes. Starting from the observation that today's design problems (for instance, in software engineering, in architecture and in urban planning) require more knowledge than any single person can possess, and that the relevant knowledge is often distributed among many people with different perspectives and background knowledge, he suggests that social capital and social creativity should be capitalized on by designing software support systems that can elicit social creativity (Fischer et al. 2004). Fischer suggests that the SER model of software design for developing systems that support social creativity be used for this, which has clear relevance for the design of online environments for CoPs.

The basis of SER is a model of the user who acts as a designer continuously. Users in the SER are seen as involved in the design of (computational) artifacts not only at the design time, when the original system is developed, but also at the use time. This goes beyond participatory design, where user involvement is strong, but only during the design phase. Structurally, this calls for models of meta-design that avoid the separation of design and use and allow users to create systems that permit continuous change to take place. The SER method is iterative in nature with cycles going repeatedly through three main phases (Fischer et al. 2001): (1) The seeding process, in which users (also called domain designers by Fischer) and developers (also called environment designers) work together to create a design environment seeded with domain knowledge; (2) the evolutionary growth process, in which users change and extend the initial seed; (3) the reseeding process, in which incremental changes are organized, reformulated and incorporated into the initial seed for the next cycle. Examples for this meta-design approach can be found in the cited literature as well as in Fischer and Ostwald (2003). DePaula et al. (2001) discuss the application of the SER model to the design of online course materials.

Information Ecologies

Nardi's (1996) notion of information ecologies is more of a stance on software design than a design framework. It does not provide one with a design method but presents a viewpoint that is quite relevant for our topic. Information ecologies are broadly defined to be "… a system of people, practices, values, and technologies in a particular local environment" (p. 49). Examples of such ecologies are libraries, offices and intensive care units; in each case, we find people interacting with each other and with technologies for specific purposes. Computers are used as a tool, but are not in the centre of practices. People usually help each other when they experience problems with the technical artifacts.

The metaphor of an information ecology refers intentionally to a number of characteristics of eco-systems. For example, like ecosystems, information ecologies are systems with strong interrelationships amongst their components – amongst people, space, and equipment. Diversity is another eco-characteristic Nardi alludes to: tools should be sufficiently specialized to fill the various niches that fields of practice offer; monocultures are to be avoided. Like natural systems, information ecologies are not static, but are dynamic equilibria. The social and technical aspects of an environment coevolve: changes in tools require practices to change; these changes in practice require the tools to be adapted. An information ecology can be seen as having keystone species, species whose presence is crucial to the survival of the ecology. An example of a keystone species is the mediators, members of organizations who build bridges across institutional boundaries. Finally, locality is an important feature of information ecologies: for technology to serve its users best it must be controlled by them and fit their practices. Nardi speaks of habitation of a technology as its "location within a network of relationships" (p. 55), comparable to Lie and Sorensen's (1996) notion of domestication.

Networked Communities

It is interesting to see that the world's longest continuously running online Master's program – the Advanced Learning Technology program at Lancaster University, UK – was, from its beginning, designed to cater to the needs of professional communities (Goodyear 2005b). In its current design, the program is built around the reification of working practices. The process starts with a student constructing a shareable representation of a working practice (typically his/her own) and of the knowledge embedded in it. Text, and increasingly video, is used to capture and represent relevant aspects of practice. This practice artefact is then shared with other students, who are then supposed to discuss and critique what is captured in the representation. Then next step involves improving upon the documented practice, and finally an attempt is made to disseminate the improved practice in the environment to which it belongs. The role of teachers in this cycle consists mainly of helping the participants to draw on relevant areas of theory or research evidence in making their contributions.

In reflecting on the experiences from running this program, (Goodyear 2005a) makes the point that increasingly all kinds of learning environments may have to include community-based elements because of the increase in the number of autonomous, self-managed learners. As life-long learning becomes a reality, an increasing number of students, in particular in the higher education and E-Learning sectors, can no longer be expected to be compliant learners; they do not necessarily work on set tasks, but are driven by their personal and immediate needs and interests. The experience gained in working with online communities of practice can therefore be helpful to a wider range of instructional designers and educators, not only those who see themselves working with CoPs. Referring to the distinction that geographers make between space and place, designers might be well advised to concern themselves with the design of online *spaces*, and leave it to the learners to create their individual or community *places*, "...their own learnplaces, configuring the physical resources available to them in ways they find most comfortable, efficient, supportive, congenial and convivial" (Goodyear 2005a).

15.4 Current Research

A good part of current research on CoPs originates from identifying limitations of the theory and limitations of its application to instructional design and software design, and attempts to overcome these limitations.

15.4.1 Limitations of CoPs

Since its original development in Lave and Wenger (1991), the concept of a CoP has attracted the interest of numerous researchers and has more recently been integrated into the method repertoire of knowledge managers. Increasingly, managers are developing and supporting CoPs as part of organizations' knowledge management strategies, even as supplementary organizational structures (Lesser and Storck 2001; Wenger et al. 2002). At the same time, researchers and practitioners have been probing into the limitations of CoPs (for an overview see Roberts 2006).

Wenger et al. (2002) mention as a downside that "...the very qualities that make a community an ideal structure for learning – a shared perspective on the domain, trust, a communal identity, long-standing relationships, an established practice – are the same qualities that can hold it hostage to its history and its achievements" (p. 141). In other words, CoPs can be a conservative force, resisting change. They can become overly exclusive, making it hard for newcomers to go beyond peripheral participation and become overly concerned with holding on to established power. Researchers have begun to study power relationships within CoPs (Fox 2000) and in the relationship between CoPs and the surrounding organizational structures (Yanow 2004).

More generally, the negotiation of meaning processes supposedly going on continuously in CoPs have come under scrutiny, based on observations that show that this kind of communication is affected by power relations, the linguistic repertoire of the employees, and habitus (Bourdieu 1990), the modes of thought endemic to professional settings (Mutch 2003). Roberts (2006) notes that despite the lip service paid to working in teams and learning in communities, a number of industries are employing management concepts that are at odds with the open flow of information and the democratic negotiation of meaning. There is also a trend in the broader socio-cultural environment towards increasingly giving weight to individual performance. This suggests that CoPs, as a form of organization for learning, might be better suited to the public and the non-profit sector rather than to business. Future research will, in particular, need to address the question of under which socio-cultural, economic and organizational factors CoPs are sustainable and effective.

15.4.2 Limits to the Instructional Use of CoPs

A first limitation from an instructional point of view is the lack of intervention studies from which designers can glean information for instructional applications. As we have seen, the very notion of designing for CoPs is problematic because the theory is essentially a descriptive social theory, not a prescriptive model for intervention and instruction. Schwen and Hara (2003), for instance, note that all of the successful CoPs reported in the literature they assessed, as well as in their students' field studies, evolved naturally. Not one of them was designed or externally managed.

A second limitation is the lack of longitudinal observations on CoPs. Clearly, CoPs are going through stages and perhaps cycles, but there are no comprehensive long-term studies on CoPs reported in the literature.

From a designer's point of view, this is highly problematic because design features that may work in the early phases of a CoP's lifecycle may turn out problematic in later phases.

A third limitation, from an instructional design point of view, is that the theory does not provide a link between micro-level learning and mid-level social processes. This renders most of the knowledge and methods accrued both in learning research and in instructional design research non-applicable. Attempts to bridge this gap have by and large led to unsatisfactory results, both when looking at the outcomes (well designed and successful CoPs are rare) as well as when looking at the pedagogy. Most of the online learning environments that use the CoP metaphor focus on individual knowledge goals, whereas CoPs are all about knowing, a relational concept. Although some years ago, in her often-cited article, Sfard (1998) warned about the dangers of using just one metaphor, acquisition or participation, a conceptually satisfying and pragmatically effective synthesis has yet to be found.

The gaps identified by Schwen and Hara (2003) provide us with an agenda for empirical and conceptual research. As in other areas of technology design and development, approaches that provide ways to reduce the distance between design/designer and use/user, as exemplified by Fischer's seed-evolutionary growth-reseed model, are particularly promising. Of interest are also approaches that provide online groups with interaction information rather than with goals, scripts and fixed structures (e.g., Reimann 2005) and approaches that allow groups to set their own norms and have them monitored by software (Kildare 2004). To the extent that the type of CoP most relevant in educational contexts is the knowledge-based learning community (Riel and Polin 2004), we can expect to see more research related to the use of knowledge technologies, in particular semantic web technologies, in CoPs. From a methodological point of view, what we urgently need are design guidelines grounded in empirical research, in particular research that looks into the development of CoPs over longer stretches of time.

References

Barab, S. A., & Duffy, T. M. (2000). From practice fields to communities of practice. In D. H. Jonassen & S. M. Land (Eds.), *Theoretical foundations of learning environments* (pp. 25–56). Mahwah, NJ: Erlbaum.

Barab, S. A., & Roth, W. M. (2006). Curriculum-based ecosystems: Supporting knowing from an ecological perspective. *Educational Researcher, 35*(5), 3–13.

Barab, S. A., MaKinster, J. G., & Scheckler, R. (2003). Designing system dualities: Characterizing a web-supported professional development community. *The Information Society, 19*, 237–256.

Barab, S. A., Kling, R., & Gray, J. H. (Eds.). (2004). *Designing for virtual communities in the service of learning.* Cambridge, UK: Cambridge University Press.

Bourdieu, P. (1990). *The logic of practice.* Cambridge: Polity.

Brint, S. (2001). Gemeinschaft revisited: A critique and reconstruction of the community concept. *Sociological Theory, 19*(1), 1–23.

Brown, J. S., Collins, A., & Duguid, P. (1989). Situated cognition and the culture of learning. *Educational Researcher, 18*(1), 32–42.

Carraher, D. W. (1991). Mathematics in and out of school: A selective review of studies from Brazil. In M. Harris (Ed.), *Schools, mathematics and work* (pp. 169–201). London: Falmer.

Daniel, B., Schwier, R. A., & McCalla, G. (2003). Social capital in virtual learning communities and distributed dommunities of practice. *Canadian Journal of Learning and Technology, 29*(3). http://www.cjlt.ca/index.html.

dePaula, R., Fischer, G., & Ostwald, J. (2001). Courses as seeds: expectations and realities. In *Proceedings of the Second European Conference on Computer-Supported Collaborative Learning (Euro-CSCL 2001)* (pp. 494–501). Maastricht, Netherlands.

Dube, L., Bourhis, A., & Jacob, R. (2006). Towards a typology of virtual communities of practice. *Interdisciplinary Journal of Information, Knowledge, and Management, 1*(1), 69–93.

Fischer, G., & Ostwald, J. (2003). Knowledge communication in design communities. In R. Bromme, F. W. Hesse & H. Spada (Eds.), *Barriers and biases in computer-mediated knowledge communication* (pp. 1–32). Dordrecht, The Netherlands: Kluwer.

Fischer, G., Grudin, J., McCall, R., Ostwald, J., Redmiles, D., Reeves, B., et al. (2001). Seeding, evolutionary growth and reseeding: the incremental development of collaborative design environments. In G. M. Olson, T. W. Malone & J. B. Smith (Eds.), *Coordination theory and collaboration technology* (pp. 447–471). New York: Erlbaum.

Fischer, G., Scharff, E., & Yunwen, Y. (2004). Fostering social creativity by increasing social capital. In M. Huysman & V. Wulf (Eds.), *Social capital and information technology* (pp. 355–400). Cambridge, MA: MIT.

Fox, S. (2000). Communities of practice, Foucault and actor-network theory. *Journal of Management Studies, 36*(4), 869–885.

Gongla, P., & Rizzuto, C. R. (2001). Evolving communities of practice: IBM Global Services experience. *IBM Systems Journal, 40*(4), 842–862.

Goodyear, P. (2005a). Environments for life-long learning: Ergonomics, architecture and the practice of educational technology. In J. M. Spector & T. M. Anderson (Eds.), *Integrated and holistic perspectives on learning, instruction, and technology: Understanding complexity* (pp. 1–18). Dordrecht, Netherlands: Kluwer.

Goodyear, P. (2005b). The emergence of a networked learning community: Lessons learned from research and practice. In G. Kearsley (Ed.), *Online learning. Personal reflections on the transformation of education* (pp. 113–127). Englewood Cliffs, NJ: Educational Technology.

Handley, K., Sturdy, A., Finchman, R., & Clark, T. (2006). Within and beyond communities of practice: Making sense of learning through participation, identity and practice. *Journal of Management Studies, 43*(3), 641–653.

Kildare, R. (2004). Ad-hoc online teams as complex systems: agents that cater for team interaction rules [Electronic Version]. In *The 7th Asia-Pacific Conference on Complex Systems*. http://eprints.utas.edu.au/152/index.html. Accessed 20 December 2006.

Kling, R., & Courtright, C. (2003). Group behavior and learning in electronic forums. *The Information Society, 19*, 221–235.

Lave, J., & Wenger, E. (1991). *Situated learning: Legitimate peripheral participation*. Cambridge: Cambridge University Press.

Lesser, E. L., & Storck, J. (2001). Communities of practice and organizational performance. *IBM Systems Journal, 40*(4), 831–841.

Lie, M., & Sorensen, K. H. (Eds.). (1996). *Making technology our own? Domesticating technology into everyday life*. Oslo: Scandinavian University Press.

Mutch, A. (2003). Communities of practice and habitus: a critique. *Organization Studies, 24*(3), 383–401.

Nardi, B. A. (1996). *Context and consciousness: activity theory and human-computer interaction*. Cambridge: MIT.

Preece, J. (2000). *Online communities: Designing usability and supporting sociability*. New York, NY: Wiley.

Reimann, P. (2005). Co-constructing artefacts and knowledge in net-based teams: Implications for the design of collaborative learning environments. In H. L. Chick & J. L. Vincent (Eds.), *Proceedings of the 29th conference of the international group for the psychology of mathematics education (PME 29)*. Vol. 1 (pp. 53–68). Melbourne: University of Melbourne.

Rheingold, H. (1993). *The virtual community: Homesteading on the electronic frontier*. Reading, MA: Addison-Wesley.

Riel, M., & Polin, L. (2004). Online learning communities. In S. A. Barab, R. Kling & J. Gray (Eds.), *Designing for virtual communities in the service of learning* (pp. 16–52). Cambridge, UK: Cambridge University Press.

Roberts, J. (2006). Limits to communities of practice. *Journal of Management Studies, 43*(3), 623–639.

Scardamalia, M., & Bereiter, C. (2003). Knowledge building. In J. W. Guthrie (Ed.), *Encyclopedia of Education* (2nd ed.). New York: Macmillan Reference.

Schlager, M. S., & Fusco, J. (2004). Online learning communities. In S. A. Barab, R. Kling & J. Gray (Eds.), *Designing for virtual communities in the service of learning* (pp. 120–153). Cambridge, UK: Cambridge University Press.

Schwen, T. M., & Hara, N. (2003). Community of practice: A metaphor for online design? *The Information Society, 19*, 257–270.

Sfard, A. (1998). On two metaphors of learning and the dangers of choosing just one. *Educational Researcher, 27*(2), 4–13.

Wenger, E. (1998). *Communities of practice: Learning, Meaning, and Identity.* Cambridge: Cambridge University Press.

Wenger, E., McDermott, R., & Snyder, W. M. (2002). *Cultivating communities of practice. A guide to managing knowledge.* Boston, MA: Harvard Business School Press.

Williams, R., Stewart, J., & Slack, R. (2005). *Social learning in technological innovation.* Cheltenham, UK: Edward Elgar.

Yanow, D. (2004). Translating local knowledge at organizational peripheries. *British Journal of Management,* 15, 89–125.

16 Business Models for the Sustainable Implementation of E-Learning at Universities

D. Euler, S. Seufert, and F. Zellweger Moser

This article indicates how business model approaches can be used in the university segment. To this end, the business model concept is initially explained and a frame of reference is introduced then aligned to the various organisational levels of universities. Further, the core questions regarding product/market combinations, the value generation chain, competitors and cooperation partners, as well as those regarding funding and income models for the university level as a whole are specified and illustrated. The interaction of the various elements concerned is illustrated by an example based on the frame of reference introduced. Moreover, systematisation in the sense of exploratory theory formation serves the identification of further research issues. The article ends with reflections concerning the limits of an economic perspective for the university context.

16.1 Point of Departure and Presentation of Problem

In many countries, sponsoring programmes have been launched with the aim of testing the potential of new information and communication technologies at universities. The initiatives concerned were linked with a wide range of objectives which proved to be of varying realism. The spectrum of objectives ranged from quality improvement in terms of academic teaching to the cooperative development of viable further education options through to the commercial marketing of E-Learning products.

In their evaluation of the German "New Media in Education" funding programme (between 2001 and 2004), Kleimann and Wannemacher made a number of findings relevant to the university segment. Their findings are far from positive. In the 540 individual projects in the programme, apart from the generation of IT tools (e.g., learning management systems, software tools and portals), it was primarily the media enhancement of separate parts of a given course and/or individual seminars that was undertaken, and then often discontinued once the public sponsorship came to an end (Kleimann and Wannemacher 2004). It is further interesting to note that only 7% of the options offered were conceived as a form of fee-based further education (Kleimann and Wannemacher 2004).

From the perspective of educational economy, this situation constitutes a risk in terms of the inefficient usage of public resources. From a business management point of view, the question must be asked as to why the available theories and tools relevant to, for instance, business models are not applied to the specific problem area.

This paper is based on the premise that the majority of theories largely concerned with corporate contexts have not yet been sufficiently systematised and specified in terms of their application for university purposes and have not therefore found the corresponding resonance as to their practical implementation. It is therefore the aim of this paper to bring the two worlds closer together and, in so doing, contribute to the generation of research findings, as well as to the practical application of the theories concerned. Against this background, this paper identifies the core issues of the business model concept, links them to a frame of reference and, via the analysis of relevant theories, develops ongoing structures with the aim of thereby achieving the differentiated identification of new questions and hypotheses. Methodologically, this procedure is closely based on the principle of "positive heuristics" as outlined by Lakatos, which, in his view, underpins the handling of research programmes (Lakatos 1974). The procedure concerned could best be described as abductive, as opposed to inductive or deductive.

The procedure breaks down into the following concrete steps: In the next section, "business models at universities", the business model concept is introduced and given a concrete form via four defining questions. The questions are used to create a still-rough frame of reference, which will help to identify theoretical arguments and empirical findings and adopt them for the purpose of the differentiated analysis of the research and implementation context.

In the section called "business models from a university perspective", the defining issues are applied to the implementation level of universities as a case in point and discussed. In this framework, the relevant points for the implementation of business models at the faculty level are identified.

In the section called "formation and application of frame of reference", the findings are recorded, and are then collated and systematised for the purposes of the differentiated analysis of the frame of reference implemented. The aim is then to use an example to illustrate the usefulness of the differentiated framework in order to assist with the conclusive formulation of research requirements. The paper ends with the section "thinking in business models – the beginning of the end?", in which a number of fundamental considerations concerning the limits of business model concepts at universities are mentioned.

16.2 Business Models at Universities

In principle, business models are management concepts by which a company is viable, i.e., earns profits (Rappa 2000). The relevant literature contains numerous presentations of the core features of a business model (cf., among others, Afuah and Tucci 2001; Bieger et al. 2002; Stähler 2001; Osterwalder and Pigneur 2002; Timmers 1998). The definitions given are primarily questions of purpose. As such, an appropriate definition depends on the objective to be achieved via the description of business models. For universities, therefore, a fundamental question is how products and services in the context of E-Learning can be put on an economically viable, sustainable footing. On the basis of this, the following four interlinked core questions are regarded as central to the development of a business model (Fig. 16.1):

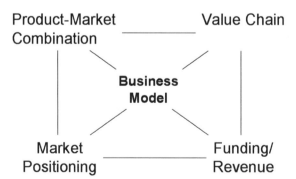

Fig. 16.1. Frame of reference for the development of a business model

Which Products and Services Are Offered in Which Market (Product/Market Combinations)?

A start can be made with the question as to which products and services are provided for which customers. This question can be answered on various levels within the context of a university. Apart from the university as a whole, individual faculties or E-Learning support centres can also see themselves as suppliers of products and services.

Which Tasks and Processes Need to be Accomplished for the Provision of the Products/Services Concerned (Value Generation Processes)?

Furthermore, one must ask *how* the given products and services are to be provided in detail. The concept of a value generation chain offers valuable indicators for the analysis of the necessary tasks, processes, responsibilities and roles (Porter 1980). An interesting approach in this connection is the breaking of the value generation chain and the innovative re-combining of individual value-generating activities (Keating 2002). For instance, education brokers specialise in the distribution of education services, in which joint ventures constitute a key issue (Baer 2002). Relevant questions in this connection are: Which of the necessary tasks are already being carried out? Which still need to be tackled? Where do they see their own core competences? To what extent can joint ventures be used to accomplish tasks (possibly better) with partners? How can a performance portfolio be drawn up efficiently for the education market?

Which Positioning Occurs in the Relevant Market Environment (Market Positioning)?

A prerequisite of the definition of a successful business model is the precise knowledge of the market potential and market environment in the various geographical markets (regional, national, international). In addition to the volume and structure of the given market, knowledge of competitors and their strategies is also of importance (Porter 1980). Are they competitors or might they be potential cooperation partners? The following are relevant questions in this area: Which characteristics does the market in which the products are to be sold have? Who are the direct and indirect competitors and what are their strategies? Which cooperation possibilities can be identified?

How Is Economic Viability Secured (Funding and Income Models)?

The focus here is on the analysis of the cost structures and potential income models in the implementation of a business model. Solid cost accounting can prevent incorrect estimates from being made (Seibt 2001). On the income side, the potential of university budgets and market proceeds need to be assessed. The fact that funds from public sponsorship programmes are only available for extremely limited periods has to be taken into account here. Central questions in this area are the following: Which additional needs are generated via E-Learning? How is the cost structure developing in the long term? Where can internal resources be released in favour of E-Learning? Which external sources of funding can be tapped, and how could they be secured in the long term?

Within a university, the four questions outlined important to various organisational units, where the issues concerned are tackled with varying levels of priority:

- At the level of the *university*, a business model should address, in particular, the question of how the resources for the development of E-Learning-supported education options are generated (question 4) and for whom the products are made available (questions 1 and 3). Also key here is the question of which units are responsible for tackling the necessary tasks in the value generation chain (question 2). The focus here is on the development of an overall strategy for universities, together with the determination of the strategic goals and the decision concerning the general conditions governing the realisation of the goals in the individual organisational units at the given university.
- At the level of *departments*, a business model should address, in particular, the question of which E-Learning-supported education options (question 1) are developed within the framework of the available resources (question 4) professionally and in a high-quality, transfer-compatible manner (question 2), in which relevant market circumstances should also be given due consideration (question 3).
- At the level of the *support centres*, a business model should address, in particular, the question of which services (question 1) both within and without the university are offered (question 2), in which market and funding conditions (questions 1 and 3) represent key decision parameters.

In the following section, concrete details of the four core questions relevant to the university's area of decision-making competence are provided.

16.3 Business Models from a University Perspective

16.3.1 Product/Market Combinations: Which Products and Services Are Offered in Which Markets?

With regard to the context discussed here, this question can be refined as follows: Which products and/or services are offered by a university vis-à-vis customers in the various market segments? Table 16.1 aims to illustrate the potential products offered by a given university and tie them to relevant market specifics.[1]

Table 16.1. Overview of products offered by universities and corresponding market segments

Products	Market					
Offered by universities	Customer segment			Market alignment		
	Private segment	University segment	Corporate segment	Region	Nation	Intern
Academic programmes						
Bachelor degree programmes						
Master's degree programmes						
Doctorate programmes						
Further education options[a]						
Master of Advanced Studies						
Diploma courses						
Certificate courses						
Further education courses						
Other services e.g., sale of education materials, courses, external avice/course options of support centres						

[a]According to the Bologna coordination team of the CRUS 2004, p. 17.

---

[1] This follows market-oriented strategy development approaches (Kotler and Bliemel 1999).

"Products" Offered by a University

The general direction of education programmes offered by a university is currently determined above all by the implementation of the Bologna Reform, and specifically by the restructuring of the courses of study with the goal of standardising the qualifications obtained. Appropriate educational options can be linked to a qualification awarded by the given university, end without certification or be tailored to a customer's specific requirements.

In this context, E-Learning can be considered a tool which facilitates the servicing of new market segments (e.g., international segments). Furthermore, E-Learning represents a possibility for structuring education options in a manner specific to target groups, which can be used as a differentiating feature with regard to other programmes. Moreover, E-Learning offers the potential of enhancing the programme profile of a given university to include other services. New education options of this sort are largely generated in the area of further education, such as the sale of course materials and further education courses via E-Learning portals, the licensing of courses as part of broker models or external advisory services offered by E-Learning support centres.

Market: Customer Segments and Market Alignment

The education market for universities is structured mainly by customer segments (private, university and corporate) as well as through market alignment in location terms (regional, national, international).

Private customers constitute those who wish to obtain an academic qualification on a full- or part-time basis (so-called "professional enhancement learners", Oblinger and Kidwell 2000). Through the qualification, they strive to enhance their careers and, as a rule, cover their own costs. Furthermore, in the further education segment, alumni represent a key target group.

Customers from other universities can also be of significance once the concept behind the Bologna process has been realised, in accordance with which mobility (both normal and virtual) between universities is supposed to be guaranteed to a large extent. Moreover, this segment is expected to generate scope of as-yet undefined proportions for partnerships between universities that may involve joint development and a division of labour, as well as the commercial marketing of study courses. A prototype in this field is presented in the project "Business Informatics Online (Winfoline)" (Uhl 2003; Hagenhoff 2002).

Customers from companies can take the form of individual persons who are supported financially by a company or institution. This market has a considerable volume, but is fiercely competitive and additionally requires more or less expensive product adaptation on the part of the supplying universities (e.g., Clarke and Hermens 2001).

New product/market combinations for universities taking special account of the usage of E-Learning are shown in Fig. 16.2.

Fig. 16.2. New product/market combinations for universities

Optimisation

E-Learning can be used for the quality enhancement of university teaching, in order to tap value-added potential (e.g., improved support of students, more intensive communication between lecturers and students as well as among students themselves). As far as resource usage is concerned, the focus here is on optimisation and professionalisation in order to achieve enhanced effectiveness and efficiency in university teaching (Kotler and Bliemel 1999).

Market Development

A given university can align its existing education options to suit new market segments (market developments). On the one hand, student mobility (the extension of education options to outside the classroom) that arises from a strategy of internationalisation can be addressed. In this context, E-Learning serves as a central communication platform and, as such, is a tool for implementing the strategy of internationalisation. On the other hand, the extension of education options can also refer to other customer segments if, for instance, further internal education seminars are opened up to external candidates from the university and corporate segments. As such, the usage of E-Learning can extend to the functionality of a distribution platform (e.g., E-Learning portals).

Apart from the efficient and effective use of resources, this product/market combination offers the opportunity of restructuring resource usage, as new revenue sources can be tapped via new market segments for investment refunding purposes.

Product Development

A further combination option for universities involves developing new education options that consider students' need for greater flexibility (product development). On many university campuses, the reality today is such that many students have to work on the side. E-Learning is a tool that supports learning without the customary restraints in terms of location and time and, as such, accommodates the changed concepts of student life. Furthermore, new programme options can be developed with the specific intention of attaining new, for instance, cross-discipline, learning goals, thereby enhancing the quality of teaching with respect to sustainable transfer activities. In this context, E-Learning should be seen as a tool addressing cross-discipline learning goals such as self-learning or social competencies within the framework of an E-Learning-supported course of self-study (cf. Euler and Wilbers 2001).

Product/Market Development

Product/market development represents the highest level of a university's expansion and/or marketing strategy. An example of an offensive and risky marketing strategy of this kind is the so-called Cardean University, a for-profit institution run by a broker (Unext). Cardean was formed by the merger of a number of distinguished universities (including Stanford, LSE, etc.), which supply curricular input in the area of business education. A new market was addressed, comprised mainly of companies whose payment preparedness was however overestimated at the outset; subsequently, the products and services concerned were also offered to private customers.[2] As far as the approach is concerned, open (remote) and/or virtual universities also subscribe to this strategy despite the fact that the conditions under which they operate are different to those classical campus-based universities are subject to.

16.3.2 Value Generation Chain: Which Tasks and Processes Need to Be Accomplished for Product/Service Provision Purposes?

Once the products and services have been defined, the form in which the services are generated needs to be clarified. The value generation chain that thus develops defines the tasks, processes, responsibilities and roles while, at the same time, offering the basis of reflection as to how the individual links in the chain can be developed in an optimum way.

As a case in point, Fig. 16.3 outlines a possible model of a value generation chain for the development of education programmes (based on Keating 2002).

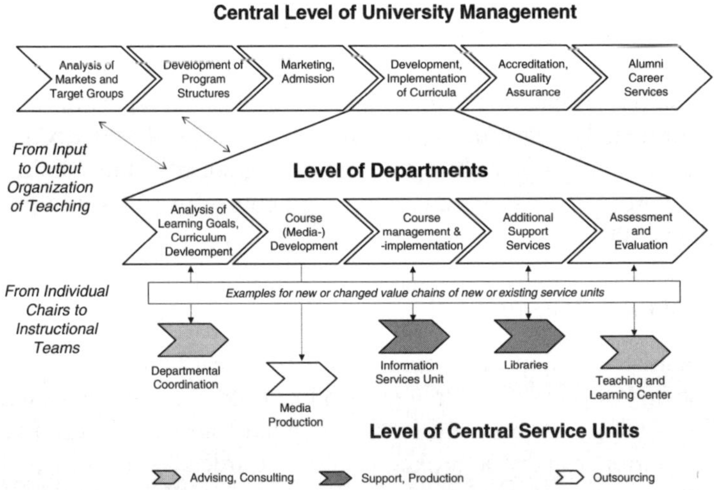

Fig. 16.3. E-Learning-supported university teaching value generation chain, taking "Development of an Education Programme" as an example

---

[2] More information is available at www.cardean.edu or the case study about Cardean published by the Center for Studies in Higher Education, UC Berkeley, 2002 http://ishi.lib.berkeley.edu/cshe/projects/ university/ebusiness/unext.html.

At the central university management level, potential changes in the spectrum of tasks within the framework of the development of new education options can be outlined as follows:

- In part, new task areas, such as the quality assurance of programmes, are created. Other tasks are intensified as a result of the intensification of the competitive environment. Marketing is a case in point here.
- Implementation of the Bologna Reform means the organisation of studies at university changes from being an input, to an output organisation. As such, credit points form the basis of calculation for study time (in working hours/output orientation), rather than the number of hours of the course (input orientation). This fundamental restructuring makes it easier for universities to define new forms of study, such as supported self-study. The calculation of the teaching deployment of lecturers is also to be adapted to this new organisation of studies. Consequently, the output study organisation creates a favourable frame of reference within which E-Learning can be integrated into the university teaching routine.
- Furthermore, general conditions are to be created at the level of central responsibility for the strategic application of E-Learning, in which consideration should be given to providing frames of reference for internal usage, i.e., structures for the integration of E-Learning into university teaching procedures as well as for external distribution structures of new products (e.g., the selling of courses).

The breaking of the traditional value generation chain of university teaching is connected, at the faculty level, to new requirements, similar to the example shown in Fig. 16.3. On the one hand, enhanced coordination and collaboration between the faculties are needed, due to the new study organisation in accordance with the Bologna Reform, which is often addressed via new functions and roles (e.g., course manager, faculty and/or bachelor degree coordinator). On the other hand, the use of E-Learning frequently increases the level of cooperation with central units such as informatics, media or didactics centres. In this way, the professional provision of education options at the faculty level promotes the move away from a departmental to a tuition team principle (Kerres 2001).

Market environment – which positioning occurs in the relevant market environment (competitors and cooperation partners)? of the relevant market environment is of central importance for a number of reasons. On the demand side, the volume and structure of the market determine whether appropriate activities carried out by a given university at a certain time have a chance of success at all. On the supplier side, relevant competitors need to be determined. These competitors should be able to act as rivals, but also as partners within the framework of joint ventures, strategic alliances or cooperation networks.

Market volume was repeatedly overestimated in past years (NFO Infratest 2003; Hoppe and Breitner 2004; Hagenhoff 2002). Against this backdrop, market estimates are to be treated with a certain caution. Nevertheless, universities are faced with the task of determining the fundamental market strategy on the basis of the estimate of market volume and structures. As far as the *market positioning* of a university is concerned, the following should be considered:

- *Profile formation, strengthening of own university brand* – in this option, clarification is needed as to the extent to which E-Learning can contribute to a university's profile formation. As such, based on Porter (1980), a strategy of differentiation can be realised in the form of demarcation vis-à-vis the competitors via unique products/services.
- *Exploitation of market potential, usage of university brand* – a university has the additional option of enhancing the existing brand to include new distribution channels under the umbrella of an "online university". Often in such contexts, sub-brands were generated, such as Harvard Business School Interactive or NYU online, which specifically addressed the further education segment. In the past, these endeavours have often failed, however (Zemsky and Massy 2004).
- *Exploitation of market potential, development of a common, new brand* – in the education market, new forms of cooperation have been generated in order to develop a new brand together with strategic, such as the E-Learning portal Fathom.[3] Experience shows, however, in the case of this option too, that it is extremely difficult to establish a totally new brand in the education market.
- *Exploitation of cost-cutting potential* – as a further market positioning option, universities can enter into partnerships to gain synergetic benefits in the development of E-Learning products and/or cost cutting via the common usage of technologies.

The strong emphasis on the creation, utilisation or reinforcement of a brands is justified by the increase in bachelor degree and, above all, master's

---

[3] Fathom (www.fathom.com) was founded as "for-profit spin-off" from the Columbia University gegründet. Since April 2003 the business activities of Fathom have been discontinued and the courses are still as freeware accessible in the fathom archive (Carlson 2003).

degree qualifications due to the implementation of Bologna structures at universities. The result is that universities no longer have rely on qualifications to stand out. Instead, other features can give them an edge over the competition when it comes to attracting good students. This is where the attempt to create a brand comes in. Creating a brand is an area of activity that is still in its infancy for universities (Gerhard 2004).

From these considerations on the market positioning of a university, as well as those on the value generation chain of university teaching, it becomes clear that *joint ventures* play a key role. Consideration should be given to the numerous forms of partnerships involving cooperation among universities themselves ("public/public partnerships") as well as between universities and private companies ("public/private partnerships"), as outlined in Table 16.2.[4]

Table 16.2. Potential forms of cooperation for universities

Cooperation level	Public/Public partnerships	Public/Private partnerships
Cooperation on a technology level	Development communities between a number of universities, e.g., open-source communities, common usage of technology platforms	Technology partnerships: Public – application partners Private – technology partners
Cooperation on a content level	Development communities, common provision of E-Learning products, teaching materials	Content partnerships: Public – content supplier Private – transfer partner (for multimedia enhancement, marketing)
Cooperation on a programme level	Programme partnerships: common development and execution of programmes, curriculum coordination for existing programmes (e.g., for double-degree programmes), common events in various programmes, common recognition of study performance of existing programmes	Programme partnerships: common development and execution of total programme, e.g., customised MBA programmes, partial value generation via programme partner, e.g., task of university: certification and quality management
Cooperation on a distribution level	Internal partnerships: Contract models with professors for marketing of E-Learning products. Brokerage models – brokerage of products, services in a university network, registration of courses	Distribution partnerships, e.g., brokerage model Private – service provider, broker Public – course supplier

---

[4] However, Cleuvers (2003, p 78) comes to the conclusion in his study that only a few univerisities are looking for a cooperation with the private sector.

The analysis of the supplier side in the education market includes the questions of whether and to what extent competition will increase in the future, from a university perspective. The following competitors can be differentiated between, as seen from a university's point of view:

- *New competitors with the same or similar services*: the establishment of private universities (e.g., International University of Bremen) is no longer a rarity, even in German-speaking countries.
- *New competitors with substitute services*: new educational institutions, such as corporate universities, are penetrating the market offering comparable education services. An example is Credit Suisse Business School, which is launching a bachelor degree programme in cooperation with a technical college in Switzerland.
- *Existing competitors with new services*: following implementation of the Bologna Reform, technical colleges, with their new degree programmes in certain market segments, represent a greater competitive threat to universities.

Additionally, the supplier side is characterised by a polypolistic market, in which a multitude of small-scale suppliers have focused on specific segments and products. Whereas universities in German-speaking countries have until now offered more or less no course options via the Internet, numerous universities, especially in the USA, Canada, Australia and Britain, have already been gathering experiences in this area. The Internet enables foreign universities and global competitors with innovative business ideas to penetrate the (formerly protected) territory of a national university system. This generates potential for a globalised education market, the dimensions of which are today only evident to a very limited extent (Van der Wende 2002).

16.3.3 Funding and Income Models: How Can Economic Viability Be Assured?

In principle, university budgets and market revenues are possible options as funding sources. In contrast, the funds from public sponsorship programmes, which were primarily used before, are available only for a very limited period of time. As far as the revenues earned from the distribution of education programmes and/or courses are concerned, differentiated analysis is needed, because the possibility of generating revenue will presumably be restricted to just a few faculties.

The following are feasible source options for revenues (Seufert and Zellweger 2004):

- The most obvious option is charging course fees (Hoppe and Breitner 2003). This can be organised in such a way that fees are only incurred for the actual usage of the services offered ("pay-per-use") – e.g., actual access of E-Learning modules, registration for certain courses).
- Another option is the member model, in which students pay a fixed amount for membership in an institution (similar to a subscription), regardless of how often they access the learning options or available services.
- The sale model generates revenues via the sale of E-Learning products and/or services.
- The brokerage or commission model generates income from the brokerage of business partners. In this way, a number of E-Learning portals have developed, focusing on the marketing and brokerage of E-Learning courses.
- Sponsoring and advertising models exploit indirect sources of revenue by, for instance, offering advertising space on Internet sites. This model has not proved successful over recent years. Its attractiveness has sharply declined and revenue margins are at very low levels.
- A further option, described by Hoppe and Breitner (2003), is the customer data sale model, which was initially generated in an e-business environment. In this model, revenue comes from the sale of the customer data and/or profiles that have been collected. Transferral of this model to universities is viewed critically, however, by the authors of this paper for legal and ethical reasons.

The experience with the sources of revenue outlined here thus provides grounds for scepticism. For example, experience with the models in the USA shows that even highly regarded universities were unable to meet their revenue targets with their online branches in the set period (Bala 2005). The eUniversity in Britain, which was set up as a broker for suitable education options offered by British universities, failed and was closed in 2004 (Garrett 2004). If such models are going to be successful, what needs to be drawn up is a differentiated market development strategy, in which joint ventures are initially agreed with pilot customers in order to provide a basis for configuring the diffusion in the market.

Funding needs to be secured primarily via university budgets, at least in the short term. This type of funding can principally be obtained via three approaches:

- Acquisition of additional funds for carrying out specific tasks, particularly in the form of state sponsorship or foundation funds. The sources concerned have not dried up completely yet, but will be available only to a very limited extent, once the comprehensive sponsorship programmes end.
- Re-distribution of funds within the framework of university budgets. This strategy is extremely conflict-ridden because, given a set total amount, it is met with the stubborn resistance of vested interests and, in view of the limited support for E-Learning concepts that universities enjoy, would not appear to have much chance of success.
- Restructuring of forms of tuition within the framework of a study reform concept that foresees a shift from "presence" self-study. In this way, funds would be freed up for use in the (further) development of E-Learning-supported forms of study (Euler and Wilbers 2001).

16.4 Formation and Application of Frame of Reference

The remarks made in the section "business models from a university perspective" can now be examined and used for further development of the frame of reference introduced. With regard to the core questions outlined earlier, a differentiated understanding has arisen in terms of the development of business models for universities, which can be summarised as follows (Fig. 16.4):

This framework can be used in two ways – first, its serves as a heuristic model for identifying and structuring the questions that need to be addressed and answered by universities in connection with the practical design of a business model. It should be noted that the individual categories are interdependently related and should therefore be structured in the form of a coordinated mix. Second, it offers support in the generation and detailing of relevant research questions that can be translated and processed into concrete research designs.

As an example, Table 16.3 shows the application of the frame of reference in three relevant examples (based on Olsen 2002; Seufert and Euler 2005; Duke Corporate Education 2005).

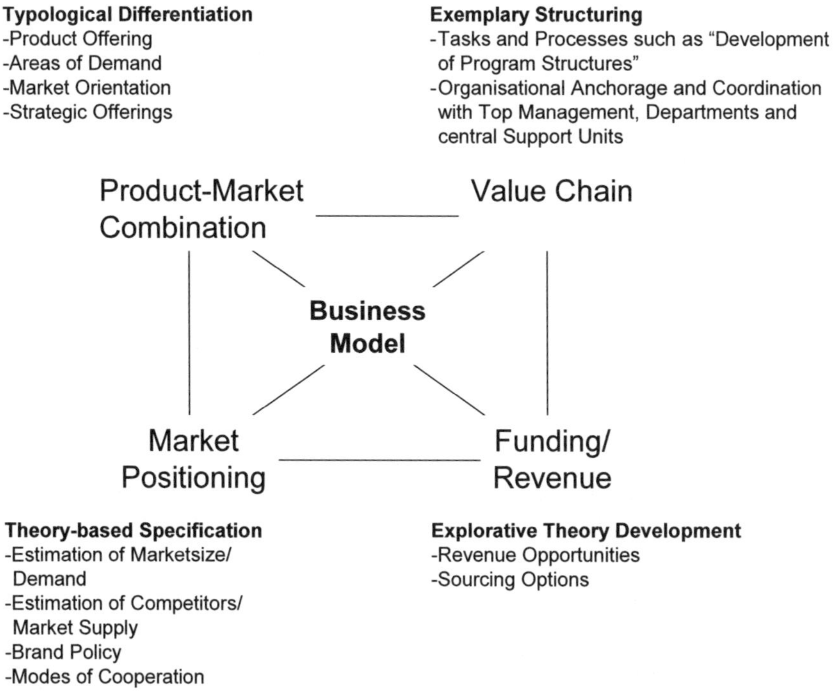

Typological Differentiation
-Product Offering
-Areas of Demand
-Market Orientation
-Strategic Offerings

Exemplary Structuring
-Tasks and Processes such as "Development
 of Program Structures"
-Organisational Anchorage and Coordination
 with Top Management, Departments and
 central Support Units

Product-Market ———— Value Chain
Combination

**Business
Model**

Market ———— Funding/
Positioning   Revenue

Theory-based Specification
-Estimation of Marketsize/
 Demand
-Estimation of Competitors/
 Market Supply
-Brand Policy
-Modes of Cooperation

Explorative Theory Development
-Revenue Opportunities
-Sourcing Options

Fig. 16.4. Differentiated frame of reference for the development of business models

The systematic generation of comprehensive research activities can merely be hinted at within this framework. Against this backdrop, the following research questions are proposed as examples in view of the four core categories the frame of reference encompasses:

- Which education needs in the various demand areas can be covered in a discipline-specific and/or interdisciplinary manner via E-Learning-supported education options (product/market combination)?
- What implications would the expanded range of education options by universities in new markets have on their internal organisation (value generation processes)?
- How can value generation processes be optimised for the development of market-oriented education options (value generation processes)?
- Which consequences do E-Learning activities have for a given university's reputation and brand (market positioning)?
- Under which circumstances do E-Learning-supported education programmes combined with reduced personnel-based teaching activities enhance a given university's economic viability (funding/income model)?

Table 16.3. Application in three examples

Frame of reference	Example: University of Phoenix	Example: University of Stuttgart	Example: Duke–LES Joint Venture
Market positioning	Focus: demand potential of "degree completion adult learners" in the American market Competitors: newly established, for-profit institutions and major public universities.	Focus: to make knowledge accessible to broad sections of the public; strengthening the competitive position of universities (incl. reaching new target groups); brand formation as a technology-oriented university.	Focus: specialisation in education options for companies (premium price segment); co-operation between complementary suppliers (Duke as corporate education supplier and LSE as research university).
Product/market combination	Small-module, distance learning options, flexible in terms of location and time, primarily with business-related content. Target group: private customers	Free content, E-Learning module options in low-cost segment, E-Learning course options with award of certificates. Target groups: regional SMEs, alumni.	International expansion strategy: new education options for international market segments (e.g., in Eastern European countries). Target group: corporate sector
Value generation process	Course provision occurs via interdisciplinary team of specialists with high-level resource deployment. Support of students provided via comprehensive adjunct faculty.	Marketing of content via service providers; based on publishing business; implementation of simple utilisation processes with lecturers as suppliers.	Joint linkage of value generation chain via the two cooperation partners (core competence of Duke in distribution segment, and of LSE in research resource access segment).
Funding/income model	Course fees, stock market capitalisation.	Course fees, commission model with service providers.	Sale model.

16.5 Thinking in Business Models: The Beginning of the End?

Economic considerations connected with the question of the sustainable integration of E-Learning into university teaching are often linked to the issue of university funding, particularly by political players, in which the focus is mainly on the search for new sources of revenue. It is hardly surprising that such reflections trigger critical responses. For instance, Bok (2003) warns of the danger of sacrificing values that are central to a university's long-term viability for the sake of short-term, profit-oriented activities.

In our view, this risk must be kept in mind while, at the same time, attention must be given to the positive benefits that reinforced consideration of economic aspects can generate. Particular emphasis should be given to an awareness of strategic issues relevant to university management as well as to pedagogical quality development issues.

At the same time, due consideration must be given to the fact that all disciplines and faculties do not possess the same prerequisites in terms of content marketing and that, a given subject's value may not be determined merely on the basis of criteria of economic usefulness. Universities also have social functions. They are both the memory and the future workshop of a given society. Business models are invigorating elements in a complex organisation such as a university. They must, however, serve a university's central remit, namely the provision of high-quality teaching and research.

References

Afuah, A., Tucci, C. L. (2001). *Internet Business Models and Strategies*. Boston: Mc Graw-Hill Irwinn.

Baer, W. S. (2002). Competition and collaboration in online distance learning. In W. H. Dutton, B. D. Loader (Eds.), *Digital academe: the new media and institutions of higher education and learning* (pp. 169–184). London, New York: Routlede.

Bala, S. (2005). Universitas 21 Global. Dogged survivor of the dotcom bubble keeps its head above water. *Financial Times Business Education*, 21 March.

Bieger, T., Bickhoff, N., Caspers, R., zu Knyphausen-Aufsess, D., Reding, K. (Eds.) (2002). *Zukünftige Geschäftsmodelle. Konzept und Anwendung in der Netzökonomie*. Berlin Heidelberg New York: Springer.

Bologna-Koordinationsteam der CRUS (Schweizerischen Rektorenkonferenz) (2004). Empfehlungen der CRUS für die koordinierte Erneuerung der Lehre an den universitären Hochschulen der Schweiz im Rahmen des Bologna-Prozesses. http://www.crus.ch/docs/lehre/bologna/schweiz/Empfehlungen/Empf.doc. Accessed 23 October 2004.

Bok, D. C. (2003). *Universities in the Marketplace: The Commercialization of Higher Education*. Princeton: Princeton University Press.

Carlson, S. (2003). After losing millions, Columbia U. Will close online-learning venture. *The Chronicle of Higher Education*, 49(19), A30.

Clarke, T., Hermens, A. (2001). Corporate developments and strategic alliances in e-learning. *Education + Training*, (43)4, 256–267.

Cleuvers, B. A. (2003). Bestandsanalyse der eLearning-Angebote der Hochschulen. In D. Dohmen, L. P. Michel (Eds.), *Marktpotenziale und Geschäftsmodelle für eLearning-Angebote deutscher Hochschulen. Bertelsmann* (pp. 29–92). Bielefeld: Bertelsmann.

Duke Corporate Education (2005). Joint Venture. http://www.dukece.com/ affiliations. Accessed 18 June 2005.

Euler, D., Wilbers, K. (2001). *Selbstlernen mit neuen Medien didaktisch gestalten.* Hochschuldidaktische Schriften, No. 1. Universität St. Gallen: Institut für Wirtschaftspädagogik.

Garrett, R. (2004). The real story behind the failure of UK eUniversity. *Educause Quarterly*, (27)4, 4–6.

Gerhard, J. (2004). *Die Hochschulmarke. Ein Konzept für deutsche Universitäten.* Dissertation, Universität St. Gallen, Nr. 2908 Lohmar, Josef Eul Verlag, Köln

Hagenhoff, S. (2002). *Universitäre Bildungskooperationen. Gestaltungs-varianten für Geschätsmodelle.* Wiesbaden: Deutscher Universitätsverlag.

Hoppe, G., Breitner, M. H. (2003). *Classification and Sustainability Analysis of E-Learning Applications.* IWI Discussion Paper Series No. 2. Institut für Wirtschaftsinformatik, Universität Hannover.

Hoppe, G., Breitner, M. H. (2004). *Sustainable Business Models for E-Learning.* IWI Discussion Paper Series, No. 7. Institut für Wirtschaftsinformatik, Universität Hannover.

Keating, M. (2002). Geschäftsmodelle für Bildungsportale – Einsichten in den US-amerikanischen Markt. In U. Bentlage, P. Glotz, I. Hamm, J. Hummel (Eds.), *E-Learning. Märkte, Geschäftsmodelle, Perspektiven* (pp. 57–78). Gütersloh: Bertelsmann Stiftung.

Kerres, M. (2001). Zur (In-)Kompatibilität von mediengestützter Lehre und Hochschulstrukturen. In E. Wagner (Ed.), *Virtueller Campus Szenarien, Strategien, Studium. Medien in der Wissenschaft 14* (pp. 293–302). Münster, Münschen: Waxmann.

Kleimann, B., Wannemacher, K. (2004). *E-Learning an deutschen Hochschulen.* Hannover: Hochschul-Informations-System.

Kotler, P., Bliemel, F. (1999). Marketing-Management: *Analyse, Planung, Umsetzung und Steuerung*, 9th edn. Stuttgart: Schäffer-Poeschel.

Lakatos, I. (1974). Falsifikation und die Methodologie wissenschaftlicher Forschungsprogramme, In I. Lakatos, A. Musgrave (Eds.), *Kritik und Erkenntnisfortschritt* (pp. 89–189). Braunschweig: Vieweg.

NFO Infratest (2003). Monitoring Informationswirtschaft. 6. Faktenbericht 2003. http://www.nfo-bi.com/bmwa. Accessed 25 October 2004.

Oblinger, D., Kidwell, J. (2000). Distance learning. Are we being realistic? *Educause Review*, May/June, 30–39.

Olsen. F. (2002). Phoenix rises: The University's online program attracts students, profits and praise. *The Chronicle of Higher Education*, 49(2), A29–A36.

Osterwalder, A., Pigneur, Y. (2002). An e-business model ontology for modeling e-business. Paper presented at the *15th Bled Electronic commerce Conference. e-Reality: Constructing the e-Economy*, Bled, Slovenia.

Porter, M. E. (1980). *Competitive Strategy. Techniques for Analyzing Industries and Competitors.* New York: Free.

Rappa, M. (2000). Managing the digital enterprise. Business models on the Web. http://digitalenterprise.org/models/models.html. Accessed 25 October 2004.

Seibt, D. (2001). Kosten und Nutzen des E-Learning bestimmen, In A. Hohenstein, K. Wilbers (Eds.), *Handbuch E-Learning. Expertenwissen aus Wissenschaft und Praxis* (pp. 1–34). Köln: Deutscher Wirtschaftsdienst.

Seufert, S., Euler, D. (2005). Nachhaltigkeit von eLearning-Innovationen: Fallstudien zu Implementierungsstrategien von eLearning als Innovationen an Hochschulen. *Arbeitsbericht 4 des Swiss Centre for Innovations in Learning.* Universität St. Gallen.

Seufert, S., Zellweger, F. (2004). Gestaltung von Geschäfts- und Kooperationsmodellen für eLearning an Hochschulen. In D. Euler, S. Seufert (Eds.), *eLearning in Hochschulen und Bildungszentren. Gestaltungshinweise für pädagogische Innovationen.* Oldenburg, München.

Stähler, P. (2001). *Geschäftsmodelle in der digitalen Ökonomie.* Lomar: Eul.

Timmers, P. (1998). Business models for electronic markets. *International Journal on Electronic Markets,* 8, 3–8.

Uhl, V. (2003). *Virtuelle Hochschulen auf dem Bildungsmarkt. Strategische Positionierung unter Berücksichtigung der Situation in Deutschland, Österreich und England,* 1st edn. Wiesbaden: Deutscher Universitätsverlag.

Van der Wende, M. (2002). *The Role of US Higher Education in the Global E-Learning Market (Working Paper CSHE1-02).* Berkeley: Center for Studies in Higher Education, University of California.

Zemsky, R., Massy, W. F. (2004). Thwarted innovation. What happened to e-learning and why? The Learning Alliance at the University of Pennsylvania. http://www.irhe.upenn.edu/Docs/Jun2004/ThwartedInnovation.pdf. Accessed 25 October 2004.

17 The Role of Competence Assessment in the Different Stages of Competence Development

J. Schoonenboom, C. Tattersall, Y. Miao, K. Stefanov, and A. Aleksieva-Petrova

This chapter discusses the role of e-assessment in the process of competence development. Its basic claim is that competence development is a process with distinct stages, and that the assessment forms and the roles taken on by those involved in the process depend on the stage in which learning occurs. More specifically, as a learner starts with competence development, self-assessment will be the most prominent, if not the only, form of assessment. This orientation stage is followed by a stage of evidence collection, which is supported by e-portfolio building. In a third stage, the learner is judged by others, and in this stage organisations make use of assessment forms such as on-the-job assessment, 360-degree assessment and assessment centres. In the fourth stage, the learner performs competence development activities. This process is supported by self-assessment and peer assessment. With each stage, examples of e-assessment are provided.

17.1 Introduction

Developing individuals' competences throughout their life is a key challenge for today's knowledge-based society. Learning activities aimed at maintaining or increasing proficiency levels, referred to as competence development activities, are a key resource in meeting the challenge. This chapter originates from work done in TenCompetence, a 4-year EU-7th framework project, which aims at developing an infrastructure for lifelong learning. It views competence development and competence assessment for the lifelong learning infrastructure that TenCompetence is developing. Yet, the insights in this chapter are not specific to TenCompetence, but apply to all infrastructures that aim at providing similar support for life-long learning.

Competence assessment is an important component of competence development. Several different methods can be used when assessing competence (Cheetham and Chivers 2005; Eraut and Cole 1993), and competence assessment occurs at several points within the learner's career (Duvekot et al. 2005).

Our basic claim in this chapter is that assessment goals change as learners make progress in their competence development. As a result, the forms of assessment that are used change, and thus the support that should be provided to the learner should change. In our view, the literature pays insufficient attention to the changing role of assessment as competencies develop. We will present a model of competence development that does account for these differences.

Competence development can be viewed from several perspectives. In this chapter, we present a model in which competence assessment is an integral part of competence development. The model distinguishes four stages of competence development and shows the different functions of competence assessment in these stages. The stages include: (1) orientation; (2) evidence collection; (3) assessment by others; (4) performing competence development activities. For each stage, we discuss the function and forms of assessment involved.

We start by outlining some general characteristics of competence development and competence assessment. As our basic claim is that competence assessment is relevant to the process of competence development in different stages, we first have to know what characterizes both. This will enable us in a later stage to indeed recognize competence assessment in the different stages of competence development.

Then, we outline the stages in competence development and competence assessment that have been distinguished in the literature. These stages are integrated into our model, which is presented in the following sections, each treating one of the stages more thoroughly, discussing the forms of assessment that are relevant to each stage.

17.2 What Are Competence Development and Competence Assessment?

17.2.1 Competence Development

In this chapter, we use a broad definition of competence development. Borrowing the general idea from Hyland (1994), we define competence development as "the general development of knowledge, understanding and cognition" in a person with respect to a specific domain. In our definition, competence development has the following characteristics:

It is about personal understanding, thus the emphasis is on the individual learner.

Competence development is an ongoing process through life, thus it is strongly related to lifelong learning.

All activities that a person undertakes may contribute to competence development. Competence development is not related to specific types of learning activities. As people learn in principle from everything they do, competence development will always include so-called informal learning, learning that occurs outside education and is not certified. Competence development may involve formal learning, and will involve formal learning in most cases, but formal learning is not a necessary component.

We agree with Brugman (1999), who, in developing his definition of competence development, states that "what is needed is not only a definition of competence development, but also an understanding of variables that affect competence development". Insight into these factors is a necessary prerequisite when thinking of how to support competence development. A first characteristic of our approach is the importance of learner goals. Learner goals are the drivers for individuals to engage in competence development. Following the TENCompetence Domain Model (Version 1.0, see Koper 2006), we claim that support for competence development should provide support to lifelong learners with any of the following goals:

1. I want to keep up to date within my existing function or job.
2. I want to study for a new function or job or improve my current job level.
3. I want to reflect on my current competencies to look which functions and jobs are within my reach or to help me define new learning goals.
4. I want to improve my proficiency level of a specific competence.

5. I want some support on a non-trivial learning problem.
6. I want to explore the possibilities in a new field (learning network) to help define new learning goals.

We consider all activities a learner undertakes to reach these goals as activities of competence development. Brugman's (1999) phrase, "competence development opportunities", captures this notion well. Note that this diversity of activities fits in well with our broad definition of competence development.

A second characteristic of our approach is that competence development is seen as a process. This is a characteristics of several approaches to competence development (see also Brugman 1999). Authors diverge in their view of what the stages in the process are. We will discuss this point in detail in Sect. 17.3.

A third characteristic is that the process of competence development may proceed along several possible routes, some more formal, some more informal. Some routes will encompass a complete trajectory which ends in a qualification, some routes will be fragmentary, in line with the incompleteness of some of the learner goals mentioned above.

17.2.2 Competence Assessment

We define competence assessment as the assessment of what a learner has learned with respect to a specific competence. Starting from this definition, we will in this section distinguish competence assessment from other types of assessment, which we loosely label "traditional assessment". Note that we use the label of traditional assessment for lack of a better one; we do not wish to convey that competence assessment is newer and thus "better" than traditional assessment.

We first note that the specific form of assessment applied does not in principle distinguish competence assessment from traditional assessment. Although it is true that competence assessment is usually based upon more advanced forms of assessment, such as 360-degree assessment and portfolio assessment, using these techniques in assessment does not turn the assessment into competence assessment. Similarly, simpler forms of assessment, such as multiple choice tests, might be used to assess competencies. Thus, competence assessment may use both more advanced and simpler forms of assessment (see also Cizek 1997).

The first aspect that distinguishes competence assessment from traditional assessment is a notion of completeness with respect to the competence involved. Competence assessment assesses the proficiency level of a specific competence as a whole, not only a part of that specific competence.

This is in line with the definition of competence proposed by Cheetham and Chivers (2005): "Effective *overall* performance within an occupation, which may range from the basic level of proficiency through to the highest level of excellence", and with their definition of professional competence: "the possession of the *range of attributes* necessary for effective performance within a profession, and the ability to marshal these consistently to produce the desired *overall* results". This idea of completeness is reflected in competence assessment practice, which typically takes into account several types of evidence. According to Eraut and Cole (1993), assessment of professional competence requires two types of evidence:

> Performance evidence, evidence drawn from the application of both specialist and generic skills in a professional context.
> Capability evidence, evidence not directly derived from the workplace, which is used either to supplement performance evidence or to ascertain a candidate's future potential.

A second distinguishing characteristic is that competence assessment is not necessarily related to specific training. Duvekot et al. (2005) describes competence assessment as assessment "of what an individual has learned with respect to a specific competence in every possible learning environment, including both formal and informal learning environments". Similarly, Wolf (1995) states that "[competence-based] assessments are not tied to time served in formal educational settings". Competence assessments differ from traditional assessments that aim at testing whether the knowledge and skills taught in a specific course or training have been acquired. The separation of training and assessment, therefore, is basic to competence assessment.

Defining competence assessment in this way reveals that the problems related to competence assessment differ from those related to other types of assessment.

> One important issue in traditional assessment is alignment, the correspondence between the content and educational formats of the training and assessment (Biggs 1996, 1999). Because competence assessment needn't be related to specific training, alignment between training and assessment isn't necessary. In contrast, alignment between competence assessment and what professionals actually do in practice is of utmost importance. According to McGaghie (1993), methods of assessment should closely match what professionals do in practice. Note that in those cases in which competence assessment is part of a formal programme of competence development activities, alignment will play a role. The content and educational formats in the programme should match the competencies to be assessed.

Traditional assessment is often a one-time event held at the end of a course or training; sometimes there will be intermediate assessments during the course. Competence assessment, in principle, recurs throughout a lifetime. Competence assessment is typically delivered in intervals ranging from quarterly to every few years.

An important issue with competence assessment is accessibility. Traditional assessment is embedded within educational or training programmes. This means that once a learner has access to the programme, the learner also has access to the assessment. Competence assessment is different. As there is often no programme related to the assessment, the question is how learners get access to the competence assessment. There are several solutions to this problem. In Norway, for example, an independent system for assessment has been set up. Every individual can have his/her competencies tested through simply sending in his/her portfolio and then being assessed. He/she gets advice, both during writing the portfolio and after the assessment (Schuur et al. 2005).

Traditional assessment is based on the content of a specific programme. Traditional assessment tests whether the learner masters the content, and is meant as finalizing the work on this specific content. On the contrary, competence assessment is based on output criteria set by the professional community. These criteria include several levels of proficiency on which a learner can work throughout his/her whole career. Thus, competence development is never closed, and competence assessment will be recurring throughout a learner's career. As a consequence, new learners have to become used to thinking of themselves not as someone starting a qualification path from the very beginning, for example, as an empty bottle (after having acquired the entrance level), but rather as a bottle, that is already partly filled (after reaching the final achievement levels) (Duvekot 2004). Making output the focus implies that changes in output also become the focus. This puts emphasis on the need for intermediate assessment when output qualifications change, and the need for alumni to regularly update their qualifications.

17.3 Processes in Competence Development and Competence Assessment

In order to substantiate our claim that competence assessment plays different roles in the different stages of competence development, we first examine the stages of competence development. Different perspectives on the nature of competence development lead to different process descriptions. We first consider four different perspectives on competence development before examining the stages in competence assessment.

17.3.1 Perspectives on Processes in Competence Development

The Learning Theory Perspective

Many approaches to lifelong learning and adult education refer to experiential learning theory, as developed by Kolb (1984). According to Hyland (1994): "Kolb offers a useful summary of the key features, noting distinctive emphases on learning as a continuous process grounded in experience, on the idea of a holistic process of adaptation through the resolution of conflicts and opposing viewpoints, and on the notion that learning needs to be regarded as a means of creating knowledge rather than merely repeating and reinforcing existing traditions. Kolb aggregates all these ideas in his broad definition of experiential learning as 'the process whereby knowledge is created by the transformation of experience'". Brugman (1999), referring to Kolb, describes the process of competence development as "consisting of a person acting in a context, observing the effects of his actions, reflecting on it cognitively, his mental and physical constitution becoming used or adapted to the actions and environment, thus slowly changing the person's capacity for subsequent performances".

According to Hyland (1994), experiential learning theory "has emerged as the preferred methodology within adult education (Mezirow 1983) and, in a slightly more practical form, is the most influential model in the further education sector (Gibbs 1988)".

Eraut (1994) discusses and integrates several models that all have experiential learning as their basis. Eraut starts with the five levels of expertise distinguished by Dreyfus et al. (1986), namely novice, advanced beginner, competent, proficient and expert. Eraut couples these to the notion of frames (Minsky 1977) or scripts (Schank and Abelson 1977), which change as learners develop expertise. The model is complemented by Hammond's cognitive continuum theory, which places the kinds of thinking that experts should be able to perform along a continuum, ranging from purely analytic to purely intuitive. Finally, regarding how expertise is acquired, the concept of deliberate reflection-on-action and rapid reflection-in-action (borrowed from Schön 1983) is incorporated.

In these approaches, the emphasis is on the learner. Brugman adds that "from the perspective of managing competence development, this notion implies that managerial attention can be given to the process of competence development, and therefore to the cycle of performance – reflecting upon the performance – subsequent performances, etc., in relation to a specific development context" (Brugman 1999).

In conclusion, from the perspectives of learning theory, at least two different process models can be derived. One directly based on Kolb, including stages of experience, observation, reflection and adaptation, and one model based on stages of expertise in which the learner progresses through the stages: novice, advanced beginner, competent, proficient and expert.

The Validation of Prior Learning Perspective

Another perspective on competence development is that of the Valuation of Prior Learning (VPL). VPL is relevant when an individual, having acquired certain competencies in both formal and informal learning, enters formal education. According to Duvekot et al. (2005), VPL aims at recognition, accreditation/validation and further development of what an individual has learned in every possible learning environment, including both formal and informal learning environments. Duvekot distinguishes a narrow or summative approach of VPL, which focuses on an overview of competences, the cognition and validation and which is retrospective. The broad or formative approach of VPL includes stimulating actual learning or knowledge development. This approach is prospective and aims at development.

Duvekot et al. (2005) distinguishes between five phases of the VPL procedure:

1. Commitment and awareness – individuals become aware of their competenies, organizations become aware of the importance of lifelong learning and VPL.
2. Recognition – identifying or listing competencies, usually in a portfolio.
3. The valuation or assessment of competencies – using the portfolio or additional assessments.
4. The development plan or the actual valuation – the valuation is turned into an action plan.
5. Structural implementation of VPL – VPL is structurally integrated into the organization.

In this approach, both learners and organizations are involved in competence development. In phase 1, both individuals and organizations become aware of their competences, and in phase 5, VPL is integrated into the organization.

This complex interplay is further elucidated by Duvekot et al. (2005), who distinguishes three levels:

Individuals need to be able to take control of their own learning and career in order to become or stay employable.

Organizations need to be able to facilitate these individual learning paths and make use this within the context of their own mission/goals. The learning system – vocational education and training (VET), guidance and counselling – and other services to individuals – labour agencies, local communities and welfare – need to adapt to rendering flexible services to these individuals and organizations.

The Organizational Perspective

From an organizational perspective, competence development is often called "competence management". Van Dongen (2003) provides an example of this approach. The introduction of competence management in an organization is depicted by Van Dongen as follows (Table 17.1):

As in the VPL approach, there is interplay between the organization and the individual.

Table 17.1. Stages in the introduction of competence management in an organization

Orientation	Inventory	Profiling	Diagnosis	Planning	Action
Plan the introduction of competence management	Determine existing core competencies (once-only)	Determine desired competencies	Measure competencies present	Plan action based on gap between competencies desired and present	Implement action plans
Management and personnel department (HRM)					
			Individual employees		

17.3.2 Perspectives on Processes in Competence Assessment

Like competence development, competence assessment is often seen as a process, with distinct stages.

The Competence Assessment Perspective

Looking at the process of the competence assessment itself, Fletcher (2000) distinguishes between the following stages:

1. State required criteria for performance (What are the required outcomes of individual performance?).
2. Collect evidence of outcomes of individual performances.
3. Match evidence to specified outcomes.
4. Make judgements regarding achievement of all required performance outcomes.
5. Allocate "competent" or "not yet competent" rating.
6. If purpose of assessment is certification, issue certificate(s) for achieved competence.
7. Plan development for areas in which a "not yet competent" decision has been made.

The TENCompetence Domain Model (Koper 2006) makes a similar distinction, distinguishing between:

(a) Identifying the competencies (given a certain function/job) that have to be estimated.
(b) Gathering evidence (e.g., by using tests, by viewing diplomas, etc.) for the competencies.
(c) Making the decision on the proficiency levels an actor has acquired.
(d) Making a decision whether a person complies to the requirements of the different function/job levels to determine at which role level he/she functions.

In Wolf's work (1995), which is entirely devoted to competence-based assessment, the stages of competence assessment remain implicit.

The Assessment Centre Perspective

From the perspective of setting up an assessment centre, the focus is on the assessment organisation. Woodruffe (2000) distinguishes between:

Competency analysis
Development of exercises
Observing and recording exercises
Feedback on exercise performance
Development planning

As stated above, competence assessment, like competence development, can be considered a process. In that process also, a complex interplay exists, not so much between individuals and their organizations, but rather between learners and their assessors.

17.4 Integrating Competence Assessment and Competence Development

17.4.1 The Cycle of Competence Development

In this section, a model is developed in which the processes of competence development and competence assessment are integrated. This model distinguishes several stages in competence development/assessment, which are based on the stages in the several perspectives presented in Sect. 17.3, and which, at the same time, are true to the definitions of competence development and competence assessment that we presented in that section. In our definition, learners' goals are central to competence development. Figure 17.1 displays our four stages of competence development. Each stage is labelled by a heading, and below the heading, the abstract learner goals corresponding to that stage are presented.

The cycle of competence development starts with a process of orientation, in which the learner determines which competences s/he wants to develop. Once this decision has been made, the learner has a choice. One very

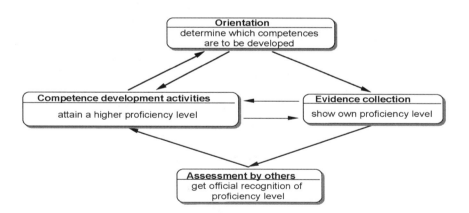

Fig. 17.1. Cycle of learner action and goals in competence development

quick route, typical for informal learning and competencies related to lei-sure activities, is to go directly to the competence development activities, based on the learner's interests with only very little knowledge on their current proficiency level. The other route, more related to formal learning and to professional development, is to proceed by collecting evidence, which shows the learner's current proficiency level. After the learner has col-lected this evidence, s/he can again choose: either the learner can have his/her proficiency level officially recognized by others, or the learner can go directly to competence development activities. Again, the latter route is the more informal learning route.

Note that if the learner takes this route, some sort of assessment is involved, as it is necessary that the learner determines what his/her own proficiency level is, and what aspects of his/her competence they should develop further. Yet, this very light form of self-evaluation is completely different from the assessment by others, which is an essential part of what we might call the formal learning route.

It is very important to realize that the formal learning route is still not completely formal. In fact, the assessment by others is the point at which the formal learning route starts, where previous learning, which might have been either informal or formal, is turned into a formal recognition. When the cycle is passed through for the first time, the moment of assess-ment by others represents the so-called intake assessment.

Also, assessment by others is the only moment in which there is direct contact between the learner and the assessor. For the rest, the contact between learner and assessor is only indirect, in that it is the assessor, or rather the assessor's organization, that determines the proficiency levels and corresponding criteria.

This cycle of competence development is, to a large extent, based on Duvekot et al. (2005). Yet, true to our focus on the individual learner, those aspects that relate to the learning organisation, such as the awareness of organisations and the structural implementation of VPL, are left out.

One remarkable characteristic of our cycle of competence development is that experiential learning theory, discussed as one of the basic perspec-tives on competence development, is not visible. This does not mean that it is absent. From our perspective, these experiential learning models refer to how learners attain a higher proficiency level. For example, learners attain a higher proficiency level by "acting in a context, observing the effects of [their] actions", and by deliberate reflection-on-action and rapid reflection-in-action. And if they do so, their scripts change and they move from being a novice to being advanced beginner, competent, proficient or expert. This means that in our model, the activities mentioned by these experiential learning models are essentially part of performing competence development activities. They reside within this stage, rather than encompassing several of our stages, and thus they do not form a basis on which our stages are built.

Note further that our stages more or less conform to the stages of the individual employees distinguished by Van Dongen (2003): profiling conforms to our orientation, diagnosis and planning together to evidence collection and assessment by others, and action to perform competence development activities. Van Dongen's stages in management and personnel department (as exemplified by Van Dongen 2003) are absent from our competence development cycle. Our focus is on the individual learner.

An important difference between our approach and approaches found in the literature is the freedom of routes that learner may follow, which is indicated by the arrows in Fig. 17.1. In literature on competence development and competence assessment, it is usually assumed that evidence collection is a preparation for assessment by others, and will thus always be followed by assessment by others, and competence development activities can only be entered after assessment by others. Duvekot, for example, takes the perspective of VPL, which is necessarily concerned with formal learning, namely with valuating former informal learning in a formal learning setting. Therefore, in Duvekot's model, the only route from evidence collection to competence development activities is through assessment by others.

Another difference with much of the literature on competence assessment is that "competence assessment" is equated with our stage, "assessment by others", so that routes without assessment by others are not included. Furthermore, as much as these papers are concerned with competency-based education, competence assessment is always linked to a programme of competence development activities, thus leaving out the possibility of learners' having their competencies assessed without proceeding by performing competence development activities (Baartman et al. 2006; Joosten-ten Brinke et al. 2007)

In conclusion, our approach to competence development is characterised by four specific stages of competence development and by: (1) being based on learner goals; (2) allowing different routes that include or exclude different stages; (3) the possibility of entering competence development activities without assessment by others; (4) the possibility of not entering competence development activities at all; (5) emphasis on all four stages, not on assessment by others alone.

17.4.2 Assessment Forms Within the Cycle of Competence Development

Figure 17.2 shows the function and forms of assessment within the competence development cycle.

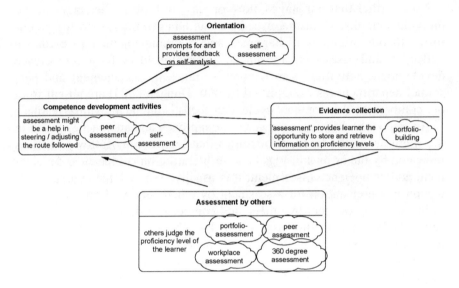

Fig. 17.2. Function and forms of assessment in the cycle of competence development

It is important to first note that the assessment stages of Fletcher (2000) and the TENCompetence Domain Model (Koper 2006) overlap with our cycle of competence development to a large extent. True to our focus on the individual learner, the competence development cycle starts with the orientation phase in which the learner determines which competencies should be developed. This first stage is the same as the first stage of the TENCompetence Domain Model, but it differs from Fletcher's first stage. Fletcher emphasises the institutional side ("state required criteria for performance"). The second stage is the stage of evidence collection, which is Fletcher's stage 2 and TENCompetence Domain Model's stage b. The third stage is the stage of assessment by others, which encompasses Fletcher's stages 3, 4, 5, and 7 and TENCompetence Domain Model's stage c and d. Note that our last stage of the competence development cycle is not included in either models on competence assessment.

An important difference between our competence development model and both assessment models is that their focus is on the assessment by others. Most of their stages are included in the stage "assessment by others" in our models. In their assessment models, collecting evidence is seen as a preparatory stage for assessment by others, whereas in our model it needn't be followed by assessment by others.

Another difference between our model and much of the literature is our coupling of assessment forms with competence development stages. In the literature, this link is absent, or at most mentioned vaguely. There is recognition in the literature that several assessment forms are needed. In the definition by Joosten-ten Brinke et al. (2007), assessment includes "classical tests, examinations and questionnaires, as well as newer types of assessment, such as performance assessment, portfolio assessment and peer assessment". Baartman et al. (2006) and Baartman et al. (2004) distinguish between newer and older forms of assessment (without specifying which forms are what). They also claim that a competence assessment programme should use both types, because all methods of assessment may contribute to the difficult job of determining whether a learner has acquired a competency. They agree with Cizek (1997) that newer forms of assessment are not meant as alternative ways of gathering the same kind of information about learners, but as ways of answering completely different questions. Many of the newer forms of assessment were developed with the idea of measuring deeper understanding. Yet, they do not link specific assessment forms to specific stages in competence development.

Duvekot comes closest to our approach, as he links self-assessment to the orientation stage. However, his emphasis is on VPL, and he does not include the stage of performing competence development activities. In our view, being assessed by others is just one option among many others. Learners may, after a short orientation, directly start with performing competence development activities, or they may want to list their competencies without having these assessed, or they simply may even want to do an orientation without a continuation. Thus, as the four stages can be entered indepedently, the functions that competence assessment might have in all of these four stages should be included in a model of competence assessment.

Traditionally, reflected in Fletcher's model and the TENCompetence Domain Model (Koper 2006), the function of assessment is to judge the proficiency level of the learner. This puts an emphasis on the "Assessment by others", which has this function and includes the evidence collection, which is seen as a preparatory stage to assessment by others. The other two stages of competence development traditionally are not included in descriptions of competence assessment. Yet, from other sources, it is clear that competence assessment may have a function in these stages as well. In the orientation stage, competence assessment might provide feedback on self-analysis of the learner as to the learner's current proficiency level regarding competences that he/she might decide to develop further. During the execution of the personal competence development plan, assessment might help in steering or adjusting the plan. The next section discusses these assessment types for each of the stages.

17.5 Assessment in the Four Stages of Competence Development

17.5.1 Stage 1: Orientation

In Duvekot's VPL model (see Sect. 17.3.1), the process through which a learner goes in the first orientation phase can be described as follows (Duvekot, p.c.):

1. Self-examination: the learner investigates his/her own current competence level. First, the learner determines the level more generally ("I am at the university education level"). Then, the learner determines his/her likelihood of success for separate domains.
2. Self-assessment: the learner determines which experiences, knowledge and skills s/he possesses.
3. Orientation: the learner looks where s/he can find information on the possibilities for competence development.

In Duvekot's view, the investigation of learners into their competencies is very much supported by self-examination and self-assessment. Comparably, Eraut (2004) states that peer assessment and self-assessment are becoming central features of professional life, and therefore need developing at an earlier stage. This is in line with McGaghie (1993), who states that more attention should be paid to what they call "pre-entry assessment". This term reflects the view of both McGaghie and Duvekot, who view self-assessment in the orientation stage as preparation to the formal assessment by others later on in the process. According to Duvekot, as much as possible, self-examination by the individual of his/her own targets, wishes and possibilities in the orientation stage increases the accessibility of the stage of assessment by others. In our model, self-assessment in the orientation stage has a broader function. Not only is it a preparation to a formal programme of competence development activities, which involves assessment by others, it may also be a preparation of an informal set of competence development activities, in which orientation is directly followed by executing a personal competence development plan. In summary: in our model, self-assessment in the orientation phase functions as a preparation for performing competence development activities, rather than a preparation to assessment by others.

An Example of E-Self-Assessment

The Belgian COBRA (index of competencies and professions for the labour market) is a classification system of professional groups. COBRA was developed on the basis of the French ROME (Répertoire Opérationnel des Métiers et des Emplois; www.anpe.fr). Professional groups are made up of professionals with the same basic backgrounds. Each of the 550 professionl groups has its own card, which describes the group and includes an indication of the competencies to which the professional group is linked. In this way, information on professions and competencies is provided in a condensed and orderly way.

On the basis of the COBRA cards a website has been built (www.vdab.be/cobra), which provides support to people who are exploring their possibilities in the labour market. The COBRA website provides several tools. The first is the already mentioned 550 professional group cards. These are complemented by 131 short videos, which show several aspects of a specific profession. Two other tools at COBRA can be considered forms of e-self-assessment. The first (tool three) is a test into the learner's interest in the various professions. On the basis of 40 questions, the learner is presented with a list of professions that fit his/her interests. The final tool consists of 50 occupational tests. Each occupational test consists of 15–20 multiple-choice questions. Combined, they give an indication of the learner's proficiency with respect to the profession. All tests can be performed anonymously.

17.5.2 Stage 2: Evidence Collection by the Learner

During the stage of evidence collection, the learner builds a portfolio, listing evidence of his/her current proficiency level. In general, assessment models recognize evidence collection as a separate stage. Done properly, the process of evidence collection may take a long time, even several years. The most important instrument in this stage is the portfolio or e-portfolio. One of the reasons for the growing importance of portfolio building is a reversal in the burden of proof. In traditional competence assessment, the assessor asks the learner to prove that s/he possesses the required knowledge and skills. This is shifting towards a situation in which learners take their portfolio to the assessor, and the assessor has to prove that the individual does not possess the required knowledge and skills. As a result, the emphasis in assessment is shifting from later assessment by the assessor to the learner's collection of evidence done earlier in the process. Learners now have the task of presenting a portfolio that proves his or her qualities. This also means a shift away from the assessor (which becomes important at the moment the assessment comes into view) to the individual, who is central in the preceding course of collecting evidence.

This shift in the burden of proof fits in very well with the idea in our model that portfolio building might, but needn't, be followed by assessment by others. The emphasis is on the evidence collection by the learner, whether or not this is followed by assessment by others.

An Example of an E-Portfolio

The Swiss Gesellschaft CH-Q Schweizerisches Qualifikationsprogramm zur Berufslaufbahn (CH-Q; www.ch-q.ch) is a national organisation that aims at developing and making available integral solutions for competence management. The organization provides support at several levels: certified development of competence management in four steps, a system of quality assurance, tools, projects related to competence management, and a national and international platform.

CH-Q provides two portfolio tools for evidence collection, presented under the category of "tools for individual competence management". The personal portfolio is meant for continuous collection of data and facts with respect to the acquired competencies and skills. It enables looking back and ahead at the personal competence development, and thus it supports competence development and career development. The demonstration record is meant to contain a specific outstanding selection of data and facts, which prove that a specific proficiency level with respect to a specific competence has been achieved; the demonstration record is meant to be used in qualification. These two tools for evidence collection are presented together with a third tool, which enables individuals to get an overview of formal and non-formal qualifications, offered by employers, schools, and (educational) institutions.

17.5.3 Stage 3: Assessment by Others

After having gone through the individual part of assessment, the learner may want to go to an assessor to have their competence level assessed. The task of the assessor is to match the output that the individual provides to the output levels of the qualification. In the model of Duvekot, assessment by others consists of three steps (1) setting the standard for valuation, which can be any standard that matches the need of the organization, be it a national or an internal standard, (2) the valuation itself, and (3) the validation of the learning evidence within the given standard. The result of valuation is a validation of the learning evidence (step 3): which can take diverse forms such as a certificate, diploma, career move, or advice on career opportunities (Duvekot et al. 2005).

McGaghie (1993) stresses that methods of assessment should closely match what professionals do in practice. According to Eraut and Cole (1993), evidence based directly on performance in the workplace should be given a high priority, but they point out that relatively few professions have clear, objective standards against which such assessments can be carried out. McGaghie (1993) criticizes current assessment methods as inadequate for addressing the complexities of professional competence. McGaghie gives primacy to direct observation of professional activity in addition to knowledge assessment of acquired knowledge. He leans towards the use of simulations, provided that they are of high fidelity, and also favours "open-ended" problem-solving exercise.

In our model, the assessment by others is the only moment when learners and assessors meet and interact with each other. This happens only after the learner has already gone through an individual process of orientation and portfolio building. This is true, even if the assessment concerned is the learner's first assessment, a so-called "intake assessment". Several people are involved in assessment by others, in different roles.

Assessment by others comes in many forms. Cheetham and Chivers (2005) list the following types of competence assessment: direct observation and production of a portfolio of evidence, sometimes verified by a senior member of the profession. In our view, these refer to assessment by others. Cheetham and Chivers further distinguish three broad patterns of assessment, which they take from Eraut and Cole (1993):

> Assessment of workplace performance during a period of practical experience, following completion of an academic qualification in higher education
>
> On-the-job assessment as an integral part of the academic qualification leading to direct professional recognition
>
> Assessment of practical performance conducted both within the academic course and during a subsequent period of professional experience

The most common assessment techniques identified by Eraut and Cole (1993) are: direct observation by supervisors; the use of role plays or simulations; observation of simplified practice; indirect observation using a video recording; interviews with candidates; and the examination of work related documents, for example, portfolios, records, testimonies.

Portfolio assessment. As mentioned above, the portfolio is a very important assessment technique. Duvekot et al. (2005) mentions the valuation of the portfolio as the most important part of assessment which is "when necessary, followed by an extra assessment". This assessment usually takes place by observation during work or by means of a criteria-based interview.

In Duvekot's model, the most important part of valuation consists of the assessment of the portfolio and its valuation with respect to the given standard and targets of the organization. Valuation of the portfolio can be followed by an extra assessment. This assessment usually takes place by observation during work or by means of a criterion based interview. Assessors compare the competences of an individual with the standard used in the organization involved.

Other forms of competence assessment identified in the literature include:

360-degree assessment. 360-degree assessment involves the assessment of an individual by a variety of stakeholders, such as peers, subordinates, supervisors, customers or clients (Cheetham and Chivers 2005). The main applications of this technique to date have been self-awareness raising, performance management and in-company development, but the technique offers a potential to be used in more formal assessment settings. Advocates argue that 360-degree assessment is fairer because it elicits perceptions of competence from people who observe an individual's day-to-day performance from different perspectives. On the other hand, there will be difficulties in achieving consistency and commonality of understanding. Some stakeholders may have insufficient evidence of the subject's performance. Not all stakeholders are experienced assessors. Finally, there is the danger of collusion amongst participants.

Assessment centres. Assessment centres administer "a suite of specially designed assessment exercises to individuals in order gauge their current or potential competence". Normally, several candidates participate in the centre at the same time since some of the exercises are group based (Cheetham and Chivers 2005). According to McGaghie (1993), the use of assessment centres should be expanded.

An Example of Assessment by Others

The Realkompetanse project (1999–2002) was a project on the validation of non-formal and informal learning in Norway, initiated by VOX, the Norwegian Institute for Adult Education. The main aim of the project was to establish a national system for the documentation and validation of adults' non-formal and informal learning, with legitimacy in both the workplace and the education system. With respect to documentation, a distinction was made between documenting in the workplace and in the "third sector", that is, outside the workplace or education. With respect to validation, a distinction was made between validation in upper secondary education and higher education. Since 2000, Norwegian adults born before 1 January 1978, who have not completed upper secondary education, are legally entitled to have their acquired competence assessed (assessment of formal and informal learning) with a view to following an individually adapted pathway for their studies.

The resulting assessment system in upper secondary education uses three types of assessment, each with their own benefits and disadvantages, and meant to complement each other. The dialogue-based method consists of a one-to-one meeting between the learner and an assessor. It is aimed at covering tacit knowledge, and is supposed to be beneficial for adults who have problems with reading, writing and mathematics. Portfolio assessment is based on written documentation provided by the learner, according to the guidelines that were developed in the project. Vocational testing consists of a specialist interview for testing the theoretical knowledge and a practical vocational test for testing the practical skills of the learner. This method aims at testing knowledge and skills that cannot be documented, in a way that is irrespective of learning and language problems.

17.5.4 Stage 4: Performing Competence Development Activities

While the learner proceeds by performing competence development activities, assessment might be a help in steering or adjusting their route. In this stage, peer assessment and self-assessment play important roles. Peer assessment, according to Topping et al. (2000), is "an arrangement for peers to consider the level, value, worth, quality or successfulness of the products or outcomes of learning of others of similar status". Self-assessment has been described under stage 1.

An Example of E-Self-Assessment

Below, an example of an assessment type is presented, which is not used for self-assessment, but which could be easily extended for use in self-assessment. The assessment type is called progress testing. Progress testing has been in use with problem-based learning for more than 25 years now.

In formal education programmes based on problem-based learning, a progress test is a general test that involves the whole competence domain. Vleuten et al. (1996) describe their use of progress testing at the Maastricht medical school in the Netherlands, as follows:

The progress test can best be conceived of considered a final examination: a comprehensive examination reflecting the cognitive end-objectives of the curriculum. Each progress test consists of multiple (approximately 250) multiple true/false questions stratified in categories based on the International Classification of Diseases (ICD). It samples knowledge across all disciplines and content areas in medicine relevant for a medical degree. Four times per year the progress test is given to all the students in the curriculum (approximately 900), regardless of their class. For each occasion, a newly constructed test is prepared. A single test question may be answered with either true or false, or with an "I do not know" (the question-mark option). The latter option is not penalized or rewarded. A correct answer is rewarded with one mark while an incorrect answer is given a negative mark. To discourage guessing, a total test score is expressed as the number of correct answers minus the number of incorrect answers. To allow comparison across tests, scores are expressed on a percentage scale. The freshmen-year students are not able to answer as many questions as the second-year students, who are not able to answer as many as the third-year students and so on.

There are several reasons why it would be interesting to deliver progress tests as a form of self-assessment with lifelong learning:

A progress test is related to a specific competence, not to specific training. This makes the progress test very suitable for testing competences in a lifelong learning situation, in which learners can follow very different routes through all kinds of competence development activities.

The progress test has been developed to be administered in long intervals, which will also be the case in a lifelong learning situation.

Once a database with multiple-choice questions has been developed and tested among groups of learners, very reliable progress tests can be derived from this database.

Delivering a progress test is easy: a set of 250 questions can be taken out of the database randomly or by any other algorithm, and be presented to the learner.

By repeatedly taking a progress test, learners can monitor their own progress, visible by an increasing score on the questions. As their score at the very beginning will be very low, it is doubtful whether progress testing would be of use for learners in the orientation stage.

17.6 Conclusions

In this chapter, we have set up a model of competence development and competence assessment with the following characteristics:

It consists of four stages of orientation, evidence collection, assessment by others and performing competence development activities.

The four stages are based on the learner's goals, which vary with each stage.

The stages that learners actually go through, and the order in which they do so, is highly variable.

After each of the first three stages, a learner can decide to enter competence development activities; assessment by others is one possible, but not the exclusive, entrance to competence development activities.

In accordance with their diverse needs, learners may go through any of the first three stages without performing competence development activities.

All four stages are important and can be followed independently.

With the distinction of these four stages, less emphasis is put on competence assessment in the form of assessment by others, but more attention to competence assessment in the other stages.

Alignment between assessment and professional practice is relevant in all stages, alignment with training is only relevant during or following a programme of competence development activities.

Different forms of assessment should not be qualified with respect to whether they are old or new but with respect to the function that they fulfil in the different stages of competence development.

Acknowledgements

The work in this chapter has been sponsored by the TENCompetence Integrated Project that is funded by the European Commission's 6th Framework Programme, priority IST/Technology Enhanced Learning. Contract 027087 (www.tencompetence.org).

References

Baartman, L. K. J., Bastiaens, T. J., Kirschner, P. A. (2004). *Requirements for Competency Assessment Programmes*. Utrecht, Netherlands: Onderwijs Research Dagen.

Baartman, L. K. J., Bastiaens, T. J., Kirschner, P. A., Vleuten, C. P. M. vd (2006). The wheel of competency assessment: Presenting quality criteria for competency assessment programs. *Studies in Educational Evaluation*, 32(2), 153–170.

Biggs, J. (1996). Enhancing teaching through constructive alignment. Higher education. *The International Journal of Higher Education and Educational Planning*, 32(3), 347–364.

Biggs, J. (1999). *Teaching for Quality Learning at University: What the Student Does*. Buckingham: Society for Research into Higher Education & Open University press.

Brugman, O. P. G. (1999). *Organizing for Competence Development in Research and Development: An Exploratory Study on Organizational Conditions for Individual Competence Development in Industrial Research and Development*. Nijmegen: Katholieke Universiteit Nijmegen.

Cheetham, G., Chivers, G. E. (2005). *Professions, Competence and Informal Learning*. Cheltenham: Edward Elgar.

Cizek, G. J. (1997). Learning, achievement, and assessment: constructs at a crossroads. In G. D. Phye (Ed.), *Handbook of Classroom Assessment: Learning, Achievement, and Adjustment* (pp. 1–32). San Diego: Academic.

Dreyfus, H. L., Dreyfus, S. E., Athanasiou, T. (1986). *Mind Over Machine: The Power of Human Intuition and Expertise in the Era of the Computer*. London: Blackwell.

Duvekot, R. (2004). Your glass is half full! Valuation of prior learning as a new perspective for life-long learning. *CIEA 2004; 24th International Course on Vocational Education and Teaching in Agriculture*, Bern, Switzerland.

Duvekot, R. C., Schuur, K., Paulusse, J. (Ed.) (2005). *The Unfinished Story of VPL. Validation and Valuation of Prior Learning in Europe's Learning Cultures*. Utrecht, Netherlands: Foundation EC-VPL & Kenniscentrum EVC.

Eraut, M. (1994). *Developing Professional Knowledge and Competence*. London: Falmer.

Eraut, M. (2004). Commentary. A wider perspective on assessment. *Medical Education*, 38(8), 803–804.

Eraut, M., Cole, G. (1993). *Assessing Competence in the Professions*. Sheffield, UK: Employment Department Methods Strategy Unit.

Fletcher, S. (2000). *Competence-Based Assessment Techniques*, 2nd revised edn. London: Kogan Page.

Gibbs, G. (1988). *Learning by Doing*. London: Further Education Unit.

Hyland, T. (1994). Experiential learning, competence and critical practice in higher education. *Studies in Higher Education*, 19(3), 327–340.

Joosten-ten Brinke, D., van Bruggen, J., Hermans, H., Burgers, J., Giesbers, B., Koper, R., Latour, I. (2007). Modeling assessment for re-use of traditional and new types of assessment. *Computers in Human Behavior*, 23(6), 2721–2741.

Kolb, D. A. (1984). *Experiential Learning: Experience as the Source of Learning and Development*. Englewood Cliffs, NJ: Prentice-Hall.

Koper, R. (2006). The TENCompetence Domain Model. Version 1.0. http://dspace.ou.nl/bitstream/1820/649/13/DomainModel-version1p0.pdf

McGaghie, W. C. (1993). Evaluating professional competence. *Journal of the American Podiatric Medical Association*, 83(6), 338–344.

Mezirow, J. (1983). A critical theory of adult learning and education. In M. Tight (Ed.), *Adult Learning and Education* (pp. 124–138). London: Routledge.

Minsky, M. (1977). Frame-system theory. In P. N. Johnson-Laird, P. C. Wason (Eds.), *Thinking: Readings in Cognitive Science* (pp. 355–376). Cambridge, New York: Cambridge University Press.

Schank, R. C., Abelson, R. P. (1977). *Scripts, Plans, Goals and Understanding: An Inquiry into Human Knowledge Structures*. Hillsdale, NJ: Lawrence Erlbaum.

Schön, D. A. (1983). *The Reflective Practitioner: How Professionals Think in Action*. New York: Basic Books.

Schuur, K., Feenstra, B., Duvekot, R. (2005). European learning cultures and VPL. In R. Duvekot, K. Schuur, J. Paulusse (Eds.), *The Unfinished Story of VPL Validation and Valuation of Prior Learning in Europe's Learning Cultures* (pp. 29–115). Utrecht, Netherlands: Foundation EC-VPL & Kenniscentrum EVC.

Topping, K. J., Smith, E. F., Swanson, I., Elliot, A. (2000). Formative peer assessment of academic writing between postgraduate students. *Assessment and Evaluation in Higher Education: An International Journal*, 25(2), 149–170.

Van Dongen, T. (2003). *Competentiemanagement. En dan?: een mensgerichte visie op competentiemanagement*. Thema bedrijfswetenschappelijke en educatieve uitgeverij, Zaltbommel.

Vleuten, C. P. M. vd., Verwijnen, G. M., Wijnen, W. H. F. W. (1996). Fifteen years of experience with progress testing in a problem-based learning curriculum. *Medical Teacher: The Journal for Educators in the Health Sciences*, 18(2), 103–110.

Wolf, A. (1995). *Competence-Based Assessment*. Buckingham: Open University Press.

Woodruffe, C. (2000). *Development and Assessment Centres: Identifying and Developing Competence*, 3rd edn. London: Institute of Personnel and Development.

Section 3:
The Organisational Perspective

18 The Future of E-Learning in Schools

G. Bull and T. Hammond

The advance of electronic technologies throughout the past century has encouraged corresponding interest in potential applications of these technologies in schools. Thomas Edison, for example, expressed a hope that invention of the motion picture might revolutionize schools (Saettler 1990). The motion picture did not revolutionize schools, nor did any of the other twentieth century technologies – radio, educational television, the audio and video recorder, etc. – that followed. The reasons for this are embedded both in the structure of schools and in the nature of the electronic media available. An understanding of both schools and electronic media is therefore needed to understand past limitations and future potential.

Recent technological advances are now altering key aspects of society itself in what has been termed an *Age of Participation*. The active participation in society at large has engendered interest in similar advances in schools through what has been termed E-Learning. Broadly speaking, the term E-Learning encompasses any form of electronic learning, such as viewing instructional videos. However, the currently understood meaning of the term is computer-mediated learning, often Internet-based. E-Learning can supplement or replace traditional, face-to-face instructional practices.

Much of the initial development of E-Learning has taken place in higher education, specifically through the evolution of online courses. The current generation of E-Learning tools and practices largely replicate previous instructional strategies and focus on delivering information. The new developments in web-based technologies in society at large, however, offer opportunities for more dynamic, interactive instructional models in schools.

18.1 Twentieth Century Learning

E-Learning does not emerge from a vacuum. The current dominant model is non-interactive, linear, and teacher-centered. The role of the instructor is to deliver information; the role of the student is to absorb it. While modern teachers employ a variety of instructional strategies, including interactive components such as simulations or dialog, the transmission paradigm controls the classroom. In history classes, the most common instructional activity for teachers is the lecture. At many universities, adjunct faculty members are termed lecturers. In medicine, interactive, teaching-by-example grand rounds are being replaced by PowerPoint-driven lectures (Altman 2006).

Changes in technology have driven changes in instructional paradigms. The proliferation of technologies in the twentieth century reinforced and accelerated the supremacy of didactic instruction. At the beginning of that century, the most recently adopted innovation in education was the blackboard. These monoliths replaced smaller and cheaper individual slates. The smaller slates encouraged groupwork or individual consultations between the students and the teacher. The wall-mounted blackboards, by contrast, allowed the teacher to present to the whole class at once. The twentieth century additions of film, radio, television, and the overhead projector added new options, but the instructional paradigm remained the same.

The microcomputer has presented a puzzle to educators. Should the computer be a tutor, a tool for composition, or a tutee to be programmed by the student (Taylor 1980)? Decades after being introduced, educators are still grappling with how to integrate one-to-one computing into instruction (Bork 2003). While computers in the classroom can support a lecture-based model of instruction, they also invite a much higher level of interactivity and student engagement than a didactic approach.

18.2 Educational Technology and Instructional Practice in E-Learning

Advancements in educational technologies have served to encourage or inhibit four characteristics in instructional design: interactivity, scalability, media-richness, and granularity. Table 18.1 presents a selection of educational technologies in rough chronological order of their introduction and notes their characteristics. (For a more encyclopedic discussion of the development of educational technologies, see Saettler 1990).

Table 18.1. Primary affordances of educational technologies

	Interactivity	Scalability	Media-richness	Granularity
Face-to-face dialog	✓			✓
Printed text		✓		
Blackboard		✓		
Film		✓	✓	
Radio		✓	✓	
Microcomputers		✓	✓	✓
Read-only Web		✓	✓	✓
Read–write Web	✓	✓	✓	✓

As the pattern indicates, advances in instructional technology have steadily addressed the problem of scalability but at the expense of interactivity. Twentieth century mass media has added media-richness, and the microcomputer added granularity. Internet-based computing, the current hallmark of twentyfirst-century education, offers the technical capacity to address all four characteristics.

One of the largest sustained efforts in development of Internet-based instruction involves online courses. Millions of higher-education students are enrolled in some form of online learning. Approximately two-thirds of graduate schools offer courses, or even entire degree programs online (Allen and Seaman 2005). K-12 schools are following suit. More than one-third of all American public school districts offer distance education courses, enrolling hundreds of thousands of students (Waits and Lewis 2003).

These courses are typically organized through specialized, Internet-based software. This software goes by many names: content management systems (CMS), learning management systems (LMS), online learning environments (OLE), and others. Regardless of variations in terminology, the functionality provided by such systems is similar: teachers make content available to students online, and teachers and students can communicate in a secure, stable, online environment. Content posted on the web can be viewed online or downloaded by the student. Communication can take place synchronously, through text or voice chat, or asynchronously, on threaded discussion boards. Teachers can also post quizzes and online tests that are linked to electronic grade books. In many instances, the LMS is now being integrated into the university or school's main website.

During the first years of the web, many universities developed their own LMS capabilities. More recently, the trend has been to acquire externally developed LMS programs. These include both proprietary systems such as Blackboard and open source systems such as Moodle or Sakai.

As indicated by this overview, these applications of Internet-based computing to education have focused on scalability more than any other characteristic of the technology. Online courses and course documents are offered to extend the scale (in time, distance, or number of students) of instruction. Certain exemplary online courses are media-rich, presenting students with appropriately blended text, images, audio, and video, but the instructional paradigm is still didactic delivery.

Some online instructional resources offer extensive granularity, such as the American Memory project at the Library of Congress, which makes nine million digitized historical artifacts (historical documents, photographs, sound recordings, moving pictures, books, pamphlets, maps, and other resources) available on the web. However, the current state of E-Learning has yet to capture the interactivity that resides in many non-educational uses of the Internet. We are at E-Learning 1.0; a new generation of web-based technologies and emerging social patterns are laying the foundations for E-Learning 2.0.

18.3 Web 2.0 and the Possibilities for E-Learning 2.0

Tim Berners-Lee, originator of the World Wide Web, conceived the web as a read–write medium for exchange of information (Berners-Lee 1999). For technical reasons, a web browser proved to be easier to develop than a web editor. The integrated browser/editor that Berners-Lee envisioned never became widely adopted, limiting use of the web as a read–write medium. Many individuals did learn to insert HTML tags into text documents to create web pages, but the technical threshold presented a barrier that others could not readily cross. For this reason (and others), the first decade of the Internet has been termed the "read-only Web".

Widespread use of the web as a read–write medium began to occur in its second decade of existence as a side effect of what has been termed the "Web 2.0" era. Expanding capabilities found in second-generation web applications are significantly affecting social interactions outside school. The changing environment outside schools, in turn, is creating an opportunity for what has been termed "E-Learning 2.0" within schools.

The phenomenon of web logs, soon shortened to "blogs", became one of the first examples of user-generated content. The number of blogs has been estimated at as many as 50 million world-wide. Blogs involve posts in the format of a diary. A survey by the Pew Foundation characterized bloggers as the Internet's new storytellers. Personal expression proved to be one of the primary reasons that many share online writing in this manner.

Approximately half of bloggers surveyed had not previously published their writing (Lenhart and Fox 2006). Blogs served as a proof-of-concept for Berners-Lee's vision of the web as an interactive read–write medium.

User-generated content can be particularly valuable in the context of a social network. Wikipedia is a premier illustration of the potential of user-generated content, employed in an application that gets better as more people use it. A resource of this type will not replace authoritative sources such as traditional encyclopedias in schools. However, its success, especially as a proof-of-concept, is undeniable.

Outside of schools, Web 2.0 applications, such as Google Docs (productivity tools) and Flickr (tagged image-sharing and annotation), are being developed and made available without charge to consumers as a result of this changed dynamic. The ease with which applications and resources can now be created and shared makes them feasible on a much larger scale than previously possible. This trend has not yet significantly influenced K-12 education, but the potential now exists.

E-Learning 2.0 will operate on the web, just as the E-Learning 1.0 tools (Blackboard, Moodle, Sakai) currently do. However, E-Learning 2.0 tools work differently to take advantage of the Web 2.0 environment. Where E-Learning 1.0 focused on the delivery of information, E-Learning 2.0 will focus on interaction and interpretation. The vignette in the section that follows illustrates some of the characteristics of such interactions.

18.4 The Future of E-Learning in K-12 Education: E-Learning 2.0

Mrs. Andersen noted that Stephen and John, like many students in her school, were technologically adept. She asked them to create a digital movie that integrated images from online primary source documents with a narration in their own voice. She accessed the script for their narrative via the web and found that, not atypically, their initial discussion was primarily a recitation of points from the textbook. She posed several questions inserted as comments in the students' script to encourage them to develop their own inferences.

The following night, Mrs. Andersen checked their work via the web. To her delight, she saw that Stephen and John had extended their dry, impersonal recitation to develop an insightful, even passionate response. Mrs. Andersen was so pleased with the results that she decided to send a link to the online digital movie to a colleague at a neighboring school who later incorporated it into his own course.

This vignette presents a composite picture of the practice of several teachers with whom we are currently working. Students who are reluctant writers sometimes are engaged by the opportunity to create a digital movie. Digital archives allow students to directly access historical documents rather than rely solely upon secondary sources and interpretations. The ability to access students' work from any location makes it possible to provide feedback more quickly and interactively than might otherwise be possible. The web also allows dissemination of work across the Internet.

E-Learning 2.0, like any other instructional encounter, involves several elements: an instructor, students, a curriculum, access to content, pedagogical tools and strategy. Several of these pieces are already established: the curriculum, for example, cannot be changed; the curriculum served by K-12 E-Learning is substantively the same as the traditional, face-to-face curriculum. Surveying the other pieces, however, requires careful thinking and suggests several propositions:

1. Teachers as well as students must be fluent with the medium.
2. Pedagogy must be adapted to the new environment, while satisfying existing curricular goals.
3. Student- and teacher-generated content will become significant beyond the classroom.
4. Teachers will have the tools to exercise greater control over their instructional design.
5. Teachers will be able to engage in an accelerated level of peer-to-peer collaboration.

These propositions provide a starting point for thinking about the potential future of E-Learning 2.0 in K-12 schools.

18.4.1 Teachers as well as Students Must Be Fluent with the Medium

Successful instruction requires a teacher who is prepared to teach and a student who is prepared to learn. In terms of preparation for E-Learning 2.0, students sometimes seem to be ahead of their teachers. The Pew research foundation's reports on young Internet users suggest different patterns of behavior. Young people (ages 12–17) are more intensive users of the Internet than adults (Lenhart et al. 2005). Teens' use of the Internet is highly interactive, as they post blogs, create and share digital media, and play games (Lenhart and Madden 2005). In addition to these extracurricular uses, students are also using the Internet to support or extend their school-related work. For K-12 students, the Internet functions as an alternate textbook and reference library, a tutor and study shortcut, a study group, a source of personal advice, and a storage space for student work (Levin and Arafeh 2002).

In contrast, many teachers report that they feel unprepared to use technology in the classroom. Teacher education programs currently focus on developing teachers' pedagogical content knowledge (PCK) as identified by Shulman (1987). PCK will remain at the heart of teacher preparation, but effective integration of technology – at present an add-on in many teacher education programs – must occur before E-Learning 2.0 becomes a reality.

Technological pedagogical content knowledge (TPCK) is an emerging concept that integrates teachers' use of technology into their practice of PCK (Mishra and Koehler 2006). An E-Learning 2.0 instructor will need a teacher preparation program that includes specific emphasis on TPCK. It cannot be assumed that the next generation of teachers will step into their teacher-preparation programs ready to reinvent their methodology classes and integrate technology. The full range of perspectives from early adopters to skeptics will always be present among preservice teachers. Teacher education students will need models of effective pedagogical use of technology to integrate it into their own instruction.

18.4.2 Pedagogy Must Be Adapted to the New Environment, While Satisfying Existing Curricular Goals

In both the classroom and in online education, the teacher is the central point of control. The teacher creates the pedagogical structure and guides students through the sequence, providing individualized support and feedback along the way. As students develop products (essays, posters, digital movies) or take assessments (quizzes and tests), the teacher is responsible for evaluating each and every item. The role of the teacher combines the functions of designer, instructor, and evaluator.

Certain styles of classroom teaching already shift the teacher from the central focus of the classroom. Online learning provides additional opportunities for independent student work. Some schools of education (such as Iowa State University's Virtual Schooling project) and organizations (such as the Concord Consortium) are thinking through the pedagogy for this environment. A consistent theme is the need for the teacher to not be the center of every interaction but to manage a learning community.

In E-Learning 2.0, therefore, pedagogy and assessment need to be restructured to serve the same curricular goals, but achieve them in different ways. Instruction will take place through tools that seamlessly integrate content and scaffolding. The authors have developed an example of such a tool, PrimaryAccess, designed to allow history students to construct digital movies that incorporate online primary source documents (Ferster et al. 2006). Many documents that were formerly accessible only to historians are now available to the public through online repositories. PrimaryAccess allows these artifacts to be accessed via contextualized online links and incorporated into web-based movies (digital historical narratives) (Figs. 18.1 and 18.2).

This historical content is integrated with a word processor as well as a web-based digital editor with pan and zoom capabilities. Writing the script while composing a digital historical narrative requires active use of language for script development, leading to increased retention of vocabulary and concepts. The complementary roles played by text and images provide an additional point of engagement for students with weak literacy skills.

Finally, PrimaryAccess incorporates a collaborative annotation feature that allows students working in pairs to post comments to one another (Fig. 18.3). The teacher can also view draft scripts and associated comments via the web at any time, contributing her own comments. This capability has been a key factor in encouraging students to go beyond recitation of facts in their narratives, considering implications and conclusions as well.

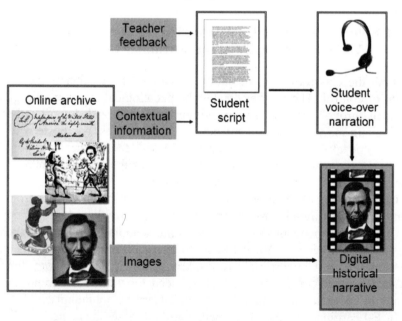

Fig. 18.1. A digital historical narrative composed in PrimaryAccess consists of a selection of online images sources (often from a historical archive) combined with a voice-over narration recorded by the student

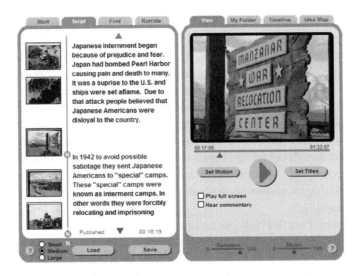

Fig. 18.2. The PrimaryAccess editor allows students to combine text and images as they create a digital movie

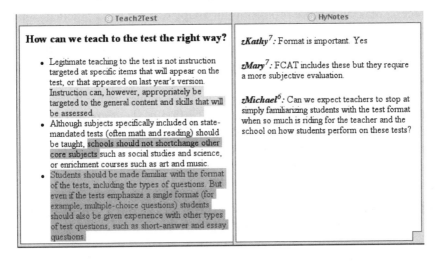

Fig. 18.3. Group annotation permits students to collectively view one another's comments on a peer product or assigned reading

Assessment is an indispensable part of effective instruction. The teacher is the most expert assessor in the class learning community. Emergent capabilities such as group annotation and calibrated peer review (CPR) provide opportunities for at least some portion of assessment tasks to usefully move into students' hands. Group annotation allows students to collectively annotate a reading in an online environment, permitting display of areas of text that one or more readers highlighted as important to develop a composite picture of where a group of readers' interests are distributed.

Lebow et al. (2003) suggest that group annotation can make activities that are normally hidden "become visible for public scrutiny, feedback, and reflection". They note that during the Middle Ages, scholars passed manuscripts from hand to hand within the community, using annotations as a mechanism for developing shared understanding and negotiated meaning. Just as technology now offers the opportunity to re-establish interactive Socratic dialog, it allows students to use a document for collective negotiation of meaning.

Calibrated Peer Review, developed by Chapman (2001), builds on the practice of peer editing and review by using a database to provide a double-blind, structured feedback process. Each student also gets an opportunity to rate the quality of feedback that they receive from their peers. Variations of this process have been conducted by means of multiple printed copies produced by faculty members in higher education in the past. A web-based version of this type of peer review automates the distribution and tracking process, making it more promising for adaptation for K-12 practice than its paper-based counterpart.

Part of the appeal of Web 2.0 is the ability of creators to work in not only text but also images, audio, and video. The proliferation of expressive media has an educational purpose; media-richness distributes cognitive load, allowing students to access meaning in multiple modes, rather than the single modality of text. However, effective instruction is about not just media but pedagogy and assessment. The heart of E-Learning 2.0, therefore, is not just media-richness but the pattern of interaction and interpretation, whether through text, images, audio, video, or a combination of all four.

18.4.3 Student- and Teacher-Generated Content Will Become Significant Beyond the Classroom

Because of Web 2.0's multi-modal capacity, E-Learning 2.0 will capitalize on new possibilities for student- and teacher-generated content. Prior to the advent of the web, it was not economically practical to widely distribute teacher and student-generated content. However, the combination of inexpensive bandwidth, inexpensive server space, and an accessible user interface (i.e., the web) has meant that the cost of distribution has approached zero for many consumers (as sites such as Blogger and YouTube demonstrate). Much of this content involves social media, but numerous efforts to make academic content freely available on the web are emerging as well.

> The "raw materials" of decentralized, nonproprietary development of open educational resources are there, ready for use. Computers and network connections are ubiquitously distributed throughout the network and around the globe, at least in advanced economies. Teachers, learners, graduate students, and amateurs populate the network in their millions, with diverse abilities, availability, time, and attention to spend on developing bits and pieces of educational resources. (Benkler 2005, p. 26)

The MIT Open Courseware initiative is one of the better-known at the university level – providing syllabi and lecture notes from more than a thousand courses. The iTunes University provides a similar function for podcasts of university lectures. The University of California at Berkeley has joined Google to make digital video content available via YouTube. Much of this content is generated by college faculty, but some content is also being produced by K-12 teachers. One of the most popular educational podcasts, *Twelve Byzantine Rulers: The History of the Byzantine Empire*, was contributed by a high school teacher, Lars Brownworth.

Teachers who use online repositories frequently have difficulty in matching available content to their curriculum, and even greater difficulty in evaluating whether the content is accurate. The time required to locate appropriate materials is one of the most frequently cited reasons that K-12 teachers do not make greater use of the Internet (Hanson and Carlson 2005). The content in textbooks has been reviewed for appropriateness and accuracy prior to adoption. If a publisher does not perform this editorial function for digital open content, it must be addressed in another manner.

One of the most crucial questions for K-12 schools is whether appropriate mechanisms can be developed to match teachers with appropriate content for the curriculum they are teaching. Filters are needed that quickly link K-12 teachers (and their students) with relevant content. Some of these mechanisms have been implemented in social media systems such as Digg and Technorati. Social media and academic media have distinctly different characteristics (Table 18.2). In the case of Internet-based video, audiences can collectively discuss, rate, and even re-mix videos, combining them with other content to author new creations. Popularity within a given peer group moves content to the top of the rankings of social media sites.

Table 18.2. Characteristics of several social media systems

	Matches needs & resources	Virtuous cycle	User ratings	Incentive for review	Non-hierarchical control	Shared organization strategies	Open content license
eBay	✓	✓		✓			
Amazon	✓	✓	✓			✓	
Netflix	✓		✓	✓		✓	
Wikipedia/ Wikimedia			✓				✓
Digg			✓		✓		
Flickr			✓			✓	✓

(Bull et al. 2006)

Academic media, however, cannot be evaluated strictly by popularity; relevance and quality are the critical factors that must be considered. Academic media must be identified as relevant to a particular level of education (e.g., K-12 vs. higher education), curricular topic (e.g., European history or world history), and even a specific learning objective or standard. The materials need to be consistent with the school infrastructure. Finally, the media's quality for this purpose must be judged (Bull et al. 2006).

The History Engine initiative at the University of Virginia illustrates one way in which user-generated content can be integrated into an academic setting with quality controls. Ed Ayers, a professor of history, has modified his course requirements to incorporate user-contributed content that continues to be useful after the end of the course. In the first half of the semester, each student catalogs events for the region and era under study. The 200 students in each class each catalog 20 events, generating a total of 4,000 entries in a database. These, in turn, are used as the basis for a term paper that each student writes in the second half of the class. Once the entries are entered into the catalog and checked for accuracy by teaching assistants, they become a resource available to anyone who might like to use them, multiplying the resources available to future students.

Applying similar methods in K-12 schools requires additional insight and ingenuity. Elementary and secondary schools are often subject to constraints that do not affect higher education. These may include centrally planned instructional objectives and high-stakes tests, as well as limited access to computers by individual students during school hours.

Properly designed databases of events such as those cataloged in the History Engine can serve as the foundation of research for history documentaries created by K-12 history students. When these types of collaborative resources and activities are disseminated through K-12 consortia such as Primary Source Learning (www.PrimarySourceLearning.org), they can readily be shared worldwide, making these teacher- and student-generated products accessible and meaningful beyond the classroom walls.

18.4.4 Teachers Will Have the Tools to Exercise Greater Control Over Their Instructional Design

For previous generations of teachers, photocopiers (or before that, ditto machines) allowed ambitious teachers to create classroom sets of their own personalized instructional materials and tests. A biology teacher covering photosynthesis, for example, no longer had to rely upon the presentation of the topic in the textbook and in other published materials but could create her own set of materials, drawing from different texts, mixing diagrams and instruction, and worksheets and lab materials as she saw fit. Today, productivity tools such as PowerPoint extend this capability. Teachers can create customized slideshows for every class session if they wish. The development of Web 2.0 will provide even more tools for these same ambitious teachers to access and modify learning materials for their students.

- *Modifying existing instructional materials*: A history teacher might use an online video streaming service such as UnitedStreaming to show selected video clips. Teachers can shuffle the order of the clips to suit the learning activities they have prepared.
- *Creating new instructional materials*: Another teacher might go a step further and custom-create a documentary, drawing together images and audio from online archives.
- *Creating new curricula*: Given the opportunity to design new materials, ambitious teachers can design entirely new curricula. The most salient example of teachers having control over the instructional design process is WikiPress, which allows teachers to design and print their own textbooks.

Teachers' design of their instructional activities is negotiated within the context of their local school administration. Ambitious teachers will, as they do now, seek to construct tailor-made learning experiences that reach their particular group of students at that specific moment in time. Web 2.0 tools expand the possibilities for these teachers, making it easier to create a variety of instructional media.

18.4.5 Teachers Will Be Able to Engage in an Accelerated Level of Peer-to-Peer Collaboration

Traditional face-to-face courses are designed for a limited audience taught for a constrained period of time, typically a semester or an academic year. Software developed to preserve this model, transferring it to an alternative delivery channel, often embodies similar constraints. This type of course brought into an E-Learning 1.0 environment becomes an electronic silo, intended for a constrained audience and a specific period of time.

This type of software fills a real need and is likely to be hugely successful for the foreseeable future. Software designed for E-Learning 1.0 environments has been successful because it leaves the framework of pedagogy and content largely intact, and simply transfers it to an alternative transmission channel. This model can incorporate limitations and constraints as well. Two adjacent school systems recently attempted to collaborate using traditional LMS software employed by both school systems. Licensing and administrative constraints made it necessary to purchase a third, jointly owned license and install it on a separate server. Usage by teachers was low, because they preferred to log into the LMS for their homeschool system. In contrast, teachers engaged in E-Learning 2.0 may be able to share their creations with one another more freely. At least three patterns exist for the development and distribution of teacher-created materials.

- *Proprietary networks* (also known as walled gardens): A walled garden is a system with restricted access. Only approved users can access the materials and services inside the system. The Blackboard LMS allows clients to create individual walled gardens. United-Streaming's Discovery Educator Network (DEN) is a walled garden that spans the entire client base. UnitedStreaming customers are invited to join the DEN and submit their teaching activities for use by others. These activities are evaluated by users, who provide ratings and comments on how the activity worked in their classroom.
- *Peer-to-peer commercial networks*: eBay provides an online marketplace that allows individual buyers and sellers to find each other quickly. The same process can be applied to instructional materials. For example, TeachersPayTeachers allows teachers to post self-created materials that others can download for a fee. As in DEN, users can rate and comment upon the materials.
- *Open educational content networks*: Finally, non-commercial systems exist to provide the same functionality. TeachersLounge, for example, is a wiki of lesson plans. Teachers can post their plans or

access others' plans. The project is open to the public and does not require payment. Most significantly, since the wiki is dedicated to open educational content, the material is freely adaptable, and adapted materials can be shared back to the group.

Teachers will continue to share content with one another through Web 1.0 activities such as posting to listservs or writing content to personal websites. Teacher-to-teacher collaboration using Web 2.0 tools will build upon these existing practices to create more powerful distributed communities of practice.

18.5 Conclusion

Historically, pedagogy lags behind technology; technological capacity evolves more rapidly than pedagogical practice. As a result of technological advances, interactive web-based applications can be developed more rapidly and inexpensively than at any other time. Countless new applications are emerging every week in an era of experimentation and creativity. This results in transitions in society in what has been termed the "age of participation".

The question is whether schools will also become communities of participation. Seymour Papert, professor emeritus at M.I.T., considered the implications of computers on schools in a seminal work, *Teaching Children Thinking*, written in 1968 at the dawn of the age of microcomputing. He correctly predicted that computers would become ubiquitous, but overestimated the influence of the technology on schools:

> We were sure that when computers became as common as pencils (which we knew would happen) education would change as fast and as deeply as the transformations through which we were living in civil rights and social and sexual relations. I still think this will happen even though the time needed is turning out to be a little longer than we imagined and the process more complex (Papert 2005, p. 366).

Schools are complex enterprises, perhaps less susceptible to change than society at large. Rogers (1995) suggests that successful innovations must be compatible with the existing system while simultaneously presenting a clear advantage that is observed to be successful. An analysis of technological innovations in schools found that the factors identified by Rogers can predict the adoption of these innovations in schools (Ferster 2006).

Technological innovations offer new affordances and capabilities, but must be integrated into existing school practice to be effective. To be successful, technological innovations in schools must address the existing curricular goals (i.e., maintaining compatibility) while adapting pedagogical practice to take advantage of new capabilities to affect learning outcomes.

References

Allen, I., Seaman, J. (2005). *Growing by degrees: Online education in the United States*. Wellesley: Sloane Consortium.

Altman, L. (2006). Socratic dialogue gives way to PowerPoint. New York Times. http//wwwnytimescom/2006/12/12/health/12docshtml?ref=health. Accessed 12 December 2006.

Benkler, Y. (2005). Common wisdom: Peer production of educational materials. COSL Press, Logan. http//wwwbenklerorg/Common_Wisdom.pdf. Accessed 18 December 2006.

Berners-Lee, T. (1999). *Weaving the Web*. San Francisco: Harper.

Bork, A. (2003). Interactive learning twenty years later. *Contemporary Issues in Technology and Teacher Education*, 2(4), 608–614.

Bull, G., Garofalo, J., Hammond, T. (2006). Connecting to open educational content. *Learning and Leading with Technology*, 34(1), 12–13.

Chapman, O. (2001). Calibrated Peer Review: A writing and critical thinking instructional tool (The white paper: A description of CPR). http://cpr.molsci.ucla.edu/cpr/resources/documents/misc/CPR_White_Paper.pdf. Accessed 19 December 2006.

Ferster, B. (2006). *Towards a predictive model of the diffusion of technology into the K-12 classroom*. Ph.D. thesis, University of Virginia

Ferster, B., Hammond, T., Bull, G. (2006). PrimaryAccess: Creating digital documentaries in the social studies classroom. *Social Education*, 70(3), 147–150.

Hanson, K., Carlson, B. (2005), Effective access: Teachers' use of digital resources in STEM teaching. http//www2edcorg/GDI/publications_SR/EffectiveAccessReportpdf. Accessed 15 June 2005.

Lebow, D. G., Lick, D. W., Hartman, H. J. (2003). HyLighter and interactive annotation: New technology to develop higher-order thinking skills. *Inquiry: Critical Thinking Across the Disciplines*, 23(1–2), 69–79.

Lenhart, A., Madden, M. (2005). Teen content creators and consumers. http://www.pewinternet.org/pdfs/PIP_Teens_Content_Creation.pdf. Accessed 7 November 2005.

Lenhart, A., Fox, S. (2006). Bloggers. http://www.pewinternet.org/pdfs/PIP%20Bloggers%20Report%20July%2019%202006.pdf. Accessed 20 December 2006.

Lenhart, A., Madden, M., Hitlin, P. (2005). Teens and technology. http://www.pewinternet.org/pdfs/PIP_Teens_Tech_July2005web.pdf. Accessed 5 December 2006.

Levin, D., Arafeh, S. (2002). The digital disconnect: The widening gap between Internet-savvy students and their schools. http://www.pewinternet.org/pdfs/PIP_Schools_Internet_Report.pdf. Accessed 21 June 2006.

Mishra, P., Koehler, M. (2006). Technological pedagogical content knowledge: A new framework for teacher knowledge. *Teachers College Record*, 108(6), 1017–1054.

Papert, S. (2005). You can't think about thinking without thinking about thinking about something. *Contemporary Issues in Technology and Teacher Education*, 5(3/4), 366–367.

Rogers, E. (1995). *Diffusion of innovations* (4th edn). New York: Free.

Saettler, P. (1990). *The evolution of American educational technology*. Greenwich: Information Age.

Shulman, L. (1987). Knowledge and teaching: Foundations of the new reform. *Harvard Educational Review*, 57(1), 1–22.

Taylor, R. (Ed.) (1980). The Computer in school: Tutor, tool, tutee. Teachers College Press, New York. In R. P. Taylor (2003), Reflections on "The Computer in the School". *Contemporary Issues in Technology and Teacher Education*, 3(2), 253–274.

Waits, T., Lewis, L. (2003). Distance education at degree-granting postsecondary institutions, 2000–2001 (NCES 2003-017). http//ncesedgov/pubsearch/pubsinfoasp?pubid=2003017. Accessed 4 December 2006.

19 An Executable Model for Virtual Campus Environments

G. Paquette and F. Magnan

In this chapter, we revisit an innovative model of a virtual campus developed and implemented in the second half of the 1990s and we compare it with the main evolution in the field of E-Learning that has occurred in the last decade. We present the vision and the orientation principles for a new virtual campus model and a conceptual framework for a virtual campus support system called TELOS. This TELelearning Operation System is service-oriented and ontology-driven and aims to support a larger set of actors than before, while generating a cascade of portals based on aggregation scenarios. We summarize the technical architecture of that system, which provides an implementation of the new virtual campus model, present some use cases and discuss its intended benefits for E-Learning systems.

19.1 Introduction

Distance education, or distributed learning, has finally acquired general support in most circles. More than a hundred countries have built distance universities. Most campus universities are developing distance education units or courses. All major companies are building training Intranets for their personnel. An E-Learning industry has developed to provide E-Learning tools and services.

At the turn of the century, distributed learning appeared to be an indispensable solution to the exponential growth of information in the knowledge society and for the support of new cognitive and learning activities it demands from individual and organizations. The extremely rapid spread of the Internet has accelerated this movement. The concept of a virtual campus, resting on the networking of actors and resources much more diversified than in the past, has become prevalent. These resources or learning objects include not only multimedia or web-based documents, but also learning scenarios and persons to interact with: instructors and tutors, subject-matter experts, training managers, and professors acting as designers.

LICEF, founded in 1992 as Télé-université's research center adopted right from the start, the many dimensions of a virtual campus model as its unifying research orientation (Paquette 1995). The first research efforts provided insights into specific applications of multimedia telecommunications in distance learning. The virtual learning center (VLC) model and architecture has been identified as the central parts of the virtual campus. Within a VLC, five theoretical actors were then identified: learners, trainers, content experts, designers, and managers. Sixty-three roles have been defined for these actors, each one being a set of use cases. Then, for some of these roles, built object-oriented graphs to design or reuse tools to be integrated in a VLC.

In 1997, the virtual campus became a powerful integrative concept at Télé-université and elsewhere. The Ministry of Education supported an ambitious 5-year plan to transform the 23-year-old distance university into a virtual campus based on a merge of hypermedia and telecommunications technologies. At the same time, we decided to re-implement the VLC architecture on a web-based platform. In 1999, we achieved the Explor@ implementation (Paquette 2001) and we started using it to develop and deliver telelearning courses and environments at Télé-université and other institutions.

Since the turn of the century, a rapid evolution has occurred marked by the convergence of three main movements. First, we are in the midst of the evolution towards a new generation of the Internet based on a services-oriented system and the semantic web. Second, an international standardization movement in the field of E-Learning has gained momentum, particularly regarding the concept of learning object repositories. Third, a growing emphasis on the use of web portals as the main information and knowledge exchange media has provided more flexible learning environments than the first generation of Learning Content Management Systems (LCMS). Taking in account this evolution, we have conducted work in the last 3 years on two fronts: implementing a new VLC system at Télé-université called Concept@, based on web-based learning portals, and launching a new R&D program, within the LORNET[1] pan-Canadian research network, aiming to develop TELOS, a new generation for a virtual campus support system.

---

[1] LORNET is a pan-canadian research network, a 5-year project aiming to developed eLearning and knowledge-based technologies for the Semantic Web.

In this chapter, the first section will revisit our initial virtual learning center model, its actors, their activities, resources and delivery models to underline its strengths and identify its limits. The second section will focus on new vision and on orientation principles, taking in account recent evolutions in the field of web-based learning. The third section will present the conceptual framework of the TELOS system, its main services and its conceptual ontology. The fourth section will summarize the technical architecture of the system as it is actually being developed within the LORNET project. The fifth section will present some cases that can already be supported by the system, to show some of the system's possibilities. A concluding section will discuss our hopes and prospects for this new virtual-campus model.

19.2 Revisiting Virtual Campus Models

We will first summarize the virtual campus model that we developed at the LICEF research center in the mid-nineties. Then we will compare this achievement with the evolution that has occurred since then. Finally, we will identify why a new virtual campus model is needed.

19.2.1 A First Virtual Campus Model

At the end of the nineties, some mega trends became prevalent. The exponential growth of information and the management of knowledge, the ubiquity of the Internet for the delivery of multimedia material, the emphasis on the acquisition of higher-order skills and new collaborative learning paradigms, all led to the advent of various form of telelearning or distributed learning. Behind terms like "distance education", "online learning", "telelearning" and "multimedia training", is a multi-facetted reality from which we can identify the following delivery models.

"High-tech" Classrooms group students and trainers in a single location, together with sophisticated multimedia and network equipment. Networked computers can give access to websites and Internet multimedia presentation, as well as videoconferencing with the outside world. Many universities and organizations build electronic campuses on this model, to help manage the many possible transitions from a predominant classroom presentation model to more interactive and flexible ways to learn and teach.

Distributed Classrooms are similar to high-tech classrooms in that learners and trainers are in two or more distant locations. Learning events use generally specialized and sometimes costly, real-time videoconferencing systems. Alternatively, desktop multi-point videoconferencing software can be used. Both of these models are close to traditional classroom teaching, some would say with more hype but not much pedagogical gain.

Hypermedia self-training on the web or CD-ROM gives preference to an individualized learning approach to Education. In the "pure" model, there is neither a trainer nor collaboration among learners in the system. A training manager supplies learning resources: self-training modules, interactive or passive websites, multimedia material on CD-ROM or DVD. The main benefit of this model is to enable the learner to progress at her own pace, wherever she is and whenever she chooses.

Asynchronous "online" training departs from this individualistic view. It is organized and led by a trainer or a teacher, priming interaction with the learners or among learners for team work and discussion groups. Unlike the above classroom-like models, these interactions are asynchronous, retaining some of the flexibility of self-training, with the exception that the pace between modules is decided upon by the teacher. The main tools and activities are forums, email, FTP transfer, together with less frequent audio or videoconferencing, online presentations, and real-time collaborative activities.

Communities of Practice focus on a professional task. The learners are basically content experts trying to extend their knowledge through the asynchronous exchange of information via forums, email, or document transfer. They progress through team problem solving and know-how sharing around projects. Unlike the previous model, there is no trainer acting as a content expert or pedagogical coach, but there is a group animator who possesses less knowledge in the subject matter than the learners, but more knowledge of methods to support group interaction.

Performance Support Systems integrate training even more closely to the actual work process and tasks in an organization. Extensive use of the organization's data banks and support software are made both ways: to use training material to help job performance and also to use real problems and tools to support training at and away from the job. Online help, adviser systems, and human supervisors are supporting these training/working activities. This model promotes just-in-time information to help the user focus, alone or in teams, on real-life problems.

We decided to design a virtual campus model that could encompass any mix of these E-Learning delivery methods, in particular to integrate the best features of the last four models.

Actors in a Virtual Campus

In this virtual campus model, we have identified five categories of actors. Each actor is personified by different persons or digitized agents playing a variety of roles and relying on a variety of resources, documents, communication, and production tools.

Figure 19.1 presents the main interactions between these actors.[2] There is a basic cycle in which an informer, responsible for the information process, investigates the structured body of knowledge in a domain to make new information available to the learner. The learner, ruling the learning process, transforms this information into personal knowledge. The other three actors, acting as facilitators, support this basic process in different ways. The designer constructs the learning environment, in particular the learning scenarios. The trainer is the pedagogical adviser, mainly coaching the learner according to the learning scenarios. The manager organizes groups and events with respect to the learning scenarios and is also an adviser on any organizational issues.

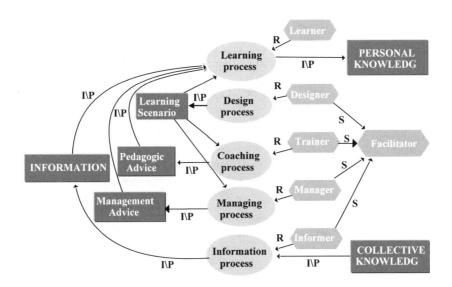

Fig. 19.1. Actors and main telelearning process

---

[2] The letters on the links have the following meanings: an R link between an actor, represented as an hexagon, and a process represented as an oval, means that the actor is responsible for the process; an I/P link between a resource represented as a rectangle, and a process either means that the resource is produced by the process or is an input to the process; an S link means that a class of actors is a sub-class of a larger class. These conventions follow those of the MOT knowledge modeling technique (Paquette 1996) we have developed during the nineties.

Interaction Spaces and Resources

Each actor, depending on the delivery model and other factors, needs resources that are distributed in interaction spaces. Table 19.1 presents a five-category distribution of resources in a learner's environment. A similar distribution would be made for a trainer's or a designer's environment.

Table 19.1. Example of resources distribution in a learner's environment

INTERACTION SPACE	RESOURCE	TYPE	DESCRIPTION
Self-management resources	Personal Profile	Java	Personal information accessible to all
	Progress status	Java	Bar graph displaying progress levels
	Calendar of events	Java	Dates where activities were looked upon
	Course schedule	HTML	Gantt distribution of activities
	Evaluation	HTML	Suggestions and course evaluation by learners
Information resources	Texts	HTML	Access to texts to be consulted or produced
	Videos	HTML	Access to video streaming
	Webography	HTML	Access to interesting web sites
	Search	HTML	To search for other web sites engines
Production resources	CBTs	EXE	Triggers seven CBTs illustrating AI concepts
	Text editor	EXE	Link to a recommended text editor
	Knowledge editor	EXE	Link to LICEF'S MOT knowledge editor
	Productions made	HTML	Simple file transfer to trainer for production evaluation
Collaboration resources	Group profile	Java	Display of other learner's progress and chat
	Email	EXE	Link to recommended email software
	Forums	HTML	Asynchronous teleconferencing system
	Showcase	HTML	Simple upload/download to a server to facilitate the exchange of productions
Assistance resources	Explora guide	HTML	Information on use of the environment
	Study guide	PDF	Access to a PDF description of the course
	Technical help	HTML	A frequently asked questions (FAQ) facility
	Resource persons	HTML	An Email list of persons: professor, tutor, manager, technician, etc.

Each interaction space offers resources grouped according to a major function in the environment: self-management of the tele-learning system, information access, production of new information, collaboration and communication with other learners (or similar actors), and assistance from other facilitators such as trainers, informers, managers, or designers or from computer agents or help files.

Figure 19.2 presents the user interface for a learner environment in the Explor@ implementation. Environments for other actors would be similar.

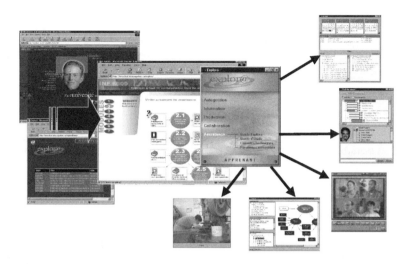

Fig. 19.2. A course website and the resources in an actor's environment

The first two windows enable a user to enter an organization's web site and choose a course and a role. The next two windows are the course entry page and the environment window. The last window provides a set of menus giving access to interaction spaces into which the resources are available, whether they are multimedia document, communication or self-management tools or access to persons to interact with. These resources are classified in a number of interaction spaces, such as the ones in Table 19.1.

19.2.2 The Explor@ Implementation of the Virtual Campus Model

Figure 19.3 presents a conceptual view of the architecture of the Explor@ system. The system deals with four types of objects: actors (roles), learning objects (resources), knowledge and competency, and operations/activity structures (functions). Actors operate functions composed of operations (activities) in which learning objects are used or produced. Knowledge and competencies describe the information owned, produced or processed by actors, which are processed in operations or contained in resources. Four corresponding managers store and retrieve information in a database, construct information structures and display information to users.

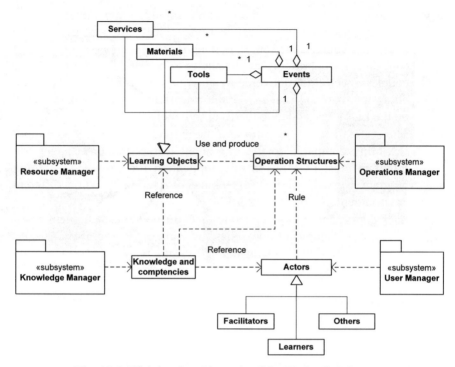

Fig. 19.3. High level architecture of the Explor@-2 System

19.2.3 Values and Limits of the Explor@ Implementation of the Virtual Campus Model

The Explor@ system, based on this virtual campus model was put into operation in 1999. Compared to distance learning platforms or the learning content management system (LCMS) as they were beginning to emerge, Explor@ had a number of innovative features:

- Explor@ operated on basic main data structures, an activity or operation structure and a knowledge and competency structure, unlike most LCMSs that provide only an activity structure. The activity structure breaks a course or a learning program into modules and units of learning, down to terminal activities. The knowledge and competency structure describes the structure of subject matter to be learnt. The association between the two structures helps learners and facilitators to target learning objectives, to obtain or provide assistance, and to evaluate the learners' progress towards these objectives.

- Explor@ was build around a resource aggregation paradigm and re-usability principle (the term "learning object" was not used at the time but the idea is the same), making it possible to assemble a set of educational support tools and resources to be reused across programs, courses or activities delivered by an organization and more generally on an international scale. In 2002, a learning object manager based on the LOM was added to the Explor@ tool set.

- The system had no limitation on the number of actors, adding more flexibility compared to the traditional learner-trainer-manager trio found in most LCMSs. In one application for a lawyers' training program, we had to design seven kinds of actors, each with a different environment.

- Each course could be designed to meet different needs implementing different pedagogical approaches, by using a variety of proprietary or third-party tools, made available to learners, course designers and other facilitators, such as instructors, content experts (informers), training program administrators, etc.

- An advisor/editor enabled the designers to build a set of rules that would trigger assistance in various forms (questions, messages, visual cues) on user demand or when certain conditions were met by values in the user properties tracked by the system.

- Explor@ was designed to support the integration of existing web-sites without changing their format, thus allowing an organization to transform its training/learning methods progressively. For example, one could take a museum website and use Explor@ to add learning scenarios, documents, communication tools and other resources very easily, without changing the website.

- Finally, the open modular structure of the system made it possible to significantly reduce design time, speeding up the implementation and allowing periodic updates by the design team or the online tutor. Environment maintenance also became much easier. Once the first course was implemented, each additional course integrated into Explor@ could be limited to a few web pages and hyperlinks to existing documents.

Despite these interesting features, Explor@ has some important limitations that explain why its use was, in the end, more limited than we had expected. First, it is not totally web-based, requiring the installation of the Java virtual machine on the client side, which created some deployment difficulties for novice users. Furthermore, the system is not multiplatform. It works well only on the Windows operating system and many times, adaptation had to be made when a new version of the operating system or a new web browser became available. On another dimension, the multi-actor capability is incomplete: each actor has his own environment but joint interfaces are not available, which makes it difficult to play some multi-actor scenarios built with the IMS-LD specification, for example. Also the transfer from the design environment to the delivery actors' environments has to be made manually. Finally, there is limited interoperability with other systems even though some SCORM export and import functionalities have been introduced.

These technical limitations to Explor@ could be mostly removed using recent advances in software engineering and E-Learning standards, while keeping most of its conceptual virtual campus model. At Télé-université, we have used DotNetNuke as a portal-generation kernel and we have integrated to it the main modules of the Explor@ system through the use of web services. This has led to CONCEPT@, the new platform that is actually replacing Explor@ and other home-made E-Learning systems as the institutional tool to generate portals for designers, for learners and for tutors at Télé-université. An interesting feature of the new architecture is that it is layered, that is, a design portal is assembled and used to generate specific portals for a program or for a course.

19.3 Vision and Orientation for a New Virtual Campus Model

At the turn of the century, a new set of concepts began to emerge from different fields, such as web-based layered learning portals, service-oriented frameworks, model-driven or ontology-driven architectures and multi-actor scenarios and workflows on which we have based a new virtual campus model, despite the technical improvements from Explor@ to Concept@. We will discuss briefly each of these developments and then present the vision and orientations of a new virtual campus model.

19.3.1 Major Innovations and Trends

From LCMSs to Web-based learning portals. In the last 10 years, hundreds of distance or e-learning platforms (or LCMSs) such as WebCT, Black-Board, LearningSpace, Docent, and Moodle have been used to deliver learning online. Recent reviews of E-Learning platforms show that there are not great differences between them. Most platforms are mainly designed for a limited set of predefined actors (author, trainer, and learner).

They are focused on a limited array of pedagogical and delivery models for self-training and online, asynchronous conferencing. Their efficiency as quick authoring tools for the web is often achieved by reducing drastically the variety of instructional strategies, each course having similar structures and components. The advent of learning portals and web services presents an interesting evolution towards more flexibility and another vision of learning, rather than just giving access to predefined, preformatted and pre-digested content. Learning portals promote learning models in which activities emerge, such as in project-based learning. New open-source tools such as DotNetNuke or Uportal have been made available to help construct courses, programs or even institutional portals more easily than before.

One level up: aggregating custom-made platforms. Compared to the evolution of generic software (text editors, spreadsheets, etc.), E-Learning systems are now in a position similar to that od the integrated software of the last decade, in which text, spreadsheets and database editors could transfer data only within the integrated suite. Similarly, E-Learning platforms offer a set of wired-in tools that are difficult to interoperate with tools from other platforms. Just as integrated suites of generic software have been replaced by integration mechanisms at the operating system level, we aim to design TELOS on the same interoperability principles. The new virtual campus model for TELOS will extend the portal assembly mechanisms to enable technologists to build their own platforms (or E-Learning desktops) in a variety of distributed learning environments or models such as electronic performance support systems (EPSS) integrated in a workplace activity, communities of practice, formal online training and technology-based classroom, and different forms of blended learning or knowledge management platforms.

Service-oriented frameworks (Wilson et al. 2004) are rapidly gaining popularity with the wide adoption of web services, and because of the lower costs of integration coupled with flexibility and simplification of software configurations. For example, a student record system may expose services defining student enrolment and registration processes and related information, which can then be used by a learning management or library system. A framework creates a broad vocabulary (an ontology) that is used to model recurring concepts and integration environments and is equivalent to the concept of a pattern in the software development community. One of the primary goals of a service-oriented framework is to encourage "coherent diversity", by providing alternate service definitions, which can then be used to meet the diverse goals of the organisation. An interesting aspect of a service-oriented framework is, for each identified service, to be able to reference one or more open specifications or standards that can be used in the implementation of the service, for example, the IEEE-LOM for resource referencing services or IMS-LD for multi-actor learning scenario composition services.

This is the case of ELF, the E-Learning Framework (ELF 2007), which is a service-oriented factoring of the core services required to support E-Learning applications, portals and other user agents. Each service defined by the framework is envisaged as being provided as a networked service within an organization, typically using either web services or a REST-style HTTP protocol. Another example is the Open Knowledge Initiative (OKI) (OKI 2007), which specifies a system architecture by identifying a set of services upon which learning tool developers can base their work. OKI takes a layered approach, defining clean boundaries between a layer of common services and an upper layer of educational service, each service made through an API to help integrate applications. The TELOS conceptual framework, which will be presented in Sect. 19.3, has also been designed as a service-oriented framework to facilitate the aggregation of services in order to create custom-made platforms and E-Learning and knowledge management applications.

Model-driven, ontology-driven architectures. Model-driven architectures involve three types of models: a platform-independent model (PIM), a platform-specific model (PSM), and a code model (Kleppe et al. 2003). The main gain is the generation of the code from the model in successive layers, the model being reusable in other context with few adaptations. Ontology-driven architectures (Tetlow et al. 2001; Davies et al. 2002) add to this paradigm an explicit ontology structuring of the objects processed by the system, acting as its executable blueprint. They therefore tend to maximize the PIM and minimize the PSM and code models. This programming style follows a pattern analogous to the Prolog programming language. Here the declarative part is encoded in the ontology, in our case through OWL-DL statements that are similar to Prolog statements. The execution part is encoded in parameterized queries prepared for an inference engine that will process the queries, the result of the query being events that trigger the execution of one of the services. In the TELOS software development process, this strategy is used to cover the most fundamental elements of the core.

Multi-actor learning designs and workflows. We pointed out earlier some weaknesses of our first virtual campus model. All kinds of actors can have their specific environment but these environments are each mono-actors. This question is now solved partly in workflow modelling languages such as BPMN, the Business Process Modeling Notation (Correal and Marino n.d.) and in a E-Learning design specifications such as IMS-LD

(IMS-LD 2003). Some instructional design graphic software, such as LAMS, and our own MISA scenarios using the MOT graphic editor, are able to represent multi-actor scenarios of workflows. Unfortunately, these representations are either informal like LAMS, semi-formal like MOT, or they are incomplete for learning design modeling, such as BPMM work-flow models. Multi-actor learning designs and workflow provide a central aggregation mechanism that groups actors, the operation they perform and the resources they use or produce from or for other actors. The notion of a multi-actor scenario is a central piece of the new virtual architecture model and its TELOS implementation (Paquette and Rosca 2003; Rosca 2005).

19.3.2 Orientation Principles

Here we present the main orientation principles (Paquette et al. 2007) that lead the development of the architecture of the TELOS system.

Solving Real Learning and Knowledge Management Problems. The TELOS system aims at facilitating learning and knowledge management activities. This entails the need to examine real educational and knowledge management problems, to analyze them thoroughly and to provide solutions to real user problems, not only in terms of system's tools, but also in terms of processes to use them effectively in real contexts. We must avoid being technologically driven instead of solution-driven, so the driving force is the careful definition of cases that guide the design of the architecture and the development of the system.

Reusing and Integrating Existing and New Tools. LORNET is a research project that aims to integrate technologies from different fields and develop new ones when they are educationally significant. We reuse, as much as we can, existing editors, communication tools, interoperability protocols and specifications from international standardisation bodies, guided by cases that underline the need for new tools or new ways to assemble or extend them. In these activities, we focus on specific TELOS core components that facilitate the reuse of existing tools by their users.

Concentrate on Essential Developments – Reduce risks. The goal of the architecture is to reduce risks by shifting the emphasis from tool development to careful analysis, evaluation and well-planned specification. This will enable the TELOS team to focus on essential developments, and leave more costly development or adaptation to industrial, university or public partners in the network.

Flexible and Pragmatic Aggregation. Pragmatic aggregation means a convergence of technological means and human intervention or interaction to achieve certain goals. Because of this, the system should have enough flexibility to be used in a variety of situations, from formal well-planned instruction, to more or less structured self-training, emerging communities of practice or performance support systems integrated with work environments. The success of TELOS will come from its demonstrated utility in a diversity of situations.

A Society of Human and Computer Agents. Software engineering sometimes sees the "system" to be solely composed of software components separated form their users. Contrary to that, we adopt a multi-agent view in which human and computer agents are interacting components of the system, providing services to each other. Extending the human-in-the-loop theory we recognize that sometimes, organizational adaptations, advising, documentation support or human communication activities can be more appropriate (and less costly) than building new tools. This approach also favors maximal results with realistic efforts.

Build Technology-Independent Models. The important work involved in the TELOS system should survive the rapid updating pace of technologies in general. At the start, it enables TELOS to operate on different network hardware and operating system configurations, and to integrate with other learning or knowledge management systems. The architecture is built to protect the conceptual models from technological instability. The conceptual specifications are kept separate from any implementation. The TELOS system should then be able to reuse such "conceptual programs" despite different previous technology environments, and adapt them to new technological implementations. So the conceptual models are not just prerequisite to building the TELOS system; they are part of the system, as one of its most fundamental layers.

Learning Ecosystem Models for Planning, Support and Evaluation. Most distributed learning systems today do not have a model of the processes, the users, the operations and the resources that they intend to support. Besides providing direct support for learning and knowledge management tasks, we aim to introduce tools to model the complex processes involved in a distributed learning system, before its use (to design it), during its use (to support users and observe their behavior) and after its use (to evaluate and maintain the system). These modeling components and tools are built-in features of the TELOS system. They aim to enable users to interact efficiently in pre-planned, as well as emerging and user-controlled events in which the initial environment is transformed, thus implementing a "learning ecosystem" approach.

Modularization and Layer Independence. The very flexible system envisioned will amount to a very small kernel, at a very high level of abstraction, capable of assembling services that generally form the core of a system, for example functions such as learning object aggregations, component coordination and control, ontology-based indexation and search, scenario modeling and so on. The architecture will promote horizontal modularity: horizontally between components, and vertical layer independence from an abstract representation, to a concrete implementation, to a run-time version of TELOS applications.

Construct Reusable and Interchangeable Models and Components. Because TELOS is model-oriented, it becomes possible to implement the model components in various forms and alternative tools, classified by their functionalities and grouped in interoperable classes. TELOS then appears as a flexible assembly system enabling the integration of tools, already existing or to be produced by various groups, to support a variety of learning and knowledge management models. Even at the kernel level, the general functions could be covered by one or more alternative kernel modules, accessible on a service bus for selection by system configurators and designers.

An Assembly and Coordination System. The TELOS kernel will then be mainly a set of computer agents capable of playing parts in "TELOS scripts", using alternative compilers or interpreters within different operating systems. TELOS will not be another huge distributed-learning platform or a system to generate rigid platforms, even though it can assemble components specific to some intended set of applications. The term TEleLearning Operating System should be seen as a metaphor. TELOS is planned essentially as a set of coordination and synchronization functionalities supporting the interactions of persons and computerized resources that compose a learning or knowledge management system.

19.3.3 System's Levels and Main Actors

Figure 19.4 shows a cascade of more and more specific system levels and their corresponding actors. The TELOS core is managed, adapted, extended by system engineers. With it, technologists in different organisations produce one or more TELOS learning and knowledge management systems (LKMS), each generalizing the idea of an online platform adapted to an organization's particular needs. Unlike in present situations, each platform is extensible, and its components are reusable in other platforms.

With a TELOS LKMS, designers can create, produce, deliver and maintain a number of learning and knowledge management applications (LKMAs), that is, courses, learning events, knowledge management portals, etc. The LKMS is a platform for the aggregation of resources, activities

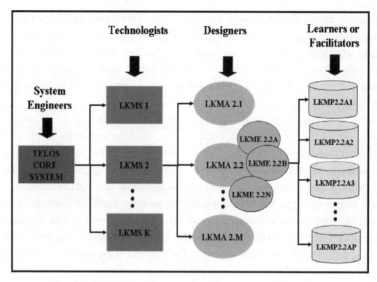

Fig. 19.4. Four-level cascade of systems and products

and actors. Each LKMA, composed using a LKMS, groups one or more actor-specific aggregates called learning and knowledge management environments (LKMEs) intended for certain types of learners and facilitators: content experts, coaches, tutors, evaluators, managers, etc. An LKME is an aggregate of documents, tools, services, operations (activities) and actor agents.

Before delivery, an LKMA and its different LKMEs are instantiated by an actor called an application administrator to start a new session involving a group of participants. Using these instances, the participants produce results that are resources and outcomes called learning and knowledge management products (LKMP), which are stored in a database for reuse or adaptive support.

The roles played by a person are interchangeable. Some persons acting as learners or facilitators can also be their own designers, and their own technologists or even engineers. Conversely, persons building environments can also be facilitators to designers. The interchange of roles can be provided by software role agents providing an interface between a human or system actor and the functionalities and data needed to achieve that role. Also some of the roles can be played by software agents, for example an intelligent advisor agent or a peer help or resource finder acting as a facilitator.

19.4 A Virtual Campus Framework and an Ontology for TELOS

In this section we present a conceptual framework (Paquette et al. 2005) for a new virtual campus model. We first present the main operations and actors in the model. Then, we identify a service-oriented framework to support these operations. Finally, the model takes the form of an ontology that will expand into the TELOS technical ontology, which is the main core element of the TELOS system.

19.4.1 Main Operations and Actors in the Virtual Campus Model

On Fig. 19.5, we present the more general use cases of the virutal campus model. A TELOS user (or a team of users), possibly helped by a facilitator providing assistance services, takes responsibility for performing a TELOS operation. In this operation, users and facilitators use or modify resources in the TELOS core and produce new resources that sometimes are embedded or referenced in the TELOS core.

Every time a user performs an operation, his/her previous knowledge and competencies are changed to new ones, which is the essence of learning by doing and doing by learning. In the TELOS system, it is possible to represent explicitly knowledge and evolving competencies related to the resources (persons, operations, documents and tools) using one or more semantic referentials. Semantic referentials can take the form of standard or specific metadata, classifications, taxonomies, thesauri or ontologies.

In TELOS, the operations are driven (or at least initiated) by human actors through user interfaces and mediated by computer programs and sometimes by software actors. There are three basic groups of operations depending on their level of granularity:

- *Basic operations on a resource* consist of asking or delivering a service using a resource either directly, or indirectly, mediated through a resource provided by the system.
- *Resource life cycle operations* consist of a series of four sub-operations (phases) in which a resource is composed, managed (prepared for use), used in some activity, and analyzed, providing feedback to start, if necessary, a new resource life cycle. These operations are generally performed in sequence by corresponding actors called, respectively, composers, administrators, explorers (resource users) and facilitators (acting as analysts to provide assistance and feedback).

- *System generation cascade operations* are even more global. They consist of using the TELOS core to produce a platform, technically called an LKMS (learning and knowledge management system), designing with it one or more LKMA (learning and knowledge management applications), such as courses, learning events and knowledge management environments, and finally, using these applications to learn and to produce results grouped in a portfolio or LKMP (learning and knowledge management products).

The combination of the resource life cycle and the system generation cascade operations are shown on Fig. 19.6.

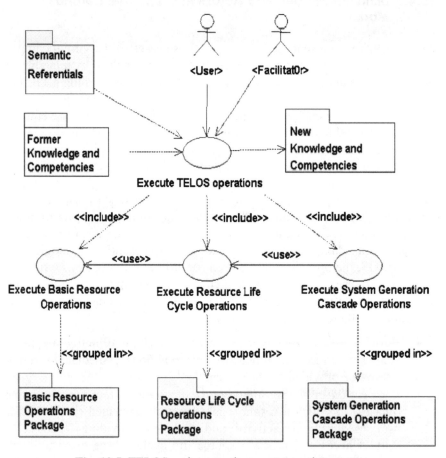

Fig. 19.5. TELOS main operations, actors and resources

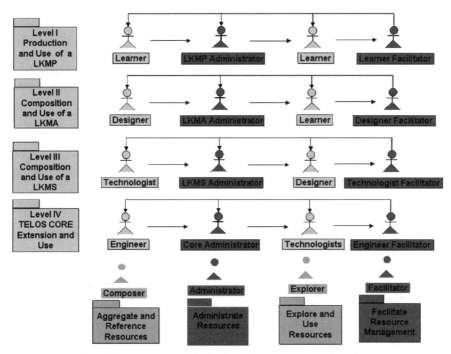

Fig. 19.6. Resource life cycle and system cascade actors

Figure 19.6 shows that the resource life cycles apply to each of the four levels of systems or products: core, LKMS, LKMA and LKMP. At level IV, the TELOS core is managed, adapted and extended by actors called engineers. It is instantiated and prepared for use by a core administrator, used by a technologist to build a LKMS, and analyzed by a core facilitator to provide assistance and feedback to the other three actors of the core life cycle. An analogous life cycle happens at level III where, this time, the technologist is the composer of the LKMS and the designer is the user, helped by a LKMS or platform administrator and a facilitator. At level II, the designer is the composer of a LKMA and the learner a user, again helped by a LKMA administrator and a facilitator. Finally, at level , within a LKMA, the composer and users are learners that produce and use resources and outcomes grouped in a LKMP.

We can use different metaphors to describe these general processes. With a manufacturing metaphor, the resource life cycle corresponds to a process in which a product passes through different production operations. For the system-generation cascade, the TELOS core is like a factory that produces machine components or complete machines. The products of this first factory are used to build machines that will be used in other factories (LKMSs) to build cars, aircrafts, and LKMAs which are used by end users to produce an outcome (e.g., to travel). Using a biological metaphor, a simple operation corresponds to a moment in the life of an organism: a resource life cycle is an ontogenesis, the process of an individual organism growing from a simple to a more complex level. Finally, a system-generation cascade is similar to the evolution of life, a process that generates new organisms from parents.

These images are important to understand the role of the TELOS core within an evolving TELOS system. As a manufacturer, the TELOS core itself starts with a complete set of components to produce LKMS factories, but it will also be open to improvement, adding new processes and operations to produce more versatile machines.

19.4.2 A Service-Oriented Framework for the Virtual Campus Model

From an elaborate set of cases, we were able to design a service-oriented framework for the new virtual campus model, bringing it closer to a possible implementation. Figure 19.7 presents the main classes of services, each being explained in (Paquette et al. 2005; Rosca 2005).

- *Kernel Communication services.* The virtual campus model is a distributed architecture on the Internet. To become a node in the virtual campus, each user installs a kernel on his machine that provides basic communication services with other nodes where resources are distributed. These services include, for example, a service registry, the location of resources on the nodes of the network, connectors to provide communication with resources built with different technologies, protocol translation and so on.
- *Resource interfacing services.* Basic resources are documents in a variety of media formats, tools to process documents, operations that can be applied to other resources and finally persons interacting on the network. All these resources usually will required to be interfaced in different ways (by a communication agent for format translation, through encapsulation for tracing, etc.) in order to be reached and to participate in the learning and/or knowledge management processes.
- *Resource life cycle services.* These services provide a number of editors for a composer to build, adapt and aggregate resources, thus producing a model of the resource. This model needs to be managed by an administrator before the instances can be explored by a user and later analyzed for assistance and feedback by a facilitator.

- *Aggregates management services.* These services provide management functionalities for the main aggregates (or web portals) used in the virtual campus: core, LKMS, LKMA and LKMP portals. For example, they will help in the storage, modification, display, evolution and maintenance of versions of core, the interoperability between platforms (LKMSs), the management of courses (LKMAs) and the LKMPs such as Portfolios.
- *Semantic services.* The services enable users to query or edit semantic resources, for example ontologies or metadata, and to create semantic referentials to be used to reference resources. Resource publication services enable users to package resources with their semantic references, enabling various kinds of resource search, retrieval and launching. With these services, a user can call upon federated or harvested search operations to jointly display documents, tools and operations (including activities and units of learning) related to some domain knowledge and competencies.
- *Common services.* We have grouped in this category all the lower level services mentioned in the preceding category. They correspond to operations that all the actors need to make or call upon while participating in the virtual campus.

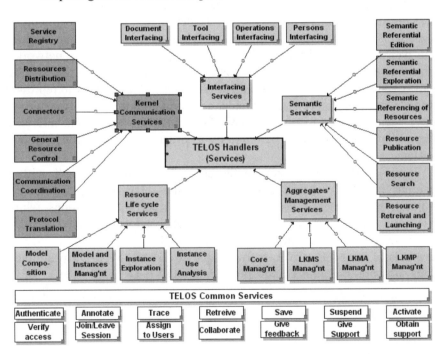

Fig. 19.7. The virtual campus service oriented framework

19.4.3 The Virtual Campus Model as an Ontology

To help the system survive the rapid pace of technology evolution, an important goal is to embed in the system technology-independent models. For that purpose, the conceptual specifications of TELOS, expressed as ontologies, should not be kept separate from their possible implementation. The TELOS system should be able to reuse ontologies as "conceptual programs". In this vision, the conceptual models are not just prerequisite to the construction of the TELOS system; they are part of the system, as one of its most fundamental layers. These considerations motivated the need for an ontology-driven architecture (ODA) combined with a service-oriented architecture (SOA), which also promotes the use of many international standards such as OWL, IMS-LD, XPDL, SOAP, LOM, SWRL and RuleML.

We have translated the use cases and the service-oriented framework of the virtual campus model into an OWL-DL ontology. We have chosen to use OWL-DL ontologies (W3C 2004) for TELOS applications for a number or reasons. OWL-DL is one of the three ontology web languages that are part of the growing set of World Wide Web consortium recommendations related to the semantic web. OWL-DL has a wide expressivity and its foundation in description logic guarantees its computational completeness and decidability. *Description Logic* (Baader et al. 2003) is an important knowledge representation formalism unifying and giving a logical basis to the well-known traditions of frame-based systems, semantic networks, object-oriented representations, semantic data models, and formal specification systems. It thus provides an interesting logical framework to represent knowledge. On a more practical side, a growing number of software tools have been designed to process OWL-DL XML files and to put inference engines at work to query the ontology in order to execute processes in a system.

Figure 19.8 presents a part of the conceptual ontology for the virtual campus model. The first graph presents the three main categories of objects, that is actors (users and handlers) that perform operations, which use and produce resources. Operations and actors are also TELOS resources (as shown by the S links). This graph is built using the graphic symbols of the MOT+OWL software that covers all OWL-DL primitives. This software translates graphs into standard OWL-DL XML files.

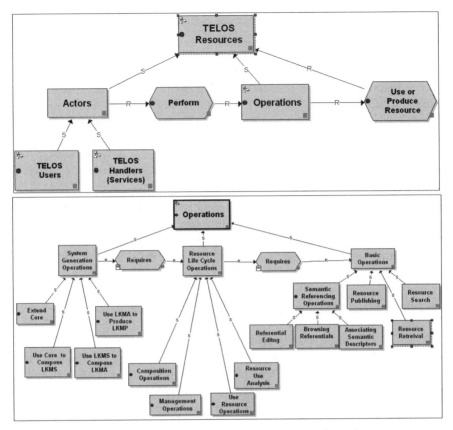

Fig. 19.8. Part of the virtual campus conceptual ontology

Each of these classes of objects is further defined in sub-models that present their classifications and properties. The second graph of Fig. 19.8 shows the taxonomy of operations that correspond to services in the service-oriented framework (Paquette and Rogozan 2006) shown on Fig. 19.7.

In the following section, we explain how this ontology was revised and expanded to build the TELOS technical ontology, a central part of the implementation of the new virtual campus model.

19.5 The TELOS Software Architecture

In the present section, we give a high-level overview of the software architecture. First, let's look at a simple picture showing the coordination of the basic concepts of the virtual campus model inside a given TELOS node.

We see in Fig. 19.9 the TELOS core, which is the central controller of a TELOS system. The core contains the TELOS Kernel basic communication services, the resources organized in libraries, the semantic layer, the local bus, the global bus and the runtime environment.

The resources are the persistent data of the TELOS node. They can be users, multimedia files, software components, learning objects or aggregations of other resources created by users. This last type of resources is of a very important nature. It enables users to create new E-Learning tools by gluing existing software components. It also enables users to model collaborative workflows describing knowledge, processes and practices in work processes or learning scenarios.

The semantic layer is where all TELOS concepts declared are related through logical constraints. The semantic layer defines the global behavior of TELOS. It also contains the domain ontologies created by users that later permit semantic classification of the resources involved in the resource libraries using semantic descriptors, that is, metadata records describing resources according to the domain ontologies of the system. The semantic layer is the foundational element of the ODA (ontology-driven architecture) behind TELOS.

The TELOS runtime contains the running instances of the resources that need some temporary data persistency such as software components and interactive learning objects. This runtime environment is connected to the core through the local bus. The local bus is the abstraction layer that lets the core speak to resources implemented in various standards and technologies

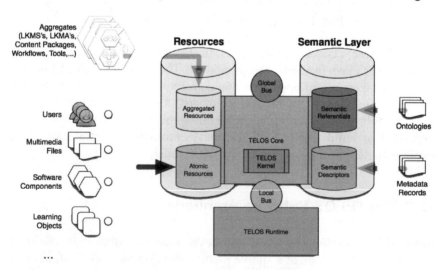

Fig. 19.9. The "Global Picture" of a TELOS node

using a uniform language: the local bus protocol. This is a key element of the SOA (service-oriented architecture) of TELOS. It enables loosely coupled integrations of rich external resources such as software components and web services.

Finally the TELOS Global bus enables the interoperability between different TELOS nodes abstracting their particular physical platform and their network configuration. By connecting the Global Bus of many TELOS nodes we form a dynamic peer-to-peer network. These networks may contain special nodes called community controllers, which are basically centralized repositories for resources.

19.5.1 TELOS Aggregates and Scenarios

We now explain one of the main principles behind TELOS: the aggregation of resources. Aggregation of resources is one of the most fundamental operations of TELOS. Roughly speaking, resource aggregation is about gluing some resources together to form resources of higher complexity. This can include, for example, building a content package from SCOs (shareable content objects, learning objects), building a specific tool from individual software components, building an LKMS from tools and interfaces, building an orchestration incorporating users and tasks, etc. The aggregates can be roughly classified into three categories: collections, integrations and orchestrations.

The software architecture has a unique formalism for describing all those types of aggregations. This is achieved with the specification of a unique XML format capable of representing all types of aggregates. This format is called XCAL.

The basic structure of the XCAL language is the structure of hierarchical directed graphs. This means that an XCAL file describes nested directed graphs (each node of a graph can contain a graph) with vertices possibly starting and ending at various graph levels. This mathematical structure has a very generic nature and can be used to model a wide variety of things: knowledge, processes, aggregates, etc. Using this generic structure as the basic aggregate format gives us a guarantee of the persistence of the format through its various usages.

Scenarios are the most common and general type of aggregate found in TELOS. The concept of scenario in TELOS is a formalism to represent multi-actor human/machine processes. Scenarios provide a high-level programming language for TELOS. This language is designed to be accessible to all TELOS actors, including students, workers, teachers, designers, technologists and programmers. This goal is achieved by materializing the language through an intuitive visual syntax. For that, we use the graphical formalism of hierarchical directed graphs. This enables both top-down and bottom-up approaches to scenario modeling.

We now look at the environment used to define and maintain scenarios: the scenario editor. To provide a basis to build a scenario editor for the TELOS system, conceptual work on function maps has been defined as a central piece of the TELOS architecture. We have developed a generic graph editor that can be used to define specific graph editors through a meta-model. These meta-models are materialized as ontologies in OWL-DL format. Then, a comparative analysis is made between business work-flows, IMS-LD learning designs and function maps, identifying the most frequent control situations for workflows encountered in software engineering literature. The MOT+LD editor, a graphic editor for IMS-LD, a specialization of the MOT graphic knowledge representation language that has been altered to suit our purpose.

The scenario editor aims to generalize both IMS-LD and business work-flow (Marino et al. 2007). The graphs produced by this editor are executable through a scenario execution engine called the scenario evaluator. The scenario evaluator will assure the coordination of actors in the enactment of the activities and the use/production of the aggregated resources at delivery time.

The scenario editor uses four kinds of MOT objects with subtypes taken from the TELOS technical ontology (Magnan and Paquette 2006). These are shown on Fig. 19.10. Concept symbols represent all kinds of resources: documents, tools, semantic resources, environments, actor resource, activity resources and datatypes. Procedure symbols represent scenario models (functions), human-based activities or software operations. Finally, principles are used both to represent different types of actors (as control human or software agents) and control conditions.

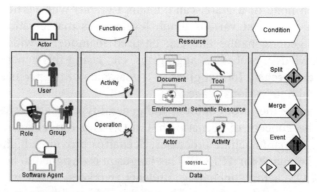

Fig. 19.10. Overview of scenario editor symbols

In Fig. 19.11, we can see an example of a simple scenario combining some of these visual symbols in which a coordinator writes the plan of a website. Then three writers write sections of the website. When the sections are complete, the flow of control is merged and a web editor builds a website by assembling the different parts. Finally, the group semantically annotates the site.

Unlike the actors, the control principles are embedded within the activity flow of the scenario model to decide upon the next activities. Figure 19.11 shows a general split condition after the first activity. After that, activities 1–3 are executed simultaneously, based on the properties of the split condition object. Later on, the flow of activities merges through the merge condition object before activity "assemble sections" takes control. This activity will wait for some or all the incoming flows to be activated before it is executed, again depending on the properties of the merge condition object.

Figure 19.12 shows another kind of condition that alters the flow of execution. In activity-2, if a time-event condition is met (the activity continues for 30 min), the flow of control will not move to activity 3 but to activity 4

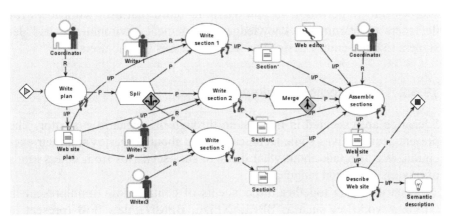

Fig. 19.11. A simple scenario model

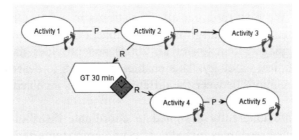

Fig. 19.12. Event-based control

and continue to activity 5. Properties of the event condition symbol provide details of the condition and action parts of the control principle. They provide the execution engine with a clear formal definition of the processing to take place.

In the scenario editor, we see a combination of a control flow and a data flow. The control flow is modeled using the MOT basic P and R links. P links are used for the basic line of execution. R links identify at which activities an event will trigger a condition to alter the basic flow of control or identify the activities controlled by an actor.

I/P links from MOT serve to model the data flow, either from resources to activities or operations where they are consulted, used or processed, or from activities or operations to product resources. This is why we need to distinguish between actors as active control entities and resource actors that will serve as data providers or be products of an activity (e.g., a new software agent added in a system). A similar distinction is made for resource activities that can be seen as resources to be transformed, for example, by other activities creating or modifying their description.

In TELOS, the scenario editor will enable engineers to combine resources into larger ones, technologists to build platform workflows for designers of learning or knowledge management environments, and designers to build course designs or work processes for end users.

19.5.2 Technological Backend

Scenarios are executed in the system through the scenario evaluator. The present section gives some technical details about scenarios and their execution. We also talk about what distinguishes scenarios from others kinds of process definition languages.

Scenarios bring together the concepts of control flow (omnipresent in business workflow such as BPEL, XPDL, BPMN), data flow (present in scientific workflow languages such as), learning design (IMS-LD type of languages) and ontologies (van der Aalst et al. 2000). In terms of control flow, scenarios actually support most of the classic patterns of control described in. We plan to cover all the patterns in a future release of the scenario evaluator. The data-flow part exhibits all the features of a classic data-flow language (Johnston et al. 2004) and provides data semantics through a technical ontology. This enables modellers to describe explicitly the data-flow relations between the different processes involved in a scenario execution.

Scenarios are inherently designed to coordinate distributed resources. These distributed resources include software components and web services each developed with possibly different technologies. The execution engine actually supports components written in C, C++, C#, Java, Scheme and all SOAP-based web services. Software component resources are connected through the TELOS local bus, which assures both connectivity and modularity between the kernel and the components. Scenarios are persistent, interruptible, resumable and traceable. Finally, scenarios have the characteristic of being mobile. This means that instances of scenarios can migrate from one TELOS node to another while they are in execution.

The key strategy is to translate XCAL aggregates generated by the scenario editor into networks of communicating processes (Magan 2005). This means that all the nodes in the scenario model will create a tiny process in the TELOS runtime when a scenario model gets instantiated. All those lightweight processes can communicate with each other by sending and receiving messages. This means that all the processes instantiating a scenario model have the ability to receive messages in a mailbox and propagate messages to other processes.

The basic building block used to implement those process networks is Termite (Germain et al. 2006), an open source implementation of communicating sequential processes (CSP) in the scheme language. Termite is itself inspired by Erlang (Armstrong et al. 1996). Using this as a basis, the implementation of the scenario evaluator is rather straight-forward and is therefore highly customizable without tremendous efforts.

19.5.3 Semantic Referential Services

The semantic layer is literally the backbone of the TELOS system. The central part of the semantic layer in TELOS is the TELOS core technical ontology presented above. All the pieces of TELOS must fit in this blueprint of the system. The TELOS ontology is not only an external representation of the architecture of TELOS with all its components and functionalities. It is an internal way to drive TELOS processes through a coherent path insured at each step by the constraints contained in this ontology. TELOS core technical ontology is the logical blueprint of TELOS. It is the TELOS "Program". Here we put forward a software development strategy in which core functionalities are programmed in ontologies and in the queries we send to inference engines working with this ontology. We therefore introduce a logic programming paradigm at the very core of TELOS. In the above sense, TELOS architecture is an ontology-driven architecture (ODA) (Tetlow et al. 2001). This approach combines very well with the SOA (service-oriented architecture) we announced above.

The TELOS semantic layer is the most fundamental module of the TELOS kernel. In fact, the very first steps of the TELOS boot process are directed towards setting up a fully operational semantic layer module so that other important modules of the system can rely on it. The main constituents of the TELOS semantic layer are displayed in Fig. 19.13.

In it, we see that the semantic layer is basically a wrapper over an OWL inference engine. It therefore provides an API to the other modules of the system that transform the API calls into queries to that inference engine. Due to the relative immaturity of OWL-DL inference engines, we decided to use the DIG protocol to communicate with the inference engine. This has the advantage of making us independent of any particular OWL inference engine.

To boot the semantic layer, we must feed the attached inference engine with all the knowledge contained in the local TELOS node. This knowledge is all contained in the TELOS core technical ontology.

Using an ontology to support the whole system provides a flexible, yet logically sound foundation for formally describing the concepts of the TELOS system. Using description logic, we can define all the various TELOS concepts. Here we must clearly outline the fact that the TELOS semantic layer makes TELOS a very innovative system in its category. The usual trend for recent E-Learning systems and information systems in general is to rely on relational databases (RDBMS) for the data persistency. The TELOS system takes a different path by proposing the formalism of description logic for data persistency. The reader will note that this doesn't exclude using RDBMS technologies underneath the semantic layer for optimization purposes. In fact, many existing RDF triples stores take this approach.

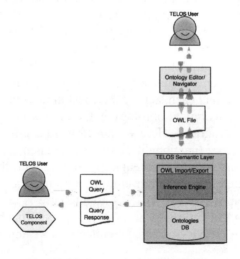

Fig. 19.13. Semantic layer overview

This innovation we propose for data persistency has many benefits. First, since we put it at the lowest level in the system architecture layers, it promotes all other system modules to rely on formal logic to implement their concepts. This has the consequence of providing a rich semantic integration of all the system concepts (users, operations, documents, processes, applications, workflow, etc.). The most interesting benefit may be the flexibility of the resulting backbone. Ontologies can change and evolve over time. When using appropriate tools, one can work on the system backbone and alter it during runtime by changing the concepts' definitions. Compared to the direct usage of RDBMS technologies, this is a very strong benefit. A relational database can be changed and restructured too, but generally at a high cost. The access to an inference engine that can prove or disprove any description logic proposition on the system is the next most obvious benefit. This conceptually outperforms the expressivity of any RDBMS query language.

19.6 Cases

To illustrate some of the possibilities of this virtual campus model and its TELOS implementation, we will now present three cases. These will take the form of three TELOS scenarios. These models can be termed "TELOS executable cases". The first one is built by an engineer to aggregate software components; the second one is built by a technologist to combine the design functionalities of more than one platform, and the third one is used by a designer to build a multi-actor E-Learning environment.

19.6.1 Aggregating Components Services

In this first use case, an engineer aggregates components to compose a new service embedded in an operation called the Batch LOM Extractor. This operation takes a set of keywords, a number of LOM to find and the name of a destination folder in a repository of learning objects managed by the PALOMA software. On the right of Fig. 19.14, these three inputs are shown as resources. The aim of this aggregated operation is to search Google with the given keywords, datamine the resulting websites to extract LOMs, insert those LOMs into the requested PALOMA folder and to open this folder into the PALOMA software interface to show the results to the user.

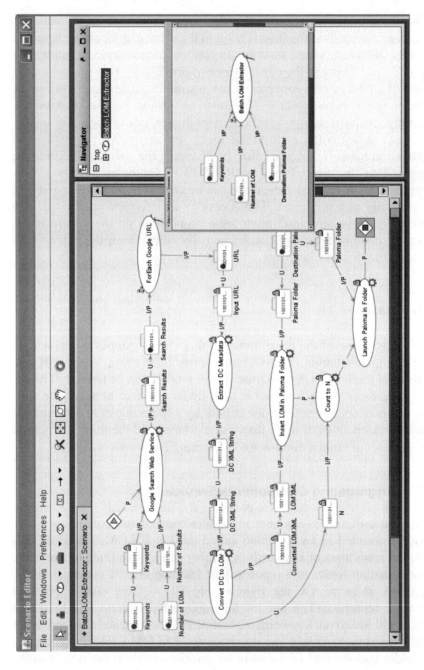

Fig. 19.14. Engineer constructing an operation aggregating services

This operation combines the services of four components embedded in corresponding operations, shown on Fig. 19.14. These operations are linked sequentially as follows:

1. The Google Search web services takes keywords and the number of results as inputs and produces a structure containing Google's search results.
2. For each URL that Google returns, extract DC metadata visits the URL and extracts Dublin Core metadata automatically through natural language processing of the web page.
3. Then this DC XML string is passed to a DC to LOM converter to produce a corresponding standard LOM XML, which is the format used by PALOMA.
4. Then, with this LOM XML and the name of a destination folder, the LOM is inserted into the PALOMA folder.
5. This cycle is repeated until all the LOMs are processed up to the number given initially; when this is finished, the PALOMA software is launched with the folder containing all the LOMs, enabling the display of LOM metadata and of the resource.

What we see here is the aggregation of components built by different groups using different technologies. The Google Search Service is launched using a SOAP web service connector provided by the TELOS kernel. The Metadata Extractor is a C# component linked to the TELOS kernel by a C# connector. The DC to LOM conversion is a scheme component linked through a scheme connector. PALOMA is a Java component linked through a Java connector.

All four components have been previously integrated into TELOS resource libraries with their semantic references to the technical ontology that are instances of some classes of resources. These semantic references describe in particular what kinds of inputs and outputs each service expects. Inputs and outputs are ports of the operation symbol. In the scenario graph, values are connected to these ports using U links. Also, the semantic references describe the technology used, so the proper connector is mobilized in the kernel to enable the execution of the component.

The result is a new aggregated operation, shown on the right of Fig. 19.14 with its three inputs. This new operation has been integrated in the TELOS library as a new digital resource. It has been referenced in the TELOS technical ontology, so it is now ready to be aggregated with other resources, for example, as a tool in an platform (LKMS) or an application (LKMA).

19.6.2 Building an E-Learning Platform

The next use case example will show how a technologist can combine functionalities from different platforms to compose a new LKMS with greater capabilities. The central component of the combined platform is a process graph for the designer used as a design scenario to produce courses. This design scenario corresponds to the central tasks of the MISA instructional engineering method (Paquette 2001; Paquette et al. 2006). Figure 19.15 shows part of this scenario that involves using Concept@, Télé-université's actual course design platform, augmented by the TELOS scenario editor and other components.

The design scenario shown in Fig. 19.15 in the TELOS scenario editor starts with two parallel functions performed by an LKMA designer: design of a course backbone using the Concept@ LCMS and development of a knowledge and competency model for the course using the TELOS ontology editor.

Let us note that Concept@ helps produce an activity tree representing the course plan with the subdivision of the course into modules and activities. This structure can be exported to a SCORM package. Many roles can be defined in Concept@ but this exceeds SCORM's mono-actor capabilities. Because of this, information on roles/actors is lost when we open the corresponding graph in the TELOS scenario editor, after the SCORM output of Concept@ is handed to the TELOS operation that translates the course structure. The next design phase proceeds graphically in the scenario editor, adding the actors designed in Concept@ manually, which is not a big task. In the scenario editor, a more advanced control flow can be added to better personalize learning.

Concept@ has no capabilities for knowledge and competency modeling. Because of this, an external editor, the TELOS ontology editor, has been integrated into the designer's environment. With it, the designer can build an ontology to represent the subject matter and add competency goals to the main concepts.

These two main design tasks proceed in parallel up to a point at which relative stability is achieved. Lists of actors, activities and resources are then made available from the scenario editor, and a list of competency is produced by the knowledge/competency modeling branch. The rest of the

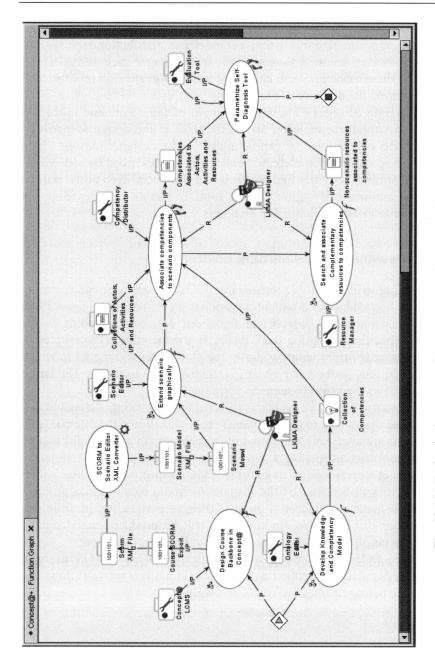

Fig. 19.15. Technologist constructing an augmented LKMS platform for designers

scenario consists of associating target competencies and knowledge to resources, actors and activities using a competency distribution tool, searching for additional resources using a resource manager such as PALOMA and using these associations to configure a learner-evaluation tool that will be used during the delivery of the course.

On the right of Fig. 19.15, we show a list of tools available in the designer's environment. Included are all the tools in the design scenario on the left, plus other tools that can be added by the designer himself. Once the design scenario is complete, with all functions described by sub-graphs down to terminal activities and operations, a designers' web portal will be produced automatically, grouping the tools in menus and providing the design scenario as a guideline for designers.

19.6.3 Designing an E-Learning Environment

Following up with a design scenario in a LKMS, a designer can construct course- or knowledge-management scenarios and environments. Figure 19.16 shows such a scenario, which had first been designed according to the IMS-LD specification, using our MOT+LD graphic editor (Paquette et al. 2006). The upper-right window shows the global scenario model in which the learning unit on the solar system is subdivided to four acts. The larger window shows the learning scenario for stage 2.

This scenario displays two teams of learners, each using a chat and different input documents to discuss planet properties. When the internal team discussions are over, both teams and the teacher join in a forum discussion. The teacher observes, manages and moderates the discussion. He stops the discussion at a certain point to start the stage 3 sub-process in which individual work will be done by the learners to find a solution to a problem that entails matching planets to some of their properties. Again, from this design, four different web environments will be produced automatically for the teacher, for each team of learners, and for the whole group.

This example shows the power and flexibility of TELOS designs. Similar designs can be applied as well to build multi-actor workflows for knowledge management activities in an organization.

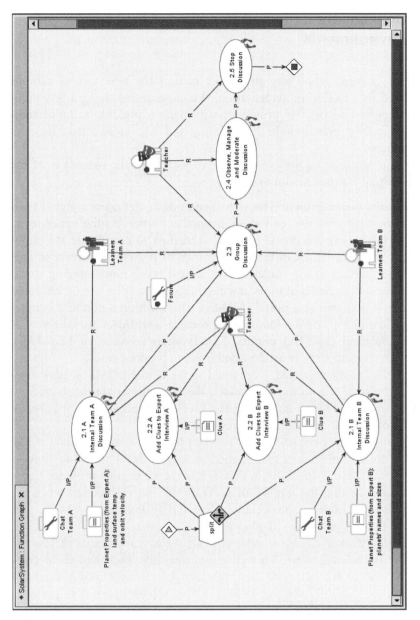

Fig. 19.16. Designer constructing a multi-actor scenario

19.7 Conclusion: Expected Benefits for E-Learning Environments

We have covered some key principles behind the new virtual campus model and its TELOS implementation. We suggest that using a low number of generic and flexible principles will make it possible to build complex yet easily manageable E-Learning and knowledge management environments.

We now summarize the benefits we expect from the extension of the former virtual campus model to the new one:

1. *Global systemic view.* The virtual campus model takes a global view to provide cohesion to virtual campus activities. At the upper level, an institution can create a global workflow to coordinate the major processes in which different categories of personnel interact to provide services to the students. At the next level, more specific workflow is designed and tools, documents and activities are orchestrated into a platform or a portal (LKMS). Then, within a portal, a number of learning scenarios (courses) or service workflows are designed as application (LKMA) portals. Finally each scenario or knowledge management flow is used by end users to produce results.

2. *Extended set of actors.* Compared to the actual LCMS in operation, and also to our initial VC model, the new global approach leads to an unlimited set of actors. At any level, in principle, any number of actors can be defined and supported.

3. *Better process coordination.* The fact that the system holds a model of the VC processes and support resources leads to better process coordination. Especially in distance universities, this provides better assurance that the quality of services will be maintained when the personnel changes, especially when the system must provide products of his activities to other actors.

4. *Visible scenarios and workflow.* Learning scenarios or workflow can always be consulted in a web portal interface, and changes to components or actors can be seen right away. Each user taking an actor's role can visually see the context of the activities he has to perform, what resources to use or produce and with whom he is to interact.

5. *Flexible and adaptable environments.* Each environment operates according to a technical ontology representing the virtual campus model, which is part of the system. This enables very flexible and adaptable environments. If a new kind of actor, activity or resource needs to be introduced, it is done simply by modifying the ontology, without changing the main operations of the system.

6. *Resource reusability* is a goal pursued by many advocates of learning object repositories, but it is not that easy to achieve. Using ontologies to model each resource within the same framework and adding connecting operations to take care of possible technology mismatches brings solutions to resource reusability problems.

7. *System interoperability.* With the new VC model, it is possible to bring different technologies and different platforms together. For example, a designer could build a course using a scenario editor in one platform and transfer it to another platform to add new functionalities, for example, personalized assistance. This process can be designed by defining the aggregation scenario between platforms and building ontology alignment operations.

8. *Modeling for all.* Modeling is not an easy task, but it is important enough to be made accessible not only to engineers and technologists, but also to instructional designers, learners and trainers. User-friendly visual modeling languages are made available at all levels of the system.

9. *Focus on learning and work designs.* Finally, we hope the proposed approach to virtual campus modeling and operation will reduce the technology noise that is often present in E-Learning applications when too much time is devoted to solving purely technological problems, instead of focusing on learning problems. We suggest that the activities be more focused on pedagogy and quality of educational services.

These approaches offer new possibilities but also pose additional challenges. The TELOS project, a 5-year research project, is now past mid-term. Some considerable refinements will occur, but our hope is that the results achieved in this project will lead the way to future developments.

References

Armstrong, J., Virding, R., Wikström, C., Williams, M. (1996). *Concurrent Programming in Erlang.* Second edition. Englewood Cliffs, NJ: Prentice-Hall.

Baader, F., Calvanese D., McGuinness D., Nardi D., Patel-Schneider, P. (Eds.) (2003). *The Description Logic Handbook.* Cambridge: Cambridge University Press.

Correal, D., Marino, O. (n.d.) *Software Requirements Specification Document for General Purpose Function's Editor* (V0.4), LORNET Technical Documents, LICEF research centrer, Télé-université, Montreal.

Davies, J., van Harmelen, F., Fensel, D. (Eds.) (2002). Towards the Semantic Web: Ontology-driven Knowledge Management. New York: John Wiley & Sons, Inc.

ELF – eLearning framework (2007). http://www.elframework.org/. Accessed 14 June 2007.

Germain, G., Feeley, M., & Monnier, S. (2006). Concurrency oriented programming in termite scheme. In *Proceeding of Scheme and Functional Programming 2006*, Portland.

IMS-LD (2003). IMS Learning Design. Information Model, Best Practice and Implementation Guide, Binding document, Schemas. http://www.imsglobal.org/learningdesign/index.cfm. Accessed 3 October 2003.

Johnston, W. M., Hanna, J. R. P., Millar, R. J. (2004). Advances in dataflow programming languages. *ACM Computer Surveys*, 36(1), 1–34.

Kleppe, A. G., Warmer, J. B., Bast, W. (2003). *MDA Explained: The Model Driven Architecture: Practice and Promise*. Boston: Addison-Wesley.

Magnan, F. (2005). Distributed components aggregation for elearning: Conducting theory and practice. ILOR2005 Conference, http://www.lornet.org/presentation i2lor 05/papers/i2lor05-03.pdf.

Magnan, F., Paquette, G. (2006). TELOS: An ontology driven elearning OS. In *SOA/AIS-06 Workshop*, Dublin, Ireland.

Marino, O. et al. (2007). Bridging the gap between e-learning modeling and delivery through the transformation of learnflows into workflows. In S. Pierre (Ed.), *E-Learning Networked Environments and Architectures: A Knowledge Processing Perspective*, Berlin Heidelberg New York: Springer.

OKI – Open Knowledge Initiative (2007). http://www.okiproject.org/. Accessed 14 June 2007.

Paquette, G. (1995). Modeling the virtual campus. In B. Collis, G. Davies (Eds.), *Innovating Adult Learning with Innovative Technologies*. Amsterdam: Elsevier.

Paquette G. (1996). La modélisation par objets typés: une méthode de représentation pour les systèmes d'apprentissage et d'aide à la tâche. *Sciences et techniques éducatives*, April 1996, 9–42.

Paquette, G. (2001). Designing virtual learning centers. In H. Adelsberger, B. Collis, J. P. E. (Ed.), *Handbook on Information Technologies for Education and Training. International Handbook on Information Systems* (pp. 249–272). Berlin Heidelberg New York: Springer.

Paquette, G., Rogozan, D. (2006). *Primitives de représentation OWL-DL – Correspondance avec le langage graphique MOT+OWL et le langage des prédicats du premier ordre*. TELOS documentation. Montreal: LICEF Research Center.

Paquette, G., Rosca, I. (2003). Modeling the delivery physiology of distributed learning systems. *Technology, Instruction, cognition and Learning*, 1–2, 183–209.

Paquette, G., Rosca, I., Masmoudi, A., Mihaila, S. (2005). *TELOS conceptual framework* V0.8. Lornet technical documentation, Télé-Université.

Paquette, G., Léonard, M., Lundgren-Cayrol, K., Mihaila, S., Gareau, D. (2006). Learning design based on graphical knowledge-modeling. *Journal of Educational technology and Society ET&S*, Special issue on Learning Design, January 2006 and Proceedings of the UNFOLD-PROLEARN Joint Workshop, Valkenburh, The Netherlands, September 2005 on Current Research on IMS Learning Design.

Paquette, G., Rosca, I., Mihaila, S., Masmoudi, A. (2007). TELOS, a service-oriented framework to support learning and knowledge management. In S. Pierre (Ed.), *E-Learning Networked Environments and Architectures: A Knowledge Processing Perspective*. Berlin Heidelberg New York: Springer.

Rosca, I. (2005). *TELOS Conceptual Architecture*, version 0.5. LORNET Technical Documents, LICEF research centrer, Télé-université, Montreal.

Tetlow, P., Pan, J., Oberle, D., Wallace, E., Uschold, M., Kendall, E. (2001). Ontology driven architectures and potential uses of the Semantic Web in systems and softrware engineering. http://www.w3.org/2001/sw/BestPractices/SE/ODA/051126/.

van der Aalst, W. M. P., Barros, A. P., ter Hofstede, A. H. M., Kiepuszewski, B. (2000). Advanced workflow patterns. In *7th International Conference on Co-operative Information Systems* (CoopIS 2000).

W3C (2004). OWL overview document. http://www.w3.org/TR/2004/REC-owl-features-20040210/.

Wilson, S., Blinco, K., Rehak, D. (2004). *Service-oriented frameworks: Modelling the infrastructure for the next generation of e-learning systems*. White Paper presented at alt-i-lab 2004.

20 Corporate Universities

V. Zimmermann

Given the importance of an organization's human capital to business success, aligning training and competency development with business needs is a key challenge. In the last 10 years, many companies created corporate universities to face this challenge. In this paper, corporate universities are presented as training or learning organizations that contribute to business objectives such as "to increase business performance" through a better short- and long-term learning approach. This is connected to many forms and methods of learning: formal learning processes, informal learning, team learning, collaboration, social networking, community building, etc. Learning needs are often driven by simply checking the training catalogue. As this is more the job of a training department, corporate universities really come into place when companies see the education of their employees as a strategic instrument to create competitiveness. As globalization creates pressure on companies, the knowledge and experience of employees become the most important difference among competitors. The resulting competition leads to better innovation, faster processes, higher productivity and fewer costs.

20.1 Business Drives Learning in Corporate Universities

In the present economic environment, enterprises are confronted with a number of vital business challenges to improve their operational efficiency. Gaining or maintaining a competitive advantage calls for new approaches with regard to how companies plan, structure and manage their activities. The quality of a company's workforce and its ability to quickly adapt to changes play important roles in all business improvement efforts, thus calling for a continuous investment in human resource development

(Zimmermann and Faltin 2006; Accenture 2006). Particularly in knowledge-intensive business environments, employees are the carriers of knowledge and represent the organization's "intellectual asset" (Nonaka and Takeuchi 1995; Davenport and Prusak 1998). Ensuring that employees have the right skills for the job is essential for the growth and success of an organization. The goal of training services is to transfer to employees all the knowledge needed to cover any deficits hindering the independent fulfilment of their daily business tasks. Accelerating skills acquisition, by means of reducing the "time2competency", can help organizations better cope with changes in processes, products and organizational structures.

Within an organization, learning (Nonaka and Takeuchi 1995; Senge, P. et al. 1994; Grace and Butler 2005) and business improvement as well as performance (Business Process Reengineering, Continuous Process Improvement) (Scheer 2000; Hammer and Champy 1993; Davenport 1993) essentially serve the same goal, that is, to improve the operational effectiveness and excellence of the organization. Nonetheless, traditionally, organizations have handled learning in their training departments very separately from the operational business. The business was very easy: "standard" courses were designed by the training departments and were then booked by the business departments.

Corporate universities were found to change this model of cooperation between the training department and the business. The idea was to drive business instead of getting driven, and to interlink learning, knowledge management and business by integrating them into the daily work at the workplace and outside of the workplace at the "learnplace". The aim was to ensure that the company's objectives got implemented through a top-down learning process. Most corporate universities, therefore, started with management training. From 1996 to 1998, Bertelsmann, DaimlerChrysler and Lufthansa were the first three German companies with "corporate universities" as specific organizations, followed by Deutsche Bank, Volkswagen and E.ON (Zimmermann et al. 2000). All over Europe, there were about 50 known corporate universities in 2000, and almost 250 the United States, which means that every large company had such an organization. Almost all of these companies still have their corporate university, but with organizational/business models and objectives different from those in effect when the universities were founded.

Today, a corporate university is usually merged with the training department, having taken over their role. An example is Volkswagen, where the VW AutoUni now gets managed by VW Coaching. Both departments profited from this merge. As a result, a new understanding of HR development came out of this process (Albrecht 2006):

- Today, corporate universities, HR developers and training departments are the architects of learning and knowledge strategies in a company.
- They are focused on the management of learning and knowledge in order to build individual competencies according to the needs within core business processes of a company.
- They have the objective to provide a solid framework, innovative programs and technologies to enable people to learn both in formal as well as informal processes.

20.2 Business View: The Role and Tasks of a Corporate University Today

As explained in the first section, corporate universities have the task of aligning business needs with learning in order to build competencies that help the company to perform, be competitive and learn faster. Aligning individual training with business priorities, to reduce the time to fill competency gaps and to build proficiency according to evolving business needs and daily work processes, is the key challenge for corporate universities. Business-oriented learning can enable organizations to adapt to changes in their organizational structure or core business processes or to effectively guide employees to new tasks to streamline business operations.

Other than the need to train existing employees or to recruit new ones, a business-driven analysis of skills deficiencies may reveal untapped potential of the existing staff, which can be mobilized to solve a specific business problem. Essentially, business-oriented learning entails integrating learning into the daily working tasks and putting in place mechanisms for the effective management of business processes and organizational roles, as well as competencies and learning processes.

To reach this goal, the tasks of corporate universities can be described as follows (Zimmermann and Faltin 2006):

- *Performance of business-driven competency gap analysis*: This comprises the identification and description of competencies or roles that are required to best perform in core business processes and functions as well as gap analysis based on assessments, audits and tests.
- *Design of learning processes, programs, communities and knowledge repositories*: This includes the instructional design, selection or development of learning content suitable to the needs and creation

of the learning process, setting up collaborative communities and integrating new methods into the learning activities.

- The *execution of the learning processes* in many different forms: as online courses, blended-learning programs, learning communities or other didactical methods.
- The learning *performance monitoring* as the evaluation of the impact of the learning process both on learning outcomes and on business performance.
- The *business value analysis*, which means measuring the business outcome of the competency improvements compared to the initial business need.

Figure 20.1 shows these tasks as the integrated learning life cycle approach of corporate universities.

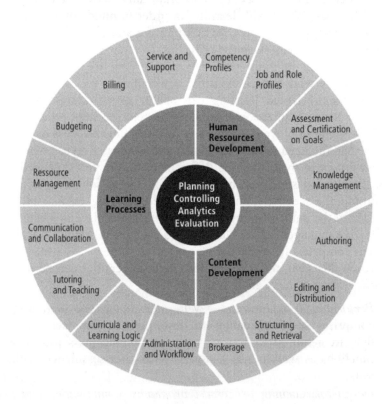

Fig. 20.1. The learning life cycle of a corporate university or business-driven learning organization (Kraemer et al. 2005)

As a result of a competency gap analysis related to business needs, corporate universities create a competence portfolio on their qualification needs. Figure 20.2 shows a sample of such a competence portfolio at GMAC for managers. Leadership, communication and interpersonal skills are the highest ranked competency needs of managers. Professional knowledge in their expertise field is seen as basic knowledge and expected as available.

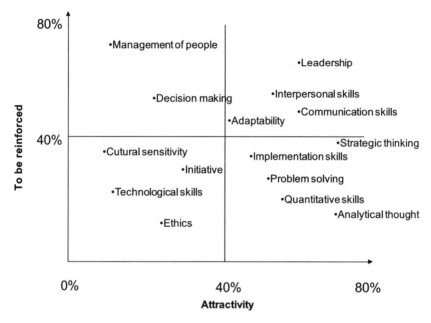

Fig. 20.2. Sample of a competency portfolio at GMAC (Cornuel 2006)

20.3 The User's View: How People Want to Learn

In order to align business needs of a company with learning needs of a person, the corporate university must know how people want to learn in addition to knowing what the company needs. According to Cross (2003), formal learning processes cover just 20% of the daily learning needs whereas most learning happens in informal processes (80%). Therefore, the question for corporate universities is how they can emphasize formal and informal learning with a shift to more informal learning. In an empirical study of Habermann et al. (2004) with more than 400 learners, the issue of how people want to learn was analyzed. In the following text, we will explain some of the key findings. The study concentrated on managers and knowledge workers as people who do not merely consume knowledge but also create it. In most knowledge-intensive businesses such as the service or consulting industry, most work is considered as knowledge work. However, the empirical study also showed that learning environments customs of managers or knowledge workers are not basically different from those of all other employees.

Result 1: Most People Want to Learn, but Are too Busy to Learn Frequently and in a Concentrated Way

It is not possible to confirm the widely held view that managers and knowledge workers, who never have time for anything, certainly have no time for learning.

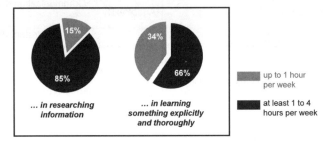

Fig. 20.3. Time dedicated to self study

What becomes clear is that the understanding of learning ranges from traditional forms of learning (seminars) to information procurement. Most people clearly place great importance on knowledge acquisition by personal initiative (self study). More than two out of three interviewees indicated dedicating a minimum of 1–4 h per week to self study.

Result 2: People Combine Learning in the Office with Learning at Home

The advantage of external conferences, company-internal forums or seminars at business schools or training centers is that they take place away from the office. This is, at the same time, the reason why such events are not attended more often than once per year. But, employees are expected to stay up-to-date and understand that self study is necessary (see Fig. 20.3 above).

In spite of remarks to the contrary, for example, "too little time is devoted to office learning", "it's not a reason for working late" and "learning is out at home; time is better spent with the family", more than half of the interviewees do their learning most frequently in both the office and at home. A small number of informants excluded home as a place for learning

(10%). Only 7% of the respondents voted the office as a place infrequently used for learning. In addition, 24% of the informants very frequently use travel periods during business trips as learning times (see Fig. 20.4).

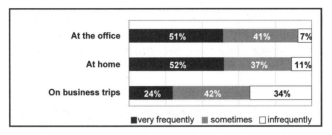

Fig. 20.4. Location preferences for self study

The most frequent stated reason for self study (73%) is the preparation of a project. Despite a general lack of time, more than half of the respondents learn for personal interest.

The Fig. 20.5 illustrates this view of the most important reasons for self study.

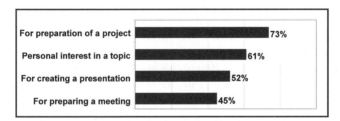

Fig. 20.5. Main reasons for self-study

Interviewees confirmed that learning is done almost always in relation to a given situation, driven by an actual business need, for example, for comprehension of a subject-related problem or to make sense of new situations/problems.

Result 3: People Are Not Hostile to Technology

More than 80% of all interviewees conduct their own searches for the knowledge they need very often. Almost every manager and knowledge worker has used an online tool in this capacity, for example, Internet search engines. All informants rate their own PC as an absolute necessity for their work.

This picture is also reflected in the study about the most frequently used information media. It comes as no surprise that specialist journals and books are an important source of new information. This resource is very often used by 61% of the interviewed people. Actually, the Internet is rated as the most frequently used source of information by almost all respondents (94%). In this regard, there also is an unexpected result: the company's own Intranet is given only very low importance in solving information needs for self study. The Fig. 20.6 illustrates this.

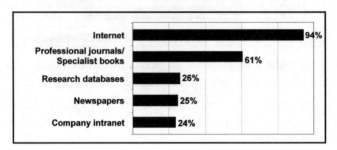

Fig. 20.6. Very frequently used information media for self study

Result 4: Poeple Do Use E-Learning

The study also looked at the question: Do managers accept interactive (online) learning modules for self study? Managers, for instance, describe media available online for downloading (80%) or printing (53%) as very frequently used for learning (Fig. 20.7). There is also a desire for online learning documentation as complementary to conventional modes of seminar (classroom training). Not so important are documents for downloading to PDA computers yet. Only 11% are using this kind of media for their self study at this time.

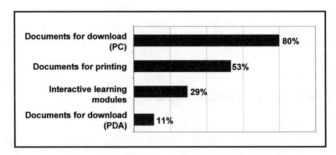

Fig. 20.7. Very frequently used online media

Didactically more complex, interactive learning modules are rated by almost 30% of the informants as appropriate for their personal learning needs.

In general, people take a critical position vis-à-vis interactive online learning media (web-based training, computer-based training). It is rated as very positive and also indispensable that such media include semantic links and optional, more-detailed, information. On the other hand, the people interviewed see a high risk in the potential loss of control regarding their own learning style and speed. Learning modules, including test options for rating personal knowledge levels, is regarded as particularly useful.

Result 5: People Want to Create a Virtual Knowledge Community

Not least important for employees are their personal networks. Many corporate universities have recognized this fact and are aiming to bring managers who are spread across the different locations of the company together in a creative exchange. This is achieved, for example, by organizing internal forums on strategic topics or completing tailored-to-requirement case studies with business schools.

The question remains: Do people form virtual knowledge and learning communities? Questionnaire results to date show that, currently, Intranet communities on common interest topics are not yet so common. At the same time, there is an unexpectedly large interest (more than two-thirds) in online networks and collaboration such as virtual meeting rooms or general network communities for business contacts (see Fig. 20.8).

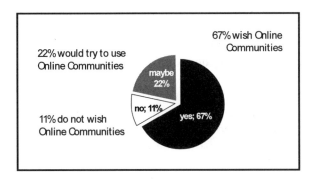

Fig. 20.8. Virtual knowledge and learning communities for managers

A majority of informants wish to use online communities to remain in contact with other participants after conclusion of a class-room seminar, for example, in online expert forums.

As a conclusion of the whole study, people do in fact learn very differently. These differences often are a question of detail. It has been shown that people do a large part of their learning in the office, frequently using the Internet, and are open to (though generally lack in experience with) both E-Learning and online knowledge communities. At the same time, the special aspects of the professional requirements in management also impact knowledge needs and learning behaviour.

People thus clearly have a special awareness in relation to the planned design of learning processes, placing high-quality demands on methods and media design. Moreover, the attention on individual issues is extremely time-restricted. Intuitively, people look for shortcuts and respond positively to options and any risks or chances to which their attention is drawn.

20.4 The Future Path of Corporate Universities

Almost all corporate universities today use software technology to support their core processes in order to enable online learning and communication. For instance, the CLIX Learning Management System from IMC supports corporate university specific functionalities and business processes. This covers the offering of blended courses delivered by special business schools, booking of courses, self-paced or blended learning, tutoring processes, assessment and testing, community support, learning performance analysis and competency management.

In the last 2 years, the integration of learning solutions with corporate HR applications and enterprise portals became more important for corporate universities. Learning management or knowledge management activities as stand-alone approaches do not fulfil the requirements of corporate universities.

In addition, one very important observation has been made: When using learning technology in a corporate university, there should not be too much emphasis on content without understanding the unique needs of learners and knowledge workers. Most people want to use a learning management platform as an organizational support tool and not only as a learning tool, integrated with company portal and HR applications.

In the future, recognizing that learning and knowledge are personal and social processes, learning and knowledge management approaches require a move away from a one-size-fits-all content-centric model towards a user-centric model that puts the learner/knowledge worker at the centre and gives them the control in the sense of Web 2.0 applications (Chatti et al. 2007).

In the past, corporate universities did act too much like education brokers, dealing with content and high-level learning programs in a blended learning mode. Some corporate universities, such as DaimlerChrysler Corporate University, integrated communities of practice in an extensive way for specific knowledge areas into their overall concept (Zimmermann et al. 1999). The experience showed that this mix was the correct strategy and led to a good integration of learning and knowledge exchange.

Consequently, the future path for using learning technology in corporate universities can be described as follows (in relation to Chatti et al. 2007):

- *Corporate universities need to be more user-centric instead of content-centric*: In a learning context, a user-centric model means the creation of self-organized learning networks that provide a base for the establishment of a form of education that goes beyond course and curriculum centric models, and envisions a learner-centred and learner-controlled model of lifelong learning (Koper 2004). This means that corporate universities need to enable personal learning experiences to every person (Hodgins 2005) and a move to learning management systems that provide very personal training.
- *Corporate universities should support a distributed and coordinated, but not central, approach*: Stephenson (2004) writes "I store my knowledge in my friends". Learners and knowledge workers are collaborating more than ever outside and across classroom and organization boundaries, which become more and more irrelevant. Centralization works well for organized knowledge or established structures. Decentralization is effective when things change rapidly, diverse viewpoints are required, and knowledge has not settled into a defined state, which is the case in today's complex knowledge spaces (Siemens 2006). To be more effective, learning solutions need to operate both with formal and central approaches as well as more decentralized and socially open approaches, based on small pieces, loosely joined, and distributed control.
- *Corporate universities should better support bottom-up knowledge approach than top-down*: In the starting phase, corporate universities did very much follow the top-down approach under the model of education brokerage. But top-down models and hierarchical controlled structures can be barriers for innovation. In general, learners

and knowledge workers love to learn but they hate not to be given the freedom to decide how they learn and work (Cross 2003). Nowadays, educational institutions and organizations follow a top-down model and put heavy emphasis on how to force users (learners, employees, customers, partners, and suppliers) to access their closed environments and join their small communities. These attempts often fail due to the "what's in it for me" factor. As a solution, Davenport and Prusak (1998) state that communities should emerge naturally and evade the control mechanisms of the formal organizations and institutions. Furthermore, learning and knowledge are dynamic and complex in nature. According to Cross (2005), emergence is the key characteristic of complex systems. It is the process by which simple entities self-organize to form something more complex.

- *Corporate universities should follow a balance of knowledge-push and knowledge-pull*: Traditional learning initiatives adopt a knowledge-push model and are concerned with exposing people to content. Recognizing that learning and knowledge are dynamic and flexible in nature, the approaches require a shift in emphasis from a knowledge-push to a knowledge-pull model (Naeve 2005). In the knowledge-pull case, people create an environment in which they can pull content that meets their particular needs from a wide array of high-value but less structured resources such as information repositories, communities, and experts, thus creating a much more flexible real-time learning and knowledge culture (Rosenberg 2006).

- *Corporate universities should enforce adaptive communities*: Learning and knowledge solutions need to be both simple and useful. To be useful, corporate universities need to provide environments that support the effective capturing of quality and context-rich knowledge as it gets created. Collaboration contextualizes content (Cross 2003). The wisdom of crowds ensures that knowledge is up-to-date and relevant. Knowledge created by many is much more likely to be of better value. Communities decide what is valuable through filtering, rating, feedback, reviews, criticisms, and recommendations. They also support the certification of people's expertise and the assessment of individual digital reputation. This collective intelligence is what is making sites such as Google, EBay, Amazon, YouTube, and Flickr so successful and popular today. Effective learning management approaches also need to develop mechanisms that ensure that learning and knowledge are embedded into the workflow of the job and in our daily activities in order to avoid any additional work.

- *Corporate universities should create a knowledge-sharing culture and trust*: Often, people tend not to share their valuable knowledge. Babcock (2004) cites two key reasons why people don't share knowledge: (a) people believe knowledge is power and (b) people don't trust each other. Motivation of learners, knowledge workers, customers, and suppliers to share valuable knowledge is based firstly on a culture that supports and encourages knowledge sharing and secondly on trust. A key requirement for knowledge sharing is a culture that allows knowledge to flow and rewards rather than punishes collaborative initiatives. Collaboration has to become the norm and a meaningful part of the performance evaluation of learners and knowledge workers. A major prerequisite for knowledge sharing is trust. Relationships foster trust. As a solution for the trust problem, Babcock (2004) suggests creating opportunities for people to meet and interact in formal and informal settings, give them time to develop relationships, to evaluate each other's trustworthiness and to learn each other's strengths and weaknesses. Similarly, Siemens (2006) states that social contact is needed to foster a sense of trust and comfort, and secure and safe environments are critical for trust to develop. A bottom-up approach and distributed control also build a base for successful knowledge sharing and trust. People only tend to share their knowledge if they don't feel that they are forced to. Therefore, encouraging people to build their personal social networks and join communities based on their needs helps to ensure trust and motivates them to share.

Taking all these future directions into account, corporate universities will become not only places to learn and to share knowledge. The whole discussion of Web 2.0 communities and social software is a very important aspect. As learning is a social process, it is important for people to create communities and collaborate. In the past, many technologies have been developed to do this, starting with virtual classroom software over collaboration and community tools. Within the web 2.0 wave, social software has emerged as a major component (Alexander 2006). The objective is to facilitate any kind of social connection and information interchange. Rapidly evolving examples of social software technologies include wikis, blogs, RSS, podcasts, media sharing, and social tagging. Social software is, however, not restricted to these technologies.

Figure 20.9 shows the components that have to be taken into account when designing learning programs within corporate universities.

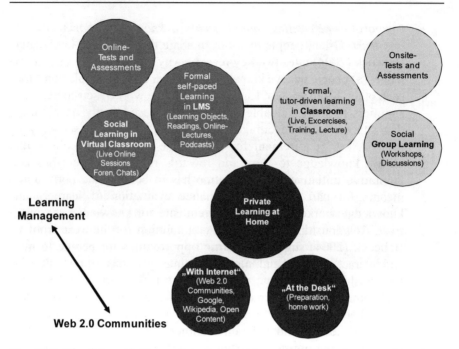

Fig. 20.9. The future platform of corporate universities unites classroom learning, learning management and web 2.0 communities with learning onsite, online and at home

There can be three distinct areas in which people learn.

- The area around *traditional classroom training* covers training sessions, workshops and learning in groups as well as onsite tests and assessments. This is the "incentive" area, in which people learn in nice locations. In this area, the aspect of community building also plays an important role.
- The area of *virtual learning*, using online content and courses, performing online tests, integrated with chats, forums and other elements for sharing knowledge as well as communicating with other people. This area covers managed learning and ensures that people perform concrete tasks to learn.
- The area of *private learning* needs to receive greater attention. In the past, this area was not taken into account by instructional designers within corporate universities. But, as explained above, people want to learn at home as well as in the office. This private learning area is more and more designed by the learners themselves. People choose and pick web 2.0 applications from the Internet to share, discover or

rate information as well authors or editors of content. People use search engines to retrieve information and use them within their formal and informal learning processes.

All three areas will merge more and more in the next years, not necessarily technically but concerning an integrated learning design. Within the design phase of learning programs, program managers of corporate universities will have to take all elements into account and manage a learning process over all three areas. The requirements resulting from this can be summarized as follows:

- *Active and social learning must be blended by instructional designers*: This is where motivation comes from. Learning takes place by activity of the learner itself. Formal learning processes give the learning process a structure, which is needed. Informal learning processes by using the web, literature, books, podcasts or online lectures allow the learner to make his or her own decisions.

- *Internet-based learning technologies move to the core of corporate universities*: In the past, the online platforms were a vehicle but not the main platform. By combining Web 2.0 technologies with learning management systems, these platforms became the heart of a corporate university. As we know, most learning takes place outside of the classroom, so corporate universities have to focus on this side of learning. The knowledge provided in the classroom should concentrate on showing interlinkage, giving the big-picture and providing experiences and stories. In the classroom, the learner should be able to benchmark himself, get feedbacks on his progress and get support concerning the priorities of learning.

- *LMS systems will be the logical linkage of all components and provide guidance*: LMS systems will deliver transparent processes to the learner within the corporate university. It is the system for official learning resources, gives an overview about the priorities and helps to track the individual learning progress. The LMS is the complementary element to the formal learning done at onsite training and in the classroom. Web 2.0 platforms will not be a "competition" for LMS systems but rather be a complementary element to link to the more private and self-organized, informal learning.

- *Everything in a corporate university will focus on personalization and individualization*: Former training approaches in large enterprises were focusing too much on large user groups, delivering to them all the same content and courses. Today, the key to success is personalization. Only if the offerings meet the individual needs and competency gaps, will the learning activity be accepted and be successful. The adoption of any standard course to an individual person is necessary. Some learners like to learn mobilely and want to subscribe to a podcast of their favorite teacher. Others prefer to learn at home at the desk by doing exercises. Others again are cognitive people that learn best by reading papers. It is important to offer a very diversified mode of access and content according to the learning style of every individual person. This does not mean that all content must be available in every kind of format. It means that corporate universities must offer flexible learning scenarios. This can only be reached if they use the potential gained by combining Web 2.0 social software elements with learning management systems and a large offering of classroom training.

20.5 Conclusion

Corporate universities are effective organizations to increase an organization's overall performance. Business-oriented learning is their mission. The instruments are a combination of learning management, knowledge management and social software. The backbone of a business-driven corporate university is the learning management system, which makes processes manageable and structured but also should incorporate the ability to create networks of experts and people to share knowledge and learning resources.

Many companies in the future will reengineer their corporate university or training organization. It will be important that these companies value this organization to be responsible for managing learning processes as a strategic instrument for enterprises to become competitive. The learning platform will be the future backbone of companies. The more digital natives come into organizations and expect the company to enable them to learn and share experiences, the greater the need for companies to make use of learning technology and Web 2.0 applications.

References

Accenture (2006). Accenture High-Performance Workforce Study 2006. http://www.accenture.com/Global/Services/By_Subject/Workforce_Performance/R_and_I/HighPerformaceStudy2006.htm

Albrecht, D. (2006). Do-it-yourself human resource management/Personalentwicklung zum Selbermachen". In *7th Learning Management Congress*, Düsseldorf.

Alexander, B. (2006). Web 2.0: A new wave of innovation for teaching and learning? *EDUCAUSE Review*, 41(2) 32–44.

Babcock, P. (2004). Five reasons people don't share. *HR Magazine*, 49(5), 47–50.

Chatti, M. A., Jarke, M., Frosch-Wilke, D. (2007). The future of e-Learning: a shift to knowledge networking and social software, *PROLEARN Whitepaper*.

Cornuel, E. (2006). Management education in Europe. In *7th Learning Management Congress*, Düsseldorf.

Cross, J. (2005) 'Educating Ourselves at Emerging', Internet Time Biog.

Cross, J. (2003). *Informal Learning – the Other 80%*, Internet Time Group.

Davenport, T. H. (1993). *Process Innovation: Reengineering Work Through Information Technology*. Bosten, MA: Harvard Business School Press.

Davenport, T. H., Prusak, L. (1998). *Working Knowledge: How Organizations Manage What They Know*. Boston: Harvard Business School Press.

Grace, A. and Butler, T. (2005) 'Learning management systems: a new beginning in the management of learning and knowledge', Int. J. Knowledge and Learning, Vol. 1, Nos 1/2, pp. 12–24.

Habermann, F., Schmidt, K., Kuechler, T. (2004). Knowledge and learning tools for managers: an empirical study. *WSEAS Transactions of Information Science and Applications*, (5)1 (ISSN 1790-0832).

Hammer, M., Champy, J. (1993). *Re-engineering the Corporation: A Manifesto for Business Revolution*. New York: HarperCollins.

Hodgins, H. W. (2005). *Grand Challenges for Learning Objects.* Presentation at Learntec, Karlsruhe, Germany.

Koper, R. (2004). Use of the Semantic Web to solve some basic problems in education. *Journal of Interactive Media in Education*, 2004(6).

Kraemer, W., Milius, F., Zimmermann, V. (2005). From WINFO-LINE to corporate learning management – sustainable transfer of ideas into competitive products/ Von WINFO-Line zum Corporate Learning Management – Nachhaltiger Transfer wissenschaftlicher Konzepte in wettbewerbsfähige Produkte. *IM Information Management*, 20(2005) Special Edition, 50–67.

Naeve, A. (2005). The human Semantic Web – Shifting from knowledge push to knowledge pull. *International Journal of Semantic Web and Information Systems (IJSWIS)*, 1(3), 1–30.

Nonaka, I., Takeuchi, H. (1995). *The Knowledge-Creating Company. How Japanese Companies Create the Dynamics of Innovation*. New York: Oxford University Press.

Rosenberg, M. J. (2006). *Beyond E-Learning*, Pfeiffer.com.

Senge et al. (1994). Presence: Human Purpose and the Field of the Future, Boston 1994.

Scheer, A.-W. (2000). *Aris – Business Process Modeling*, 3rd edition. Berlin Heidelberg New York: Springer.

Siemens, G. (2006). *Knowing Knowledge*, Lulu.com, ISBN: 978-1-4303-0230-8.

Stephenson, K. (2004). What knowledge tears apart, networks make whole. *Internal Communication Focus*, 36.

Zimmermann, V., Faltin, N. (2006). Integration of business process management platforms and learning technologies: The PROLIX process-oriented learning life cycle. In *Proceedings of eLearning 2006 Conference*, Helsinki 2006.

Zimmermann, V., Kraemer, W., Milius, F. (2000). Virtual corporate universities. In U. Beck, W. Sommer (Eds.), *Learntec Proceedings Bd.1* (pp. 337–350). Karlsruhe.

21 Lessons from Africa

J. Cronje

This chapter will consider the current rationale for implementing Internet communication technology (ICT) in an educational context in developing countries, by looking firstly at the problems that people were traditionally hoping to solve with ICT, and then looking at the opportunities that are being created by ICT implementation.

Following upon the rationale the chapter considers relevant literature, in context of Friedman's notion of a world "flattened" by ICT (2005). Thereupon follows a selection of lessons learnt and reported in the literature. Then, ten case studies showing current developments of winning schools in South Africa are analysed to answer the question "What do successful ICT integrations in schools have in common?"

Finally, the chapter is concluded by considering the success stories in terms of the contextualize, apply, transfer and import model of ICT integration, developed primarily in Tanzania.

21.1 Introduction

Over the past 10 years, the implementation of computers in Africa has increased in frequency and sophistication. The "missionary" approach of dumping computers in rural communities and hoping that the people will somehow become literate and internationally competitive, has worn off. The honeymoon seems to be over, and there is a move towards a much more scientific approach to infusing ICT into developing communities.

A strong argument can be made for seeing Africa as a case study for the integration of ICT in education in the world. On the one hand, there are countries such as South Africa with its strong, emergent economy. On the other hand, there are countries such as Sudan, torn by civil war. This chapter will integrate lessons learnt from various African countries, in the hope that it may resonate with the experiences of other developing countries.

21.2 Why ICT for Education in Africa?

Often the rationale for the deployment of ICT for education in developing countries is to solve problems. While there certainly is some merit at throwing technology at problems and hoping that they will go away, there seems to be a growing realisation that the greater reason for using ICT is a positive one. Instead of using ICT to solve problems, we should be using it to create opportunities. The following sections will discuss some of the problems that ICT claims to solve for developing countries, and then move onto a discussion of the opportunities that are likely to be created.

21.2.1 The Problems

The three most frequently listed problems in developing countries are large classroom sizes, lack of infrastructure and inadequate teaching staff (Osin 1998).

While it is true that schools in developing countries often have class sizes of over 50 learners per teacher, it does not necessarily hold true that putting those learners in front of a computer will improve their chances of passing. Even in developed countries such as the United States of America, authors such as Larry Cuban and Todd Oppenheimer deplore the waste of financial resources on ICT. In direct contrast with Osin's (1998) enthusiastic support of computers in a developing country such as Israel, Angrist and Victor (2002) found that "on balance, it seems, money spent on CAI in Israel would have been better spent on other inputs". They argue that, in their earlier research, they found that reduction of classroom staff and improvements in teacher training have led to significant gains in learner performance. Thus, one must conclude that adding computers to over-full classrooms is not likely to solve any problems.

The second problem mentioned relates to lack of infrastructure. Schools in developing countries often lack electricity, telephones, lavatories, and even classrooms (Osin 1998). However, what is unclear is how ICT is supposed to solve these problems. With no electricity or telephones, how will the computers work? The money involved in installing solar electricity and satellite-based Internet could be better spent in reducing class size. Adding computers is unlikely to improve classroom structure or the availability of lavatories.

The third problem, lack of adequately trained teaching staff, is not solved, but complicated by the addition of computers. Inadequately trained staff firstly lack subject skills, then they lack methodological skills. Adding ICT to the mix will mean that they now also lack computer skills.

There seem to be two clear errors in thinking involved in using ICT to "fix the problems" in education in developing countries. The first is that, as has been shown thus far, the problems are usually systemic and not necessarily aligned with ICT as solutions. The second is philosophical, relating to an approach to developing countries that suggests that they are pools of problems that need to be solved. Once the problems have been solved, the countries will stop having poor people and disappear from the radar. Fundamental to the use of computers in developing countries is the need to erase the problem-based mindset that often forms the point of departure for development goals and replacing it with a more positive mindset of stimulation of growth.

21.2.2 The Opportunities

It is in the arena of the stimulation of growth that the work of Thomas Friedman (2005) presents a powerful rationale for ICT in education for developing countries. In his provocative work, *The World Is Flat: A Brief History of the Twenty-First Century*, Friedman argues that ICT has leveled the playing field between developing and developed countries. He uses the example of India and China as emerging economies and shows how these countries have used the Internet specifically, and ICT in general, to become low-cost preferred suppliers to the developed world. Friedman (2005) identifies six trends that define the flattening of the playing field: outsourcing, offshoring, open-sourcing, insourcing, supply-chaining and informing. Outsourcing means that digital work such as programming or running a call centre can be done over the Internet, independent of time and space. Offshoring means that entire factories can be moved to countries where labor is cheaper. Open-sourcing refers to the use of software of which the code is developed on a shared basis and is free to anyone – thus breaking the monopoly of large software houses in developed countries on secret code. Insourcing means that specialist companies can work inside other companies to perform non-key functions. Supply-chaining means that as one product is sold, another is being created – even on the other side of the world. Informing refers to the use of powerful easy-to-use and ubiquitously available search capabilities that allow companies (or even countries) to easily mine their own information.

Friedman goes on to show how these six tendencies can have alarming consequences for the United States, because all the work for which it currently gets money could eventually be moved away to developing countries that do it more cheaply and even better. Of course, what Friedman sees as a threat to the US could well be seen as an opportunity for developing countries.

In discussing the lessons learnt, this chapter will follow an optimistic view by showing how Friedman's tendencies are coming to fruition in developing countries. This is not to say that there are no drawbacks. It is just that the chapter focuses on the successes and the opportunities. The greatest element of success in Edison's invention of the light bulb was not the 2,500 filaments that failed in his experiments, but the one that succeeded.

21.3 The Literature

This section will commence with a selection of examples based on the rationale presented by Friedman (2005). It will then continue with a number of lessons learnt during such implementations and draw certain conclusions from which a future scenario may be developed.

21.3.1 Outsourcing

The African Virtual University (www.avu.org) is an example of an institution that outsources its development of course materials (Ondari-Okemwa 2002). The chief benefit of such a system is that the university is able to acquire coursework of an internationally recognized high quality, at a reasonable cost. Nevertheless Ondari-Okemwa (2002) points out that "flexibility, technology, adaptation, skilled human resources and dynamic information policies are some of the hurdles that must be overcome".

21.3.2 Offshoring

Calling itself "Australia's most internationalised university" Monash University, established in 1958 in the state of Victoria, has eight campuses around the world, including one in Malaysia and one in South Africa (Monash University 2007). Marginson (2002) points out that "the United States has seventeen times the population of Australia but less than four times the number of foreign students". The reason for Australia's development of offshore campuses was to develop another form of export. The relative weakness of the Australian dollar compared to the American and British currencies of the 1980 meant that Australia was in a position to compete strongly in terms of price.

One serious downside of this offshoring of the knowledge factory is that it is in direct competition with local institutions. The competition lay mainly in the fields of ICT and business training. In 1995 there were only two institutions providing an MBA in Pretoria, South Africa. By 1997, this number had grown to 40. MBA courses, being prestigious but also concentrating on highly motivated students who pay a premium for their studies, could be seen as cash cows from which more expensive courses can be cross subsidized. An attack upon the MBA of a university in a developing country may be seen as an attempt to internationalise the quality of such training in the country, but one has to be wary of its consequences upon the other academic offerings.

21.3.3 Open-Sourcing

The rise of the Linux operating system, as well as the Moodle learning management system, and the Open Office productivity suite has had a tremendous impact upon teaching and learning in developing countries. Entire universities are able to run their systems without expensive licensing. Noronha (2003), citing Rajani (2003), points out that "teachers, journalists and democracy activists have been using computers, e-mail, web publishing, desktop publishing and the Internet to get their messages out to the world, participate in societal debates and acquire as well as disseminate knowledge and skills". Although open-source software is cheaper, its adoption is dependent on a number of factors. For Hafström and Hofbauer (2004) these are "addressing real, experienced problems, making the technology sensible to its users, providing sustainable solutions, controlling that the infrastructure supports the technology, realising the importance of local champions, focusing on the right target group, avoiding technical distanciation and understanding attitudes and structures of the society".

21.3.4 Insourcing

Where outsourcing means that a business gives non-core activities to specialist providers, insourcing involved imbedding outside providers seamlessly into your own environment. Cronjé (2006) describes the presentation of a master's course in ICT for education by the Sudan University of Science and Technology (SUST) in Khartoum. The course was insourced from the University of Pretoria (UP), South Africa. Three South African professors from Pretoria were contracted to adjust the South African curriculum for approval by the SUST senate, and then to present the course in Khartoum on an Internet-supported basis, with a few contact visits. In this way, SUST was able to present a master's course for which they had no local expertise whatsoever.

On an even larger scale, RMIT University of Melbourne, Australia, presents an African Virtual University programme in computer science, directly from Australia (RMIT 2002).

The advantage of insourcing over outsourcing, in the case of the co-operation between SUST and UP, is that the administrative control of the course remained with the insourcing institution. Contractual agreements, however, had to be drawn up to deal with issues of intellectual property. In effect, though, the process was as simple as the appointment of visiting professors from another university.

21.3.5 Supply Chaining

Leh and Kennedy (2004) point out that their respondents in Papua New Guinea indicated some reluctance towards ICT in general, stating that they fear it may be disruptive to their agrarian lives. Some tension exists between the fact that technology could lead to more productive agriculture and higher standards of living, and the erosion of indigenous culture. They see a particular benefit of instructional technology in that it makes local students realize the importance of spending a year or two of their studies abroad. However, it would seem that their respondents were not all that interested in participating in any sophisticated supply chain.

By contrast, Mbambo and Cronje (2002) showed that women in the textile industry in Botswana, when shown the power of the Internet in providing them with information about suppliers and markets, immediately wanted to create their own websites to assist them in selling their products. They wanted to be producers of information as well as consumers.

21.3.6 Informing

Perhaps the most innovative experimentation with computers in developing countries takes the form of the series of "hole in the wall" experiments of Mitra (2003), which he calls "minimally invasive education". The experiments take the form of public access computers that are made available to children without adult supervision. Mitra (2003) hopes to demonstrate that "If given appropriate access and connectivity, groups of children can learn to operate and use computers and the Internet with no or minimal intervention from adults". Mbambo and Cronje (2002) have shown that adults are quite capable of peer-tutoring in computer and information literacy skills.

The constant work that is being done on simplifying the user interface of computing, coupled with the fact that peer tutoring seems to be an almost natural occurrence in front of a computer, has important implications for information behavior in developing countries when people can obtain free information for themselves.

21.4 Lessons Learnt the Hard Way

Hawkins (2002) presents 10 lessons learnt in putting information technology into developing countries. These are:

- Computer labs in developing countries take time and money, but they work.
- Technical support cannot be overlooked.
- Non-competitive telecommunications infrastructure, policies and regulations impede connectivity and sustainability.
- Lose the wires.
- Get the community involved.
- Private–public sector partnerships are essential.
- Link ICT and education efforts to broader education reforms.
- Training, training, training.
- Technology empowers girls.
- Technology motivates students and energizes classrooms.

Linking their results to the literature, Hafström and Hofbauer (2004) give five suggestions to facilitate the integration of open source technology into institutions:

- The technology must address real, experienced problems in the country.
- The technology must make sense for the people who are going to use it.
- The technology must provide sustainable solutions.
- It is important to investigate the level of infrastructure in the country.
- It is important to realise the importance of local champions.
- It is important to focus on the right target group.

- The technology is implemented to solve people's problems, not to increase them.
- It is important to see to the bigger picture and try to understand (socio-political) attitudes and structures where the technique is going to be used.

As far as sustainability is concerned, Thomas (2006) presents an interesting case study of a school district where a project of implementation of computers in schools was started in the late eighties, and continued with enthusiastic government support for 5 years. Thereafter, a change of government saw all support withdrawn. Ten years later, a number of schools were still functioning effectively. Thomas conducted a series of interviews to determine what factors during the implementation phase may have contributed to the sustained use of computers after withdrawal of support. He identifies four influences on the project: personal, programmatic, physical and systemic.

Personal factors in this particular project included the enthusiasm of the participants, coupled with the continued support that they received from their superiors. Although it is commonly agreed that it is necessary to have "champions", very little has actually been done about what a champion really is. More research is necessary to determine the characteristics of champions in developing countries so that those characteristics can be designed into the system, rather than relying on individuals.

Programmatic factors deal with the complex nature of the implementation program. Thomas (2006) concludes that each implementation needs to be designed for its own peculiarities, although one must guard against the possible chaos that can ensue if the level of customization is too high.

Physical factors comprise infrastructure. Infrastructure goes beyond the IT infrastructure, or even the architecture. Some infrastructural elements such as electricity (solar, wind, hydro or network), seem obvious, but there are numerous workarounds. There are examples of schools that moved their computer laboratories into the local village library. In this way, the school has access to physical space in school time, and the community has access to computers after school. The telecommunications backbones of developing countries are notoriously poor. Satellite connectivity is becoming increasingly viable, and organizations such as NEPAD are negotiating for low-cost bandwidth (Sakoana 2005). Some researchers such as Cossa (2002) warn against using old, donated computers, while there are many examples of schools that actually use the maintenance and upgrading of older machines as a learning opportunity. On the other hand, especially in underdeveloped areas and particularly poor areas, it may even be necessary for other infrastructure to be developed. There are examples of rural African schools that grow vegetable gardens in order to nourish the children who stay after school to work on computers.

Thomas (2006) notes further that the systemic positioning of the implementation occurs within the context of larger systems. This concurs with other authors' conclusions regarding socio-political issues. The implementation of computers in a district needs to take cognizance of the power relationships within a community, as well as general community involvement.

21.5 Ten Case Studies

An analysis of presentations by the 10 winning ICT-using schools in South Africa's Gauteng province in February 2007 showed that the winning schools had the following tendencies in common:

21.5.1 Learners Learn by Doing

A project-based approach is followed whereby learners design and build PowerPoint slideshows, websites, or various other technology-based artefacts. The development of such artefacts usually requires teamwork and multiple technologies such as digital cameras, digital voice recorders, etc. The computer forms the platform for integrating the technologies and the individual contributions of team members. In disadvantaged schools, a clear balance is kept between the level of technology and the quality of work. Students who own digital cameras, for instance, would contribute photos, while those who have Internet connections at home would contribute data. During evaluation, emphasis is placed on what learners had *learnt* rather than on what they had produced.

21.5.2 Learners Produce Learning Materials

There is a tendency towards using materials made by senior students as learning materials for junior students, as well as towards using peer-learning materials. Thus a group may well be given a project to design and develop a lesson on a certain topic for their classmates.

21.5.3 Schools Develop Their Own Software and Websites

More and more schools are using professional software such as Authorware, and Dreamweaver, or regular productivity software such as Excel and PowerPoint, to produce drills, tutorials and even simulations that they share freely with other schools. In South Africa, the Thutong (www. thutong.org.za) was created to facilitate such sharing.

21.5.4 Research Done by Learners

The current South African school curriculum shows a marked emphasis upon research-based learning. In the digital environment, this has led to three manifestations. Firstly, learners use the Internet to do research that would previously have been done in libraries with encyclopaedias. Secondly, learners engage in physical research projects by following research protocols published on the Internet. Finally, learners publish their results on the Internet, or contribute to large, existing Internet-based collaborative school-based research projects such as the Globe Program (www.globe.gov).

21.5.5 Focus on Learning, Not on Technology

What was particularly striking during the analysis of the winning schools was that, while vendors of the technologies used in the schools concentrated on demonstrating "exciting new technologies", the educators and administrators from the winning schools, almost without fail, hardly said anything about the technology they were using, but concentrated on the products that were produced by the learners in the learning process. They did not talk about the cell phones, they talked about the pictures the learners took with them and the text messages that they exchanged. They did not talk about the computers, but about the websites that they learners created and the new knowledge that they generated.

21.5.6 Computers Across the Curriculum: Integrated and Thematic

Many of the participants demonstrated projects whereby a certain local phenomenon was investigated by the learners, from various perspectives. A central focus of these phenomena is usually some form of entrepreneurship. It would seem that the central question driving much of the research done by the learners is "How can we turn the current situation around and even turn it into a profit-making venture?" In this way, for instance, local battlefields become the terrain for an integrated history, geography, biology, accounting and mathematics lesson. The technology is used to obtain data from geographical information systems or the GSM cellular phone network. The web is searched for historical background and the biomass of the area is calculated using a spreadsheet.

21.5.7 Educator Training

The united cry from all the delegates is "Train, train, train". Slideshows presented by the delegates show one picture after another of staff, not learners, in front of computers. Three modes of training are in evidence. State-provided training, training by non-governmental organisations, and peer training by fellow staff. Anecdotal evidence also exists.

21.5.8 Community Involvement, Outreach and Sharing

The communities around participating schools were involved in a two-way sharing process. On the one hand, they were the sponsors of the project, and on the other hand, they were the benefactors. Sponsorship came in the form of equipment, labour and expertise, while the benefit was reaped in the form of training. Some schools even placed their computer laboratories in the community libraries some distance away from the school because they did not have the available space and the library was in a more secure environment, particularly after hours.

21.5.9 Focus on Girls

The focus on girls ranges from a reporting on participation by girls to the active encouragement of girls to participate in what many consider to be an essentially male pastime: working with computers. It would seem, though, that the use of cellular technology has no gender stereotyping.

21.5.10 International Links

Most of the winning schools report some international cooperation. In the simplest form, this is through international sponsorship of equipment. The next level involves some form of Internet-based exchange of information between schools, be it on the level of emails to and from learners about school subjects or cultural-geographic information (what's it like living in your country?) or collaborating on web-based projects on topics of mutual interest, such as global warming or terrorism. One school's international cooperation included participating in a project that took a number of representatives from the school in Pretoria, South Africa, to NASA in Florida, USA.

21.5.11 Future Plans

All the schools report future plans. While reporting on the current situation always focuses on learning rather than on technology, it would seem that future plans invariably focus on improving infrastructure. Improvements may involve constructing a new laboratory, or upgrading existing computers. In schools where there are already more than one laboratory, the trend is for individual computers to be placed in classrooms. Some schools are beginning to report on integrating the use of cellular technology.

This section began with lessons learnt by outsiders working on the incorporation of technology into schools in developing countries. Then the focus shifted to an analysis of a number of cases in which schools took their own initiative in the implementation of technology. What is occurring at the moment is that the incorporation of technology is happening from both sides. Somehow the traditional missionary approach with outsiders bringing technology and then disappearing is losing ground in favor of a model whereby current viable initiatives are sought out and supported.

21.6 Contextualizing Computers for Developing Countries

The previous section dealt with two types of introduction of ICT into classrooms in developing countries: from outside and from within. It would seem that a model is needed that would integrate both these types of development. Such a model would concentrate on contextualizing the integration of ICT into developing countries. In this respect much has already been done by the University of Joensuu, Finland, as a result of their experience in Kenia, Tanzania, Namibia, Singapore and South Africa.

Vesisenaho et al. (2006) describe a four-stage model called CATI (contextualize, apply, transfer, import) shown in Fig. 21.1.

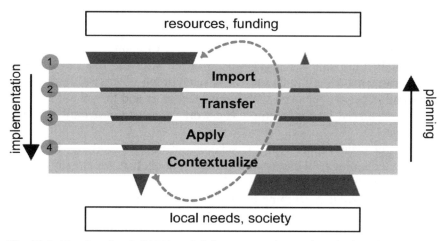

Fig. 21.1. The four-level CATI model for representing and analyzing the planning and implementation processes of ICT (Vesisenaho et al. 2006)

The model shows a two-way relationship between resources and funding and local needs and society. Moving from local needs to funding occurs during the planning phase, while implementation sees a movement from funding to society. This model seems to explain, for instance, why schools, reporting on their successes, concentrate on the learning (application and context) that took place as a result of a successful implementation, but in their planning they report on the technology that they wish to import.

To conclude this chapter, it might be a good idea to filter all the information from the literature and the case studies through the CATI model and see what lessons can be extracted.

21.6.1 Import

Vesisenaho et al. describe the import phase as the importation of a technology "before any local needs analysis has been undertaken" (Vesisenaho et al. 2006). Such uncritical importation is often criticized by the literature (Hafström and Hofbauer 2004; Hawkins 2002; Thomas 2006). Yet the experience from the case studies show that a number of schools, while first objecting to foreign technology in their environment, started little by little to embrace the new technology until they eventually started to ask for more.

21.6.2 Transfer

In the transfer stage, generic ICT that has been imported is used in local content. In this way, the users start working with the technology to do things more effectively than they have been doing otherwise. In this way, pens and paper are replaced with word processors and the school encyclopedia is replaced by the Internet. The work, however, essentially remains the same.

Transfer occurs more easily if schools are already working differently without technology. In other words, those schools that are already following a research-based curriculum and that are already letting their learners work in groups on developing products, are more likely to incorporate the technology that enables group work and research.

21.6.3 Apply

Vesisenaho et al. (2006) point out that application means that the potential of ICT innovation is being realized by the users. International participation facilitated over the Internet is an example of application.

Another example of application is the cross-curricular use of ICT. This involves the recognition of the fact that technology is an enabler, but that the technology per se is not as important as how it is applied.

21.6.4 Contextualize

Community involvement, a focus on learning and the inclusion of girls are the strongest features of contextualization from the case studies. "If ICT is to be sustainable, it needs to be contextualized to serve the local community" (Vesisenaho et al. 2006). The teachers at participating schools have realized that the purpose of computers is to improve learning. Therefore they report, not on the computers, but on the learning. Similarly, one of the biggest problems in developing countries is the exclusion of girls, thus, technology that enables girls is likely to be adopted and nurtured.

21.7 Conclusions

The biggest barrier to ICT integration in Africa remains the lack of resources, both physical and human. One cannot try to use ICT to bypass educators. If ICT is to be used successfully, then educators have to be trained more, not less. They need to learn how to teach better, how to teach with technology and, of course, how to maintain the very technology that they are using.

While the role of ICT in "flattening" the world has to be recognized, it can become a double-edged sword. While ubiquitous Internet connectivity provides opportunities for rapid growth, particularly in the ICT sector, it also poses a serious threat to local industry. Educators need to realize that they are preparing learners to compete, not only locally, but globally.

Case studies in South Africa have shown that the technology is not as important as what is done with the technology. The focus lies on learner activity, with learners learning by doing, as they produce their own research products. Success is dependent upon community buy-in, educator training, international networking and future plans.

From all the above, it becomes clear that, as was stated at the beginning of this chapter, there is a move towards a much more scientific approach to integrating ICT into developing countries and the need to contextualize such integration cannot be overemphasized.

References

Angrist, J., & Victor L. (2002). New evidence on classroom computers and pupil learning. *Economic Journal*, 112(482), 735–765.

Cossa, G. C. (2002). Implications of introducing Information and Communication Technology in Mozambican schools. Unpublished M.Ed essay, University of Pretoria. http://hagar.up.ac.za/catts/learner/generossa/cossaessay.doc.

Cronjé, J. C. (2006). Pretoria to Khartoum – how we taught an Internet-supported Masters' programme across national, religious, cultural and linguistic barriers. *Educational Technology and Society*, 9(1), 276–288.

Friedman, T. L. (2005). *The World Is Flat: A Brief History of the Twenty-first Century.* New York: Farrar, Straus and Giroux.

Hafström, C., & Hofbauer, J. (2004). IT adaptation in developing countries: An ethnographic study of the open source initiative SchoolNet Namibia. Unpublished Masters Thesis, University of Gothenburg. http://www.handels.gu.se/epc/archive/00003927/01/Nr_39_CH,JH.pdf. Accessed 1 February, 2007.

Hawkins, R. J. (2002). Ten lessons for ICT and education in the developing world. In G. Kirkman (Ed.), *The Global Information Technology Report 2001–2002: Readiness for the Networked World.* Oxford: Oxford University Press.

Leh, A. S. C., & Kennedy, R. (2004). Instructional and information technology in Papua New Guinea. *Educational Technology Research and Development*, 52(1), 96–101.

Marginson, S. (2002). Education in the global market. *Lessons from Australia Academe*, 88(3), 22–24.

Mbambo, B, & Cronje, J. C. (2002). The Internet as information conduit for small business development in Botswana. *Aslib Proceedings*, 54(4), 251–259.

Mitra, S. (2003). Minimally invasive education: a progress report. *British Journal of Educational Technology*, 34, 367–371.

Monash University (2007). A brief history of Monash University. http://www. monash.edu.au/about/overview/brief-history.html. Accessed 4 February 2007.

Noronha, F. (2003). Developing countries gain from free/open-source software. http://www.linuxjournal.com/article/6884. Accessed 1 February, 2007.

Ondari-Okemwa, E. (2002). Challenges of harnessing virtual information resources in Kenya: the case of the African Virtual University. *Journal of Information Science*, 28(4), 321–329.

Osin, L. (1998). Computers in education in developing countries: Why and how? *Education and Technology Series*, 3(1). Washington, DC: World Bank. http://maple.ubc.ca/mapletest/revisions_ded/downloads/v3n1.pdf. Accessed 1 February 2007.

Rajani, N. (2003). *Free as in Education – Significance of the Free/Libre and Open Source Software for Developing Countries*. Ministry for Foreign Affairs, Helsinki, Finland.

RMIT University (2002). African Virtual University computer science programme. http://www.international.rmit.edu.au/avu/. Accessed 1 February 2007.

Sakoana, T. (2005). Nepad to link African schools. South Africa.Info. 26 October. http://www.southafrica.info/ess_info/sa_glance/education/update/eschools.htm. Accessed 6 February 2006.

Thomas, H. E. (2006). The sustainable implementation of computers in school districts: A case study in the Free State Province of South Africa online. Ph.D. thesis, University of Pretoria. http://upetd.up.ac.za/thesis/available/etd-11092006-185713. Accessed 1 February 2006.

Vesisenaho, M., Kemppainen, J., Islas Sedano, C., Tedre, M., & Sutinen, E. (2006). How to contextualize ICT in higher education: A case study in Tanzania. *African Journal of Information and Communication Technology (AJICT)*, 2(2), 88–109.

22 The African Virtual University

P. Bateman

22.1 Introduction

In addition to the widely reported digital divide between sub-Saharan Africa and the rest of the world, there also exists an ever-widening knowledge divide. It is imperative for the future economic and social development of the region that appropriate and effective measures be taken to bridge this divide. This implies that African countries need to create a critical mass of professionals who are skilled in using and adapting new knowledge and information in order to be able to (a) participate effectively in the global knowledge-based economy and (b) address many of their social, technological and political challenges. To achieve this, it has long been recognized that there is a need for these countries to invest in quality education and training at a tertiary level.

Regrettably, most tertiary education institutions in sub-Saharan Africa are overwhelmed with challenges that have led to their inability to adequately service the burgeoning demand for higher education in their respective countries. As a result, universities in Africa are looking to resolve a number of issues restricting their efficacy. Key among these are their inability to accommodate excessive student enrollment demand, their limited ability to train (and retain) faculty, their limited research capacity, their lack of access to quality educational materials, the generally poor state of their physical and technological infrastructure, and the prevalence of academic programs that do not always meet the requirements of their national development objectives. It is in this context that in 1997, the African Virtual University (AVU) arrived on the education scene in Africa with a mandate to seek to address some of these challenges.

22.2 A Short History

The AVU is not a university in the traditional sense. It is, rather, an educational organization that is part of a network of African partner institutions that aims at supporting the development and delivery of open, distance and eLearning (ODeL) programs for a wide array of learners, including traditional students, life-long learners and active workers and professionals.

The first phase (1997–1999) of the AVU was launched as a World Bank project wherein a campus-based learning center model was adopted for the delivery of academic programs that were brokered from universities located outside Africa. During this proof-of-concept stage the AVU established 19 learning centers in 15 African countries. The campus-based model was useful in countries where infrastructure and basic computing facilities were scarce and/or where particular subject disciplines were not readily available.

All teaching and learning resources for the project were managed from the AVU Unit of the World Bank in Washington, DC. The Chief Academic Officer procured, coordinated and managed the delivery of courses to AVU learning centers at partner institutions in Africa. The AVU deployed a technical infrastructure that integrated satellite technologies to transmit video and data resources from its external content providers to multiple sites in Africa. A combination of live and videotaped instruction, supported by textbooks, a digital library and course notes, was provided by leading international universities and content providers. Students interacted with their instructors and other students via phone, email, discussion forums or fax.

Phase 2 (1999–2003), constituted a period of consolidation and expansion as the AVU established learning centers in 34 partner institutions in 18 countries. Significantly, this period also saw the AVU transfer from the World Bank in Washington, DC, to Nairobi in Kenya to become an African-led and African-run initiative. Its program offerings grew to include training in information technology, journalism, business management, computer science, languages and accounting. The other main achievements during this phase were: (1) the affiliation to a global network of leading universities; (2) about 3,000 h of instructional short-course programs delivered by leading overseas universities; (3) about 23,000 students enrolling in semester-long courses; (4) close to 2,500 professionals enrolling in executive business seminars; (5) close to 45,000 e-mail accounts being created; and (6) the establishment of a digital library including about 1,000 journals together with a website, with an average of over 1 million hits (number of times accessed) per month.

Also during this phase (in 2002), the AVU became an intergovernmental organization, with its own charter affirmed by the governments of five African countries: Kenya, Senegal, Mauritania, Cote d'Ivoire and Mali. In addition to its headquarters in Nairobi, Kenya, the AVU later established a regional office in Dakar, Senegal, to service its partner institutions in Francophone and Anglophone West Africa. After the transfer of the AVU headquarters to Nairobi, the management, staffing, budget (including fund-raising) and learning resources were coordinated from Nairobi.

22.3 Adapting to a Changing Educational Environment

Early E-Learning programs supported by Web 1.0 were noted for the characteristic push methodology that they adopted via the use of learning management systems (LMS) (Porter 2006). Rarely did these programs fully exploit the communication potential of networked computers that would enable the types of reflection, communication and collaboration espoused in social theory (Coleman 1990) and/or active learning theory (Vygotsky 1978). In what may be viewed as a lost opportunity, the col-laboration tools built into the LMSs being used did not feature highly in the program design for E-Learning programs.

More recent developments in Web 2.0 tools and practice have served to increase the awareness of the value of peer learning that encourages students to share and negotiate ideas in order to reach a deeper understanding of their subject discipline and develop a range of different skills such as criti-cal inquiry and reflection. Earlier studies by Blum (1999), Ryan (2000), and Wegner et al. (1999) indicated that new pedagogical strategies needed to be devised for E-Learning programs that aimed at developing this reflec-tive construction of knowledge and active participation by students as auto-didacticians.

To some extent, the process of devising new E-Learning strategies is now being undertaken by some of the early adopters or more experienced instructors, including some in Africa, albeit mainly in those African coun-tries with the requisite ICT infrastructure that would support such strate-gies. Porter (2006) notes that instructors with experience in online course delivery are now beginning to investigate wikis, blogs, and various media-casting tools for their application to social-constructivist aspects of learn-ing (Porter 2006). In acknowledging the potential impact the Web 2.0 environment on E-Learning, Porter notes the following:

"Newer social software systems may provide a medium for instructional activities that instructors may have done without when they focused their online and distance teaching activities around production-based learning management systems that place a high emphasis on content development and its transmission" (Porter 2006).

There are, therefore, signs of a significant paradigm shift among educationalists towards establishing social networks or communities of practice (Wenger and Snyder 2002) that provide a collaborative environment that facilitates the creation, organization, dissemination and use of micro-content (O'Reilly 2005). This shift increasingly includes the active involvement of students in remixing micro-content and thereby constructing their own learning in collaboration with each other and their instructors. Downes (2005) points out that

"Learning is [increasingly] characterized not only by greater autonomy for the learner, but also a greater emphasis on active learning, with creation, communication and participation playing key roles, and on changing roles for the teacher, indeed, even a collapse of the distinction between teacher and student altogether" (Downes 2005)

Students in the west, who have ready access to the Internet, are part of a generation of learners whose awareness of the socializing aspects of the World Wide Web rival that of any previous generation's – including most of their instructors/tutors at university. As a result, they are searching for and finding a wealth of course materials and resources online, not all of which emanate from their designated course instructors, who tend to overlook the pedagogical effectiveness of the vast array of learning resources that do not originate from the formal university content production system.

A further issue yet to be fully addressed in this new learning paradigm is the significant potential of open educational resources (OER). Currently most approved OER content emanates from universities in developed countries and is designed for campus-based program use. Such content is published and distributed to the web and could therefore be made widely available for use in Africa for open, distance and e-learning (ODeL) programs if it were to be pedagogically reworked and recontexualized for ODeL program delivery. Heller (2006) suggests that the benefits to universities of making this transition between the formal development of purpose-made educational content for ODeL that they *own*, to using remixed OER for formal courses may not be widely understood as yet. Universities, says Heller, like to have ownership so that they can charge fees and compete for students. Much of the development of OER will take place outside the formal university setting as a result of the move towards new forms of education. Universities will have to "catch up later" (Heller 2006).

Keats (2006) voices his concern that the educationalists involved in the OER movement may remain locked into the consumer/producer model for developing and using open educational content. He believes this model arose from a time when production and distribution were difficult and, despite the fact they no longer are as a result of wider access to easy-to-use online publishing tools, the model persists mainly out of habit. He cautions that "[i]f we do not change this view, then we will be guilty of superimposing 20th Century ... ... pedagogical models onto 21st Century technologies and onto the digital native generation" (Keats 2006).

Stacey (2007) suggests that open educational resources themselves may be a catalyst for change by instigating a positively disruptive effect on current educational delivery paradigms:

"OER are recognized as disruptive changes to traditional educational practice. Socio-cultural factors around faculty and institutional support and involvement in developing and using OER significantly influence the potential of OER ... ... Personal interaction with a teacher is seen to be part of the for-credit offering and learning experience which typically has a fee associated with it. To date OER support lifelong learners, but only in a non-interactive, non-credit fashion" (Stacey 2007).

Applying the blogging and podcasting practices to the online learning environment in the form of ePortfolios enables learning content to be created and distributed in a very different manner. As today's students become active participants in designing their own learning as members of a community of practice, their expectation is that they will have free access to the wealth of knowledge resources available on the Internet and beyond. Universities will need to involve themselves in making choices now to shape how this so-called E-Learning 2.0 unfolds. The extent to which they recognize the changing level of involvement of their students and respond effectively to this will be a determinant of their impact on the future of knowledge and learning.

The OLCOS Roadmap for OER (2007) suggests that the level of involvement by students may also be a contributing factor in the sustainability of OER initiatives:

"OER projects are more likely to flourish if they support learners in doing something themselves, for example creating, managing and sharing some content within a community of practice. Sustainability of a community-based OER project will often be not so much a matter of financial resources as of removing barriers that hinder the community from growing and maintaining momentum" (Baumgartner et al. 2007).

Success Factors for E-Learning 2.0 in Sub-Saharan Africa

The potential impact of E-Learning 2.0, particularly the increasing availability of and access to knowledge resources as a catalyst for development, is not yet clear. In the higher education sector, the mode of access to education is still heavily reliant on a campus-based model. In 1998, Daniel (1998) suggests that for this model to work, "a sizeable new university would now be needed every week merely to sustain current participation rates in higher education". Almost a decade on, there has been no indication that the establishment of universities has taken place anywhere near this rate. This begs the question as to how to cater to the 150 million or so individuals (most of whom reside in the developing world) who aspire to undertake a higher education but cannot access a campus-based education system.

The educational environment in Sub-Saharan Africa (SSA) indicates a high, yet largely hidden, demand for educational services. In response, the countries of SSA have moved to expand traditional tertiary capacity rapidly. Between 1990 and 1997, the overall tertiary education population grew by about 60%, from 1.4 million to approximately 2.2 million, while the number of universities expanded from six in 1960 to 97 in 1992. This number was estimated to be over 156 in 2002 (UNESCO 2002). Enrolment in tertiary education is estimated at 2.2 million people in Sub-Saharan Africa, with a gross enrolment rate of only 4%, the lowest rate for any region in the world (UNESCO 2005). This indicates that there are many more qualified people leaving the secondary school system than spaces in the tertiary education system can absorb. A survey conducted on behalf of the AVU in 2001 indicated that only one of four or five qualified African student gains admission into tertiary education (Accenture 2001).

The African Virtual University has developed a model for the expansion of tertiary educational opportunities for Sub-Saharan Africa that was premised on the notion that the high demand will only be met through a corresponding expansion in the development and delivery of open, distance and E-Learning programs. The model was ideally designed, developed and implemented as a collaborative effort among consortia of African universities (Bateman 2005).

The consortium model for collaborative ODeL program development involved participating universities working towards achieving economies of scale, increasing access to high quality and relevant ODeL programs developed for and by African tertiary institutions while ensuring stringent quality assurance mechanisms would be in place to satisfy the requirements of the individual universities. The model recognized the potential of sharing knowledge resources (both human and material) through ODeL programs that aimed at providing large numbers of students with access to the best of what the continent has to offer.

By collaborating to pool limited resources, consortium members also recognized the gains to be made in efficiency and cost. The scenario in which each university independently invests in the "odelification" (the conversion of content to digital and ODel formats) of its own campus-based programs represents an enormous duplication of efforts by African institutions that have limited access to resources. Research undertaken by DfID confirmed that "a severe impediment to achieving economies of scale can be caused by non-communication between institutions. The result of this is that materials and/or courses are often produced competitively, markets are split, resources are not shared and the costs increase as a consequence" (Bilham and Gilmour 1995).

The AVU Gap Analysis Report (Bateman and Murray 2004) and subsequent concept paper (Bateman 2005) both indicated that a collaborative model for the development (and possibly for the implementation) of ODeL programs was both possible and encouraged by African universities. However, a major obstruction to the collaborative development and delivery of ODeL programs has been the need for content/materials that assume an alternative form of copyright and therefore can become more widely available across the network of participating institutions.

Often, the copyright costs attributed to higher-learning resources soar far beyond the annual tuition rates for African tertiary educational institutions. Initially, the goal in establishing the current global IPR structure, outlined in the WIPO Trade-Related Aspects of Intellectual Property Rights (TRIPS) agreement, was an attempt to provide the legal context necessary to promote the development of entrepreneurial societies (WIPO 1995). However, it has done so almost exclusively in the developed world and at the expense of the developing world. The education sector in many developing countries experiences the current IPR regime in terms of an increase in costs, rather than in increased opportunities for learners and users of educational materials in general.

More recently (from 2005), the AVU, in conjunction with its network of partner institutions, has re-thought the external program delivery model adopted during its initial phases. This model proved to be costly, difficult to scale, economically unsustainable and in terms of student numbers, did not lead to the level of skills and knowledge transfer anticipated. Following a detailed analysis, it became clear that the real problem was no longer the absence of programs on African campuses but the availability of these programs in modes other than the traditional classroom-based methodologies. As a result, the AVU sought to discover how it might change its emphasis from offering externally delivered programs to AVU learning centers to supporting African universities in increasing access to their *own* programs that make increasing use of new Web 2.0 environments to develop and implement E-Learning 2.0-type programs.

The AVU's response to the changes in the higher education environment in Africa was that its efforts should increasingly be directed towards enhancing institutional capacity across its network of partner institutions. As described later in this chapter, the need to develop ICT infrastructure remains a critical impediment to the wider adoption of alternative learning models in Africa, including open, distance and E-Learning. The AVU has, since its inception, been involved in supporting the development of ICT in its partner institutions. However, with the ongoing efforts of governments and universities to expand the ICT infrastructure, the question arises as to how best to use it once it is in place. Accordingly, the AVU has concentrated its efforts in the implementation of a carefully targeted skills and knowledge transfer program aimed at developing and supporting communities of practice that foster more systematic patterns of thinking regarding distributed, blended or mixed modes of teaching and learning that adopt the emerging E-Learning 2.0 paradigm.

The AVU has gradually moved from an external delivery model to a model that seeks to work with African institutions in the development of intellectual capital for open, distance and eLearning (ODeL) program development and delivery. By working collaboratively with its partner institutions, the AVU seeks to shape the future of higher education and training in Africa in an affordable, scalable, flexible, cost-effective and sustainable manner through the use of innovative education methods. The AVU has dubbed this approach the in-country strategy.

22.4 The AVU In-Country Strategy

The AVU in-country strategy commences with the contextualization of existing externally brokered programs from universities in Australia, Canada and the USA and then uses these resources to scale up existing local programs for which African universities have excess demand and limited capacity. This will be achieved by redeveloping the local campus-based programs and supporting their delivery as open, distance and eLearning programs. The resultant in-country programs will be designed, developed, implemented, monitored and evaluated under the guidance of two governance bodies[1] whose membership comprises a consortium of Africa universities.

Within the consortium governance framework the development and management roles for particular programs are undertaken jointly while delivery and accreditation take place at each partner institution. This enables the AVU and its partner institutions to collaborate effectively in program development and credit portability on programs that are jointly developed and owned by all. In designing the in-country strategy, the AVU recognizes that the processes involved in the conversion of existing degree and diploma programs from print-based materials designed for face-to-face delivery to open, distance and eLearning format is by no means straight forward for those universities with little or no experience and expertise to undertake this process. As a result, the AVU has developed the AVU Capacity Enhancement Program (ACEP) to be implemented at participating partner institutions.

22.5 The AVU Capacity Enhancement Program

The ACEP (Phase 1) is a project designed to enable the AVU's partner institutions to design, develop, deliver and manage their own ODeL programs. The project is a result of the AVU's experience in delivering similar programs in collaboration with various African and international institutions of higher learning. The aim of the ACEP is to create a critical mass of skilled ODeL professionals, as well as a vibrant community of ODeL practice in Africa. Subsequent to implementation of the ACEP, it is anticipated that the AVU's partner institutions will be able to create high-quality ODeL programs, delivery mechanisms and strategies for managing and financing their programs, which will be shared and updated by the whole AVU network. Eventually, the co-developed ODeL programs and resources will be incorporated into the AVU's open educational resources portal to facilitate access and review by any member of the AVU network of institutions.

---

[1] The AVU Partner Institution Consortium Advisory Council or *APICAC* in Anglophone Africa or the Conseil Academique or *CA* in Francophone Africa.

The ACEP adopts a comprehensive and holistic approach to institutional capacity enhancement and includes the following:

ODeL Workshops

Initially, trainees from each participating institution will attend a workshop in one of the following three domains: materials development for ODeL programs; delivery and technology for ODeL programs; and governance, management and financing of ODeL programs.

This first set of workshops will serve as an initiation to the respective domains, and will help participants to develop the skills and understanding they will require to successfully participate in the year-long professional development programs that follow. Towards the end of this year-long program, the AVU will run a second series of ODeL workshops designed to ascertain the level of competence of the participating partner institutions and as remediation for any gaps that would otherwise limit the partner institutions' progress.

ODeL Professional Development Program

From experience, the AVU recognizes that workshops alone are not an effective mechanism to guarantee the development and effective use of a critical mass of skills, understanding and knowledge in ODeL. The one-year ACEP Professional Development program has been devised to provide participants with in-depth, up-to-the-minute training that leads to the award of an internationally accredited post-degree certificate in one of the following domains: ODeL program development, ODeL program delivery, or the management of ODeL programs. Furthermore, the training received will enable those who wish to continue with further research and study in the field at master's or doctoral level to do so.

ODeL Tool Kit

In addition to the above, every participant will receive a customized ODeL toolkit relevant to their domain that is designed to enable them to develop and support their institution's ODeL programs as well as to transfer the knowledge and skills they have gained during the ACEP to their colleagues via cascade training workshops at each partner institution. The toolkit will combine different types of media (print based, video, CD-ROM, etc.) as well as online support and interaction via the AVU OER portal. The formation and participation in these structured communities of practice

(CoP) is viewed as being an important part of the overall professional development process. It is hoped that these CoPs will continue after the formal training is complete.

The AVU's approach of working collaboratively with its network of partner institutions to enhance their capacity to develop and use open, distance, and eLearning programs has the potential to significantly increase access to higher education across the continent while limiting the resource input required by any one institution. In doing so, the AVU and its partner institutions will promote and adhere to strict quality assurance procedures in all aspects of the ODeL program development process to ensure that the confidence and willingness of partner institutions to use (adopt) and/or re-use (adapt) these resources remains high.

22.6 The AVU Learning Architecture

In keeping with its paradigm shift towards a supportive role for its partner institutions, the AVU has developed a learning architecture that describes the general pedagogical elements and principles of the ICT-supported open, distance and eLearning models that it seeks to implement across its network.

How teaching and learning is conceptualized and delivered has a significant impact on the number and diversity of students the AVU network of partner institutions can support. The AVU's learning architecture forms the structure within which the AVU program development and instructional design, as well as pedagogy, delivery and technology models are framed. It is based on the broad principles of lifelong learning, learner centeredness, learning to learn, contextualized learning, customized learning, transformative learning, collaborative/cooperative learning and just-in-time learning for its program design and delivery. In keeping with these principles and in recognition of the varied educational contexts existing in different African countries, the AVU applies the following range of pedagogy and technology models within the learning architecture:

- *Model 1: Distributed classrooms:* Interactive telecommunications technologies extend a classroom-based course from one location to a group of students at one or more other locations. The typical result is an extended class set that mixes on-site and distant students. The facilitator and institution control the pace and place of instruction.

- *Model 2: Independent learning:* This model frees students from having to be in a particular place at a particular time. Students are provided a variety of materials, including a course guide and detailed syllabus, and access to a facilitator, who provides guidance, answers questions and evaluates their work. Contact between the individual students and the instructor is achieved by one or a combination of the following technologies: telephone, voice-mail, computer conferencing, electronic mail and surface mail. Students will arrange their study time to suit individual circumstances.
- *Model 3: Open learning + class:* The model involves the use of a course guide and other media (such as DVD, CD ROM or videotape) to allow the individual student to study at his her own pace, combined with occasional use of interactive telecommunications technologies for synchronous group meetings between all enrolled students.

To have a significant impact on access to higher education and training on the African continent, the AVU works with its network to regularly realign its learning architecture to lower costs to a level that is within the reach of more students, and to provide increased access to those who are unable to attend a campus-based classroom each day.

Therefore, the AVU's focus will increasingly be on flexible delivery modes that make the programs more affordable and cost effective for both academics involved in capacity enhancement, research and professional development programs and students registered in programs that the AVU jointly develops together with African and global partners. Currently these programs include the Secondary Teachers' Education Program in 10 countries across Africa, the Teacher Education in Sub-Saharan Africa (TESSA) project for primary teachers in nine other countries and the Short Professional and Continuing Education (SPaCE) programs. In the future, the AVU intends to offer additional materials in the form of open educational resources (OERs) that its partner institutions will be able to contextualize as ODeL programs. Hence the learning architecture as depicted in Fig. 22.1 takes into account a range of learning and technological contexts predominant in Sub-Saharan Africa.

Fig. 22.1. The AVU learning architecture

22.7 The Dual Challenges of Connectivity and Bandwidth

In its early phases, the AVU used digital video broadcasting over an asynchronous (downlink only) satellite network. The network had many shortcomings, including the extremely high cost of satellite bandwidth (broadcasting digital video requires high levels of connectivity), inefficient use of the network (which was largely idle after-hours), high telephony costs, problems with audio feedback and limited access to Internet at the learning centers. The high cost of operating the network compared to its return in terms of program delivery was a major criticism from donors and other AVU partners at this time.

As a result of these initial lessons learned, the AVU no longer accentuates technology to the degree at which it dictates pedagogy or student-support and program-delivery models. However, the selective and appropriate use of ICTs will continue to be a marked feature of the AVU's in country strategy in terms of how these support the needs of the learner, the educational context including specific discipline requirements, and the institutional and national ICT contexts. Accordingly, and in line with the AVU Learning Architecture, ICTs that support collaborative and constructivist modes of learning are now preferable.

An appropriate technology for developing regions like Sub-Saharan Africa has to consider several constraints facing the adoption of technology in these regions. These constraints include:

- Cultural and language issues
- Geographical reach
- Poor telecommunication infrastructure
- High bandwidth and connectivity costs
- Unreliable power
- Lack of computers
- Lack of trained technical personnel to manage and maintain the technology
- A largely undefined policy environment for ICT-supported distance education

With this in mind, the AVU has revised its delivery approach and re-designed and upgraded its satellite network to provide video broadcasting (synchronous and asynchronous) capacity and Internet access using a full duplex asymmetric VSAT solution. The AVU's adoption of VSAT technologies helps to support more effective program delivery and alleviates the serious constraints imposed by poor Internet access at the partner institutions. It also reduces the dependency by its partner institutions on the local communication infrastructure, which may be unreliable. While VSAT is not an inexpensive solution, nor is it preferable to a robust, affordable and widely accessible fibre optic network, the added benefits to the quality and management of the learning process in the medium term are considered well worth the expense.

Access to the Internet via a VSAT network offers seamless delivery of all formats of content (video, audio, text, image data, etc.) making it ideal for AVU's mixed-mode pedagogical approach. The interaction between students and lecturers is now supported by Internet-based communication solutions such as email, chat and discussion forums. The VSAT network also supports the development of national research and education networks (NRENs), which are a key part of the collaborative program-development process described earlier in the section, AVU In-Country Strategy. A schematic representation of the AVU VSAT network follows (Fig. 22.2):

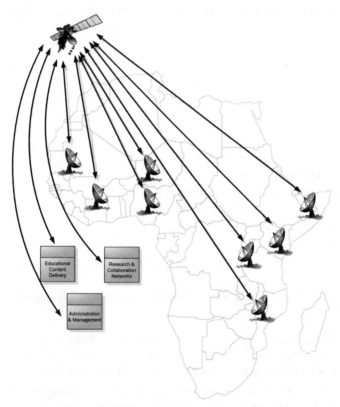

Fig. 22.2. The AVU VSAT Network (schematic)

The Bandwidth Consortium

One of the major technological challenges the AVU has been able to overcome through deploying the VSAT network solution has been the excessive cost and low availability of bandwidth and connectivity. It is widely known that some universities in Africa make do with less than one megabyte of bandwidth and pay considerably more for it than their European or North American sister institutions. Although the AVU has deployed some 20 VSATs across Africa, most universities still do not have access to reliable and affordable bandwidth that would promote the uptake of open, distance and eLearning programs. Part of the solution that the AVU and its partners have put in place in the medium term (until a ubiquitous fibre optic network is in place across Sub-Saharan Africa) is the development of a consortium to purchase bandwidth via VSAT.

The AVU has aggregated the demand from several participating universities in order to purchase bandwidth at a price of US$2.3 per kilobyte per second (2005) (Table 22.1). With increased numbers of universities participating in the consortium, the ability to leverage further economies of scale and purchasing power also increases. The AVU is hopeful that additional universities will join the consortium, thus reducing the costs of bandwidth for all consortium members. This situation will also have very positive effects on key aspects of the AVU's activities, such as implementing the ACEP and increasing accessibility to the open educational resources portal by students and researchers across the AVU network.

Table 22.1. Lowering of bandwidth costs for African Universities

Year	Bandwidth cost (US$ per Kbps)
1997–2001	20
2002	13
2003	8.90
2004	5.0[a]
2004	4.2
2005	2.33
Future	1.00 or less

[a]The AVU commenced bandwidth cost negotiations with satellite service providers in 2004

22.8 The AVU Open Educational Resources (OER) Strategy

Another key part of the AVU's future collaboration with its network of partner institutions revolves around increasing their access to quality open educational resources (OERs). The AVU's OER architecture lays out the general components of the nascent OER movement within the higher education sector on the African continent. The OER architecture is grounded in two experiences: a thorough analysis of the existing theories and perspectives concerning the global open content movement and the AVU's own current experiences in establishing processes, systems and frameworks of design, development, management and sharing of OERs on the African continent. The combination of these elements constitutes the empirical and theoretical foundation on which the AVU OER architecture is based.

The constituent parts of the architecture (creation, organization, dissemination and utilization) are held together by several elements or scaffolding (see Fig. 22.3). From this basic framework, the dimensions of the architecture are formed to create knowledge spaces in which meaning and information about ODeL initiatives and methodologies converge. These knowledge spaces, however, are neither restrictive nor prohibitive entities. They are punctuated by hallways and paths allowing for the free flowing of ideas from space to space (i.e., between the institutions and individuals within the communities of practice that the AVU is developing in Africa).

These virtual and physical spaces form vital lines of communication within the community of practice in that they are often the site of engagement, exploration, pilot testing and innovation of ideas around OERs and open, distance and eLearning methodologies. Indeed, they encourage and generate discourses between those occupying the different spaces, gradually re-shaping new relationships and strengthening old ones within the AVU's network of partner institutions.

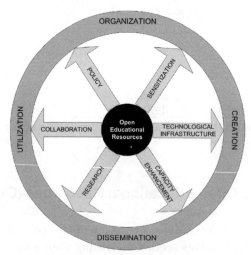

Fig. 22.3. The AVU OER architecture

The components supporting the AVU OER Architecture include:

Creation:
- Localization and contextualization OER of content
- Using/re-using/re-authoring/re-purposing of content
- Developing capacity to create OERs from scratch
- CoPs: structured communities of users and producers
- Interoperability and compliance
- Iterative and collaborative processes for OER creation

Organization:
- Governance, management and financing models
- Storage/portal mechanism
- Tagging & metadata systems
- Repository development
- Institutional development: developing a knowledge-sharing culture

Dissemination:
- Sensitization campaign at each partner institution
- Delivery methods for remote and local access to OERs
- Packaging
- Building and nurturing CoPs
- Scalability of delivery
- Decentralization vs. centralization or a combination of both

Utilization:
- Mechanisms for accessing and updating OER repositories
- Quality assurance mechanisms
- Accreditation of materials
- Sustainability of use, reuse
- Business modeling

For each of the above, it is possible to determine the necessary support (scaffolding) activities that are required in terms of six key areas: capacity enhancement, sensitization, technological infrastructure, policy, research and collaboration.

It is also important that the AVU OER architecture provide space for future developments, because the OER movement has yet to mature and will inevitably develop beyond its current limits. The growth of OERs in Africa will rely on the free flow of ideas, both within the hallways and paths of the African OER architecture and globally among the neighboring OER architectures. Figure 22.4 illustrates the planned trajectory for the AVU OER Strategy over the next few years (2006–2008).

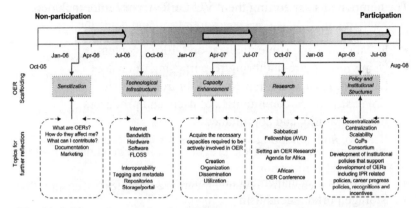

Fig. 22.4. The trajectory for the AVU open educational resources strategy

22.9 Conclusion

Evidence shows that countries that have succeeded economically have also invested heavily in tertiary education and training. The AVU believes that, without extensive investment in higher education and training, Africa will not be able to develop an innovative basic and applied research and development base that is necessary to succeed in today's technological, networked and global marketplace.

As a result of its experiences, the AVU has several recommendations to make in terms of how African governments and higher-education institutions might approach open, distance and eLearning program development and implementation. There are three broad areas under which these recommendations fall:

- Strategic planning and policy frameworks
- Research and knowledge sharing
- Developing and implementing new pedagogical paradigms for ODeL program provision and offering capacity enhancement opportunities that support them

Strategic Planning and Policy Frameworks

Without adequate planning, the ability of countries, institutions, educators and indeed the learners themselves to benefit from strategies and policies that will support the cost-effective provision of quality ODeL programs will be severely curtailed.

A supportive policy environment is essential to the success of education provision particularly when this needs to inform and guide the levels of transformation required in Sub-Saharan Africa. Policy formulation and implementation are key considerations for many countries in SSA that seek to regulate educational quality within the institutions they govern in order to ensure that their development objectives are met. Appropriately designed ODeL policies should therefore form part of existing education and development policy and support the following:

- Increasing access to ODeL programs while regulating ICT-supported cross-border education
- Developing capacity enhancement programmes to ensure that the requisite skills are readily available
- Developing quality assurance (QA) frameworks
- Developing workable business models and budgetary frameworks that result in cost-effective ODeL teaching and learning approaches
- Supporting and coordinating the expansion of education-related infrastructure, including information and communications technology (ICT)

Research and Knowledge Sharing

There is a need for further research into ODeL program design and delivery that, ideally, emanates from African institutions themselves. Currently, there is little formal research available that analytically describes and evaluates good practice for ODeL programs in Sub-Saharan Africa. More specifically, there is need for further research into ODeL program costing, financing, management (including learner support systems, assessment and cross-border accreditation), pedagogy (including the impact of Web 2.0 tools and collaborative learning environments), technology (including mobile learning), access (including issues surrounding gender equity), and the value chain of teaching and learning provision in terms of its impact of realizing national development goals.

Knowledge is becoming an increasingly important commodity in the economic, social and cultural development of a globalized world. Higher-educational institutions in Africa, as centres for innovation and the creation of knowledge, must continually and progressively set the pace and direction for this development. Knowledge sharing and collaboration strategies are required both within the institutions themselves and among the education ministries that support them.

Demonstrating New Teaching and Learning Paradigms

The AVU experience suggests that there is a sure benefit to enhancing the capacity of institutions to design, develop and implement new ODeL programs that make appropriate and effective use of ICTs. However, given the dynamic nature of ICT-supported education and the "on the horizon" impact of Web 2.0 environments, rather than launching into this process largely unprepared and risking scarce resources, a step-by-step progression is required. This progression should include needs analyses, feasibility studies and pilot programs that demonstrate current models of demand-driven, cost-effective, affordable, and quality teaching and learning through the appropriate and contextualized use of ODeL methodologies.

To this end, inter-institutional collaborative partnerships should be considered since they enable the:

- Sharing of developed courses (such as open educational resources) in order to reduce development costs
- Joint development of new resources that are appropriate to the developing world context
- Sharing of facilities such as libraries and learning centres (for learner registration, distribution of study material, and examinations) to reduce duplication of costly resources
- Collaborative delivery of programmes to promote cross-border accreditation and, in turn, a mobile labour supply
- Establishment of joint partnerships with external agencies providing professional development and/or funding (such as the Partnership for Higher Education in Africa [PHEA])

Higher education institutions and several NGOs in Sub-Saharan Africa are entering into the process of developing and/or supporting open, distance and eLearning programs. Most of the larger African universities have embraced the possibilities the Internet enables in terms of expanded education provision via E-Learning. To a large extent, however, they do so using content-push methodologies based on Web 1.0 paradigms. There is yet to be wide-scale roll out to the extent the AVU has attempted due in part to lack of extensive ICT infrastructure beyond the urban context and in part to an ongoing lack of credibility (by students, employers, university administrators and even some academics) of ODeL programs as being of the same caliber as their campus-based counterparts.

Equally, there are few universities that are actively adopting the Web 2.0 tools and environments in the creation of the ODeL programs. Some notable exceptions are the Commonwealth of Learning's WikiEducator[2] project, the South African Government's Thutong[3] Education Portal, the University of the Western Cape's AVOIR[4] project (mainly in the development of its Knowledge Environment for Web-Based Learning[5] [KEWL] LMS platform) and Teacher Education in Sub-Saharan Africa[6] (TESSA) program. Notably, each of the above also adopts, to one degree or another, a consortium development approach.

The AVU regards itself as an institution that can contribute to the development of a critical mass of Africans with the necessary knowledge, skills and understanding that are required to bring about the desired acceleration in economic and social development in African countries and to assist in their transformation into knowledge-based economies. Throughout its short existence, the AVU has needed to adapt and even reinvent itself to stay in line with the changing higher education and training environment in Africa. In the future it will continue to do so while seeking to be at the cutting edge of innovation and practice.

References

Accenture (2001). *African Virtual University Strategic Review*. Washington: Accenture.

Bateman, P. T. (2005). *The AVU/Partner Institution Consortium Program Development Model*. Nairobi, Kenya: Unpublished Concept Note for the African Virtual University.

Bateman, P. T., Murray, L. (2004). *The African Virtual University Gap Analysis of Open, Distance and eLearning in Higher Education in Africa*. (unpublished).

Baumgartner, P., Naust, V., Canals, A., Ferran, N., Minguillón, J., Pascual, M., Rajalakso, M., Väliharju, T., Behrendt, W., Gruber, A. (2007). *Open Educational Practices and Resources: OLCOS Roadmap 2012*. Salzburg Research/ EduMedia Group.

Bilham, T., Gilmour, R. (1995). *Distance Education in Engineering for Developing Countries*. UK: Overseas Development Administration, Education Division.

---

[2] http://www.wikieducator.org.
[3] http://www.thutong.org.za.
[4] http://avoir.uwc.ac.za.
[5] http://kewl.uwc.ac.za.
[6] www.tessaprogramme.org.

Blum, K. D. (1999). Gender differences in asynchronous learning in higher education: Learning styles, participation barriers and communication patterns. *Journal of Asynchronous Learning Networks*, (3)1. http://www.aln.org/publications/jaln/v3n1/pdf/v3n1_blum.pdf. Accessed 15 May 2007.

Coleman, J. S. (1990). *Foundations of Social Theory*. Cambridge: Harvard University Press.

Daniel, J. (1998). *Mega-Universities and Knowledge Media: Technology Strategies for Higher Education*. London: Routledge.

Downes, S. (2005). E-learning 2.0. eLearn Magazine, ACM, 2005. http://elearnmag.org/subpage.cfm?section=articles&article=29-1. Accessed 11 May 2007.

Heller, R. F. (2006). OECD study of OER-Week2 (21 November 2006). Email to: iiep-oer-opencontent@communities.unesco.org.

Keats, D. (2006). Users as producers of Open Educational Resources – scorecard (18 November 2006). Email to: iiep-oer-opencontent@ communities.unesco.org.

O'Reilly, T. (2005). What Is Web 2.0: Design Patterns and Business Models for the Next Generation of Software. http://www.oreillynet.com/pub/a/oreilly/tim/news/2005/09/30/what-is-web-20.html. Accessed 14 March 2007.

Porter, D. (2006). Innovations, Trends, and Creativity in Distance Learning – Paper presented at the 4th International Congress on Education and Technology: Inter-American University of Puerto Rico (UIPR) September 7, 2006. http://www.bccampus.ca/Assets/BCcampus+Whitepapers/Innovations$!2c+Trends$!2c+and+Creativity+in+Distance+Learning+report.pdf. Accessed 26 March 2007.

Ryan, R. C. (2000). Student assessment comparison of lecture and online construction equipment and methods classes. *The Journal*, 27(6), 78–83.

Stacey, P. (2007). Open educational resources in a global context. *First Monday*, 12(4). http://firstmonday.org/issues/issue12_4/stacey/index.html. Accessed 15 May 2007.

UNESCO (2002). Forum on the Impact of Open Courseware for Higher Education in Developing Countries, UNESCO, Paris, 1–3 July 2002: final report. Paris: UNESCO. http://unesdoc.unesco.org/images/0012/001285/128515e.pdf. Accessed 23 April 2007.

UNESCO (2005). Draft Final Report from the Second Global Forum on International Quality Assurance, Accreditation and the Recognition of Qualifications. http://portal.unesco.org/education/en. Accessed 23 April 2007.

Vygotsky, L. S. (1978). *Mind in Society: The Development of Higher Psychological Process*. Cambridge, MA: Harvard University Press.

Wegner, S. B., Holloway, K. C., Garton, E. M. (1999). The effects of internet-based instruction on student learning. *Journal of Asynchronous Learning Networks*, 3(2). http://www.aln.org/publications/jaln/v3n2/pdf/v3n2_wegner.pdf. Accessed 15 May 2007.

Wenger, E. C., Snyder, W. M. (2002). *Cultivating Communities of Practice: A Guide to Managing Knowledge*. Boston: Harvard Business School Press.

WIPO (1995). Agreement Between the World Intellectual Property Organization and the World Trade Organization. http://www.wipo.int/treaties/en/agreement/trtdocs_wo030.html. Accessed 25 April 2007.

Index

Printing: Krips bv, Meppel, The Netherlands
Binding: Stürtz, Würzburg, Germany